SPEECH COMMUNICATION

and Human Interaction

SECOND EDITION

Scott, Foresman's
Consulting Editor in Speech Communication

DOUGLAS EHNINGER
The University of Iowa

For this edition,

BRIAN R. BETZ, Indiana University Northwest,
contributed Chapter 12.

JOSEPH M. FOLEY, The Ohio State University,
contributed Chapter 15.

GORDON C. WHITING, Brigham Young University,
contributed Chapter 16.

ALAN MEYERS and KAREN CARLSON, Wright College,
Chicago, contributed Study Probes for
Chapters 1–6.

SPEECH COMMUNICATION

and Human Interaction #6

SECOND EDITION

Thomas M. Scheidel

UNIVERSITY OF WISCONSIN

SCOTT, FORESMAN AND COMPANY

Glenview, Ill. · Dallas, Tex. · Oakland, N.J.
Palo Alto, Cal. · Tucker, Ga. · Brighton, England

All photographs in this book are by Thomas England.
Page 84: The woodcut by M. C. Escher from the
    collection of C. V. S. Roosevelt, Washington, D.C.
Cover painting by Robert Amft.

Library of Congress Cataloging in Publication Data

Scheidel, Thomas Maynard, 1931–
    Speech communication and human interaction.

    Includes bibliographies and index.
    1. Oral communication. 2. Interpersonal relations.
3. Public speaking. 4. Mass media. 5. Intercultural
communication. I. Title.
P95.S3 1976   808.5   75-35982
ISBN 0-673-15005-4

1 2 3 4 5 6 7 8–VHS–82 81 80 79 78 77 76 75

PREFACE

Often, when we pause and look back on our efforts to communicate with others, we wish we had a second chance: "I should have said . . . I would have added . . . I could have made the point better if . . . ." It is the same in writing a textbook. Happily, this Second Edition of *Speech Communication and Human Interaction* provides me with that "second chance."

In this Second Edition, I have tried to maintain and, wherever possible, expand those features of the First Edition that users of the text identified as significant strengths. Throughout, the focus is again upon speech communication as a *process*—an ongoing, dynamic phenomenon in which many variables are acting and interacting. The major elements of the speech communication process treated are (1) communicating *agents* who (2) *interact* in (3) a *context.* That setting in which two persons converse is presented as the archetype of all oral communication contexts; the principles which apply there are applicable also and can be extended and generalized to all other settings. This emphasis upon the unity of principle underlying all the speech forms continues to be a major theoretical touchstone of this text.

An overall practical point of view predominates again in this Second Edition. The book is written and designed for maximum usefulness to students. Appearing throughout most of the chapters are *Study Probes* closely threaded with the text and aimed to help clarify, expand, and reinforce the reader's understanding of the key concepts being presented. *Self-Assessment Scales* and other structured guides for communication analysis and evaluation are provided. Textual illustrations, both photographic and diagrammatic, are used to illuminate and vivify various facets of the textual content. A second color adds a special dimension and allows the highlighting of important or difficult concepts.

Although I am gratified by the response to these features in the First Edition and by the wide use of the text in beginning speech communication courses in a variety of institutions across the country, there are things "I wish I had said . . . added . . . developed differently." In this Second Edition there are three major modifications or additions:

First, an improved organizational scheme has been employed to simplify and better integrate the presentation of the material. Part One covers *intrapersonal* aspects of speaking/listening communication agents. Part Two treats

v

interpersonal aspects of communicative interaction. Parts Three, Four, and Five cover the important *contexts* in which speech communication occurs. These contexts range from the dyadic encounter in which two persons converse to those special concerns introduced by the attempt on a worldwide scale to communicate across cultures. The reordered material of the First Edition has been interwoven with additional material and new chapters to produce a whole with unity, coherence, and a natural flowing development starting with intrapersonal communication and moving outward through interpersonal, public, mass, and intercultural concepts and contexts of speech communication.

Second, an attempt has been made to simplify the text presentation so that the whole is more personalized and readable. Terminology has been simplified and complexity of necessary theory reduced. In format as well, a simpler and clearer appearance has been adopted for greater ease in reading. The Study Probes, for example, now appear consistently at the bottom of the pages to which they relate, and footnotes have, wherever possible, been placed at the end of the chapters.

Third, new substance has been added throughout the text in both general and specific ways. To reflect current interests and trends in the field, for example, the material on public speaking has been expanded from one chapter to two. In addition, three entirely new chapters have been contributed by specialists in content areas not treated in the First Edition: Professor Brian R. Betz of Indiana University Northwest wrote Chapter 12 on Managing Conflict in Interaction; Professor Joseph M. Foley of The Ohio State University wrote Chapter 15 on Mass Electronic Communication; and Professor Gordon C. Whiting of Brigham Young University contributed Chapter 16 on Intercultural Communication. These chapters all add substantial new coverage to the work, and I am especially grateful to their authors.

Many persons, through their critical analyses and professional advice, have contributed significantly to the restructuring and revising of this new edition. In particular, I want to thank the following users of the First Edition who provided detailed critiques which proved so helpful to me in effecting some of the changes I've made: Professors Howard Dorgan of Appalachian State University, David L. Swanson of the University of Illinois, Blaine Goss of The University of Oklahoma, and David M. Jabusch and Instructor Don Ellis of The University of Utah. My visits to Lamar University in Texas and to the University of South Florida, during which I discussed the use of my text in basic courses, produced a number of useful suggestions which I have tried to incorporate here. I wish to express my appreciation also to Professors Alan Meyers and Karen Carlson of Wright College, Chicago, who contributed Study Probes for the first six chapters. Finally, several colleagues, past and present, and numerous students have offered suggestions and encouragement during the preparation of this edition. I am indeed grateful to all.

T. M. S.

OVERVIEW

I

FOUNDATION
AND
PERSPECTIVE

II

INTRAPERSONAL
DIMENSIONS
OF THE
SPEAKER/LISTENER

III

INTERPERSONAL
INTERACTION:
SENDING
AND RECEIVING
MESSAGES

IV

INTERPERSONAL
CONTEXTS
OF SPEECH
COMMUNICATION

V

PUBLIC CONTEXTS
OF
SPEECH
COMMUNICATION

VI

MASS
AND INTERCULTURAL
CONTEXTS
OF
SPEECH COMMUNICATION

CONTENTS

III   INTERPERSONAL
                                          INTERACTION:
                                          SENDING
                                      AND RECEIVING
                                          MESSAGES

IV

V

PUBLIC CONTEXTS
OF
SPEECH
COMMUNICATION

VI

**MASS
AND INTERCULTURAL
CONTEXTS
OF
SPEECH COMMUNICATION**

ILLUSTRATIONS

TABLES, CHARTS, ASSESSMENT SCALES

FOUNDATION
AND
PERSPECTIVE

Chapter 1

THE
SPEECH COMMUNICATION
PROCESS

*Speech communication is a process involving
speaking/listening agents who, by sending and
receiving verbal and nonverbal messages,
interact within a physical and psychological
context to achieve a meaningful effect.*

The world energy crisis is one of the chief concerns of our time. The term *energy crisis* is, in fact, a label for a number of interrelated problems which demand our attention now more than ever before. The growth of world population, the increasing rates of energy consumption, the ultimate limits of certain energy resources, and the pollution of our environment are problems which influence one another, and which combine now to produce a genuine threat to human survival.[1] Starvation in one country, high fuel prices in another, and the death by pollution of a great lake in yet another can be seen to share some common causes and effects.

We must, and we can, learn to manage many of the problems included under the label *energy crisis*. Let us consider pollution as an example. Until recently, the haphazard and wholesale disposal of wastes into the earth, water, and air was considered to be "the inevitable price of progress." Now we are finding that pollution is approaching dangerous levels in many areas. We unintentionally created an environmental problem of great severity, and we must now develop swift and far-reaching solutions to control it.

3

Problems such as these demand accurate information, sound thinking, and skillful speech communication. They are too complex to be solved by any single individual. They demand prompt *social cooperation* and *united action* of unprecedented proportions. And the primary means by which individuals are brought to cooperative effort is meaningful interaction through speech.[2]

It's true, of course, that many of our social problems, including pollution, have been with us a long time. In every era groups have had to solve the dilemmas of the day. But in our day, there are more *people* than ever before and fewer *resources*. This magnifies our problems manyfold.[3] Hence the need for new solutions and the interactive skills to make them work is increasingly urgent. Today, as never before, we must recognize the difficulties, discuss probable causes, identify possible solutions, weigh alternatives, agree upon the most desirable courses of action, and promptly put them to work.

DEFINING SPEECH COMMUNICATION

Because the communication process is so fundamental to relating our own lives to the lives of others, we might feel that we already understand what the term *speech communication* means. After all, we have been involved with the process from a very early age; all of us have had a good deal of firsthand experience both as senders and receivers of oral messages; almost every day we have observed its successes and failures. As a test of our understanding of what speech communication really is, let us see if we can devise a satisfactory definition of it. 1 *

Study Probe 1
Exploring a Definition of Speech Communication

Stop reading and consider carefully what the term *speech communication* means to you personally. Then write out your own definition. When you're satisfied—for the moment at least—with what you've written, resume reading the chapter and compare your definition with those listed in the following paragraphs. Don't cheat by reading ahead, or this exercise won't work. When, however, you have concluded your comparison and have finished reading the chapter, return to *your* definition. Examine it critically and determine how, if at all, you would want to alter it. But don't. Bring it to class with you for discussion; it won't be graded.

---

*These symbols appear throughout this edition as a means of keying the text to the Study Probes. For the sake of textual continuity, the Probes are always positioned at the bottom of the pages. If a Probe is not on the same page as the key or the facing page, it can be easily located on a closely following page.

If you compare your definition with those of other students in the class, you will probably discover that no two definitions are identical. Previous classroom experience with this Probe has produced the following fairly typical descriptions:

Speech communication is the process of transferring one's ideas, facts, or theories through the use of language, gestures, and vocal intonation to another person or group of persons.

Speech communication is the meaningful exchange of thoughts, feelings, ideas, emotions, etc., through verbal stimuli, with production by one person (or more) and received by one or more others.

Speech communication is the process by which thinking beings are able to convey their thoughts and emotions to others.

These are adequate definitions. They compare favorably with many found in published works on communication. Consider, for example, the following:

Communication is the verbal interchange of thought or idea.[4]

Communication: the transmission of information, ideas, emotions, skills, etc., by the use of symbols—words, pictures, figures, graphs, etc. It is the act or process of transmission that is usually called communication.[5]

Every communication act is viewed as a transmission of information, consisting of discriminative stimuli, from a source to a recipient.[6]

There are, of course, many usable definitions. The idea of *process* is basic to most of them although some speak of "transferring" and others of "transmitting"; some refer to "act" and others to "interchange." All list several *elements,* too—although these differ from example to example. Now, you might very well ask: "But do these distinctions make any difference? If I define speech communication in a different way, will I understand it differently?" The answer is decidedly yes.

How we define the terms we use determines to a very great extent the *meaning* we give them in our own mind. The clearer and more specific that meaning is, the more successful we are likely to be when we try to communicate about it with somebody else. That's why we say that the ability to define with "mutual" meaning lies close to the heart of really effective speech communication. Unless you can understand what I want my terms to mean and how I use them, we can't hope to interact very intelligently or constructively.

Let me suggest how I would like to use speech communication in this book:

Speech communication is that process which occurs when speaking/listening agents interact by transmitting and receiving verbal and nonverbal messages in communication contexts.

Our definition is lengthy and includes many concepts which themselves need defining. Since this definition identifies both the foundation and the superstructure for this book, it will be helpful if we develop some explanation and analysis of the central terms. Let's look first at the notion of *process*.

THE PROCESS OF SPEECH COMMUNICATION

Most contemporary writers refer to speech communication as a "process." The concept of *process* implies a dynamic, changing, ongoingness; something which develops, which never stands still. Process implies an operation in which many elements are involved, and to view something as a process is to pay particular attention to the interrelatedness of its elements.

Our understanding of the process character of speech communication can be heightened by noting some contrasts between written communication and spoken communication. As instances, consider these three opinions:

1. *Writing, you know, . . . has this strange quality about it, which makes it really like painting; the painter's products stand before us quite as though they were alive; but if you question them, they maintain a solemn silence. So, too, with written words; you might think they spoke as though they made sense, but if you ask them anything about what they are saying, if you wish an explanation, they go on telling you the same thing, over and over forever.*

2. *. . . all great, world-shaking events have been brought about, not by written matter, but by the spoken word . . . the speaker gets a continuous correction of his speech from the crowd he is addressing, since he can always see in the faces of his listeners to what extent they can follow his arguments . . . the writer does not know his readers at all. Therefore, to begin with, he will not aim at a definite mass before his eyes, but will keep his arguments entirely general. By this to a certain degree he loses psychological subtlety.*

3. *. . . in speech we tend to react to each situation that occurs, reacting in tone and gesture even to our own act of speaking. But writing tends to be a kind of separate or specialist action in which there is little opportunity or call for reaction.*

The first statement comes from the Greek philosopher Plato. It appears in his dialogue *Phaedrus*,[7] which was written about 370 B.C. and which deals in some detail with suggestions for speech communication. The second quotation is from Adolf Hitler's *Mein Kampf*,[8] written during the early 1920's. The work includes a number of comments revealing Hitler's emphasis on the value of the spoken word. The final quotation is from *Understanding Media*[9] by Marshall

McLuhan, one of the most influential contemporary spokesmen on the communication process. The differences between Plato, Hitler, and McLuhan can hardly be overstated. The ages in which they lived, their national origins, their languages, their political and ideological orientations, and their general circumstances of life reveal little in common. Yet the same thread of meaning connects their thoughts, expressed or implied, on the unique nature of speech communication. Their common emphasis is upon the dynamic, changing, and adaptive process that is distinctive of speech communication.

What comes to mind when we think of a painting or a piece of writing? Probably we visualize a particular painting or call to mind a certain book. We probably think of a *completed product* existing in a fixed and visible form. And if we fail to understand the "product," we can only go on looking at the object or reading the puzzling passage over and over again. Obviously, the painting or the printed word is not going to change in order to adapt to *us* and our questions. By the time we view a painting, it has been finished. By the time we read a poem, it has been written. There it is—finished and done with, insofar as the sender of the "message" is concerned.

In contrast, spoken interaction is an active, adaptive, and dynamic process. When we listen to somebody speaking, we hear what is happening rather than what has happened. We are *directly* and *personally* involved at that instant. We *participate*. We are simultaneously producers and consumers of communication. The process is a live "happening" in which living people are taking part: acting and reacting. The effective speaker strives to stimulate a continuous reaction from the listener, a reaction to which the speaker will then try to adapt. If, as listeners, we are puzzled or are unable to understand, we can ask questions or at least let the speaker know by our actions that we want more information. The speaker can modify her meaning or change his behavior at that very moment.

Speech interaction, unlike a painting or a piece of writing, brings together *interacting participants*. The mutual involvement of living, speaking human beings and their continuing interaction—one with another—are exclusively characteristics of speech communication. They are what we mean by *process*. Fundamentally, the process "operates" on three identifiable levels: (1) *intra*personally, within the self; (2) *inter*personally, between two persons or among a relatively small number of persons within a group; and (3) *publicly*, between one speaker and a sizable number of listeners.

Even handwritten manuscripts or printed transcripts of the world's greatest speeches can't tell us very much about *speech as process*. Consider for a moment the Gettysburg Address, a beautiful expression of man, printed in thousands of books and even carved in granite and marble. The process view of speech communication will lead us to argue that the real Gettysburg Address existed only once, and that the speech as we now know it is a monument to the Gettysburg Address of November 19, 1863. For instance, Lincoln apparently had not planned to speak the phrase "under God," and had not written it in the copy held in his hands as he delivered the speech. But he did insert that phrase as he uttered the speech, and he included it in the later copies he wrote out. Another phrase, "our poor power," appears in all written copies of the speech. Although Lincoln seemingly intended to use this phrase, the evidence of a written transcript of his words on that occasion indicates that he *said* "our power" when actually delivering the speech.[10] Such adaptations characterize the communication process, and an awareness of them can increase our understanding of its dynamic aspect.

It is true that printed versions of such speeches can be valuable when we want to study formal speech *preparation.* They can teach us something of message-content, use of language, rhetorical structures, and strategies. But they tell us almost nothing of the "life" of the actual speaking event, of what really went on at the scene. To understand speech communication, we must try to see the *whole* of it and the activity *within it*—the give and take, the interacting and transacting that speaking/listening agents engage in—the *dynamics* of the process.

THE ELEMENTS OF THE SPEECH COMMUNICATION PROCESS

If you will look again at our basic definition of speech communication on page 5, you will see that it points out the essential elements that go together to make up the process. These key elements or factors are: (1) *speaking/listening agents,* (2) *interaction,* (3) *message,* and (4) *context.* Actually, as we have already seen and will continue to emphasize, in the functioning of the speech communication process all these factors work together interdependently and inseparably.

Speaking/Listening Agents

If you observe for a moment a situation in which interpersonal speech communication is taking place, you will readily recognize some of the essential elements. Fundamentally, there will be:

A speaker
A message
One or more listeners

Probably you will then note that the person who is speaking at one moment is listening during the next, and vice versa. Actually, each person (let's say there are three of them) is both speaker *and* listener. The roles of speaker and listener shift back and forth. So you modify your list slightly, thus:

Speaker/listener
Message
Listener(s)/speaker

Now focus your attention upon one of the listeners. As an attentive participant in the process, this person—Listener No. 1—probably isn't saying anything *aloud.* But she is, nonetheless, nonverbally showing the speaker something of what she is thinking and feeling about the speaker and/or about what the speaker is saying. You, therefore, extend your list to include the essential element of:

Listener feedback to speaker

As the communication process continues, direct your attention back to the speaker of the moment. Note that very probably he is sensing or becoming aware of his listener(s)' reactions. Perhaps he hesitates, or glances at his notes, or adjusts his glasses. Possibly he interrupts the flow of his words, or he may merely alter the pace of his utterance, adjust his vocal tone, raise or lower his volume. But perceptibly or imperceptibly, *he* changes; he modifies his behavior because of the reaction of his listener(s), and by so doing he reveals still another element of the process:

Speaker adaptation to listener feedback

Shift your observation back to Listener No. 1 again. How is she reacting to the speaker's reaction? Perhaps she's leaning forward. Maybe her frown is gradually changing into a more agreeable expression. She may even be nodding affirmatively. And so you add to your list of elements:

Listener adaptation to speaker adaptation

But suppose that another listener—Listener No. 2—happens to disagree with the reaction of Listener No. 1 and makes this clear, either verbally or nonverbally, to Listener No. 1. Better enlarge your list to include:

Listener feedback to other listener(s)

In the final analysis, if the oral interaction goes on long enough, you will become increasingly aware of the extent to which this adjustment of listener-to-speaker and speaker-to-listener—this *reciprocity of reaction*—determines the success or failure of the participants to achieve a meaningful interaction.

In the formal, public communication contexts, of course, the roles of speaker and listener(s) are more arbitrarily defined. In less formal conversation and small group discussion, the roles are alternated as the speaker at one moment becomes the listener in the next. In fact, the roles may shift back and forth so rapidly as to become almost indistinguishable in terms of the process as a whole. And, often, because the interplay and switching of roles takes place so swiftly, we can see each of the participants in the speech communication process not so much as a speaker *or* a listener, but rather as both speaker *and* listener— that is, as a speaking/listening agent.

Thus far in our considerations, then, we have identified the following key factors and subfactors:

Speaking/listening agents   Speaker adaptation to listener feedback
Message   Listener adaptation to speaker adaptation
Listener feedback to speaker   Listener feedback to other listener(s)

Interaction in Speech Communication

The *interaction* element in our definition highlights the "transactional" nature of speech communication. Over all, our emphasis in this book will be upon *interpersonal* speech communication between and among speaking/listening agents who are interacting in a particular context. Thus the root of our definition is *joint participation*. Therefore, with face-to-face communication serving as our ideal case and model, we can appropriately—and most usefully—study what happens in all kinds of interpersonal interaction: dyadic, small group, public, and even mass-media communication. A television speaker and a television viewer, for example, can be considered as being joined together (conjoined) and participating jointly in the communication process, even though they are not in direct, physical, face-to-face contact.

Psychiatrist Joost Meerloo throws some additional light on the transactional nature of communication by describing it as:

> a cluster of transactional functions whereby a state of body and mind is conveyed from one person to another, and responses evoked. Both sender and receiver are supposed to take part in the rhetorical operation.[11]

Another psychiatrist, Jurgen Ruesch, views the transactional aspect of communication in a slightly different manner, speaking of "the perception of perception" as the key:

> The perception of the perception, as we might call this phenomenon, is the sign that a silent agreement has been reached by the participants, to the effect that mutual influence is to be expected.[12]

Finally, sociologist Erving Goffman sees the speech transaction as following a system of rules and conventions which are "understood" by the participants:

> In any society, whenever the physical possibility of spoken interaction arises, it seems that a system of practices, conventions, and procedural rules comes into play, which functions as a means of guiding and organizing the flow of messages. An understanding will prevail as to when and where it will be permissible to initiate talk, among whom, and by means of what topics of conversation. . . . When this process of reciprocal ratification occurs, the persons so ratified are in what might be called a state of talk—that is, they have declared themselves officially open to one another for purposes of spoken communication and guarantee together to maintain a flow of words.[13]

Obviously, the transactional impulse—the open interaction between two or more persons who expect and exert mutual influence—is what activates and sustains the speech communication process. *Real communicative interaction begins only with the recognition of and reaction to feedback.* It begins when both agents realize they are sending and receiving, interpreting and reacting to the stimuli from each other—when *both are aware* that they are jointly participating in the communication act. This mutual awareness and receptivity are involved in the "ground rules" of speech communication. Without them, there can be no productive interaction. Without their mutual acceptance, the process won't work. Communicative interaction is something like a "game" which can be played only if the players will accept the rules and agree to abide by them. In short, speech communication interaction occurs when speaking/listening agents recognize a common bond or goal, mutually accept the situation, and expect and exert mutual influence.

Transmitting and Receiving Speech Communication

Speech communication, as we noted earlier, is sometimes described as a *transferring* process, in the sense of "transferring one's ideas, facts, or theories." But the word *transfer* too often implies the conveying of an image or idea intact from one person to another. If you think about this for a moment, you will see that, although the speaker may largely shape and control the message he *sends out,* he cannot exercise any direct control over the *receipt* of that message by those who hear it. The speaker cannot predict with any certainty that the ideas, images, impressions, and information that he or she holds and speaks about will be the same ideas, images, impressions, and information held by listeners following the communication. Thus the word *transfer* may distort our view of what occurs during the speech process. Instead, let's use the word *transmit,* with the implication of "sending out." All a speaker can do is transmit, send out, stimuli. The speaker can—and must—take the nature of each listener into account as he speaks, and should attempt to adapt his message material to that specific listener. But once having sent a message out, a speaker can do no more with it. If it fails, he or she can only adapt it further and send it out again in somewhat different form.

We are reminded here of the old question of the tree in the forest: If a tree falls in a forest and no living being is present to hear it, is there any sound? The answer obviously depends upon the definition of *sound.* If we define it as the creation and transmission of sound waves, then in this case there is sound. But since we wish to focus on those instances in which at least two persons are conjoined—in which sender and receiver are present—if one person shouts in a forest and no other person is present to hear, speech communication does not occur. Transmitting by speaker and receiving by listener are complementary processes, and both are necessary for the speech communication act as we have defined it.

Let's push this point a bit further and ask: *What* is transmitted and *what* is received? In this book we take the view that ideas, facts, theories, images, impressions, and information are *not* what is transmitted or sent out by a speaker. Images, impressions, and information are qualities existing *within persons.* These elements do not exist in the channels which link persons during the communication act. A speaker transmits *only* visible and audible stimuli—sends out audible sounds in combination with factors of vocal quality and inflection, along with visible postures, gestures, and facial expressions. Since, as listeners, we can receive only patterns of audible sound and visual appearances, we can perceive only the *sounds* and the *sights* of communication. It is strictly up to us as listening agents to interpret them and give them meaning. 2

Verbal and Nonverbal Messages

If only sounds and sights are transmitted during the communication process, then how do we gain ideas, impressions, and information from that experience? We can find a part of the answer, at least, by considering for a moment the manner in which a listener attaches meaning to audible and visible stimuli.

Language is often described as a *code*. The visible and audible stimuli of speech communication are somewhat like the dots and dashes of the Morse code. These marks or sounds are quite meaningless in themselves, and to someone unfamiliar with the code would represent nothing more than a series of dots and dashes or audible dit-dahs. But the person who knows the Morse system "receives" and recognizes the dots and dashes as signs or symbolic cues, and attaches meaning to them.

Often, the terms *encoding* and *decoding* are used to describe what takes place. A speaker is said to encode a message when he transforms his idea into words and gestures to be transmitted to another; that is, the changing of an idea into visible and audible stimuli by a speaker is labeled the process of *encoding*. As a listener perceives the transmitted stimuli and attaches his own meaning to them, he is employing the *decoding* process.

Study Probe 2
Investigating the Process of Transmission

At home, list three or four people in government, past or present, under the headings of both *politician* and *statesman.* Then, bring your list to class, where your instructor will write all the names you and your classmates have listed on the board. Your various lists should disagree considerably, with several names appearing in both the politician and statesman categories. After discussing and debating your choices, consider these questions:

1. How did your assumptions about a specific governmental figure differ from those of other students?
2. Did you share the same assumptions about the meanings of the words *politician* and *statesman* that were held by others in the class?
3. Given the variety of assumptions and opinions in the class, how would you convince *everyone* that one of your choices clearly belongs on one list?

Now, for a further test of how assumptions differ, try discussing the meaning of the word *democracy* in class. See if you and the others can arrive at a common definition.

In speech communication, the idea held by the speaker and the idea formulated by the listener are not necessarily the same. The "idea" represents the meaning each has attached to the symbolic cues transmitted and received during the communication process. The thoughts behind a speaker's statement and the thoughts of a listener as he interprets that statement can never be identical. This fact again emphasizes why we should not think of speech communication as a process of *transferring* ideas. The linkage between speaker and listener simply is not that direct and mechanical, nor is the relation between signs and meanings wholly predictable. As Colin Cherry writes, "If I push a man into the lake, he inevitably goes in; if I tell him to jump in, he may do one of a thousand things."[14] Think, rather, of speech communication messages as the meanings or the interpretations given to transmitted and received stimuli by the speaking/listening agents.

There is another useful distinction that we can make: the difference between the *verbal* and *nonverbal* aspects of messages. The verbal aspects of the message are determined by the language itself—the words used and the ways in which those words are arranged. As we all know, these verbal elements carry meaning; that is, they may hold "commonality" of meaning for both speaker and listener. But the *non*verbal stimuli also provide cues that are given meaningful interpretation. Many stimuli, ranging from tone of voice and vocal inflection to posture and gesture to the physical setting in which the communication takes place, can work to make up potent nonverbal messages. These elements, because they carry their own special meaning for the speaking/listening agents, are important components of the communicative process. We will have more to say about verbal and nonverbal messages in Chapters 4 and 6.

Communicative Contexts

Every communication event occurs in and is bounded by a context: an *occasion,* a *place,* a *setting,* a *situation,* and a *time.* What may and what will occur is limited by the immediate circumstances of context. Because context exerts very powerful influences on the communication process, we need to be aware of some of its basic dimensions.

Physical dimensions.   The physical size and seating arrangement in a lecture hall will, for example, determine in part what goes on there. The listeners may be favorably disposed toward the speaker; but the barnlike size of the auditorium, its draftiness, and the remoteness of the seats from the podium—the environmental factors—may alienate them from the speaker despite his or her best efforts.

These physical dimensions of context also affect the speaker. Most teachers will tell you that there are certain classrooms which have the "right feel" for them, a physical setting which seems to "work best" for them. These judgments are based upon the physical characteristics of the room and the conscious and subconscious reactions of the teacher to those physical conditions.

The vantage point from which we, as speaking/listening agents, view other participants in the process and from which they view us can be especially influential, too. We have already noted the advantages of face-to-face, spoken communication over written communication. Part of this advantage stems from the fact that the proximity of the participants permits each of them to perceive more cues and thereby to gain more "information" from the speech communication event. By seeing what is "going on," the communicator is able to add the meanings of nonverbal messages to the meanings of the verbal messages he or she receives. We must, therefore, take careful note of the placement of participants within the communicative context. ⌷3⌷

In general, we prefer to speak with people close to us and with whom we can maintain easy eye contact. In one study, subjects were asked where they would seat themselves at a table if someone they disliked were already seated there. They tended to choose a seat at some distance from the person and not directly opposite. From such studies we can see that physical, spatial barriers can generate psychological barriers which, in turn, become barriers to communication.

Psychological dimensions. Just as the physical aspects of the room or communicative setting are often significant factors in the communication context, so too are the size and feelings of the audience—the numbers of listeners and their predispositions, biases, and emotional states. Political speakers and evangelists, as well as demagogues, do not seek large, assembled throngs as audiences solely for the purpose of spreading their messages widely and efficiently; they recognize the possible contextual advantages of a "mass" audience. Although there is no general agreement as to the psychology and operational validity of "mass mind" and "crowd effects," there is at least one aspect of these ideas which is useful to our consideration here. This factor has been called *social facilitation.*

Social facilitation refers to the effects which the members of an audience have upon one another because of their physical and emotional proximity. For instance, when a few individuals in the audience begin to applaud, others tend to join in. In *Mein Kampf* Hitler wrote of the effect of the atmosphere of the meet-

Study Probe 3
Considering Some Physical Dimensions of Context

Compare the various classrooms you use this term, and try to assess their effects upon the communication which has taken place there. Consider all physical aspects of the rooms—size, shape, color, furnishings, view from the windows, etc. How do the settings separate the teacher from the students? Do these settings seem to facilitate or impede productive social interaction? In general, try to determine how the physical characteristics of each classroom can mold the speech communication which can occur there.

ing hall and of the influence of the crowd upon the individual. He recommended night meetings because at night an audience will "succumb more easily to the dominating force of a stronger will."[15] In a large group all behavior is magnified, and our attention is drawn more strongly to factors outside our own person. In a sense, then, we can lose a measure of control-by-self in that psychological setting. So powerful are such crowd-unifying, nonverbal symbols as uniforms and robes, flags and medals, and music that speakers who use them as the central, environmental conditioners of large group activity can get listeners to behave in ways that are completely counter to their own instincts—like laying down their lives for a cause.

Audience composition is another significant factor influencing the speech communication context. What listener or listeners will hear you when you speak? Who will *overhear* you? With parents present, teenagers may feel constrained in what they say. If the parents leave the room, the subjects of conversation, the language used, and the "tone" of voices may all change. As this case suggests, the alert and sensitive speaker will adjust not only to listeners who are physically present but will also make adjustments to *overhearers* who are likely to be within earshot. Some interesting studies could be made of speakers' adaptation to overhearers. Consider the way people speak in the presence of waitresses and taxicab drivers. Some carry on a conversation with their companions as if these overhearers did not exist. Others will draw the overhearers into conversation. Still others will sit in embarrassed silence, unable to reconcile what they interpret as their conflicting roles.

Time is still another crucial variable of a communication context or setting. What you may say, for instance, during the last five minutes of a half-hour's conversation with a comparative stranger might be highly inappropriate during the *first* five minutes. How long you pause to let a point sink in and how rapidly you speak are other aspects of timing. A pause following a humorous comment or a joke must be timed with precision. If it is too brief, the "punch" of the jest may be lost; if it is too long, your speaking may lose momentum. If you have elected to say too much in the time available, or if you feel that your role as speaker may be preempted too quickly, you may speak too hurriedly and thereby reduce your effectiveness. If you speak too slowly or leisurely, the attention of your listeners may wander, or your words may be cut off by another.

Social dimensions. Finally, to our catalog of contextual influences we must add cultural characteristics and social values, for they, too, determine norms for communicative behavior. In certain cultures, for example, persons stand closer together when conversing than they do in ours. Edward Hall, who has studied these matters extensively, describes the meeting of two men from cultures with different norms for what they regard as "proper" conversational distance.[16] The European, he says, takes a step forward to achieve what he deems the correct intervening space. The American takes a step backward. And so it goes, with the American backing up the entire length of a corridor until he is finally cornered. Hall is exaggerating, of course, but his point is significant: A cultural element in a context may impede or even prevent communicative interaction without either agent realizing why he "just cannot seem to get on well conversing with that other fellow." These intercultural differences in communicative behavior will be dealt with more fully in Chapter 16.

In sum, then, communicative acts must occur in a context having physical, psychological, and social dimensions. We should be continuously sensitive to the elements of that context which may be influencing the course and the outcomes of any communicative interaction. Not only must we recognize the effects of the more obvious factors in the physical setting—such as place and space and numbers—but we must also seek to learn what we can of the psychological context and the possible influences exerted by time and timing, by the culture, and by the prevailing social values.

Many of the matters we have touched upon briefly thus far will be developed more fully in later chapters. The aim of this preliminary examination has been to define quite fully what we mean by speech communication and to describe the essential process so that we will have a common point of view and a mutual starting point from which to build our future considerations. What we have considered in these opening pages should enable us to attach new and fuller meanings to the idea of speech communication as a process which occurs when speaking/listening agents interact by transmitting and receiving verbal and nonverbal messages in communication contexts.

A MODEL OF SPEECH COMMUNICATION— TWO PERSONS CONVERSING

A method frequently employed to depict the essential elements of the speech communication process and the interaction of those elements is the illustrative abstraction, or *model*. Perhaps you have already seen a few of these models. Some are verbal, some are pictorial, and some are diagrammatic and graphic. Many are quite complex, and because they attempt to show all the elements and all interrelationships, are too detailed for our purposes. Some also run counter to our conception in that they show the process as a static and linear activity with a sender and a receiver as separate elements, rather than emphasizing that all communicative agents simultaneously are both senders and receivers.

What, then, would best serve us as an adequate, contemporary, graphic model of the speech communication process? Ideally, such an illustration should be as simple as possible without omitting any major elements, and as accurate as possible in depicting the essential elements and their interrelatedness. In terms of our definition, the simplest and most accurate illustration would be one in which we see (1) *speaking/listening agents* who (2) *interact* within (3) a *context*.

The conception of *agents interacting within a context* does not impose an artificial and absolute distinction between "sender" and "receiver." It does not imply a linear process, but attempts instead to point to simultaneous, multidirectional, and multidimensional activity. It focuses upon *interaction* as the cen-

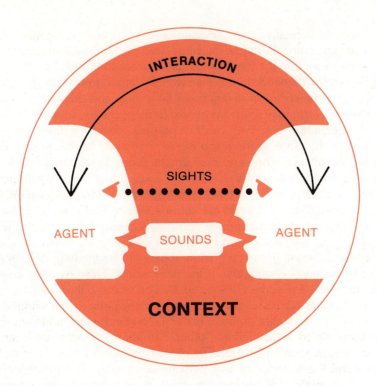

tral criterial aspect of the process. Although it is not, strictly speaking, a "scientific" model, as a representation of process it possesses the useful qualities of clarity, flexibility, and simplicity. Our model is made up of people rather than boxes and arrows, although the personalities involved are abstracted and generalizable. To make this a "living model" you have only to visualize *two persons conversing.* 4

Mark Hopkins, the American educator, once observed that an ideal educational setting would consist of a teacher on one end of a log and a student on the other, both talking in close interrelation. Similarly, we can view two people conversing (dyadic communication) as an ideal communicative context because the essential elements of the process seem to be most pronounced in it. This general "model" of speech communication is the simplest instance of speech, in

Study Probe 4
Exploring the Essential Factors of Speech Communication

List what you consider to be the essential factors involved in effective speech communication in two-person settings. What facilitates good communicative interaction between two people? What impedes it? Now consider a public speaking setting. How well would the criteria you listed for the two-person setting apply to the one-to-many public communication setting? Explain.

that it permits us to analyze with comparative ease the context, agents, and inter-action in such a setting. It may at the same time be the most complex of speech forms, in the sense that the interchange taking place in this setting may produce more interpretable *feedback stimuli* than would a larger group setting.

That two persons conversing could be at once the simplest and the most complex speech form may seem a paradox. Perhaps the explanation lies with our central concept: interaction. With only two persons conversing, there will be more feedback and therefore more *response* to feedback. In this setting there is greater participant interaction and involvement. A good case can be made for the claim that a person can establish maximal contact and meaningful interaction with only one other person at a time. In research related to this question, Profes-sor Laura Crowell and I have found some evidence that even in a discussion group of only five or six persons, a participant cannot interact with the entire group all at once, but seems rather to interact with only one person at any given moment.[17] Thus, small group discussion appears to be made up largely of frag-ments of interaction between two of the participants. This possibility could also serve as the basis for some challenging studies of the public-speaking context where one speaker addresses an audience of many persons. To whom does he or she speak? To the entire group at once? To one individual, and then another, and another? Or to a generalized "other"? In short, to better understand the speech communication process in all its phases and occurrences, we must first try to understand the instance of two persons conversing. The principles discov-erable in this model will be seen to apply in all communication forms and settings. 5

Study Probe 5

Observing Two People Interacting Within a Given Context

To develop an understanding of the model, two members of the class should volunteer to discuss, perhaps for five minutes, the difficulties in communicating. While the rest of the class observes, their discussion should be videotaped, or at least tape-recorded.

Then, with the tape as a reference and guide, the class should analyze the discussion, with the following questions, or any others that occur to you, in mind:

1. To what verbal and nonverbal cues did each speaker respond in the other?
2. Did one speaker's tone of voice communicate any messages? How did the other speaker respond?
3. Did the postures of the speakers communicate any messages? Did the postures change? Why?
4. What did the pauses and silences communicate? Why did they occur?
5. Were the speakers' involuntary gestures and facial expressions commu-

The case of two persons conversing, fortunately, is a form of communication with which all of us have had much experience and can also observe readily. At first thought, we may be inclined to consider our one-to-one speech experiences to be quite unlike participating in a group discussion, or the giving of a speech to a large audience, or taking part in a television interview. If we think further about the matter, however, we will realize that, since nearly everyone feels comfortable enough when conversing with a friend, there is no real and valid reason to become fearful when we find ourselves conversing with a stranger, or taking part in a business meeting, or giving a short speech to an assembled audience. After all, the differences between the converser, the discussion participant, and the public speaker are merely matters of *degree*, and no sharp dividing line can be drawn between them. To illustrate this point, the late James Winans of Cornell University wrote:

> Let us imagine all speeches and all memory of speech-making to be blotted out, so that there is no person in the world who remembers that he has ever made a speech, or heard one, or read one; and there is left no clue to this art. Is this the end of speech-making? Here comes a man who has seen a great race, or has been in a battle, or perhaps is excited about his new invention, or on fire with enthusiasm for a cause. He begins to talk with a friend on the street. Others join them, five, ten, twenty, a hundred. Interest grows. He lifts his voice that all may hear; but the crowd wishes to hear and see the speaker better. "Get up on this truck!" they cry; and he mounts the truck and goes on with his story or his plea.

nicating different messages than their words? Did the speakers respond to these messages?

6. Did the topics shift during the discussion? Why?
7. Did one speaker begin to imitate the other's mannerisms? Why?
8. Did one speaker dominate the conversation? Why?
9. Did the speakers know each other well? What effect did this seem to have on their interaction?
10. Did the sex of the two speakers seem to influence the interaction?
11. Did the context of the situation—two people speaking on an assigned topic for a given number of minutes before a videotape machine or tape recorder and an audience—affect the interaction? How?
12. Did the discussion begin easily? If not, why not?

Don't be surprised if your analysis of the discussion requires quite a bit of time and that with each replay of the tape you notice something further. Afterward, your instructor may ask you to write a paper on the complexities of communication.

When does the converser become a speech-maker? When ten persons gather? Fifty? Or is it when he gets on the truck? There is, of course, no point at which we can say the change has taken place. There is no change in the nature or the spirit of the act; *it is essentially the same throughout, a conversation adapted, as the speaker proceeds, to the growing number of his hearers. There may be a change, to be sure, if he becomes self-conscious; but assuming that interest in story or argument remains the dominant emotion, there is no essential change in his speaking. It is probable that with the increasing importance of his position and the increasing tension of feeling that comes with numbers, he gradually modifies his tone and his diction, and permits himself to launch into a bolder strain and a wider range of ideas and feelings than in ordinary conversation; but the change is in degree and not in kind. He is conversing with an audience.*[18]

There are obviously some typical *situational* differences between conversation and public speaking; but these, as we have said, should be viewed as differences of degree only. For example, we usually speak more loudly in a public speech than in a conversation. But not always. A teacher, for instance, may speak much more loudly, carefully, and distinctly when conversing with an 85-year-old neighbor than when lecturing to a class of twenty young students. The general principle is that, in any speech context, one tries to speak loudly enough to be heard. The same is true with other general principles of speech communication. We try to speak in terms that will be clear and appropriate for our listeners, to adapt our ends to the interests of our listeners, to be in a position if possible to look at them, to react to their reactions. These are desirable goals and behaviors in *any* speech setting. All that we try to do in good conversation we should try to do in a small group discussion or in a public speech or on radio or TV.

In support of this view are the results of a study made of the perceptions and feelings students have toward participation in (1) conversation, (2) group discussion, and (3) public speaking.[19] The outcomes of this analysis indicate how similar these activities were deemed to be by two groups of students: Group A having completed course work in speech communication, and Group B having had no such work. In diagrams shown below, representing the general conclusions reached by the two groups, the length of the lines between the basic contexts (C = conversation, GD = group discussion, PS = public speaking) indicates the extent of difference perceived between these respective speech settings by the students.

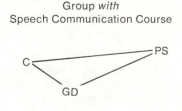

Group *without*
Speech Communication Course

Group *with*
Speech Communication Course

Note that both groups gave similar *placement* to conversation, group discussion, and public speaking in relation to one another. The basic difference is that, following a speech communication course, students tended to see these different situational forms of speech as *much more closely related* and more alike.

The findings of this study further reinforce our belief that the various speech communication forms *are* alike in the essentials and come to be seen as such by persons with speech communication training. The study also suggests that we will progress more quickly in our speech training if we see and understand these close relationships. All of our past experience in speech—primarily in the one-to-one setting—should be considered as something significantly and usefully related to what we are learning now.

In summary, the goal of this opening chapter has been to provide the foundation for an understanding of speech communication. We have presented and developed a definition of the speech communication process and emphasized as key elements the speaking/listening agents, interaction, transmitting and receiving, messages, and context. We have examined a model of these elements and their interactive relationships, and have emphasized that we can usefully consider *two persons conversing* as the basic conception of all speech communication, both as the archetype or pattern of all speech forms and as the foundation for our future efforts toward learning to interact effectively through speech.

Suggested Readings

Theodore Clevenger, Jr., and Jack Matthews, *The Speech Communication Process* (Glenview, Ill.: Scott, Foresman and Company, 1971). This paperback book provides a clear and comprehensive overview of all the significant elements in the speech communication process, including a chapter which synthesizes them into a usefully detailed model.

Frank E. X. Dance, ed., *Human Communication Theory* (New York: Holt, Rinehart & Winston, Inc., 1967). This work contains chapters outlining the contributions of various disciplines to human communication.

Giles W. Gray and Claude M. Wise, *The Bases of Speech,* 3rd ed. (New York: Harper & Row, Publishers, 1959). This excellent reference contains chapters on the social, physical, physiological, neurological, phonetic, linguistic, psychological, genetic, and semantic foundations of speech communication.

C. David Mortensen, *Communication: The Study of Human Interaction* (New York: McGraw-Hill Book Company, 1972). Chapters 2 and 8, especially, develop some interesting views of the speech communication process in terms of visual models and diagrams and their significance in communicative interaction.

Raymond S. Ross, *Speech Communication: Fundamentals and Practice,* 3rd ed. (Englewood Cliffs, N.J.: Prentice-Hall, Inc., 1974). Chapter 1, "The Communication Process," presents a number of the better-known models and provides usefully concise information about the process elements and how they may be put together in various ways.

Alfred G. Smith, ed., *Communication and Culture* (New York: Holt, Rinehart & Winston, Inc., 1966). The work contains a number of significant readings on speech communication. It touches, for instance, on contributions made by mathematics, social psychology, and linguistics; and it ranges from intrapersonal to intercultural settings.

Reference Notes

[1]D. Meadows et al., *The Limits to Growth* (New York: Universe Books, 1972). This book resulted from a study which attempted worldwide predictions based on critical variables such as available natural resources, food supply, population, and pollution. Using M.I.T. computer simulations and projections, the study predicted a collapse of the world system within a century unless we modify the present exponential growth and use rates for a number of these variables.

[2]An example of the success that can be achieved by concerned citizens working together can be found in *The Unclean Sky,* by Louis Battan (Garden City, N.Y.: Doubleday & Company, Inc., Anchor Books, 1966).

[3]See, for example, Thomas R. Detwyler, *Man's Impact on Environment* (New York: McGraw-Hill Book Company, 1971).

[4]John B. Hoben, "English Communication at Colgate Re-Examined," *Journal of Communication* 4 (1954):77.

[5]Bernard Berelson and Gary A. Steiner, *Human Behavior: An Inventory of Scientific Findings* (New York: Harcourt Brace Jovanovich, Inc., 1964), p. 254.

[6]Theodore M. Newcomb, "An Approach to the Study of Communication Acts," *Communication and Culture,* ed. Alfred G. Smith (New York: Holt, Rinehart & Winston, Inc., 1966), p. 66.

[7]Plato, *Phaedrus,* trans. W. G. Helmbold and W. G. Rabinowitz (Indianapolis: Liberal Arts Press, Inc., 1956), p. 69.

[8]Adolf Hitler, *Mein Kampf,* trans. Ralph Manheim (Boston: Houghton Mifflin Company, Sentry ed., 1943), p. 469.

[9]Marshall McLuhan, *Understanding Media: The Extensions of Man* (New York: McGraw-Hill Book Company, 1964), p. 79.

[10]David C. Mearns, "Unknown at This Address," *Lincoln and the Gettysburg Address,* ed. Allan Nevins (Urbana, Ill.: University of Illinois Press, 1964), pp. 118–133.

[11]Joost A. M. Meerloo, "Contributions of Psychiatry to the Study of Human Communication," *Human Communication Theory,* ed. Frank E. X. Dance (New York: Holt, Rinehart & Winston, Inc., 1967), p. 131.

[12]Jurgen Ruesch and Gregory Bateson, *Communication: The Social Matrix of Psychiatry* (New York: W. W. Norton & Co., Inc., 1951), p. 23.

[13]Erving Goffman, *Interaction Ritual* (Garden City, N.Y.: Doubleday & Company, Inc., Anchor Books, 1967), pp. 33–34.

[14]Colin Cherry, *On Human Communication* (New York: John Wiley & Sons, Inc., 1961), p. 220.

[15]Adolf Hitler, *Mein Kampf,* trans. Ralph Manheim (Boston: Houghton Mifflin Company, Sentry ed., 1943), p. 475.

[16]Edward T. Hall, *The Silent Language* (New York: Fawcett World Library, 1969), p. 160.

[17]Thomas M. Scheidel and Laura Crowell, "Feedback in Small Group Communication," *Quarterly Journal of Speech,* 52 (1966): 273–278.

[18]James A. Winans, *Public Speaking,* rev. ed. (New York: Appleton-Century-Crofts, 1921), pp. 20–21.

[19]This was a graduate-student project completed by Marylee Bradley Wallace.

INTRAPERSONAL DIMENSIONS OF THE SPEAKER/LISTENER

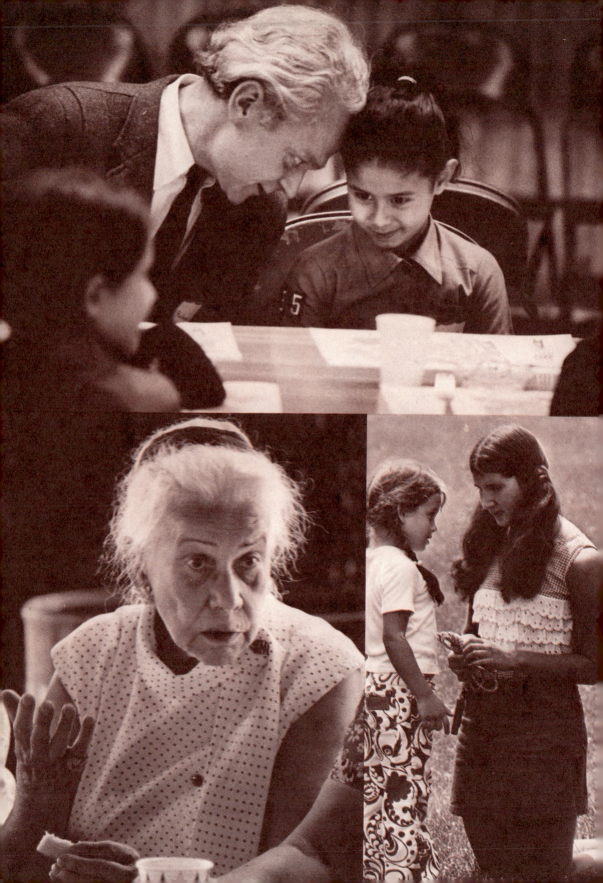

We communicate mainly to assert and support our
self-identity, to establish social contact with the people
around us, and to influence others to feel,
think, or behave as we want them to.
But our overriding purpose is to gain control of our
physical and psychological environment.

When we ask, "Why do we communicate?" we are, in fact, posing a very broad question. In this chapter, we will take up that question and attempt to identify some of the major purposes served by speech communication. We will inquire into such matters as: What inner values and needs move us to speak? What benefits do we gain from speaking in a particular speech context? To what extent does speaking contribute to our self-satisfaction? How are we influenced by such factors as our self-image, our experiences, the situations in which we communicate, and the people with whom we interact? Then, too, what influences *inhibit* us as speakers and *limit* our range of possible speech behaviors in a given situation?

In trying to discover what the purposes and ends of communication are—what lies behind and prompts the impulse to speak—let's begin by trying to identify the basic purposes: the widely inclusive motivations common to all human utterance. If we can do that, we can use that understanding as a vantage point from which to view some of the equally important but not so generally recognized purposes which impel people to speak and interact.

Here are some purposes you should keep in mind as you study this chapter: (1) to assert and support the self; (2) to establish social contact with others; and (3) to exert influence on others. These purposes, taken together, fit within one overriding, all-encompassing purpose: to gain control of our physical and psychological environment.

ACHIEVING SELF-IDENTIFICATION AND SELF-FULFILLMENT

As human beings we use speech for purposes other than establishing contact with other people and exerting influence upon them. Frequently, our purposes turn *inward:* We use speech to influence the thinking we do about *ourselves.* We employ it to serve *intrapersonal* needs or drives. Among these "self"-serving and self-actualizing purposes we find:

> Asserting self-existence
> Establishing a self-concept or self-image
> Achieving self-satisfaction
> Diminishing tensions within ourselves and others

Asserting Self-Existence

Of the many ways that speech can be used to serve the self, one of the most important is to proclaim our existence. We could modify Descartes' famous phrase and say: *I speak, and therefore I am.*[1] If we are silent, others may treat us as if we do not exist. But when we speak we assert—along with everything else—that we *are.*

In a study conducted for an undergraduate speech course, a student research worker made detailed observations of the speech behavior of preschool children as they played together.[2] She observed in particular a small child who was playing alone and talking aloud to himself. He wasn't addressing anyone; nor, apparently, was anyone listening. Eventually, the other children drifted out of the room, one by one. When all the others were gone, the observer noted that the lone child stopped talking. Later, as the other children came back into the room, the "loner" started talking aloud to himself again.

The research worker set up a situation in which the same conditions were repeated, and noted the same results. When alone, the child played silently; when others were present but playing independently in the room, the youngster talked aloud to himself. In the presence of the others, he used speech not to influence anyone, but to assert for others, and especially for himself, that he was there—that he *existed.*

Psychiatrist Joost M. Meerloo explains this assertion of self-existence by noting that:

The built-in intention and goal of communication is always to arrive—at least for oneself—at a greater feeling of certainty and security. In short, to a better adaptation . . . . Besides the information imparted, communication should contain an actualization of the self, a creative rhetorical assertion.[3]

Another indication of the need to assert self-existence can be seen in small group discussion. If one member of the group does not speak and elects to remain silent for an extended time, the other people begin to act as if the "nontalker" were not there at all. They do not look to the nontalker for comment, nor do they address him or her. And if this member of the group suddenly decides to say something, the other members often react as if the heretofore silent member were intruding. They pay little, if any, attention. They have come to expect the nontalker *not* to speak. This kind of response by the group is less likely to happen if the nontalker has made some comment early in the discussion and then merely waits for a long time before speaking again. But if this "nonparticipating" participant says nothing at all in the beginning and stays silent for an extended interval, his or her existence seems almost to be denied by the active, participating "talkers." The nontalking individual has failed to use speech to assert self-existence.

The significance of this for you as a speaker is that any time you attempt to interact with others you will—often must—assert your self-existence in varying ways and with varying emphases from time to time. Sometimes you may feel impelled to make the assertion openly; often you will do it subtly. If you overdo it, of course, you may be marked as an egotistical bore; if you fail to do it sufficiently, you may be completely ignored. And neither of these conditions is conducive to useful oral communication.

Still another way in which we sometimes use speech to proclaim self-existence is to "stake out a territory"—real or imaginary—and warn off would-be trespassers. Prompted by this ego-centered purpose, we sometimes speak to lay claim to certain social or psychological or even physical "domains" which we want to dominate or control verbally. On occasion we may feel that if we talk loudly and insistently enough we can establish the boundary lines around ourselves and keep out all would-be "trespassers." Other earthly creatures do this

Study Probe 1
Observing Nonparticipating Agents and Their Relationships in a Group

As you participate in classroom, community, or family groups, observe the "silent" or rarely participating members of these groups. Make notations as to the frequency or infrequency with which they attempt to interact orally with others. Also, on those occasions, note in particular the ways in which other, more active agents react to the "silent" ones.

too. Male birds sing not only to attract female birds, but also to make territorial claims, to establish audibly the boundaries they wish to control. Speech serves a similar purpose for us human beings. You may have known persons, for instance, who used nonstop speech and a loud voice to dominate a conversation (and, often, the surrounding ones as well). Like birds, they chattered and chirped to make their presence known and noisily tried to lord it over what they seemed to view as their private verbal domain. You may be one of those few people who are able to use this particular self-assertive tactic skillfully, subtly, and creatively—particularly if you are clever at "games" and oneupmanship. Since most of us probably are not, we have to be cautious, so that what we *are,* or are trying to be, does not speak so loudly that others cannot hear what we *say.*

Establishing a Self-Concept

You cannot hate, it has been argued, until you can love, and you cannot respect another unless you can respect yourself. Similarly, you will find it difficult to establish contact and interact meaningfully with another "self" unless you have some conception of your *own* self. George Herbert Mead has suggested that each of us develops his or her concept of *self* as a result of interaction with others in society—largely in the speech communication setting. As he puts it, "Our contention is that mind [the self] can never find expression, and could never have come into existence at all, except in terms of a social environment."[4]

In support of the notion that establishing a self-concept or self-image through speech communication can develop only in a social setting, consider the rare examples of children who—through accident, neglect, or other circumstances—have been reared in comparative isolation from other people.[5] The few available reports on such individuals, usually termed "feral" or "wild" children, point to a single striking conclusion: such children appear to be "unhuman." Their behavior seems more that of animal than of human. Their "speech" often consists only of grunts and isolated sounds. These reports on feral children provide some insight into the profound and far-reaching effects which other persons have upon us in the communicative setting. And they suggest that if we really want to understand self-concept and how it "works," we need to be fairly well aware not only of the influence we try to exert upon others but also of the influence those others exert upon *us.*

To better understand the nature of these influences, remember that, essentially, we utilize the self-conceptualizing purpose of speech communication (1) to establish in the judgment of others the image that we have—or want to have—of our "self," (2) to discover the image that others have of or wish to impose upon our "self," and (3) to try in a great many instances to align—to pull into sharper focus—these two differing images. To *preview* this purpose in even more direct and specific terms, your effectiveness as a speaking and listening communicator will depend in no small degree upon your discernment of your own self-image, the extent to which that image is accepted and affirmed by other people, and by the interplay of *your image* and *the images those others have of you.* [2]

Beginning in early childhood and continuing throughout our lifetime, we "fantasize" a great deal about the self we would like to be, or the "picture" we would like others to have of us. Much of the time, these self-images and self-concepts tend to slip in and out of focus with great frequency, and often may be lost or changed entirely—especially during our more formative years. But regardless of the concept of the self that we hold or would like to hold, we continue to test that concept through oral communication. In nearly all of our speech acts, one of our insistent purposes will be to discover or affirm whether listeners' judgments and expectations concerning us agree with our own continually developing self-concepts. This need to *be*—or *appear* to be—what we like to believe that we are cannot be denied or minimized.

Also very early in our childhood we become aware of how others see us and what they expect of us. Through the subtleties of their communication, we learn the image they have of us. And, often, if we do not conform to that image, we feel threatened either in a physical or psychological sense. We are coerced into conformity. If, for instance, we feel that we are "expected" to be the butt of others' jokes, we may tend to play the clown. Or we may try to develop the wit and skill to turn jokes back on others.

In nearly every society, and especially in the structured ones, people try to "live up to" the expectations of their fellows, to "fit in," even to *be* what others want them to be. While we can never be (and ought not hope to be) totally what others expect of us, we will discover when we try to interact with them that their expectations, their "impression," their image of *us* exert a powerful force in shaping what we become. These others characterize and "type" us. So, at least, we assume; and on the basis of such assumptions, we begin to play the roles we are "expected" to play. If and as this role-playing becomes habit, we "internalize" it: We incorporate it within the self as one of the guiding principles of our behavior. We make it a part of our self-concept.

 Study Probe 2
Discovering a Concept of Self

On a sheet of paper write what you consider to be your image of "self." How do you see yourself? What image do you believe you project to others? What "type" of person do they see you to be? Do their typical reactions to you present any consistent pattern which might reveal how they think of you? Try to recall interaction with your parents, relatives, siblings, and peers when you were a child. How do you perceive that you were perceived? What seemed to be expected of you? Can you make any connections between your self-image now and roles and behaviors expected of you when you were a child?

Come back to this Probe when you have completed the Speech Assessment Scales in Chapter 3. See if your stated views here coincide with your observations using the scales.

In this role-imposed way, our original intent to create a self-concept may be validated, or altered, or even destroyed. In this way, others' interpretations of what we should be contribute to determining what we will be. And, in this sense, we may become—to a greater or less degree—what others *say* we are. Probably most of us cling tightly to our most cherished self-images because of a kind of self-pride. But despite our best efforts to the contrary, we will be categorized, stereotyped, and pigeonholed by images *imposed upon us by others.*

Examples of these "other-imposed" self-concepts are all around us. In elementary school, the skinny kid with glasses may become a "brain" because he is assigned that role by his classmates. If he accepts it, he is likely to spend more time on his homework, get better grades, and thereby verify the impression held by his peers. Or, as another example, according to one theory (debatable, but probably not wholly wrong), a child may become a stutterer if his parents call him one or treat him as one. Or, as still another example, if you have brothers or sisters, you probably discovered at a very early age your "pecking order" in the family. Studies of families having several children show clearly that significant role differences between first-born children and those born later evolve and are learned through family interaction.[6]

Often, of course, an interpersonal encounter starts out with no preconceived notions or images on anyone's part. Others are not trying to impose an image upon us—not at first, at least. Rather, while we are speaking, they are trying mainly to "discover" who we are—a discovery made possible by the multidirectional nature of human interaction. Implicit in the self-conceptualizing purpose of speech, therefore, is the fact that—whether we like it or not—others are constantly observing our communicative behavior and trying to sift out information and clues that will help them put together an impression or "picture" of us. Just what *are* some of these clues? What types of identity-data do we intentionally or unintentionally reveal to others as they try to shape and confirm their conceptions of us as speakers and as persons?

Some of these clues are provided by the working together of the *patterns of words* we choose and the *vocal dynamics* we use. In societies where "class" differences are drawn fairly sharply, speech patterns tend to reveal a speaker's socioeconomic origin and status almost immediately. He speaks as he "should." His choice of words and his manner of enunciating them may strongly suggest that he is from the "working" class. If he "sweats," for instance, he is likely to be a "member" of the lower class or the upper class; if he "perspires," he probably comes from the middle class. When I attempted to speak Dutch in the Netherlands, my accent was so clear (clearly American) that by the time I had managed to utter only a very few sentences, an Amsterdammer would smile tolerantly and begin to speak English to me.

Sometimes, for understandable reasons, we try very hard not to reveal our self to others. At such moments we use speech for the purpose of *concealing* ourselves. We all may—and sometimes do—try to portray ourselves as something we're not, usually in an attempt to mislead or deceive our listeners as to our true identity, role, motivations, and/or values. And, conversely, we have observed speakers who were attempting to deceive us, or themselves, about the reality of a situation. Most of us, for instance, have known of people in public life who were notorious for their duplicity and who seemed to have made a career out of maintaining multiple public identities.

Some people may resort to a certain glibness for the sake of self-concealment, whereas others may try to exclude from their speech behavior all clues about the self. The speaker who tries this usually tends to be defensive and tense—constantly on the alert *not* to "give himself away." He is not likely to succeed, however, for as psychiatrist Joost Meerloo points out, "We can recognize the psychic level of such well-guarded expressions by its different sound. The musical tone is gone, and the voice sounds mechanical, monotonous, and stripped of emotion." [7]

Taken all together, then, as both speakers and listeners we have to be continuously aware of the self-conceptualizing/self-assertive purpose of speech communication. We must be aware that when this purpose is at work there are "two sides to the coin": As we use speech to develop and present our *own* self-image, so do we use it to investigate and understand the self-images and self-concepts of others. Within a given situation, *all* communication agents share in the inputs and the "outtakes" of communicative exchange. Through interaction with others we find out what they are and what they would like to be or to feel, and thus we are better able to predict and to judge the nature and possible dimensions of our relationships with them. In sum, the self-assertive and self-conceptualizing purpose of speaking serves the very useful function of revealing to speakers and listeners their *common bonds*—the *mutuality* of their knowledge, background, experience, and values. 3

Study Probe 3
Comparing Self-Concepts

Spend five or ten minutes getting to know another person in the class. Tell each other something about yourselves, and ask each other questions. Soon afterward, write a two- or three-paragraph characterization of the person you met and one of similar length describing yourself. Did your partner or you seem shy? Was your partner, or were you, easy to talk to? What interests do you share? Be honest but tactful.

In the next class period, you and your partner should exchange your characterizations of each other and compare them to your self-descriptions. Are they approximately the same?

Since this exercise potentially can damage feelings, keep in mind that first impressions are often erroneous. Rather than taking offense at an uncomplimentary or inaccurate characterization, you might more profitably consider what elements in you, the other person, and the initial communication experience led to the misperceptions.

Achieving Self-Satisfaction

As we have illustrated, the fulfillment that we experience from identifying ourselves through speech and asserting our self-image contributes much to our self-satisfaction. Related to—but extending beyond—that purpose is the *creative* motivation for speaking. It is true, of course, that speech in nearly all of its aspects involves some degree of creativity. But sometimes, as its "creators," we derive a special, added satisfaction—a kind of deeply felt inner satisfaction that can come only from the realization that we have created something special.

Creative speech.   Most of us take pleasure in producing and creating. When we are speaking, we experience a glow of pride when we sense we have said something "just right," something uniquely suited to the circumstances. The remark doesn't have to be poetic, certainly; it doesn't even have to be clever. Or, again, if our attempts to create interaction succeed, or if the desired response from a listener is greater than we had anticipated, we know that we "have done something": We have *created orally.* The speech process thus allows us an opportunity for almost unlimited self-fulfillment. If successful, every communicative interaction can be an intensely satisfying, self-actualizing experience in creativity. As we mentioned earlier, psychiatrists—Meerloo among others—have stressed the psychological importance of this creativity-potential. The personal experiences and intimate glimpses of famous speakers also emphasize frequently the special feeling of creativity and great inner gratification to be derived from facing and moving an audience. Clarence Darrow (1857–1938), celebrated defense attorney, champion of the underprivileged, and antagonist of William Jennings Bryan in the Scopes "monkey" trial, revealed a measure of this feeling as he described one of his early speeches:

> I had discovered enough about public speaking to sense that unless a speaker can interest his audience at once, his effort will be a failure.
>
> The audience hesitated and began to sit down. They seemed willing to give me a chance. I had at least one advantage; nothing was expected of me; if I could get their attention, it would be easier than if too much was expected. Not one in twenty of the audience knew much about me. As a matter of fact, I had taken great pains to prepare my speech. The subject was one that had deeply interested me for many years, one that I really understood. In a short time I had the attention of the entire audience, to my surprise. Then came the full confidence which only a speaker can understand; that confidence that is felt as one visits by the fireside, when he can say what he pleases; when the speaker can, in fact, visit with the audience as with an old-time friend. I have no desire to elaborate on my talk, but I know that I had the people with me, and that I could sway those listeners as I wished.
>
> I have talked from platforms countless times since then, but never again have I felt that exquisite thrill of triumph after a speech. That was

forty years ago, and even now I occasionally meet some one who tells me that he heard my speech at Central Music Hall the night I was there with Henry George.[8]

Darrow's statements, in addition to making clear the memorable pleasure he experienced in interacting with his audience, strongly supports a key point we made on page 20. A speaker addressing a large audience is much more likely to be effective if he can see the communication situation as similar to a visit with "an old-time friend"—as closely related to our model of *two persons conversing.*

Another highly persuasive speaker in this century, Malcolm X (1925–1965), a leading spokesman for the black nationalist movement, described a similar inner awakening and exciting self-discovery in being able to move and influence others:

Standing up and speaking before an audience was a thing that throughout my previous life never would have crossed my mind. Out there in the streets, hustling, pushing dope, and robbing, I could have had the dreams from a pound of hashish, and I'd never have dreamed anything so wild as that one day I would speak in coliseums and arenas, and the greatest American universities, and on radio and television programs, not to mention speaking all over Egypt and Africa and in England.

But I will tell you that right there, in the prison, debating, speaking to a crowd, was as exhilarating to me as the discovery of knowledge through reading had been. Standing up there, the faces looking at me, the things in my head coming out of my mouth, while my brain searched for the next best thing to follow what I was saying, and if I could sway them to my side by handling it right, then I had won the debate—once my feet got wet, I was gone on debating. Whichever side of the selected subject was assigned to me, I'd track down and study everything I could find on it. I'd put myself in my opponent's place and decide how I'd try to win if I had the other side; and then I'd figure a way to knock down those points.[9]

Obviously, both of these effective speakers found speech making a uniquely creative and self-satisfying experience. We should also note, in passing, that (1) they had something they wanted very much to say, and (2) they prepared carefully for the speech event.

Emotional-outlet speech.[10]   Some speakers—usually much less effective than Darrow and Malcolm X—mouth words as if they were good food. By being excessively wordy and repeating themselves over and over, they savor what they consider to be a good phrase or thought. Quite often, the speaking they do is done for its own sake, as if the words were made to be tasted—delicious morsels to be turned temptingly on the tongue. *Real* communication, as we have been trying to describe it, is rarely their goal.

In describing this kind of speech, some writers use the word *consumatory* (coming from the word *consume)* and others use *consummatory* (from *con-*

summate). Regardless of the name given it, this kind of speech is largely—and certainly initially—"internal," in that its primary purpose is *to generate satisfaction within the speaker.* It enables the speaker *to derive some inner gratification, to relieve his innermost emotions or feelings* because—first of all—to do so somehow allows him to "feel better."

Theodore Clevenger, Jr., and Jack Matthews make a useful distinction between what they call "consummatory" and "instrumental" speech by noting that:

> *Even when the primary purpose of the communication is instrumental—for instance, to secure concessions or to quell a riot—such consummatory elements as profanity, irrelevant attacks on "the establishment," moralistic generalizations, etc., are very likely to manifest themselves. Thus, we may say that whenever content appears in a communication without regard to its intended effect on some group of receivers, it represents consummatory communication.*[11]

This description is similar to ours in a number of respects and suggests, among other things, that the consummatory or emotional-outlet purpose of speech works in a *variety* of directions and is not always readily recognizable. In certain situations, for instance, such as those involving direct and very personal salesmanship, legal argument (especially as it is addressed to jurors), auctioneering, and carnival huckstering, the consummatory speech purpose may take a highly *competitive*—almost *combative*—turn. You might call this the "go-getter" variation. We've all met the "high-pressure" life-insurance or automobile salesman who insists on giving us the "hard sell" even though we've obviously made up our minds to buy what he has to offer. He is typical of some speakers, especially those whose work is by nature aggressive or combative, who seem unable to accept victory without a contest. For them, a large part of the reward is to be found in the *verbal battle.* The means have thus become an end in themselves.

From what we have been saying, we do not mean to imply that the emotional-outlet purpose of speech tends to produce only negative effects. While it's true that at its worst it can seriously damage or even destroy desirable human relationships, at its best it can provide a much-needed measure of self-stabilization and self-reassurance for the user. In fact, as we are about to see, this kind of intrapersonal motivation often generates some very positive and beneficial results—especially as it bears upon the release of our inner tensions.

Diminishing Tensions

In an overpopulated and tension-ridden society such as ours, people must have the means to reduce their frustrations and feelings of being "uptight." Otherwise they can't hope to maintain their mental balance and a sense of well-being. Psychologists and behavioral scientists have, in fact, shown us that much of human behavior is motivated by the need to balance or reduce internal tensions. To the extent that speech communication helps us "let off steam," it can reduce our frustrations and help us retain our emotional stability.

When you bark your shin, for instance, you yell "Ouch!"—or something stronger. And somehow that makes it hurt less. Probably there have been times, too, when—using speech as a pressure-escape valve—you have "told someone off," and have experienced a great deal of satisfaction for the effective way you did it. You were probably so proud that you recalled the incident over and over, at first silently to yourself and later telling your friends, co-workers, or anyone else who would listen. Your pleasure in telling and retelling that story of your verbal prowess—like the pleasure of chewing a good piece of steak—gave you considerable satisfaction while, at the same time, it reduced the tensions created by the original conflict. At other times, if the telling off didn't turn out so well, you may have repeated over and over what you "should have said." In either case, you feel better—you are less "uptight."

Similarly, guilt or frustration or the anxious desire to see social change can produce inner tensions which can be reduced appreciably only by "speaking up" about them. Like most of us, you have no doubt experienced that satisfying relief that comes from discussing a distressing personal problem with a friend. *Saying* it—"getting it off your chest"—dissipates some of the emotional and physical tautness associated with the problem. In like manner, if you feel strongly that one candidate for a job or political office is much better qualified than another, that inner conviction can create tensions which will drive you to speak up for the person of your choice. In situations of these kinds, you feel the *need* to say something—and you say it.

In contrast, if you have nothing that you feel you simply *must* say, if you are not moved to speak from a burning *desire* to speak, your listeners may well detect your lack of conviction. When this happens, your uncertain feeling—rather than your intended message—will communicate itself to them. This is why we say so emphatically: In any speech communication situation, whether inside the classroom or out, your chances of being really effective will be far greater if you choose a topic that is so *vital to you* that you experience an emotional release when you are speaking about it.

Prolonging speech. One of the tension-relieving uses of speech is to prolong consideration of an important question or issue. You may, for example, find yourself in a situation in which the ideal "timing" for the desired action is not quite yet. So, because you feel that the proposed action is so important to all concerned, you talk—and you *keep on* talking. Or you manage to have others keep it going. You prolong the talking just as long as you can to prevent the matter from being dropped or lost sight of. Legislators often use this talk-much-and-delay-action approach, hoping that a final vote on the matter can be postponed until tensions have "cooled off," until more information can be collected and "better" judgments arrived at.

If unfairly used, this kind of stalling tactic or filibustering should be condemned. But, if used sensibly and sparingly, this tension-reduction approach to human relationships can be a valuable tool. Speaking for the purpose of prolonging a decision is especially useful for the individual or the group that wants a social or economic change which, though justifiable, doesn't as yet have broad support. For all concerned, speaking for this purpose helps maintain tensions at a "live-withable" level. It can hold the group together. And it can provide the hope that *eventually* a perplexing problem can be solved or an unfair condition corrected. In the history of our country, for example, a number of third-party or minority movements have led ultimately to significant social, economic, and political adjustments. Usually these efforts began with a high talk-to-action ratio. By prolonging talk, such groups have been able to keep a key issue in the public ear until the proposed action became more generally acceptable and achievable.

To the extent that you use prolonging talk to diminish your own inner tensions, its dimensions will be largely *intra*personal; to the extent that you may be trying to diminish tensions in others, its dimensions will be *inter*personal.

Avoiding silence. Silence can communicate, both constructively and destructively. And it can either create or diminish tensions. Certain societies cultivate the practice of "communing" in silence. Some religious groups encourage periods of silence and meditation. Individually, from time to time many of us may feel the need to reflect quietly—that there is, at such moments, no need for speech. Quite properly, we believe, we need not speak until we have something to say.

In our society, however, silence is not necessarily golden. Not uncommonly we punish one another by giving the "silent treatment." Frequently parents use silence to punish children by seeming to withhold attention and, therefore (in the child's eyes), affection. Children, in turn, use silence to register their rebellion. In these and similar ways, silence can create deep and lasting tensions.

You won't have to look very hard to find other instances of this negative, tension-producing purpose of silence. It's evident in a huge number of human relationships and at almost every level of our society. What, for instance, is more stressful than being hostess at a very quiet party where the guests refuse to converse—if not wittily, at least perfunctorily? What is less enjoyable than finding yourself at a party where most of the people—strangers all—arrive in cultural or professional or conversational straitjackets and most of the "good spirits" are contained in bottles? In very many communications settings—especially in social contexts—we place such a high premium on *not* being silent that we are willing to engage in *any* kind of talk, however empty, fatuous, caustic, malicious, or ego-shattering it may be. The main thing is to fill the void so as to relieve our tensions and soothe our fears.

Most of us probably would agree how pointless and even harmful such void-filling chatter can be. But the fact that we are willing to put up with it for the sake of preventing an awkward silence is proof enough of the tension-triggering potential of silence. As you study the pages of this text, you will become increasingly able to inform and train yourself to react appropriately and productively in both the silent and the speaking "domain" of human interaction. That, at least, is one of the reasons why this book has been written. If you know when and how to be silent when the situation calls for it and—perhaps even more important—when and how to *break* silence by having something interesting, intelligent, and constructive to say, you will have taken two very important steps toward becoming a better communicator. 4

ESTABLISHING SOCIAL CONTACT

Speech communication becomes necessary, in part, because people are psychologically isolated from one another. In the psychological sense, people are quite alone and self-dependent. At the same time, they realize that as human beings they *need* other human beings—that they are essentially interdependent. Perhaps this "contradiction" between isolation and interdependency—this ambivalence—is what Kenneth Burke had in mind when he wrote:

> *If men were not apart from one another, there would be no need for the rhetorician to proclaim their unity. If men were wholly and truly of one substance, absolute communication would be of man's very essence. It would not be an ideal, as it now is, partly embodied in material conditions and partly frustrated by these same conditions.*[12]

From this interdependency we can infer another of the major purposes served by speech communication: *to establish social contact in order to achieve human understanding and cooperation.* Through speech communication, human beings can express their interdependence, can create and proclaim their *mutuality*—their common interests and common understandings. Psychologist Grace De Laguna emphasized the importance of this purpose when she described oral

Study Probe 4
Observing the Results of Silences

In the cafeteria, your dorm, or wherever else a "bull session" is in progress, take a back seat, and, with a pen and some paper, listen to the conversation. If someone notices your seemingly bizarre behavior, supply whatever alibi you need: you must complete a speech assignment; you are using your friends as guinea pigs in an experiment; or you are just "writing something." You be the judge of how to handle it. As you listen, each time a pause occurs in the conversation, record the first remark *immediately* following it.

Later, look at your list of remarks and write a short paper describing the communication situation you observed—the time, the place, the people involved (were they friends or strangers?), and the seriousness of the discussion (was it mostly idle chatter?)—and, within that context, evaluate which comments seemed most and least appropriate for breaking the silences. Indicate the times when the speakers were most obviously struggling to maintain the conversation. Hand in your paper, along with your list of remarks.

communication as "the great medium through which human cooperation is brought about."[13]

Of course, *cooperative action* will not automatically follow from every attempt at communicative interaction. Not every failure in human relationships is a sign of "failure to communicate." This age-old myth, which is so deeply embedded in our cultural roots, should be critically reexamined. We may have to recognize that sometimes differing systems of government, different people, different values, and different ideas really *are* incompatible. Sometimes, in fact, human differences can be aggravated by open and full communication. Sometimes it is better to remain silent—to avoid communicative interaction. But just because speech communication can't resolve all differences and solve all problems is no reason to underestimate its potential for bringing about human cooperation.

To see how apart—how really isolated and lonely—people can be in our society we have only to look about. All around us we can see many groups, large and small, in which people have distressing differences and interact not at all or with severe constraint. Such groups are disrupted by feelings of hate, distrust, or indifference. Therefore, despite our caution against viewing communication as a cure-all for human ailments and conflicts, we see it as the only means by which to reduce our social, economic, intellectual, religious, and generational gaps and "bring ourselves together." Only in speaking together can we hope to allay our fears and fulfill our longings and expectations. To this end, speech must play an increasingly productive role.

 Study Probe 5
Analyzing a Social Grooming Ritual

In social grooming or verbal stroking rituals, the *words* exchanged often bear little or no relationship to the *messages* actually communicated. Consider, for example, the following ritual which often opens a conversation:

First Speaker: Hi. How are you?
Second Speaker: Can't complain. And you?
First Speaker: Just fine, thanks.

Though both speakers seem to be inquiring about the other's health, they really aren't. Wouldn't either be surprised and perhaps irritated by a 15-minute medical report in response to the other's initial inquiry?

The ritual really is an exchange of two verbal strokes: an empty question traded for an empty answer, followed by a similar trade of question and answer. Roughly translated, the conversation may actually mean:

First Speaker: I'd like to open the conversation and establish my presence.

How—in a real and practical sense—do we go about this "social contacting"? Animals, in their wild state, can be observed in the act of grooming one
another. This "social grooming" helps them establish cooperative, nonaggressive, social contact. Writing in *The Naked Ape*, anthropologist Desmond
Morris finds the human equivalent of such behavior in "grooming talking," which
he describes as

> . . . the meaningless, polite chatter of social occasions, the "nice weather
> we are having" or the "have you read any good books lately" form of talk-
> ing. It is not concerned with the exchange of important ideas or informa-
> tion, nor does it reveal the true mood of the speaker, nor is it aesthetically
> pleasing. Its function is to reinforce the greeting smile and to maintain so-
> cial togetherness. It is our substitute for social grooming. By providing us
> with a nonaggressive social preoccupation, it enables us to expose our-
> selves communally to one another over comparatively long periods, in
> this way enabling valuable group bonds and friendships to grow and be-
> come strengthened.[14]

By means of such "grooming talking" (also known as "verbal stroking"),
human beings establish contact—a touching-together which describes itself in
such terms as *openness, friendliness, personal warmth, congeniality and con-
viviality,* and even *simple courtesy.* [5]

We are not suggesting, certainly, that all social-contact speech has to

---

Second Speaker: OK, I acknowledge your presence and give you permission to continue the conversation. Please acknowledge my presence
as well.
First Speaker: Permission accepted and presence acknowledged.

Having completed the ritual, the two speakers can safely discuss more
serious matters (including the *real* state of their health!) or the conversation can
end—a mere exchange of strokes between people passing each other on the
street.

Try to analyze a similar social grooming ritual, writing out and translating
the exchange in a few paragraphs. Then, in class, your instructor will call on
each of you to read your papers aloud and to collect a large list of the rituals
you discuss. Feel free to disagree with or modify each other's interpretations of
the rituals.

As preparation for the class discussion, read Study Probe 6.

be pointless politeness. What we are emphasizing is that people must establish contact and affirm their social nature, and the speech communication process provides them with the most direct and personal means for accomplishing this.

In research related to small discussion groups, Professor Laura Crowell and I found that nearly half the comments made by participants in problem-solving situations were statements confirming, or further clarifying or substantiating, ideas already before the group.[15] In other words, much of the talking that went on was not—in terms of actual substance—logically necessary for the development of a decision by the group. What did appear to be psychologically necessary, however, was the participants' need for *oral play on an idea* and the *voicing of concurrence.* Such psychological needs are, of course, related to "grooming talk." One thing that we can be sure of, in any case, is that comments made for the purpose of mutual clarification and confirmation of agreement are important in establishing social interchange. This sense of contacting and social bonding, basic to small group interaction and the loyalty of its members to the group's decision, is equally apparent and influential in one-to-one (dyadic) and one-to-many (public) speech communication.

To sum up what we have been saying here, another of the primary and basic purposes of speech communication is that of *social contact*—the bringing together of communicative agents for interaction that can lead to common and cooperative effort.

EXERTING MUTUAL INFLUENCE

As human beings attempt to *maintain* and *extend* the emotional and intellectual contact they make with one another, they recognize a need *to inform: to exchange information and share ideas.* Desmond Morris, again writing in *The Naked Ape,* describes this sharing and exchanging as "information talking" and maintains that such talking is the most important form of vocal communication for our species.[16] His view differs from that of some others, including both classical and contemporary rhetoricians, who say that the overriding purpose of speech communication is *to persuade.* "Rhetorical study in its strict sense," they note, "is concerned with the modes of persuasion." [17]

With this distinction we are not deeply or immediately concerned here. If people really want to share information and proclaim their ideas, very likely they are going to have to inform *and* persuade—and, quite likely, they will do *both* at the same time. To inform a person, you have to convince that individual by means that are either direct or indirect that your information is accurate, trustworthy, and worth knowing. To persuade someone, you have to inform that person of the facts on which you base your argument or claim; you have to give him or her the information pertinent to your case or cause. Usually it is more useful, we think, to view these purposes as working *in combination* because ultimately both are concerned with the *mutual influencing* of communication agents. In this view, communication agents influence and are influenced.

At the same time, however, we should realize that in a given context or circumstance one or the other of these purposes may appear to predominate. In public communication, for instance, where the message is often highly structured and uninterrupted, the speaker will give unmistakable emphasis to an informative purpose or a persuasive purpose. In the classroom, the lecturer will frequently want—above all—*to inform*. At a political rally, the speaker customarily will try *to persuade*. There will be variations and extensions, too, of the informative/persuasive intention. In a church, we may expect the sermonizer *to stimulate* and *to inspire*. In a night club, we may expect a comedian *to entertain*. If we seek advice from a friend, we expect her *to share* our feelings and *to counsel* us as to the best course of action. ⑥

But even so, as you can quickly see, these variant or extended purposes will overlap. Entertainment often accompanies information. Inspiration may combine with stimulation. Stimulation may join forces with persuasion. And persuasion, as we've said, rarely occurs without information. What is important here is that in interacting with others, we will be more effective in getting our message across if we are clearly aware of the purposes—and cross-purposes—that are at work in the situation. And very probably, we will be more successful in our interpersonal relationships if we reveal—rather than conceal—the specific and immediate purpose we have in mind.

Study Probe 6
Classifying Communication

Tape-record the in-class discussion of social grooming rituals mentioned in the previous Study Probe, and appoint three or more people to serve as secretaries. For a few of the more lively exchanges, the three secretaries should, on a signal from the instructor, attempt to classify each remark into one of the following categories, using whatever shorthand method they wish. The tape recording will contain the full remarks.

Essentially Informative	Essentially Persuasive	Essentially Oral Play or Concurrence
1.		
2.		
3.		
4.		
5.		
6.		
7.		
8.		

Since these arbitrary categories overlap, the lists should differ among the secretaries, who should report their findings to the class for full debate.

To summarize briefly, in this section and the one immediately preceding, we have considered two fundamental purposes which speaking/listening agents will have in all interpersonal/public communicative contexts—establishing social contact and exerting mutual influence. In looking at these purposes, we need to dwell more on their common features than on differences between them; we need to focus on their central rather than peripheral aspects. This perspective, you will recall, parallels the one we took in Chapter 1, where we suggested that all speech communication, regardless of variations in form or setting, can be best represented by the model of two persons conversing.

CONTROLLING OUR ENVIRONMENT

In a very broad sense, all of the purposes for which we speak are concerned with controlling our environment. Intrapersonally, all of our striving to proclaim our existence and maintain a reasonably convincing self-image will strengthen us—or so we like to believe—in our struggle to shape and reshape our surroundings. By enlarging and enriching our sense of self-satisfaction and cutting down on our tensions, we think we can better cope with and adjust to our world. These, as we have said, are primarily "internal" purposes. And interpersonally, of course, all of our efforts to establish social contact with other human beings and to influence each other have the overriding goal of controlling the environment into which we are born and with which we must successfully interact if we are to survive. These purposes, obviously, involve the interaction of communicative agents.

In considering this final, control-of-environment purpose of speech communication, we are thinking primarily of the means—the specific "tools," actually—by which each one of us, as a single communicative agent, is able to exercise some degree of control. There are, of course, a number of means by which we can achieve this. Let's look at just one of them—a major one—*language.* Much of our ability to shape and dominate our physical and psychological environment is bound up in the nature of language itself. Later, in Chapter 4, we will look in a more critical and detailed way at the relationship of language to speaking and thinking. The implications are many, but a brief comment on only one of them will serve to demonstrate the kind of control-of-environment purpose we are talking about here.

At one time or another, you have probably been told that if you cannot express an idea clearly, you do not have the idea clearly in mind. This correctly implies that when we attach a word-label to an object, we gain a measure of control over that object. Once we provide the label, with all that *that* implies, we are able to manipulate the object *symbolically:* We can think about it in the abstract and in its absence. We are able to freeze it in time and place. We are able to communicate with others about it; that is, we can "put it into words."

To cite an example, if we did not have a word *dog,* we could still collect sensory impressions of the animal and create an "internal" image which would enable us to *think* about "dog." However, if we wanted to *talk with others* about this particular kind of animal, we would have to invent a "dog" word or devise a label of some kind. The same is true of all objects and concepts that we name, label, and symbolize. In this way, the use of language and speech gives us a certain control over a portion of our enviroment. ⬚7⬚

In response to our original question, "Why do we communicate?" we find that there is not one answer, but many. The conscious desires of one person to make contact with and to influence another are by no means the only purpose served by speech communication. If, as students of speech behavior, we are to make a meaningful *analysis* of the speech process, we must be aware of all the factors and forces which produce it. If, as practitioners of oral communication, we are to produce meaningful messages, we must intelligently and discriminantly *utilize* these factors and forces. And, finally, we must combine them in such ways as to ensure to the greatest extent possible the interaction we desire and the purposes we hope to accomplish.

In trying to answer the other questions we raised at the start of this chapter, we have examined some of the influences which motivate speakers and which, at the same time, limit the range of possible speech behaviors in a given situation. We have analyzed some of the influential effects which self-image, experience, the specific speech context, and other persons can have upon a speaker. We have considered the inner drives and tensions which move the speaker. And we have attempted to determine the ways in which speaking can contribute to self-satisfaction and help us to maintain social contact. Specifically, we have considered the following purposes of speech communication:

1. To assert self-existence.
2. To establish self-concept.   } Self-identifying and
3. To achieve self-satisfaction.   self-fulfilling purposes
4. To diminish tensions.
5. To establish social contact.   — Social-contacting purpose
6. To exert mutual influence.   — Mutual-influencing purpose
7. To gain control over the   — Control-of-environment purpose
   environment.

Study Probe 7
Identifying Language That Controls a Private Environment

Sometimes you invent words to share with friends, relatives, or co-workers, thus controlling a small portion of your private environment. Write a paper to hand in listing and defining five or ten such words. If you can, explain what experience originated each word and speculate about why you continue to share the word with others. Is the word's purpose mostly humorous? Does it establish more intimacy between you and others? Does it identify an object or experience for which no word existed previously?

On the basis of this list and the lines of inquiry we have pursued in this chapter, we must conclude that speech communication clearly serves a great many purposes. We encourage you to continue to search out and investigate these purposes and possibly discover others. We also urge you to think seriously about the implications and applications of these purposes as you work to improve your own speaking and as you observe and evaluate the *effects* they produce upon the speech of others.

Suggested Readings

Martin P. Andersen, E. Ray Nichols, Jr., and Herbert W. Booth, *The Speaker and His Audience* (New York: Harper & Row, Publishers, 1974). Chapter 3, especially pages 55–63, affords some insightful extensions of the behavioral-response purposes inherent in human speech.

Charles T. Brown and Charles Van Riper, *Speech and Man* (Englewood Cliffs, N.J.: Prentice-Hall, Inc., 1966). This small but meaningful paperback volume pursues in some detail the varied purposes served by oral communication. Inspiring as well as informative.

George Herbert Mead, *Mind, Self, and Society,* ed. Charles W. Morris (Chicago: University of Chicago Press, 1962). This work, especially Part III on "The Self," contributes significantly to an understanding of the social-communicative nature of humankind.

Alan H. Monroe and Douglas Ehninger, *Principles and Types of Speech Communication,* 7th ed. (Glenview, Ill.: Scott, Foresman and Company, 1974). For an interesting and practical consideration of the conventional, rhetorical reasons why we communicate—to inform, to persuade, to actuate, etc.—see especially Chapters 7, 19, 20, and 21.

Jean Piaget, *The Language and Thought of the Child,* trans. Marjorie Gabain (New York: World Publishing Company, 1955). This authoritative volume develops some challenging notions about the emergence of the child's thinking and speaking and the purposes which strongly influence them.

Lev S. Vygotsky, *Thought and Language,* ed. and trans. Eugenia Hanfmann and Gertrude Vakar (New York: John Wiley & Sons, Inc., 1962). Vygotsky offers some thought-provoking ideas about why human beings speak and how speech communication develops. His views contrast interestingly with the theories of Piaget.

Reference Notes

[1]René Descartes (1596–1650) was a French philosopher, mathematician, and author. The basis of his philosophy is summed up in the words: *Cogito ergo sum.* ("I think, therefore I am.")

[2]The student's research was prompted by the writings of Piaget and Vygotsky concerning social-versus-egocentric speech behaviors—specifically: Jean Piaget,

The Language and Thought of the Child, trans. Marjorie Gabain (New York: The World Publishing Company, 1955); and Lev S. Vygotsky, *Thought and Language,* ed. and trans. Eugenia Hanfmann and Gertrude Vakar (New York: John Wiley & Sons, Inc., 1962).

[3]Joost A. M. Meerloo, "Contributions of Psychiatry to the Study of Human Communication," *Human Communication Theory,* ed. Frank E. X. Dance (New York: Holt, Rinehart & Winston, Inc., 1967), p. 132.

[4]George Herbert Mead, *Mind, Self, and Society: From the Standpoint of a Social Behaviorist,* ed. Charles W. Morris (Chicago: University of Chicago Press, 1934). See especially Part III on "Self."

[5]If interested in this topic, you could begin your reading with Susanne K. Langer, *Philosophy in a New Key* (New York: The New American Library, Inc. Mentor Books, 1948), pp. 97–99.

[6]Edward Zigler and Irving L. Child, "Socialization," *The Handbook of Social Psychology,* 2nd ed., ed. Gardner Lindzey and Elliot Aronson (Reading, Mass.: Addison-Wesley Publishing Co., Inc., 1969), v. III, pp. 547–548.

[7]Joost A. M. Meerloo, "Contributions of Psychiatry to the Study of Human Communication," *Human Communication Theory,* ed. Frank E. X. Dance (New York: Holt, Rinehart & Winston, Inc., 1967), p. 142.

[8]Clarence Darrow, *The Story of My Life* (New York: Charles Scribner's Sons, 1932), pp. 46–47.

[9]Malcolm X, *The Autobiography of Malcolm X* (New York: Grove Press, Inc., 1966), p. 184.

[10]Some of these thoughts have come from the author's interaction with Edmund C. Nuttall.

[11]Theodore Clevenger, Jr., and Jack Matthews, *The Speech Communication Process* (Glenview, Ill.: Scott, Foresman and Company, 1971), p. 162.

[12]Kenneth Burke, *A Grammar of Motives and a Rhetoric of Motives* (New York: World Publishing Company, 1962), p. 546.

[13]Grace Andrus De Laguna, *Speech: Its Function and Development* (New Haven, Conn.: Yale University Press, 1927), p. 19. Reissued by Indiana University Press, Bloomington, 1963.

[14]Desmond Morris, *The Naked Ape* (New York: McGraw-Hill Company, 1967), p. 167.

[15]Thomas M. Scheidel and Laura Crowell, "Idea Development in Small Discussion Groups," *Quarterly Journal of Speech,* 50 (1964): 140–145.

[16]Desmond Morris, *The Naked Ape* (New York: McGraw-Hill Book Company, 1967), p. 166.

[17]Aristotle, *Rhetoric, The Basic Works of Aristotle,* ed. Richard McKeon (New York: Random House, Inc. 1941), p. 1327. For a contemporary view emphasizing the role of persuasion as one basic, encompassing speech purpose, see *The Prospect of Rhetoric,* ed. Lloyd F. Bitzer and Edwin Black (Englewood Cliffs, N.J.: Prentice-Hall, Inc., 1971).

Chapter 3

SELF-DISCOVERY
AND
SELF-ACTUALIZATION

Develop *self-awareness*—a sensitivity to
your own potential as a communicator—and an
active desire for *self-actualization.*
Prefer to act for yourself—to be all that you
can be—and to be accepted on your own terms
for what you *are.*

Our focus in Chapters 1 and 2 has been upon *the speaking/listening agent as an individual,* with definite emphasis upon the *intrapersonal* factors—that is, those factors within the self—involved in the speech communication process. We have also noted that among the essential elements of this process are *agents* who *interact* within a *context.* And we have looked rather closely at the reasons *why* we communicate, namely:

To achieve self-identification and self-fulfillment
To establish social contact
To exert mutual influence
To control our environment

In this chapter we will look even more closely at the role of *the self* in communicative interaction. We will be centering our concern upon what the interactive self is and does—the "dimensions" it takes on—in order to accomplish and actualize the important purposes of communication. In other words, the self will be the core of our immediate "universe" as we try to relate it as closely as we can to the purposes we have identified and the "dimensions" of self we are about to explore. The following diagram may serve as a useful starting point:

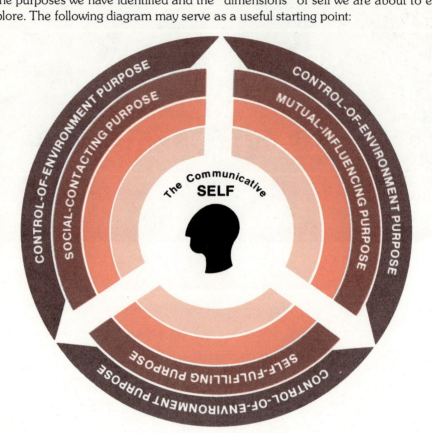

With these general relationships in mind, let's begin to explore some of the ways in which as speaker/listeners we can through (1) careful *self-assessment* gain (2) greater *self-awareness* and thereby achieve (3) greater *self-actualization* as communicators.

DIMENSIONS OF THE SELF IN SPEECH COMMUNICATION

"Know thyself" is ancient and sound advice. As speaking/listening agents, certainly, we can be more effective as we become more fully aware of our own abilities, interests, knowledge, and especially of the impressions we make upon others. Every communicator has to strive for this enlarged awareness.

Our self-image is our touchstone—our standard reference and the basis for many of our recollections and judgments. Reference-to-self is the pivotal point when we recall our experiences, and we usually date events from the viewpoint of how they involved us. We see and judge others first of all in terms of our self-image. And above all—when we really want to make the most of communication—we must see ourselves in terms of our relationships to and interaction with others.

Suppose, for a moment, that you are a player in a baseball game. It's the last half of the last inning. The opposing team is at bat. There is one out. The score is tied. The winning run is on third base. The pitcher throws. The batter connects. As an outfielder going deep for a high fly ball, you must keep your eye on the ball, run to it, catch it, and get set to throw it to home plate without having to watch the other players move into position to make the put-out. You must depend on their knowing how to complete the play and upon their ability to do so. You and each of the other players must not only know your "place" or individual role in the game, but you must also know how your "position" relates to all the other "positions" and the people who play them.

In this regard, communication is very much like a ball game. There are "understood" roles and rules for the interaction, "player" relationships to be maintained, and actions to be accomplished. The understanding of *self,* as we are using the term here, means that as a speaking/listening agent you understand clearly your "place" in the communicative interaction—that you understand what you can do, what you are expected to do, and how others will be acting and reacting toward you.

Analyzing Communicative Self-Dimensions

The "self" is extremely complex and, because it is unique to each individual, very difficult to describe. Yet if we are to provide some adequate means for self-assessment, we need a classification system which will reduce the complexity and simplify the description of self-as-communicator. If we are going to try to assess our communicative capacities and possibilities, how do we begin? Just what should we *look* for—what tendencies, inclinations or predispositions, factors, and relationships? What kinds of "positions" or roles do we take with others when we are trying to relate *our* self with *their* self? Well, for one thing, we can try to evolve a set of "measurements" or "dimensions" and apply them to *our* self to see how—as individuals—we stack up as communicators in a variety of communicative situations.

This won't be easy. But, fortunately, we aren't the first to face this problem. The desire to develop some sort of communicative-self-analysis system began long ago, and over the years a number of people have suggested some interesting interrelational dimensions within which to see and understand the "connections" between *our* self and the self of *others* when communication is happening or about to happen. Taking a very brief look at a few of them may help us put together a useful scheme of self-analysis.

The Greek philosopher Aristotle, in his famed *Rhetoric,* was apparently suggesting some such system when he pointed out the susceptibility of the self to certain "appeals" or "modes" of persuasion in the public-speech setting. The factors that are at work in the persuasive relationship, he said, are: (1) *ethos,* or the personal character and perceived credibility of the speaking agent, (2) *emotional appeal,* as the speaker touches upon those elements that motivate behavior, and (3) *logical appeal,* made up of evidence (substance) and argument (reasoning) to the case at hand.[1] In short, Aristotle's "system" provided three "dimensions" or interrelationships that we can think about when we try to relate our self to some other self. These include a *personal* dimension, an *emotional* dimension, and a *cognitive* or "substance-for-reasoning" dimension.

In much more recent times, sociologists Kenneth Benne and Paul Sheats, in describing the functional relationships of individuals in a small group setting, have also laid out a three-dimensioned system of interactional analysis.[2] In the Benne/Sheats system, the self is seen as a kind of "role alternator." In interacting, the communicating self plays various roles depending upon whether the individual is engaged in (1) establishing and sustaining a strongly self-centered "individuality," (2) helping the group as a whole to do its job or "task," or (3) helping to hold the group together—to "build it up" and maintain itself. This brief sampling will give you an idea of the Benne/Sheats role classifications:[*]

THE SELF'S "INDIVIDUAL" ROLES   **ROLE FUNCTION**

1.	Aggressor	deflates status, attacks others
2.	Blocker	negates, disagrees, opposes
3.	Recognition-Seeker	boasts, calls attention to self
4.	Dominator	asserts authority, superiority, control
5.	Self-Confessor	gives personal, non-group-oriented insight

THE SELF'S "GROUP-TASK" ROLES   **ROLE FUNCTION**

1.	Initiator-Contributor	suggests new ideas, new proposals
2.	Information Seeker	seeks information, clarification
3.	Information Giver	gives facts, "authoritative" generalizations
4.	Elaborator	develops and extends ideas of group
5.	Coordinator	pulls ideas together, shows relationships

THE SELF'S "GROUP-BUILDING-AND-MAINTENANCE" ROLES   **ROLE FUNCTION**

1.	Encourager	praises, agrees, provides solidarity
2.	Harmonizer	mediates differences
3.	Compromiser	offers compromise involving his/her position
4.	Gate-Keeper	keeps communication channels open

[*]Adapted from Kenneth D. Benne and Paul Sheats. "Functional Roles of Group Members," JOURNAL OF SOCIAL ISSUES, Vol. 4, No. 2 (1948), pp. 41–49. Reprinted by permission of JOURNAL OF SOCIAL ISSUES and the authors.

As you can readily see, the *individual roles* are primarily self-assertive, self-actualizing, and turned inward. The self's *group-task roles* are more concerned with the positive ways in which the self can contribute to the substance and reasoning needed to accomplish the group's goal. And the self's *group-building-and-maintenance roles* generally are more social-emotional and supportive of others.

In another analysis of the self as it is involved in group interaction, social psychologist Launor Carter has come up with a three-factor system that—overall—is quite similar to that of Benne and Sheats. Carter sees his "factors" as follows:

> *Factor 1. Individual Prominence*—the behaviors which point to the individual self as he or she stands out from the group. Such traits as aggressiveness, leadership, self-confidence, and self-assertiveness are seen as the self's attempt to achieve individual recognition from the group.

> *Factor 2. Group-Goal Facilitation*—the behaviors which are effective in helping the group as a whole achieve the goal toward which it is oriented. Efficiency, adaptability, cooperation, etc., are viewed as traits which facilitate group action in solving the group's task.

> *Factor 3. Group Sociability*—behaviors which indicate the positive social interaction of the individual self in the group. The important traits here include sociability, a striving for group acceptance, and an adaptability, which—taken all together—represent a friendly, interpersonal behavior pattern of the individual self toward the other members of the group.[3]

Similarly, psychologist Robert F. Bales, in his *Personality and Interpersonal Behavior,* offers what he describes as "a three dimensional spatial model which may be used to visualize and describe the participants in a group and to infer what their relations with each other are likely to be."[4] Basically, Bales contends, when an individual is taking part in a decision-making or policy-making group, the *position* taken by the self can be located and described in terms of three factors: (1) a "Personal Dominance" factor, (2) an "Interpersonal Friendliness" factor, and (3) a "Task-Work Oriented" factor.

Perhaps the most widely-referred-to system for analyzing what happens to the self in interpersonal relations, is the one worked out by William Schutz.[5] Schutz' system, too, has three dimensions; and while not identical to those of Benne and Sheats, Carter, or Bales, it has some implications in common with them. Schutz bases his analysis on the needs-of-the-self: *inclusion* (to have the attention of others), *affection* (to have friendliness from others), and *control* (to have acceptance-of-influence from others).

Now let's try to pull together—to summarize—the essential characteristics of "dimensions" of the five systems we've taken note of. The most useful way to do this, probably, is to put the somewhat similar elements of each into a table which may serve to dramatize the comparison and conclusions we hope to make; thus:

Table 1.   DIMENSIONS OF THE SELF IN COMMUNICATIVE INTERACTION.

System and Source	Self-Centered, Self-Actualizing Dimension	Affective, Emotional (Feeling) Dimension	Substantive, Task-Related Dimension
ARISTOTLE	*Ethos*	Emotional Appeal	Logical Appeal
BENNE/SHEATS	Individualistic Role	Building-and-Maintenance Role	Task-Centered Role
CARTER	Individual Prominence	Group Sociability	Group-Goal Facilitation
BALES	Personal Dominance	Interpersonal Friendliness	Task-Work Orientation
SCHUTZ	Inclusion/Control	Affection	Inclusion/Control

Admittedly, the people whose systems are cited here are not all saying exactly the same thing. The fit of each scheme in our table is not exact and absolute. For instance, Schutz' Inclusion and Control dimensions seem to overlap in relation to the general headings of Task-Relatedness and Self-Centeredness. But despite the minor discrepancies, it is helpful and encouraging to see that so many systems designed to describe the dimensions of the self in interpersonal behavior have arrived at such remarkably similar results.

Three Dimensions of Your Communicative Self

From our brief survey of these five systems, we can conclude, certainly, that one very useful way to describe the communicative self and the selves of other speaking/listening agents is to do it in terms of:

1. A personal, self-actualizing dimension
2. An affective, feeling dimension
3. A task-related, substantive dimension

These three dimensions or interrelationships can be viewed as being relatively independent of each other, and the communicative predispositions and behaviors of any speaking/listening agent can be measured, we believe, along each of the three. Also—to come back to a point we emphasized at the outset of this chapter—these three dimensions are closely correlated with the major *purposes* of speech communication. Perhaps we can see more clearly now just what those correlations are by adding them to the simple diagram we used on page 50; thus:

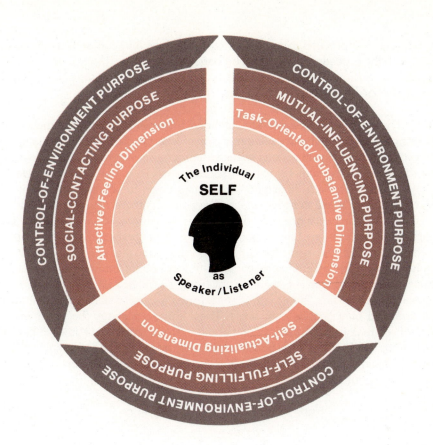

As you can see in this scheme of things, the self-actualizing dimension of communicative behavior is continuously involved in accomplishing the *self-identifying/ self-fulfilling purposes*. The affective/feeling dimension relates directly and significantly to the *social-contacting purposes*. And the task-oriented, substantive dimension is clearly connected to the achievement of the *mutual-influencing purposes* of human interaction.

ASSESSING YOURSELF AS A COMMUNICATOR

The three dimensions-of-self at which we have arrived served as the bases of the "Speech Communication Assessment Scales" which follow. These scales are designed to assist you in discovering and measuring some of the important aspects of your "communicative self," how that "self" relates to the judgments of others' "selves," and more about your "place" as a speaking/listening agent in certain communication contexts. Take time now to study carefully the following instructions for using the Assessment Scales (pages 57–61) and begin to respond to them. Once you have completed them, score them as explained on pages

61–62, and then proceed to make the interpretations and comparisons in accordance with the procedures described on pages 63–65.

Using the Self-Assessment Scales

The Assessment Scales are intended to provide you with a means for analyzing some of your own self-dimensions: your predispositions, inclinations, and probable reactions in various speech-communication settings. By discovering and measuring these dimensions you should begin to understand more clearly how you interrelate with other people; you can begin to see some adjustments you may need to make in order to actualize your communicative abilities and attain your communicative goals. Involved in this measurement—in addition to you yourself, of course—are six important *other communication agents* (father, mother, friend of the same sex, friend of the opposite sex, job supervisor, teacher); four speech *settings or contexts* (talking about future plans, receiving criticism, discussing current events, conversing socially); and three *dimensions* (pleasant/not pleasant, informative/not informative, self-fulfilling/not self-fulfilling) arranged on a "continuum" scale. These three scales tap the three dimensions-of-self that we have been talking about in this chapter: the Affective-Feeling dimension; the Task-Related, Substantive dimension; and the Personal, Self-Actualizing dimension. Study the following example as an illustration of the procedure you should use:

SPEAKING WITH A SMALL CHILD

a.	pleasant	⑦	6	5	4	3	2	1	not pleasant
b.	informative	7	6	5	④	3	2	1	not informative
c.	self-fulfilling	7	6	5	4	3	②	1	not self-fulfilling

First, try to imagine yourself in the given context (in this example, "Speaking with a Small Child"). Then, for each of the three dimensions (a, b, c), circle the appropriate number of the continuum-scale. That is, for the first of the three dimensions (a) circle the number of the continuum-scale which best describes how you think you would "feel" in that situation—how it would affect the emotions you would experience. For the second dimension (b), circle the number on the scale which indicates your assessment of the "substance" or substantive value that would grow out of the interaction insofar as *you* are concerned. And for the third dimension (c), circle the number which suggests the "amount" or degree of self-fulfillment or self-satisfaction that you would probably achieve by interrelating with the other person.

Let's follow through, for example, with the Affective/Feeling dimensions (a). If either of the descriptive terms at the beginning or end of the continuum-scale *describes your feelings completely,* circle the number (7 or 1) next to that term. If one of the terms *describes your feelings fairly well*—but not completely, circle the number one scale-position away from the descriptive term (6 or 2). If one of the terms *describes your feelings only somewhat*—but better than does the other term, then circle the number (5 or 3) two scale-positions from the appropriate term. If neither scale seems appropriate, or if both terms *describe your feelings equally well,* then circle the number 4.

In somewhat similar fashion, proceed to assess yourself in terms of the other two dimensions (b) and (c). In the example above, the person marking the scale as indicated would be describing his/her experiences in speaking with a small child as (a) thoroughly pleasant, (b) neither especially informative nor uninformative, and (c) for the most part not self-fulfilling.

Now try to imagine yourself in each of the twenty-four speech-communication situations listed in the Assessment Scales. For each situation, try to analyze the extent of the feeling or emotion you would have, the substantive or task-related values that would accrue to you, and the degree of self-fulfillment you believe you would experience in that circumstance. There are no correct or incorrect responses because the only purpose of these self-assessments is to provide you with *a better understanding of yourself as a communicator*—a positive step toward "knowing yourself" as a communicative agent.

SPEECH COMMUNICATION ASSESSMENT SCALES

1.   A TALK ABOUT YOUR FUTURE PLANS WITH YOUR FATHER

a.	pleasant	7	6	5	4	3	2	1	not pleasant
b.	informative	7	6	5	4	3	2	1	not informative
c.	self-fulfilling	7	6	5	4	3	2	1	not self-fulfilling

2.   A CRITICISM FROM YOUR MOTHER

a.	pleasant	7	6	5	4	3	2	1	not pleasant
b.	informative	7	6	5	4	3	2	1	not informative
c.	self-fulfilling	7	6	5	4	3	2	1	not self-fulfilling

3.   A DISCUSSION ABOUT CURRENT WORLD EVENTS WITH A CLOSE FRIEND OF THE SAME SEX

a.	pleasant	7	6	5	4	3	2	1	not pleasant
b.	informative	7	6	5	4	3	2	1	not informative
c.	self-fulfilling	7	6	5	4	3	2	1	not self-fulfilling

4. A CONVERSATION AT A SOCIAL AFFAIR WITH A CLOSE FRIEND OF THE OPPOSITE SEX

a.	pleasant	7	6	5	4	3	2	1	not pleasant
b.	informative	7	6	5	4	3	2	1	not informative
c.	self-fulfilling	7	6	5	4	3	2	1	not self-fulfilling

5. A TALK ABOUT YOUR FUTURE PLANS WITH A CLOSE FRIEND OF THE OPPOSITE SEX

a.	pleasant	7	6	5	4	3	2	1	not pleasant
b.	informative	7	6	5	4	3	2	1	not informative
c.	self-fulfilling	7	6	5	4	3	2	1	not self-fulfilling

6. A CRITICISM FROM A CLOSE FRIEND OF THE OPPOSITE SEX

a.	pleasant	7	6	5	4	3	2	1	not pleasant
b.	informative	7	6	5	4	3	2	1	not informative
c.	self-fulfilling	7	6	5	4	3	2	1	not self-fulfilling

7. A DISCUSSION ABOUT CURRENT WORLD EVENTS WITH A JOB SUPERVISOR

a.	pleasant	7	6	5	4	3	2	1	not pleasant
b.	informative	7	6	5	4	3	2	1	not informative
c.	self-fulfilling	7	6	5	4	3	2	1	not self-fulfilling

8. A CONVERSATION AT A SOCIAL AFFAIR WITH A TEACHER

a.	pleasant	7	6	5	4	3	2	1	not pleasant
b.	informative	7	6	5	4	3	2	1	not informative
c.	self-fulfilling	7	6	5	4	3	2	1	not self-fulfilling

9. A TALK ABOUT FUTURE PLANS WITH YOUR MOTHER

a.	pleasant	7	6	5	4	3	2	1	not pleasant
b.	informative	7	6	5	4	3	2	1	not informative
c.	self-fulfilling	7	6	5	4	3	2	1	not self-fulfilling

10. A CRITICISM FROM A TEACHER

a.	pleasant	7	6	5	4	3	2	1	not pleasant
b.	informative	7	6	5	4	3	2	1	not informative
c.	self-fulfilling	7	6	5	4	3	2	1	not self-fulfilling

11. A DISCUSSION ABOUT CURRENT WORLD EVENTS WITH YOUR FATHER

a.	pleasant	7	6	5	4	3	2	1	not pleasant
b.	informative	7	6	5	4	3	2	1	not informative
c.	self-fulfilling	7	6	5	4	3	2	1	not self-fulfilling

12. A CONVERSATION AT A SOCIAL AFFAIR WITH YOUR MOTHER

a.	pleasant	7	6	5	4	3	2	1	not pleasant
b.	informative	7	6	5	4	3	2	1	not informative
c.	self-fulfilling	7	6	5	4	3	2	1	not self-fulfilling

13. A TALK ABOUT YOUR FUTURE PLANS WITH A CLOSE FRIEND OF THE SAME SEX

a.	pleasant	7	6	5	4	3	2	1	not pleasant
b.	informative	7	6	5	4	3	2	1	not informative
c.	self-fulfilling	7	6	5	4	3	2	1	not self-fulfilling

14. A CRITICISM BY YOUR FATHER

a.	pleasant	7	6	5	4	3	2	1	not pleasant
b.	informative	7	6	5	4	3	2	1	not informative
c.	self-fulfilling	7	6	5	4	3	2	1	not self-fulfilling

15. A DISCUSSION ABOUT CURRENT WORLD EVENTS WITH A TEACHER

a.	pleasant	7	6	5	4	3	2	1	not pleasant
b.	informative	7	6	5	4	3	2	1	not informative
c.	self-fulfilling	7	6	5	4	3	2	1	not self-fulfilling

16. A CONVERSATION AT A SOCIAL AFFAIR WITH A CLOSE FRIEND OF THE SAME SEX

a.	pleasant	7	6	5	4	3	2	1	not pleasant
b.	informative	7	6	5	4	3	2	1	not informative
c.	self-fulfilling	7	6	5	4	3	2	1	not self-fulfilling

17. A TALK ABOUT YOUR FUTURE PLANS WITH A JOB SUPERVISOR

a.	pleasant	7	6	5	4	3	2	1	not pleasant
b.	informative	7	6	5	4	3	2	1	not informative
c.	self-fulfilling	7	6	5	4	3	2	1	not self-fulfilling

18. A CRITICISM BY A JOB SUPERVISOR

a.	pleasant	7	6	5	4	3	2	1	not pleasant
b.	informative	7	6	5	4	3	2	1	not informative
c.	self-fulfilling	7	6	5	4	3	2	1	not self-fulfilling

19. A DISCUSSION ABOUT CURRENT WORLD AFFAIRS WITH YOUR MOTHER

a.	pleasant	7	6	5	4	3	2	1	not pleasant
b.	informative	7	6	5	4	3	2	1	not informative
c.	self-fulfilling	7	6	5	4	3	2	1	not self-fulfilling

20. A CONVERSATION AT A SOCIAL AFFAIR WITH A JOB SUPERVISOR

a.	pleasant	7	6	5	4	3	2	1	not pleasant
b.	informative	7	6	5	4	3	2	1	not informative
c.	self-fulfilling	7	6	5	4	3	2	1	not self-fulfilling

21. A TALK ABOUT YOUR FUTURE PLANS WITH A TEACHER

a.	pleasant	7	6	5	4	3	2	1	not pleasant
b.	informative	7	6	5	4	3	2	1	not informative
c.	self-fulfilling	7	6	5	4	3	2	1	not self-fulfilling

22. A CRITICISM BY A CLOSE FRIEND OF THE SAME SEX

a.	pleasant	7	6	5	4	3	2	1	not pleasant
b.	informative	7	6	5	4	3	2	1	not informative
c.	self-fulfilling	7	6	5	4	3	2	1	not self-fulfilling

23. A DISCUSSION ABOUT CURRENT WORLD AFFAIRS WITH A CLOSE FRIEND OF THE OPPOSITE SEX

a.	pleasant	7	6	5	4	3	2	1	not pleasant
b.	informative	7	6	5	4	3	2	1	not informative
c.	self-fulfilling	7	6	5	4	3	2	1	not self-fulfilling

24. A CONVERSATION AT A SOCIAL AFFAIR WITH YOUR FATHER

a.	pleasant	7	6	5	4	3	2	1	not pleasant
b.	informative	7	6	5	4	3	2	1	not informative
c.	self-fulfilling	7	6	5	4	3	2	1	not self-fulfilling

Scoring the Self-Assessment Scales

In the Communication-Profile Scoring-Matrix on page 62, the six agents and the four settings are listed in the column at the extreme left. The numbers printed in the next column refer to the Title-Numbers of the twenty-four separate scales to which you have responded. For example, Scale Numbers 1, 11, 14, and 24 deal with your communicative interaction with your father. So, in the first blank space at the top of the third column write in the *total* of the "Pleasant/Not Pleasant" scores from each of these four scales. Proceed in this manner for all of the agents and all of the settings. Do likewise for the fourth and fifth columns, thus completing the entire matrix. Some interpretations will then be possible.

YOUR COMMUNICATION-PROFILE SCORING-MATRIX

From each of the 24 scales numbered in the second column, write in—in the appropriate spaces—the total of the scores you recorded for each dimension.

COMMUNICATION AGENTS	TITLE-NUMBERS OF THE 24 SCALES	Pleasant/ Not Pleasant	Informative/ Not Informative	Self-Fulfilling/ Not Self-Fulfilling
Father	1, 11, 14, 24			
Mother	2, 9, 12, 19			
Friend— same sex	3, 13, 16, 22			
Friend— opposite sex	4, 5, 6, 23			
Job Supervisor	7, 17, 18, 20			
Teacher	8, 10, 15, 21			
COMMUNICATION SETTINGS				
Talking About Future Plans	1, 5, 9, 13, 17, 21			
Receiving Criticism	2, 6, 10, 14, 18, 22			
Discussing Current World Events	3, 7, 11, 15, 19, 23			
Conversing at a Special Affair	4, 8, 12, 16, 20, 24			

Interpreting the Self-Assessment Scales

You now can note the place you expect your feelings to occupy along each dimension in interaction with each of the six speaking/listening agents in each of the four settings or contexts. For each *agent,* possible scores could range from 4 to 28, with a midpoint of 16. For each *setting,* possible scores could range from 6 to 42, with a midpoint of 24. *Compare your scores with these possible ranges and midpoints.*

Notice, however, that the actual averages obtained from a group of men and women students differ somewhat from these theoretical midpoints. Study Table 2, page 64, where these actual midpoints are shown, and *compare your scores with the averages listed there.*

Next, *compare your self-assessment scores in terms of how you interact with each of the six different agents.* With which one do you find communication most self-fulfilling? *Make similar comparisons in terms of the four different settings.* Which situation do you find most informative? Which is most self-fulfilling? Do you—in general—agree with the interpretations which have emerged from this self-analysis?

Third, *compare your self-assessment profile with that of a classmate.* In which respects are the two profiles most similar? Most different? How do your scores compare with the scores of Student X and Student Y (Table 3, page 65) who participated in this self-assessment program in a previous classroom situation? What interpretations would you make of their scores?

Finally, using a different colored pencil, go over the twenty-four assessment scales again; but this time, score the items in terms of how *you suppose each of the six other speaking/listening agents would feel, evaluate, react, etc.,* when talking with you in the four communicative settings. Then compare the profile from your point of view with that from the other agents' point of view. Would the other agent, in each case, tend to see the situation similarly? How might you account for the differences you detect? Spell out some of the implicit "rules" of communicative interaction on which you and each of the other agents apparently would agree.

Who initiates topics most often? Who is permitted to interrupt? On what levels are status differences maintained, and on which levels do you speak more or less as equals? Which of the other agents seems most like you? Most unlike you? In what specific settings do you provide the most information, pleasure, and opportunities for self-improvement for the other?

Your work with these Speech Communication Self-Assessment Scales is intended to sample only a few of the possible Affective/Feeling, Task/Substantive, and Personal/Self-Actualizing dimensions of yourself as a communicator. To extend your explorations, you could prepare a list of additional agents, or of other settings and contexts. You could also devise a somewhat different set of scales to measure some of your other interactive dimensions. The possibilities are limitless.

TABLE 2. A COMPARISON OF SOME ACTUAL SELF-ASSESSMENT, MIDPOINT SCORES OF COLLEGE MEN AND WOMEN.

	MEN			WOMEN		
	Pleasant/ Not Pleasant	Informative/ Not Informative	Self-Fulfilling/ Not Self-Fulfilling	Pleasant/ Not Pleasant	Informative/ Not Informative	Self-Fulfilling/ Not Self-Fulfilling
Father	18.4	19.4	17.6	18.0	20.4	19.0
Mother	18.4	17.6	16.6	19.1	18.6	19.0
Friend— same sex	21.3	22.0	20.0	22.4	22.5	21.3
Friend— opposite sex	20.9	20.6	19.8	21.5	22.6	21.6
Job Supervisor	15.1	18.2	16.5	15.3	18.4	16.9
Teacher	19.0	21.4	18.8	18.5	22.0	20.4
Talking About Future Plans	30.5	29.9	28.6	31.2	31.4	31.5
Receiving Criticism	19.8	29.4	26.1	19.8	30.4	26.4
Discussing World Current Events	30.4	31.6	27.9	30.2	32.6	29.7
Conversing at a Social Affair	32.4	28.3	26.8	33.6	30.1	30.5

TABLE 3. A COMPARISON OF THE COMMUNICATION-PROFILE SCORING-MATRIX OF STUDENTS X AND Y.

	STUDENT X			STUDENT Y		
	Pleasant/ Not Pleasant	Informative/ Not Informative	Self-Fulfilling/ Not Self-Fulfilling	Pleasant/ Not Pleasant	Informative/ Not Informative	Self-Fulfilling/ Not Self-Fulfilling
Father	10	14	16	10	14	13
Mother	17	13	12	10	13	13
Friend— same sex	23	21	19	21	21	23
Friend— opposite sex	19	17	19	15	16	19
Job Supervisor	13	14	12	17	20	19
Teacher	16	21	17	15	17	16
Talking About Future Plans	21	23	22	23	31	26
Receiving Criticism	18	30	21	15	28	26
Discussing Current World Events	29	29	24	21	25	22
Conversing at a Social Affair	30	18	28	29	17	29

ASSESSING YOURSELF AS A SOURCE OF KNOWLEDGE

There are of course other practical approaches to self-assessment—to gain self-knowledge that will supplement what you learn from the Assessment Scales. Very frequently, as a communicator you must attempt to "size up" the substantive and task-related contributions you can make, both generally and specifically, to a given communicative interaction. You must ask yourself: What do I *know?* What are my *interests?* What *controversial issues* excite me to the point that I would like to have others agree with my view? What *social problems* are most urgently in need of solution? These are the kinds of knowledge-appraisal questions that demand critical self-searching. Many communicators, particularly when they are inexperienced, neglect or ignore this kind of useful "brain search." They prefer to ask others, rather than themselves, what to talk about. For many student speakers—whether asked to participate in an interview or a group discussion or to give a public speech—the problem of "getting the topic" becomes the most difficult part of the assignment. This problem therefore deserves some attention here.

When preparing for a particular communicative situation or assignment, have you ever said, "But what can *I* contribute? What can *I* say? My life has been so *typical,* just like the others, and I have nothing really to offer"? This is, in large part, a rationalization. Remember, first of all, that most of us feel challenged and somewhat threatened by a speaking obligation or assignment, and we must all wish that we had greater resources at hand. Remember, too, that actually no one's life is really typical and so like another's. We haven't all lived in the same places, done the same things, experienced the same excitements, sensed the same dangers, liked or disliked the same companions, enjoyed the same interests and hobbies, had the same unusual relatives employed in the same unusual occupations, and so on. In these and an endless number of other ways, the life you have led is far from typical. [1]

What often *is* typical, however, is the feeling of inadequacy that each of us experiences when faced with a speaking event or experience. We should recognize this feeling for what it is and not allow it to bring our search for communication substance or a speech topic to a frustrated halt. We mustn't allow it to cut back on our capabilities or cramp our style. If we take time to assess our accumulation of knowledge about ourselves and our ideas, we can readily sort out those subjects on which we are already prepared to speak and those subjects for which we will have to make some additional preparation. Obviously, there's a significant difference between *being* prepared to speak about a topic and *becoming* prepared to speak about it. This is the difference between what we call *general preparation* and *specific preparation.* This distinction applies equally to giving a public speech, taking part in a group discussion, or being interviewed for a job. The backlog of your prior experience, observation, reading, and deliberation about a topic constitutes your *general* preparation for speaking about it. Once you have in mind the subject you want to talk about, the additional fact-hunting, organizing, planning, and practicing you do for the actual communicative event make up your *specific* preparation. It stands to reason, doesn't it, that most young speakers—for reasons of age alone—will probably have had fewer prior experiences and will therefore need a greater amount of specific preparation for any given speech interaction.

Your memory, naturally, will furnish much of the task-related substance you will need for your general preparation for communicating. But, despite its exceptionally retentive capacities, don't rely on memory too heavily. In addition, collect and file away in some *concrete, tangible form* those interesting bits and pieces of potentially useful information regarding a number of your major interests in life. Do this often, and do it immediately when you come across such items. Systematically file for future reference notes on the lectures you listen to, on your reading, on your conversations, and your observations. Hang on to pertinent newspaper clippings, letters-to-the-editors, magazine articles, cartoons, etc.; and organize them in an easy-to-get-at fashion. And for *everything* you collect and file, be sure to list the source, author, date, and any other necessary identification. Moreover, once you have collected data for a topic or completed a course, do not discard your research materials, class papers, and class notes. *Hold on to them, too.* Such research, even though carried out for an assignment of the moment, is almost certain to have future value and relevance for your work in speech.

Call this "pack-ratting," "squirreling," or what you will, but a methodical procedure of this kind will provide you with both a general background and—when you need it—a readily available source of ideas and substance you can use in your speech preparation for a specific subject. Few things are more inefficient and frustrating than to have to waste valuable time in a frantic and often futile

Study Probe 1
Preparing an Interests Inventory

As a first step in ascertaining your potential communicable knowledge, prepare a written inventory of your interests, experiences, and family background—in short, a kind of autobiography, though not necessarily in essay form. What jobs have you had? Where have you lived, traveled, wanted to go? What are your hobbies, pastimes, interests? What do you read, look at, listen to? What are your talents: painting, skiing, baking, macramé, playing rhythm guitar in a rock band? What traumas and ecstasies have enlivened your childhood? What social issues interest or anger you? What do you know about politics, pollution, evolution, astronomy, theology?

Is your family large or small, and what are your responsibilities within it? Do your parents work? At what? In her spare time, does your mother collect antiques? In his, does your dad fix his own car? Are any of your relatives famous or in unusual occupations? Are your friends?

Once you have completed such an inventory, you'll have a much better idea of what you do and do not know.

search for vaguely remembered materials. While *some* searching for "just the right thing" is both desirable and necessary, the systematic practice of collecting and filing reference items will reduce it to a minimum. These and the other suggestions we have made for assessing and storing communicable knowledge are aimed at making you more aware of your assets and capabilities. By following through on them, you will find that they can contribute a great deal to your self-actualization as a communicator.

ASSESSING YOUR CONTROL OF EMOTIONS

As a part of your self-appraisal when you were reacting to the Self-Assessment Scales on pages 57–61, you probably asked yourself—especially when you were weighing the *Affective/Feeling dimensions* of an interaction—"How do I *feel* when I'm faced with a communicative situation? What is my *emotional and 'mental' state* when I engage in a communicative interaction with others?" In certain of the contexts you probably felt at ease, calm, and in a positive frame of mind. And it no doubt occurred to you that a confident, positive mental attitude can carry a speaker a long way toward success. In some of the other agent/context relationships, however, you probably were somewhat ill-at-ease, off-balance, and even quite anxious about what might happen.

Understanding Your Anxieties

Anxiety, of course, is a feeling common to nearly *all* speakers, regardless of age or experience; and it is especially troublesome among beginning speakers. In fact, it is not altogether unusual for the beginner, when anticipating a communicative interaction, to visualize himself or herself with quivering knees, trembling hands, a sweat-beaded brow, dry mouth, and a breaking voice. There is much that we don't know yet about speech fear—or stage fright, as it is sometimes called. It is a prevalent problem, however, and one that has persisted for so many centuries that we can be sure that such fear is a part of the general anxiety and tension that affects *every* man and woman to some degree. Psychologists who have investigated the problem extensively cite evidence that general anxiety fluctuates in early childhood, rises quite consistently in adolescence, declines considerably through early and middle adulthood, and then rises once more as people progress to and through old age—especially after they reach their sixties.[6] What this emphasizes for our purposes here is that *the level of general anxiety is high when most persons in our society are just beginning their formal speech communication training.*

Reducing Speech Fears

Because all of us are "afflicted" with speech fear to a greater or less extent, what positive steps can we take to overcome it? Obviously, there can be no one solution, no one pat answer. We can begin—as we have here—by trying to recognize it for what it is. In addition, we believe, there are a few helpful ideas we can keep in mind as we attempt to sort out, appraise, and alleviate our communication anxieties.

1. *Learn to take a "two-persons-conversing" approach to* ALL *communication forms and situations.* You will compound your speech-fear difficulty if, in your first classroom efforts at oral communication, you imagine that your task is very unlike all of your previous speaking experience. Constantly remind yourself that it *isn't.* As we noted on pages 20–21, students who have taken a course in speech come to see the various classroom-speaking situations—even the more formal ones—as being very much alike. And in their essentials they *are* alike; all of them easily fit our basic model of "two persons conversing." For example, the sooner you can learn to visualize a public speech as "conversing" with an audience, the more at ease and effective you are likely to become.

2. *Remember that fear "feeds" on fear.* As with a self-fulfilling prophecy, undue concern about speech fear may only intensify the existing level of your anxiety.

3. *Realize—as we have suggested—that speech anxiety is a very common feeling* and that it will rarely, if ever, be as apparent to your listeners as you may suppose.

4. *Before and during the speaking situation, focus primarily upon the ideas you want to communicate and upon how those ideas are being received by the people for whom you intend them.*

5. *Prepare thoroughly for every speech occasion, and gain as many varied speech communication experiences as possible.* In a sense, fear of speaking is like fear of swimming, a fear which is usually lost in water rather than on land.

6. *Make a list of those circumstances which provide anxiety or speech fear in you, and rank them according to the level of their severity.* Very probably you will discover that you experience greater anxiety in some speech situations than in others. Then try to analyze, with your instructor's help if necessary, why the levels vary from situation to situation. Once you have pinpointed the "why," you will have found a fairly sound basis for ameliorating the difficulty.

7. *Finally, take comfort in the realization that a limited amount of anxiety or tension may work to your advantage.* If not excessive, it helps keep you alert and concerned about sustaining meaningful interaction.

We have discussed anxiety at some length here because often it is the dominating emotion for a beginning speaker. Once that fear is under your control, other more positive and productive emotions begin to predominate, and they will play more significant roles in the development of your self-actualizing communicative behavior.

ACTUALIZING YOURSELF AS A COMMUNICATOR

In these pages we have considered only a *beginning*—a starting point from which to launch a systematic appraisal of your tendencies, preferences, and possibilities as a speaking/listening agent in the many communicative situations in which you will find yourself during your lifetime. A major objective of all the self-assessment we have suggested is of course *increased self-awareness*. This increased awareness should, in turn, contribute significantly to your *self-actualization through communication with others*. By "self-actualization" we mean, first of all, that you be able to achieve as fully as possible the self-identifying, self-enriching, social-contacting, and mutual-influencing purposes of speech that we talked about in Chapter 1. Psychologist Abraham H. Maslow stated the idea aptly when he said:

> *A musician must make music, an artist must paint, a poet must write if he is to be ultimately at peace with himself. What a man can be, he must be. This need we may call self-actualization.*[7]

As a speaking/listening person, you—like the musician, painter, or poet—must strive to be all that you *can* be. This is both your potential and your right as a human being.

Psychologists—Maslow and Hamachek among others—suggest that the self-actualizing person possesses certain important perceptions, attitudes, feelings, and reactive qualities which help to "actualize" that individual in communicative involvement with others.[8] These include: the ability to perceive reality; an acceptance of self, others, and reality; spontaneity of behavior; problem-centeredness; autonomy and detachment; and a sense of humor.

1. *An accurate and deep perception of reality.* The self-actualizing person is more likely to perceive accurately what is real and to be less influenced by selfish concerns and anxieties. Self-actualizing people are sensitive to unspoken, unconscious "messages," realizing that the uttered meaning is not necessarily the true or intended meaning. Being especially sensitive to the needs of "reality," they listen actively and accurately. Generally, these individuals are not frightened by the unknown. They are able to feel (and accept) a broad spectrum of emotions and impulses, ranging from anger to love, from joy to sorrow, from despair to delight, etc. Hence they experience continually fresh perceptions and have a greater intensity of feeling and appreciation. For them *every* sunset can inspire a sense of wonder and awe.

2. *Acceptance of self, others, and reality.* The self-actualizing person tends to be more open-minded and to accept things *as* they are and for *what* they are. Such persons show less defensiveness and self-protective covering than do others. That is, they usually prefer to act in accord with their own best judgment and do not react with excessive guilt-feelings if others disapprove. Although they are aware of and regret their shortcomings, they are not beset by self-doubts. They are not paralyzed in the face of failure. As persons they feel equal—not su-

perior or inferior—to others, despite differences in attitudes, aptitudes, and backgrounds. In short, they accept other people, social customs, and themselves—all in an interactive setting.

3. *Spontaneity of behavior.* The self-actualizing person tends to behave in a natural and direct manner. These individuals exhibit less artificiality and stereotyped behavior. They can take for granted that they are persons of value and interest to others, and they do not worry unduly about what happened yesterday or might happen tomorrow. They are now-oriented. They can enjoy various activities—of work, play, creative self-expression, or simply relaxing with friends. They are able to accept praise without pretense or false modesty, and they know how to pay a compliment honestly. They can communicate freely and openly, actualizing themselves in nonaggressive, nondefensive ways.

4. *Problem-centeredness.* The self-actualizing person is problem-centered rather than ego-centered. These individuals are better able than others to control their ego-involvement in problem situations; they are better able to keep their own personal feelings and emotions from influencing policies and solutions. They try to see issues from the point of view of other people and refrain from hastily judging and stereotyping them. Well-suited to membership in task groups, they are able to lead unobtrusively in a search for solutions to problems and encourage contributions from others.

5. *Autonomy and detachment.* The self-actualizing person usually has an inner core of quiet self-certainty. Such persons are able to concentrate on the essential features of a situation and to maintain a degree of detachment about it. They value solitude more than do most other people and need time to be alone. They have a strong belief in their values and principles and will defend them in interaction with others. But they are not stubborn or unyielding; they are secure enough to modify their beliefs when new experiences or evidence suggests the desirability of doing so. Even when they fail, they can maintain confidence in their abilities and judgments, and will ordinarily resist the attempts of others to dominate them.

6. *A well-balanced sense of humor.* The self-actualizing person has a healthy and unhostile sense of humor. Although characteristically purposeful and intense, such persons are able to laugh at themselves. They are able to poke fun at their own efforts and mistakes. They appreciate the value of a joke but are careful not to create laughter at the expense of someone else.

To restate the major principle of this chapter, as a speaker/listener you should develop an improved *self-awareness*—a sensitivity to your own position and potentialities as a communicator. Without an accurate self-assessment, you cannot hope to interact with maximum effectiveness. But in addition to self-awareness, to communicate well you must have a *self-concern*, an active desire for *self-actualization*. You must prefer to act for yourself—to be all that you *can* be—and to be accepted on your own terms for what you *are*.

All that we have said thus far in this book is aimed toward helping you achieve that end; what we shall be saying in future pages is directed toward that same goal. But no one else can tell you what your self-concept is or should be. No one else can—in the final analysis—tell you what your special needs are and what you must do about them to achieve a greater measure of self-actualization. The effort must be yours.

Suggested Readings

Eric Berne, *Games People Play* (New York: Grove Press, Inc., 1964). This book introduces Berne's system for transactional analysis. The mental states of speaking/listening agents (parent, adult, and child) are considered as they influence the communication context.

Erving Goffman, *The Presentation of Self in Everyday Life* (Garden City, N.Y.: Doubleday & Company, Inc., Anchor Books, 1959). Using the theater as an analogy, Goffman discusses the ways in which speaking actors present or portray the self to others.

D. E. Hamachek, *Encounters with the Self* (New York: Holt, Rinehart & Winston, Inc., 1971). This book takes an evaluative look at the human self and examines some dimensions and factors which can help in achieving a greater sense of self-understanding and self-attainment.

A. H. Maslow, *Motivation and Personality* (New York: Harper & Row, Publishers, 1970). Maslow's work on this subject is both authoritative and highly regarded. Chapter 12, "Self-Actualizing People," is especially to the point here.

Reference Notes

[1]Aristotle, *Rhetorica,* trans. W. Rhys Roberts, in *The Basic Works of Aristotle,* ed. Richard McKeon (New York: Random House, Inc., 1941), pp. 1329–1330.

[2]Kenneth D. Benne and Paul Sheats, "Functional Roles of Group Members," *Journal of Social Issues,* 4 (1948), 41–49.

[3]Launor F. Carter, "Recording and Evaluating the Performance of Individuals as Members of Small Groups," *Personnel Psychology,* 7 (1954), 477–484.

[4]Robert F. Bales, *Personality and Interpersonal Behavior* (New York: Holt, Rinehart and Winston, 1970).

[5]William Schutz, *FIRO, A Three-Dimensional Theory of Interpersonal Behavior* (New York: Holt, Rinehart and Winston, 1958).

[6]Raymond B. Cattell, "The Nature and Measurement of Anxiety," *Scientific American* (March 1963), 96–104.

[7]A. H. Maslow, *Motivation and Personality* (New York: Harper and Brothers, 1954), p. 91.

[8]For a more detailed consideration of this matter, see the works by Hamachek and Maslow which are cited in "Suggested Readings."

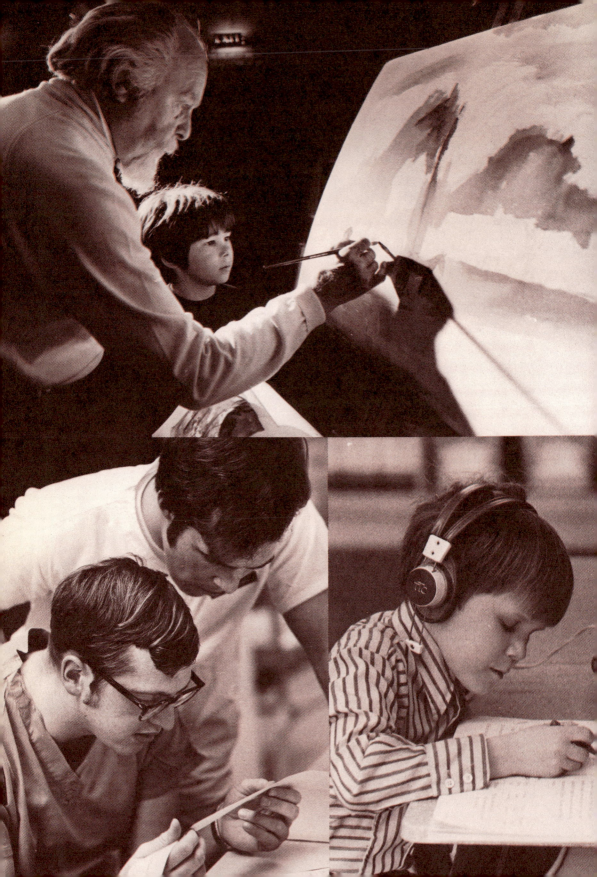

Chapter 4

SENSATION, PERCEPTION, AND LANGUAGE

From what we sense in the world around us,
the feelings and ideas these sensations produce in us,
and the categories, labels, and symbols we devise
for them—from all of these we acquire and develop
the substance of speech communication.

In this chapter our central concerns will be *the acquiring and developing of speech communication substance.* In the speech communication process, speaking/listening agents interact within a context which both *influences* and *is influenced by* the outcome of that interaction. That is, the context—the physical and psychological environment—is constantly influencing and shaping the human self while, at the same time, the self is also constantly striving and scheming to influence and shape *it.* And out of this kind of alternating stimulus-response interaction comes the "substance," the "communicable stuff" of speech communication.

Necessarily, therefore, not only do we *speak* and *listen* within contexts—we also *live* within them from moment to moment. Our thoughts, behaviors, and potential actions depend on and are limited by the ranges of our seeing and hearing and other senses, by the breadth of our reading and experience, by the extent of our travel, and by the nature and frequency of our contacts with others. Our particular human ways of interpreting, adjusting to, and ordering our environment powerfully influence the kinds of ideas we "think up" and develop. They determine, in large part, the attitudes, opinions, beliefs, preferences, and priorities we bring to any specific communicative situation. In short, the contexts in which we live and function will determine in large part the what-and-how that we try to communicate.

75

Our emphasis in this chapter, then, will be to create an understanding of (1) how the self senses, perceives, and classifies the potentially communicable *substance* coming to it from the environment, and (2) how the self systematically arranges and orders this substance so as to present to others the ideas or claims it wants to make. We will try to broaden this understanding by highlighting some fundamental ideas about *sensation, perception,* and *language.* These are the processes which bear most centrally upon how we form our ideas and feelings, and how we arrive at our convictions and values. So . . . let's begin at the beginning—with the processes by which we receive and organize stimuli from our environment. [1]

SENSATION AND PERCEPTION

Sensation is the "intake" process by which we draw information and experience from our contact with our environment. It is the much-studied process

Study Probe 1

Determining How Contexts Influence Communication

Imagine the following communication situations:

1. You and several friends playing cards in the school cafeteria, with cokes and French fries in front of you.
2. You and a friend at midnight in late December before a crackling fire.
3. You and several friends of the same sex at a football game, late in the fourth quarter, with the score tied and your team on the opponent's 10-yard line.
4. You and many strangers your age in a social science class, with the teacher at the chalkboard asking who can explain the concepts of the id, the ego, and the superego.
5. You and your family at the dinner table, with the television set tuned to the evening news, and your father just home from work.
6. You meeting an elderly aunt for the first time at an elegant restaurant luncheon to celebrate your cousin's confirmation.
7. You in your room with someone of the opposite sex studying for a biology examination.
8. You sitting on the lawn during spring with a person of another race.
9. You and your friends at a club meeting after the minutes have been read and the chairperson has asked, "Is there any old business?"
10. You sitting in your room one morning with your best friend and your dog, after both you and the friend had dates the night before.

Write a few sentences about each of these situations, discussing the probable subjects you would discuss, and how you might communicate. Or, better yet, try role-playing each of these situations in class.

of the ways in which our sense organs respond to stimulation by light, sound, touch, pressure, taste, and smell, thereby producing the individuality and totality of our so-called sensory experience. By reason of these stimulations we become aware of such sensations as color brightness, vocal pitch vibration and loudness, tactility, tangibility, weight, warmth, pungency, and so on. *Perception is the complex process by which we select and organize our sensations into patterns that are more or less complete and "understandable."* It is at this basic level of sensation and perception that speech ideas and "propositions" are born. By *speech proposition* we mean "an expression in language or signs of something that can be believed, doubted, or denied or is either true or false."[1] We use the term also to refer to a communicative claim, project, or situation which calls for acceptance, rejection, or some other kind of interactive result.

In any consideration of sensation and perception within a communication framework, there are at least five key aspects that we need to keep in mind: (1) We are made aware of sensation because of a change in the physical or psychological environment; (2) we must have sensory intakes to help us hold onto our *self-identity* and our sense of "reality"; (3) we are endowed with a central nervous system that has a remarkable ability—and agility—to *adapt* to the quantity and nature of the sensations it will "accept" and the perceptions we will make; (4) we achieve this adaptability, in part, by "filtering" sensations and perceptions; and (5) we achieve this adaptability also, in part, by "completing" or filling in the "missing" parts of our perceptions.

Sensation and Environmental Change

We experience sensation as a change in the environment. Basically, sensation is a response to *energy change.* A change in stimulation, rather than the sheer amount of stimulation, is what attracts our attention. To experience warmth we must have known cold; to be aware of sound we must distinguish it from silence. A perfectly homogeneous or absolutely unchanging environment would be like none at all. This is why many animals—for safety's sake—"freeze" when frightened, rather than run from danger. By remaining motionless, they not only help to camouflage their presence, but they also produce minimal change in the sensation of their enemies and thus are more likely to remain unseen by those who would threaten them. When confronted with the need to communicate, human beings often respond in similar fashion. Instead of speaking up in various communication settings, some persons "freeze" like any other fearful animal. They are frightened by the occasion, and hope not to be noticed. The participant in a group discussion, for instance, who says little and does little attracts little attention and so remains unnoticed. In contrast, the animated, energetic speaker—because he or she provides many energy changes (potential sensations) in the communicative environment—has numerous natural advantages in attracting and holding listeners' attention.

Energy change—movement and differentiation—is a significant factor, then, in activating and sustaining the speech process. Such change accounts in no small measure for our capacities to stimulate other agents in a speech communication context. In short, it is one of the key *factors of attention.* ②

Sensation and Self-Orientation

Through sensation we are able to orient ourselves to our environment. Sensory intakes help us hold onto our self-identity and sense of reality. We must make some differentiations and distinctions among a bewildering array of these intakes in order to orient ourselves appropriately to our environment and maintain the necessary physiological/psychological balance. We must have sensation to know who and where we are and what is happening. This need was made strikingly evident in experiments on the effects of *sensory deprivation.* Typically, each of the subjects in these studies was isolated in a separate room and placed in bed. Each was blindfolded, and the subject's hands were padded, and the arms encased in cardboard tubes. The temperature of the environment was maintained at a comfortable and stable level. Aside from being properly fed and allowed to take care of bodily functions, the subjects were kept as free as possible from changes in external stimulation.

The results of this sensory deprivation were remarkable. The great majority of those subjected to it experienced hallucinations and other unusual sensations. They reported seeing weird geometric designs and strange figures. Their minds, without differentiated inputs to guide them, seemed able to supply only an *unreal* set of sensations.[2] In the literal sense of the phrase, these subjects truly lost contact with reality.

It is clear that we humans must have sensory intake as a condition of "normality." In the speech communication process, this means that as speaking/listening agents we must receive and be aware of continuing feedback-response (sensory inputs) from each other if we are to be fully aware of where we are and how effectively we are interacting with others in our physical/psychological environment.

Study Probe 2
Analyzing Movement and Attention in Speaking

Observe persons who are conversing. Catalog the postures and gestures they appear to use frequently. Do the speakers "mirror" one another's nonverbal behavior, employing similar stances, postures, and gestural activities? Identify and contrast animated and lifeless conversationalists. Describe the types and specific examples of movement which seem to attract and hold the attention of others in the conversational interchange.

Suggest several guidelines for effective speaking which might be derived from the fact that it is a *change* in stimulation rather than the amount of stimulation that tends to attract our attention.

Sensation and Adaptation to Stimuli

We humans have senses capable of wide-ranging adaptation to the stimuli directed toward them and the perceptions made from them. Our central nervous system can regulate the quantity and nature of the sensory inputs to which it is subjected, becoming more sensitive or less sensitive to suit the conditions of the moment. Three factors appear to govern this sensory adaptability: (1) the *intensity* of the stimulus, (2) the *duration* of the stimulus, and (3) the *comparative magnitude* of the stimulus. ⬚3

If there is very little energy change in the environment because of the low intensity of the stimulus—if our senses receive very little stimulation—we may become maximally sensitive, able to detect the low intensity and small stimulus-differences. Human hearing, for instance, is not as acute as that of many other animals, but in a very quiet auditorium we can, with normal acuteness, hear a pin drop at a considerable distance. On the other hand, when we are bombarded with intense stimuli, we have internal protective devices—"stimulus thresholds"—which will effectively reduce our sensitivities. Our middle-ear mechanism, for example, has features which hinder the transmission of harmfully intense stimuli—a most useful and necessary protection in a society subject to many varieties of "noise pollution."

A comparable adaptive capability characterizes all of our sensing mechanisms, of course.

Not only do our senses adapt to changes in stimulus intensity; they also adapt to the *duration* of the stimulus. We may receive a sensory shock, for instance, when we dive into the cold water of a swimming pool, but we soon adjust and no longer feel the cold.

 Study Probe 3
Testing Adaptability to Stimuli

In class, try concentrating on tactile, visual, or auditory phenomena you normally are not sensitive to—for example, the pressure of your chair against your thighs, or the clatter of a pencil dropping. Your instructor will ask each of you to supply one such observation for a list to be classified into the following three categories:

Phenomena of Small Intensity	Phenomena of Short Duration	Phenomena of Small Magnitude

In different circumstances, which of your observations might you have noticed without special efforts of concentration?

Furthermore, our senses establish adaptation levels on the basis of the *comparative magnitude* of the stimuli. That is, we judge the magnitude of one stimulus against that of other stimuli considered to be in the same class. For instance, we may see a certain foreign car as small when we view it beside an American car, but large when we view it alongside any one of several other European makes.

Now, let's apply this notion of adaptability levels to *communication* specifically. As an illustration of the way in which the human senses adjust to stimuli-input and develop adaptation levels, let's consider for a moment the popular, contemporary preference for *short public speeches.* In our society today, a one-hour speech may seem too long. But in many other contemporary societies, and in our own country only a few decades ago, a one-hour speech would be considered too brief. In the short "speechettes" which we modern Americans seem to insist upon, a speaker doesn't have time to explore adequately a major question or issue and to present supporting facts and evidence. In the twenty to thirty minutes to which the public speaker is usually limited, there is merely enough time to present an "image"—a public presentation of the self that the speaker wishes to assert or establish. It would be desirable, we venture to say, if the sensory mechanisms of the listening public *could* adapt once again to speeches long enough to feature substance, structure, and stylistic grace rather than mere speaker-image. However, this would call for a change in our present patterns of sensing and perceiving public speeches—a greater range of adaptation levels, especially for those speeches aired on TV or radio.

Broadly speaking, we human beings achieve the sensory adaptation we need for satisfactory functioning and survival in one of the two ways we shall now consider: by *filtering* our sensations and perceptions, or by *completing* many of our perceptions which for one reason or another seem to have "something missing."

Filtering Sensations and Perceptions

We achieve sensory adaptability, in part, by "filtering" our sensations and perceptions. Within fairly general ranges, as we have noted, our central nervous system can regulate the kind and number of the sensory imputs it will accept, and hence the perceptions we can make. In making this "acceptance," it seemingly *selects* and *facilitates reception* of certain sensations; and—at other times—it appears to *block out* certain sensations entirely. This is what we mean when we say that our sensations and perceptions are "filtered." We can see a fairly obvious example of involuntary filtering in a listener who is slightly hard-of-hearing. This listener may miss some of what the speaker says, perhaps a great portion of it. Or, again, you may see this sensory filtering at work in a listener who is foreign-born and is only now acquiring the use of English as a second language. The vocabulary or syntax in some parts of the speaker's message may be confusing or meaningless to the foreign-born listener, and he or she may not receive any useful sensory impressions of them at all. In fact, a certain amount of such filtering of sensations and perceptions will occur in almost *every* speech communication situation: The speaker may have among his or her listeners the person who is slightly deaf, the person of foreign birth, a person who is intellectually dull, another who is sleepy, still another whose thoughts continuously wander to personal problems, and so on. Because of these possibilities, large portions of the speaker's message may make only an incomplete sensory impression upon the intended receivers, or may even fail to create *any* sensory impressions upon some of them.

The human nervous system can also filter out sensory materials and perceptions that are a *threat* or a potential threat to the self. These materials can be the actual sensations (the fear that a hacking cough—caused perhaps by too much smoking—might be signalling the onset of lung cancer), or they might be *images* (the image of a menacing knife-wielder with upraised blade) that are recalled or associated with an earlier experience and the attendant sensations recreated by the central nervous system. To many people, for example, profanity or pornography is a threat, or potential threat, even though it may not be directed toward them personally or specifically. They fear it; they associate it (perhaps) with evil, violence, guilt, or some other dissonant feeling; and so they build what is called a perceptual defense.

Typically, in studies of perceptual defenses, the investigator flashes words and pictures onto a screen for very brief periods.[3] Some of these words and photographs are "neutral" in the strength of their emotional stimulation, whereas others are "loaded." Profane or "dirty" words, for instance, appear to be loaded—sometimes overloaded—with stimulus ranges and strengths which greatly excite the individual's central nervous system. Thus, when some persons hear profanity or see a pornographic photo, they experience stronger sensations and greater excitement than they feel they can safely handle. This feeling may be conscious or subconscious, but in either case they feel threatened and try to build a set of counter-perceptions or a perceptual defense against it. In contrast to the profane word or the obscene photograph, the neutral materials—those having less exciting stimulus ranges—appear to be more easily and quickly accepted by the human nervous system. In sum, our sensory receptors help us filter out excessive excitation, thereby defending us against stimulation which may be threatening to us and/or our values, or which might lower our status, or which might insult our self-esteem.

Just as our central nervous system can block out threatening or "unsafe" perceptions, so it may also *facilitate* those that support our beliefs and values or bolster our biases. We may *see* and hear what we *want* to see and hear. This is "selective perception." Suppose we were to perform an experiment in which we presented to a general audience a speech that advanced some arguments favoring the Democratic party and some arguments favoring the Republican party. If we then administered a retention test to all members of the audience, what would you expect to happen? As numerous repetitions of this experiment have clearly demonstrated, the Democrats in the audience will tend to remember more of the arguments favoring their position, and the Republicans will tend to remember more of the arguments favoring their views. This selective perception will occur even when the audience is cautioned prior to the speech to remember *all* of the content for a test to be given immediately following it.

The effects of *facilitative filtering* during the receiving phase of the communication process will almost always be evident: Listeners favorable to an issue will selectively perceive those arguments and data which support their stand, thereby reinforcing their positive perceptions. Listeners opposed to an issue will selectively perceive those claims and pieces of information that support their objections, thereby reinforcing *their* perceptions of it. As one of these classic studies concluded:

> . . . it is almost impossible to expect objectivity and accuracy in perception, learning, remembering, thinking, etc., when ego-involved frames of reference are stimulated. Our behavior is too much determined by our desires, wishes, beliefs, attitudes, and values for us to expect anything other than what we find, namely, highly subjective responses.[4]

From this and other studies on *selective perception,* we can conclude that as listeners we tend to filter speech communication messages according to our needs, our expectations, and our prior knowledge. In almost any kind of communicative interaction, we will be partisans and will receive from a speech more easily and retain longer those materials to which we are favorably inclined and/or with which we are familiar, while forgetting or "filtering out" the material less favorable to our cause. If we're hungry, we may focus on that part of a speaker's message which promises food, and may fail to hear with equal clarity that part of the message which prescribes or implies the violence needed to get it. In these and similarly selective ways we can, as listeners, perceive elements we will use in putting together our *own* messages. By perceiving selectively the messages we

Study Probe 4
Testing Your Own Filtering

Your instructor will rapidly read aloud a list of one hundred words. Immediately afterward, write down as many as you can remember. Then, you and others in the class should read your own lists aloud, trying to explain what factors seemed to influence what words you recalled. Did some words seem to fit your experiences better than others? Were some shocking or unusual? Were the last words the instructor read easier to remember?

What words did most people recall? Why? What words did most people filter out? Why?

Enumerate several steps that a communicator might take to combat listeners' tendencies to filter out sensory stimuli and perceptions essential to their reasonably full comprehension of the message. Compare your suggestions with those of your classmates.

receive from others, we will be able to reconstruct the perceived elements in accordance with our personal predispositions and preferences. 4

Completing Perceptions

We extend our sensory adaptability, in part, by "completing" our perceptions with supposed or "missing" parts. Given the natural limitations of human sensing mechanisms, our sensory impressions and resultant perceptions can never be really *complete.* But, nevertheless, we constantly try to fill them in and *make* them complete. In the process of perceiving, we organize incoming stimuli into what we like to believe are *whole* and *complete* patterns. This is both an advantage and a disadvantage. On the one hand, it helps us maintain a sense of balance and "certainty" in our lives. On the other hand, it can deceive us—trick us into believing that something exists when it doesn't, into trying to communicate about "substance" that has no basis in fact or reality. In short, because our perceptions are necessarily incomplete, we must recognize that they are not fully reliable.

We "complete" our perceptions, usually, in one of three ways: (1) by *adding supposed elements* to what we perceive, (2) by *interpreting ambiguous elements* in such a way as to give meaning to our perceptions, and (3) by *"generalizing" or transferring the effect of one perception to one or more other perceptions.*

For example, when we look at the figures below, we tend to complete our perceptions of them by seeing—and talking about—not an arc or a group of dots, but a circle and a triangle. We sense that something is missing, and we *add* what we suppose that missing "something" to be.

If adjacent dots of light flicker alternately, we may "see" movement. In this *phi phenomenon* we complete our perceptual experience by adding nonexistent, intermediate dots of light and thus "see" motion. Many advertising displays and street signs utilize this principle of incomplete-perception-made-complete. When still pictures are flashed before us in rapid succession, we see motion in the pictures *as such.* The illusion of "in-motion" images seen on movie screens is made believable by this means. In the process of completing our perceptions, we are not filtering something *out* of a message directed our way; we are *adding something* to it as we hear it or see it or otherwise sense it. This seems to be what McLuhan is getting at when he writes about viewer-involvement and the manner in which the viewer "completes" what he or she sees on a television screen.[5]

There are, of course, variations and extensions of this way of completing our perceptions. If, for instance, our perceptions are ambiguous, we may interpret them and try to add meaning. That is, if initially we perceive what appear to be meaningless elements, we try to reorganize those elements in such a way as to give them meaning for us. What, for instance, do you see when you look at the illustration below, and what meaning do you add to it?

The woodcut "Heaven and Hell" by Escher.[6]

We may also complete our perceptions by *generalizing* or *transferring* the result of one perception to another perception. If we receive a certain stimulus, perceive it, and learn to respond to it in a particular way through repeated experience, we say we have learned it by *conditioning*. If we then receive a stimulus similar to (but not exactly like) the one to which we have been conditioned, we tend to respond to the similar stimulus as if it were the one we first learned. Studies of learning by conditioning refer to this transfer-of-effect response as *stimulus generalization*. That is, once a conditioned response has been established for a given stimulus, that same response may be elicited not only by the controlled, original stimulus but also by a fairly wide variety of like or nearly-like other stimuli. In a speech communication setting, for instance, if we are "persuaded" (conditioned) by the speaker as to the soundness of two or three specific cases in support of a given issue, we tend almost automatically to draw on our own experiences to discover other similar cases. We add them to the speaker's cases, generalizing all of them together, transferring the persuasiveness of one case to another. We thereby complete our perception of the persuasiveness of the speaker's argument *as a whole*. This generalizing or transferring of response is of course still another instance of our human tendency to seek internal consistency by trying to complete our perceptions. It demonstrates, again, our human need to infuse our perception of the environment with order and balance.

Finally, we need to remember that in all of our conscious and subconscious efforts to complete our perceptions, the *needs, previous experiences,* and *expectations* of the self are continuously at work. All of these will significantly influence how and what we will add to our perceptions, how we will interpret what seems ambiguous, and—finally—how we will generalize and transfer our responses in order to round out what we hear, see, and otherwise sense. Note, for instance, the potency of our expectations in helping us fill the gaps in our perceptions (and, incidentally, to nurture our biases). In a public communication setting, if we *expect* "illogical ranting" from "that buffoon on the platform," we will probably hear it. If we expect "common sense," we are likely to hear *that*. If we approve of the viewpoint of a speaker, we may see him as wiser or taller or handsomer than he really is. If a speaker says something which—coming from a different speaker—would be objectionable, we excuse and defend her by saying, "But she doesn't really *mean* that! What she's *actually* saying is . . . ." In these and other "unreal" ways we add to the message transmitted by the speaker and thus fulfill our own personal expectations.

Thus far in this chapter we have considered how, as human beings, we sense and receive stimuli from the world about us. We have looked at some of the basic aspects of sensation and perception as they are more or less directly involved in speech communication. Specifically, we have noted that: (1) We are made aware of sensation because of a change in the physical or psychological environment; (2) we can maintain a sense of self-identity and reality because of our sensory intakes; (3) our central nervous system is highly adaptive to the number and kinds of sensations we can take in and the perceptions we can make therefrom; (4) we can achieve this high adaptability in part, because we can filter sensations and perceptions; and (5) we can achieve this high adaptability also, in part, because we can complete or fill in the missing portions of our perceptions.

We have noted further, that a knowledge of these matters is important to us as students of speech communication because it is through the processes of sensation and perception that the self forms its initial reactions to the environment and "decides" what to do about it at any given moment. Through these processes we begin to develop the feelings and ideas which will—eventually—make up the substance of the messages we will be sending to others. However, long before these messages can take on anything near a final form, the sensations and perceptions in which they are grounded must be organized into *classes* or *categories*. As we have suggested before, one of the chief ways in which this classifying and organizing is accomplished and made *meaningful to others* is through the use of *language*.

LANGUAGE: CATEGORIES, LABELS, AND SYMBOLS

Let us now consider how language—as the "expression" of speech substance—affects our adaptation to our environment.[7] Earlier, we pointed out that all of the efforts we exert in establishing social contact with other human beings and in trying to exert mutual influence upon each other have but one overriding goal: *control of the environment* (see Chapter 2, pages 44–45). And we say again, as we said then, that one of the major means by which we can hope to accomplish this goal is *language*. With language we can impose *order* on those aspects of nature which we can perceive. As we are about to explain in some detail, we can create this order by developing "categories" or meaningful groupings of the products of our sensing and perceiving and giving them names. We can then use these names as *symbols* with which to understand and talk about the things we have sensed and perceived. The implications of this capability are of course far-reaching.

Categories

In a practical sense, to find a word with which to name or label *everything*—every sensory or perceptual experience encountered by the human self—is obviously impossible.* Let's just consider one example. Science tells us that our human senses are capable of discriminating seven million different colors. That is, if we could be shown all possible degrees of color brightness, hue, and saturation, we would be able—theoretically at least—to perceive seven million different "colors." If we had to provide a name for each one of them, we would need seven million different words to describe or refer to all of the distinguishable colors. Imagine trying to learn the names of seven million colors! If we were to find it necessary to treat each color possibility as a separate and equal entity—with a name for each—obviously our understanding of color would break down. We could never learn the needed vocabulary or remember it, much less communicate with it. So, because of the vastness of this problem, we have had to find some other way—some simpler, shorter, and less detailed way—to cope with this always-present, ever-demanding difficulty. We categorize.

The ability to categorize.   *We can organize our sensations and perceptions into categories and thus reduce the complexity of our environment.* Having this ability, we do not always have to consider each person, object, or experience as unique and separate. We may *group* or "classify" these entities or some aspect of them—take a shortcut. By combining them into "sets" or "classes" or "categories" we can deal with them more simply and efficiently. With this process we

---

*Notice that we are already having to use "words," "word-labels," "terms," etc., even to talk about categories. In a theoretical framework it is possible—necessary, actually—to separate the concepts of *category* and *word-label;* in actual practice, of course, it *isn't.* The two processes of classifying/categorizing and "languaging" with word-labels for them are bound together—probably inextricably for all practical purposes. That is, to be aware of a category is to try to *name* it.

are able to (a) provide a measure of *order* and *relationship* to the ways in which we perceive our environment; (b) organize our perceptions into meaningful awareness, knowledge, and judgment; and (c) try to communicate this substance to others.

Let's go back to our "color" illustration for a moment and see how this works. With the categories of *red, orange, yellow, green, blue, indigo,* and *violet*— seven names rather than seven million—we find it possible to do much of our necessary thinking and communicating about color. By subdividing these seven categories or sets and adding the classifications *brown, black, white,* etc., we can—with only sixty or seventy terms—carry on a very specific conversation about the colors, say, of sweaters or paint for a dining room. Thus we can see that categorizing is both a necessary and a desirable process for enabling us to better understand and manipulate our environment. If we couldn't categorize, we would be overwhelmed by the number of sensations which constantly bombard us. If we couldn't organize and "sort out" our sensory and perceptual experiences into meaningful and simple groupings, we couldn't reason efficiently or communicate at all. In sum, the categorizing process permits us to reduce the complexity of our environment.

We accomplish this reduction in complexity—basically—by *abstracting* and *generalizing.* In abstracting, we draw not upon a specific instance or case or item but upon *general classes* or *groups* of instances or cases or items. Then, on the basis of these classes or groups we *generalize:* We draw a general principle from them or make a conclusion about them. Always, when we abstract and generalize we are dealing with the notion of classes or groups—never with our perception of the individual thing. If we "reason" that women live longer than men, we are not talking about a *particular* man or a *certain woman;* we are talking about *numbers* of men and women. We are generalizing about a key characteristic aspect or criterion of a fairly large class of men and a fairly large class of women; namely, comparative age.

When Aristotle wished us to perceive *young* men as being different from *old* men, he concerned himself with *classes* and not with individuals. When he "classified" young men, he noted that ". . . they have strong, but unsteady desires; they look on the good side rather than the bad; they look more to the future than to the past; they are easily deceived; all their mistakes are on the side of intensity and excess."[8] In this description Aristotle abstracts: He does not describe everything about every youth, but focuses rather upon those *key criterial aspects* of all youth as he sees them. He generalizes: He extends his ideal description to cover *all* entities in the class (*all young men*). Exactness, the precise specific, is lost in the process of abstraction and generalization, but this loss is necessary. In categorizing, to make our terms or word-names generally applicable we must sacrifice a measure of precision and completeness in describing the individual case.[9]

If you stop and think for a moment about the ways you abstract and generalize, you will recognize that *selectivity,* too, figures importantly in categorizing. Consider the variety of perceptions you could choose to include in your categories for "dog," "school," and "politician." What *characteristic aspects* would you choose to attribute to each class? What features or qualities must any specific entity have for you to classify it in one of these categories? What features or qualities are usually associated with the entity, but not essential? Must a "dog" have four legs, hair, and be man's best friend? Must a "school" have a building, a teacher, a desk, and a football team? Must a "politician" be a speaker, an opportunist, a wheeler-and-dealer, and have powerful friends in City Hall? 5

You can see that the essential traits on which you base your classification must really be few in number. You can also see that to abstract them from the many possible, specific characteristics which you can perceive in any particular entity, object, or idea, requires a high degree of *selectivity*. When we abstract, we *select* from among the many characteristics or qualities which we can perceive; and then we say, in effect: "These are all of the characteristics needed to understand what I mean when I use the word 'dog'; these qualities are 'common' to *all* 'dogs.' " Thus, when we speak of "dog" in the abstract, we are not talking about Fido, or Spot, or Rover; we are generalizing on the basis of a few canine qualities in order to distinguish a *class* of creatures which we arbitrarily name "dog."

Validity of categories. *Categories, being largely "inventions" of the human self, can never be exact or entirely accurate; but they should, nevertheless, stand up under the tests of appropriateness, practicality, and consistency.* As must be obvious now, our categories or sets are personal *inventions*, not discoveries; they exist in us as persons rather than in nature. Again consider the color spectrum. The boundaries for *green* certainly do not exist within that spectrum. These boundaries are established *arbitrarily* by individuals, and the single label *green* is applied to all shades falling within those boundaries. We *suppose* these boundaries, these dividing lines, to exist; but actually they may not. Moreover, even the most carefully defined categories can overlap. The greater the perceptual range of our knowledge and the broader the scope of our sensory experiences, the less

---

Study Probe 5
Testing the Effects of One Form of Categorizing

In a role-playing exercise, your instructor will take turns introducing several of you to the class by using a certain label: *an orphan, an educator, a divorcee,* etc. The rest of the class will then ask questions of each person and try to carry on as natural a conversation as possible. Of course, the interaction will be influenced by the label by which the person was first introduced, but you might consider afterward what "normal" subjects of discussion were left out or not emphasized.

What are normal subjects of discussion when people are first introduced? To find out, try repeating this experiment *without* the instructor's using any labels in the introductions.

distinct are the categorical boundary lines likely to become. As laymen, we speak freely and easily about the "living" and the "dead," and about "animals" and "plants." But scientists are hard pressed in some cases to label a single instance as "living" or "dead," as "plant" or "animal."

Conveniently for us, most of the instances we perceive appear clear-cut and relatively easy to categorize. Because we human beings have a great many of the same or similar experiences and because we are often subject to more or less the same conditioning in our homes, schools, churches, etc., our personal categories often coincide quite closely with those of other people. However, even when we examine what we suppose to be exceptional cases, we can see how the dividing line between categories is not fixed in nature, but is determined and imposed by human beings. This is one of the reasons why thought and communication—to the extent that they are dependent upon the use of language—can never be exact. Room for error is inherent in the very nature of language because there is so much room for error in the perceiving, categorizing, abstracting, and generalizing that we do.

Although the boundaries of our categories frequently are established arbitrarily, they are not set capriciously or without meaningful, workable purpose. Very often the categories we use and talk about are set up to satisfy standards of some kind or meet certain requirements. Scientific categories especially are of this type. Other categories are set up to satisfy our need for internal consistency and balance—especially those involving a desire for a comfortable either-or relationship, neat parallelism between concepts, and a sense of completeness. In reasoning and communicative situations, we are constantly testing the validity, accuracy, and appropriateness of our categories, subjecting them to considerable adjustment and readjustment.

Psychological categories. *Categories necessarily include the psychological as well as the physical "properties" and aspects of entities we perceive and try to talk about.* We can—and often must—form categories or sets which reflect our reactions to *physical* objects or to sensations resulting from external influence. However, not all categories are tangible; many of them do not refer to discernible objects or events. Frequently, that is, our communicative impulse requires that we create categories also for nonobservable or even hypothetical concepts and imaginary objects—for entities that we can't see, hear, touch, taste, or smell. For example, just as we form categories for physical qualities, aspects, or properties of color, so we also form categories for *psychological* qualities or properties—categories which involve sets of feelings or values or other internal responses. The expression "a blue Monday" suggests but one of hundreds of instances of this property of the color *blue*. As another example, to certain circumstances or events or feelings we attach the labels *just* or *fair*. To an even larger set of circumstances, happenings, and reactions we attach the labels *good* or *bad*. These categories represent psychological attributes—feelings and values—just as *green* and *hard* reflect physical properties. Again, we do all of this—in part—in order that we can talk about sensory data and impressions that we are made aware of.

Language Labels

Naming or assigning word-labels to our categories is fundamental to human communication. To form groupings and classifications of our sensory experiences would be pointless if we couldn't talk about them—couldn't communicate with others about them. This is where *language* comes into the picture. Categories, as we have seen, provide boundaries for grouping our experiences; they "fence off" sets of experiences. To communicate, we have to let others know the fencing-off we are doing. And we accomplish this—and facilitate it—by means of word-labels. In short, to assign labels or names to these categorical groupings or sets of human experience is one of the primary functions of language.

The processes of categorizing and labeling are *interdependent:* Categorizing establishes the boundaries; labeling establishes the names. Labeling, like categorizing, involves the processes of generalization and abstraction. A language label must identify the "territory" covered by the category. In a sense, it has to be an almost instantaneous "map" of the categorical territory. The label should, of course, be as descriptive and as accurate as possible. It must suggest details but not too many because, as we have emphasized, the category that it names applies not so much to the total of the individual entities in the set as to certain real or imagined properties of that *grouping* of entities. Since the important common elements or properties are combined and narrowed in the making of the category, it is this narrowed "meaning" of it to which the label applies. The word *bottle,* for instance, may prompt us to think not of *every* bottle we have ever seen but rather an abstractively narrowed set of generalized "meanings" which we have come to associate with and attach to that word.

We human beings tend to give labels to all the different categories we discriminate; and, conversely, we discriminate among the different categories for which we have devised labels. Anthropologist Franz Boas has pointed out, for example, that Eskimos discriminate among many different categories for snow and ice and have dozens of labels for their various conditions. Fine shades of difference in the condition of ice and snow are extremely important to the Eskimos' daily functioning and survival; and the ability to make those discriminations is more necessary to them than it is, for example, to people who live in warmer areas. All of this again emphasizes how we use categories and language to impose order upon our environment. With this order we can of course better understand and control our own existence and communicate with others concerning the many common features of existence.

Language as Symbols

We use language labels as symbols. As we use a label to name the perceptions we have organized, abstracted, and generalized into a category, the label becomes a linguistic *symbol* for the category: It "stands for" the category. Taken together, the labels we apply to categories thus provide us with a *language system* or *linguistic code.* With this code, we can manipulate *symbolically* all of the groupings into which we have analyzed our universe. This code of symbols enables us to deal with the physical world more efficiently and—we may hope—more effectively.

Imagine the enormity of the difficulties we would experience if we could communicate only about those objects, entities, and processes which we would have immediately at hand or before us at the moment we wanted to converse with someone. Jonathan Swift reveals something of what our dilemma would be when he refers in a humorous, satirical vein to the linguistic theories of the wise men of his mythical Laputa. Two of these sages, he tells us, would carry along with them, in large sacks, all of the various objects to which they might wish to refer in their speaking. Swift describes the plight of the pair as "almost sinking under the weight of their packs . . . and who, when they met in the streets, would lay down their loads, open up their sacks, and hold conversation for an hour together; then put up their implements, help each other to resume their burdens, and take their leave." [10]

Advantages of language symbols.   Thanks to the *symbolizing* capacities of language, we don't have to carry around in a sack the things we want to talk about. Because we can use the "word" in place of the "entity"—the symbolic in place of the real—within practical, workable limits we are able to handle at least three extremely important communicative functions: (1) We are able to control and cope with our environment in sensible ways; (2) we are able to communicate with others more speedily and directly; and (3) we are able—because our linguistic symbols often reflect common and shared experiences of other human beings—to facilitate the speech communication process as a whole.

We can use language symbolically to mediate—work between—our self and our environment. Obviously, language is the great facilitator of human action and communicative coping. Suppose, for example, that two of us are trapped in a burning building. One of us is familiar with the place; the other is a stranger to it. Under these circumstances, we needn't race randomly about and try all potential or imagined escape routes solely by trial and error. Language—used first, perhaps, as "inner speech" and later as meaningful utterance—makes it possible for us to travel each route *symbolically.* We can stand for a moment, "think through," and—if necessary—talk about each particular escape route, and take the trip symbolically to its possible consequences. Then we can choose the route that seems to offer the highest probability for safe escape. In this manner, among many others, language can mediate between human beings and their physical world.

We can use language symbolically to mediate—work between—our self and the selves of others. As the "burning building" incident also illustrates, by means of the labeling code which language provides, we can communicate with other human beings more speedily and directly. I can, for instance, vocally transmit to a listener the symbol *fire* and hope that, because of the common cultural environment in which both of us learned that label, *fire* will call up in that listener a set of reactions essentially similar to those that *I* experience in response to that symbol. The internal reactions we feel when confronted with a symbol are probably the best definition of the "meaning" that symbol has for us. And to the extent that our utterance of that symbol causes our listeners to experience similar internal reactions, they will understand the "meaning" we are trying to communicate to them. If genuine communication is taking place, our "meaning" and their "meaning" will *coincide* rather closely. And this brings us to our third and final point about the symbolism of language.

Clearly, the common experiences which human beings share for linguistic symbols underlie and greatly facilitate the speech communication process. This, in large part, is what the study of language—etymology, linguistics, semantics, imagery, etc.—is all about. Some commonalities are readily arrived at; others are much more difficult to achieve. As we have already suggested, some categories— and the labels for them—are seemingly more "appropriate," "fixed," and "verifiable" than others. The likelihood that a speaker and a listener will have essentially similar reactions is greater for the symbol *fire* than it is for the symbol *freedom.* The sensations which produce a response of *fire* are easily and quickly identifiable: We smell the smoke; we see the flames; feel the waves of heat emanating from them. If necessary—as in the instance of a stove, furnace, or an electric iron—we can measure the intensity of these emanations with scientific instruments such as thermometers. We can, if we wish, stabilize our judgments on the label *fire* with relatively high reliability; and if we are willing to exert the required effort, we can obtain fairly general agreement in setting the boundaries of *fire* in terms of thermal units. ⁶

But the symbol *freedom* stands for a broader and higher level of abstraction. In contrast with the boundaries of the "hotness" and "coldness" of fire, the boundaries which encompass the category labeled *freedom* are not nearly as clear. In fact, since for many of us *freedom* isn't really a single-dimensioned concept, it probably has no "single" meaning for us. To understand what it "means" might require that interacting agents be familiar with *clusters* of categories, all having somewhat different labels but all interrelated and all interacting. But no matter how we might go about trying to define *freedom,* the intangible boundaries designated by the label very probably will never be as clear and definite as are the wavelength of reflected heat or the other distinctions we can draw for *fire.*

Inexactness of symbols. It is this lack of tangible, readily discernible, and commonly agreed-upon boundaries for meaning, we must admit, that creates one of the most serious *limitations* of language. (This point will be developed more fully in Chapter 6.) It must inevitably prohibit the exactness which makes possible "perfect" communication between one human being and another. The fact that our language labels are, first of all, derived from fallible or incomplete perceptions, that they have to progress through fairly high levels of abstraction and generalization, and that ultimately their "meanings" must emerge as symbolic and often complex representations makes it impossible for such labels ever to be as precise as we'd like them to be. Add to these limitations the fact that the "interpretation" of labels is so dependent upon the almost-always-incomplete perceptions and the fragile sharing of experiences which two or more mortals are capable of, and you can readily see why many of the significant barriers to effective communication are imbedded in the very nature of language.

Actually, though, these limitations are a relatively small price to pay for the *advantages* which the symbolism of language affords. As we conclude this brief exploration of how we use language, and before we move on to its relationship to thinking and reasoning, let's reflect for a moment upon a few of those advantages and their implications; namely:

With language . . .

1. We can devise and attach suitable word-labels to the perceptions we make and the categories we invent.
2. We can impose a sense of order and selectivity on our categories and the concepts related to them.
3. We can improve our adaptability to the environment. This is made possible, in part, by the fact that
   a. We can evolve a code of "meanings" with which to manipulate *symbolically* the categories and word-labels describing our environment and relationships to it.
   b. We can eliminate the need to manipulate *real* entities and *actual* objects because language, being symbolic, enables us to use the *word* in place of the *entity*.
   c. We can think about people, events, and objects even in their absence, and communicate about these matters with others.
4. We can discover and interrelate *commonalities* of perceptions, categories, language labels, and—therefore—"meanings." The greater the commonality of language and "meaning," the greater the likelihood of effective communicative interaction.
5. We can, to a large extent, count on its *flexibility*—that language will *change* with the increased inputs of information by speaking/listening agents, with shifting perspectives, and with the passage of time.

Study Probe 6
Finding Common Meanings

Look at the following list of words:

1. death	5. beer	9. flag	13. education
2. cancer	6. Hitler	10. roach	14. politician
3. abortion	7. football	11. home	15. clouds
4. liberal	8. rock music	12. hot dogs	16. springtime

Now write a *single word* which best describes your feelings for *each* of the words above. Compare your list with those of your classmates. Which reactions seemed most universal? Which least? How can you explain the differences?

In this chapter we've attempted to trace the origins of the substance of speech communication and the processes by which we acquire and label it with language. In particular, we've looked rather carefully at those processes by which we receive stimuli from our environment, perceive them as sensations, categorize and organize those perceptions, and attach language symbols to them. As we move on into the next chapter, we will concern ourselves with some of the ways in which we *systematize* speech communication substance, noting especially how we manipulate those language symbols in reasoning, thinking, and communicating about our existence.

Suggested Readings

The following works provide varied and informative materials which will supplement the content of this chapter.

Peter Farb, *Word Play: What Happens When People Talk* (New York: Alfred A. Knopf, Inc., 1974). This book presents an informative and very entertaining discussion of language. Many readers will complete the book in one sitting, in spite of its 320 pages.

Bernard F. Huppé and Jack Kaminsky, *Logic and Language* (New York: Alfred A. Knopf, Inc., 1957). An introductory work which interrelates the study of logic and language. As such, the presentation is most useful for beginning students in speech communication.

Philip G. Zimbardo and Floyd L. Ruch, *Psychology and Life,* 9th ed. (Glenview, Ill.: Scott, Foresman and Company, 1975), Chapter 4, "Language, Communication, and Memory," pp. 142–183, and Chapter 6, "Perception," pp. 232–273. These chapters from this basic psychology textbook present introductory and useful background materials on sensation, perception, and language. You may also wish to consult some of the other chapters of this text. Any information gained about psychology will be helpful in understanding the speech communication process.

Reference Notes

[1]*Webster's Seventh New Collegiate Dictionary* (Springfield, Mass.: G. & C. Merriam Company, Publishers, 1965), p. 486.

[2]Floyd L. Ruch and Philip G. Zimbardo, *Psychology and Life,* 8th ed. (Glenview, Ill.: Scott, Foresman and Company, 1971), pp. 299–300.

[3]Ibid., pp. 296–297.

[4]Allen L. Edwards, "Rationalization in Recognition as a Result of a Political Frame of Reference," *Journal of Abnormal and Social Psychology,* 36 (1941): 224–235.

[5]Marshall McLuhan, *Understanding Media: The Extensions of Man* (New York: McGraw-Hill Book Company, 1964), pp. 268–294.

[6]When you are looking at the devils, the angels become background; but when you are looking at the angels, the reverse happens. Despite attempts to keep from shifting, you are likely to see one and then the other alternately. This demonstrates the foreground-background phenomenon, a subject discussed in connection with this woodcut in Floyd L. Ruch, *Psychology and Life,* 7th ed. (Glenview, Ill.: Scott, Foresman and Company, 1967), p. 304.

[7]If you want to explore further the fascinating world of human language, take a look at *The Speech Communication Process* by Theodore Clevenger, Jr., and Jack Matthews (Glenview, Ill.: Scott, Foresman and Company, 1971). In Chapter 3, "Meaning in Language," pages 33–47, these authors present a clear, concise analysis of various kinds of "Content" and "Structure" words and their importance in communicating.

[8]Aristotle, *Rhetoric, The Basic Works of Aristotle,* ed. Richard McKeon (New York: Random House, Inc., 1951), p. 1331.

[9]A good source of information about language from the view of General Semantics is Harry L. Weinberg's *Levels of Knowing and Existence* (New York: Harper & Row, Publishers, Inc., 1959).

[10]Jonathan Swift, *Gulliver's Travels* (Garden City, N.Y.: Doubleday & Company, Inc., 1945), pp. 186–187.

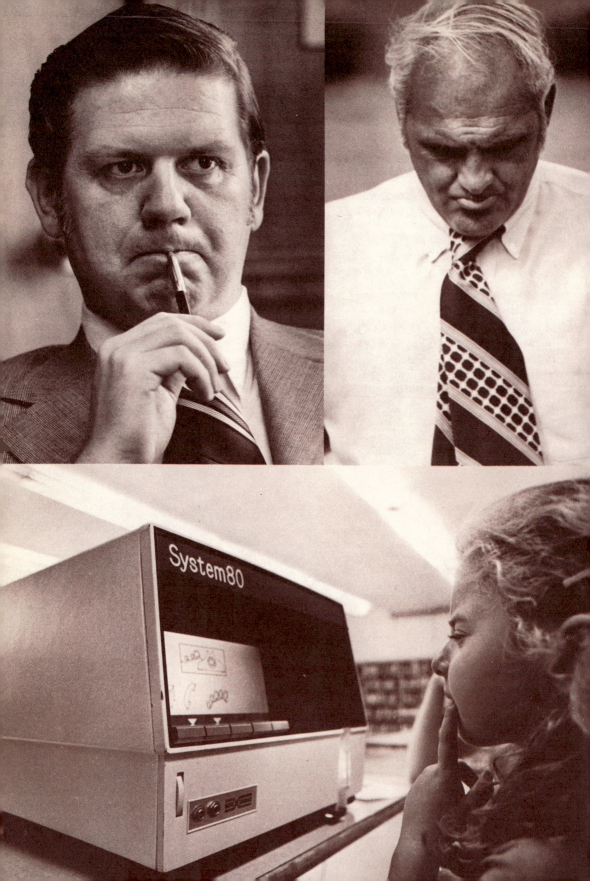

REASONING

Before we can communicate the substance
of speech, we must put it into some kind of
reasonable and commonly understood
system—two useful systems being deductive
and inductive reasoning. But however logical and
consistent we are, we must remember
that reason and emotion are inseparable,
working together in every speech act.

Now that we've acquired the stuff and substance of speech communication and labeled it, what do we do with it? How, more specifically, do we communicate with it? Obviously we can't just randomly string together one word-label or language symbol after another without regard to their relative *meaning,* comparative *importance,* or useful *sequence.* We can't assemble the bits and pieces with no thought of their interrelationships or the informing, persuading, or actuating functions we'd like them to serve. No, we've got to consider how to put the substantive elements together into some kind of meaningful, communicable *system.* We must endow them with "reason" and "reasonability." For want of a more precise and accurate word-label, this process of systematizing and sequencing is usually called *reasoning* or *thinking.* And as we are using the words here, they are—loosely speaking—synonymous.

As we proceed, we'll need to keep reminding ourselves, of course, that when we try to "reason" or "think" we often are climbing even higher into the clouds of abstraction and generalization that we talked about in Chapter 4. Sometimes, however, we have to go into reverse, so to speak, and come closer down to earth as we move from the generalized to the specific, from the abstract to the more concrete and individualized aspects of our categories. But in any case, we must never lose sight of the fact that in synthesizing and systematizing speech substance it is the *symbols,* the language labels and not the realities, that we are adjusting and manipulating. Essentially, to make any system of reasoning or thinking work within a communicative context, we have to "arouse" in others an awareness of the language symbols in our code of meaning and then manipulate those symbols into the most meaningful relationships that we can. Thus, along with psychologist Norman Munn, we are defining *reasoning* as "the sequential arousal and manipulation of language symbols."[1]

IMPOSING SYSTEM AND SEQUENCE ON SUBSTANCE

There are numerous systems for reasoning and thinking, and you are doubtless already familiar with a good many of them. As you probably know, one way we reason is by *associating*—in some kind of pattern or order—the language labels we have applied to categories of experience. This association, or the relating of these symbols one to another, allows for *inference,* the process by which we derive new propositions* or conclusions from previously established or assumed propositions and facts. In this section, we will review three of the well-established and useful approaches to reasoning and inference-making: (1) *deductive reasoning,* (2) *inductive reasoning,* and (3) *Toulmin's inferential pattern.* Then, later in the chapter, we will consider briefly some common misunderstandings about the reasoning process.

Deductive Reasoning

Deductive reasoning aims at *valid* or *necessary* conclusions. The term has been defined roughly as "inferring from the general to the particular case." If we accept certain premises and follow certain rules for relating these premises, we arrive at necessary conclusions. A deduction is an inference in which the conclusion *necessarily* follows from acceptance of given premises.** Consider the following dialogue:

GIVEN   John: I think water-skiing is a dumb sport, and everyone who
PREMISES   likes it is stupid.

---

*You will recall that on page 78 we said that by *proposition* we mean "an expression in language or signs of something that can be believed, doubted, or denied or is either true or false." Also, we said, "We use the term to refer to a communicative claim, project, or situation which calls for acceptance, rejection, or some other kind of interactive result."

**A proposition that is "pre-existent" and that may be supposed or proved as the basis of an argument or inference is called a *premise.*

> Bill: Why, I was just talking with your fiancee, Mary, and she said she loves to water-ski!
>
> John: Oh.

The conclusion (although unstated) is obvious, logically unavoidable, and pre-determined by the premises—and John knows it. He is trapped by a necessary deductive inference. If he—and Bill—accept the given premises, there is no way to avoid the "obvious" conclusion that John's fiancee is "stupid" because she loves the "dumb sport" of water-skiing.

Aristotle gave much attention to the deductive form of reasoning, and his efforts are nearly always associated with what he called the "categorical syllogism" and the rules for its application. The categorical syllogism is a deductive scheme or system for arranging categories and subcategories. It consists of three main statements—a *major premise,* a *minor premise,* and a *conclusion*—each of which is usually stated in the form of a simple, declarative sentence. With this rhetorical invention, Aristotle was attempting to develop standards or tests to be applied to thinking in order to insure its validity. Given major and minor premises, stated in proper form and meeting certain standards, then the "proper" conclusion must "inevitably" follow; and it will be "valid." Surely the most frequently cited categorical syllogism is:

All men are mortal.	*(major premise)*
Socrates is a man.	*(minor premise)*
Therefore, Socrates is mortal.	*(conclusion)*

Over the years, the structure of the syllogism and its appropriate tests have been applied to the analysis of speech communication messages. It doesn't always "work," however. One of the major difficulties is that often a speaker, in developing a deductive, "syllogistic" line of reasoning, will *omit* a significant premise. And then, as listeners we are faced with the job of analyzing the message material and searching out the *unstated premise.* Aristotle anticipated this circumstance and described a syllogism in which one premise is implicit—but missing—as one form of "enthymeme."

On a practical, workaday level, we must admit, one of the real obstacles to analyzing messages in terms of syllogisms and enthymemes is that we rarely find a fully stated syllogism *as such* occurring in conversations, discussions, public speeches, or other communicative contexts. This happens, largely, because in many "incomplete" syllogisms the *unexpressed* parts or premises frequently deal in probabilities, potential understandings, and implied premises which are already familiar to listeners and accepted by them.

Supposedly, because of this listener familiarity and ready acceptance of at least one of the premises in a syllogism, a speaker can present the "incomplete" syllogism in a short form, or even omit part of it entirely, and still be fairly certain that the listeners will supply the missing or "unstated" premise. For example, a speaker may declare that "Socrates is mortal because he is a man," thereby requiring his or her listeners to fill in for themselves the unstated major premise, "All men are mortal." In making the kind of analysis we are talking about here, a two-step procedure is required: (1) we must *recognize* the "incomplete" syllogism when we hear or see it, and then (2) we have to be able to *complete* it by mentally supplying the *unstated premise.* This filling in of an unstated premise is another example of the *perception-completing* behavior discussed on pages 83–85 of Chapter 4. 1

In the Middle Ages the deductive system of reasoning was predominant to the point of being extreme, and it is still occasionally condemned for some of the excesses of that period. In those times, the "absolute truth" of too many premises was assumed, and the unquestioning acceptance of the resulting conclusions often was demanded by church and government. We now recognize, of course, that the deductive method is only a *part* of the total reasoning process. So long as we intelligently mix and balance our methods of making inferences and drawing conclusions, deductive reasoning can be of real help to us.

Inductive Reasoning

Induction offers another inferential—and somewhat more flexible—system for putting together the speech substance we've acquired. With it, too, we can develop lines of reasoning by associating—in a *different* kind of pattern of order—the language symbols we've assigned to the categories and subcategories of our sensory experience. With it, too, our communicative objective is to reach clear and convincing conclusions. With the inductive system, however, we take a slightly

Study Probe 1
Determining Premises

Write down the premises which warrant each of the following statements:

1. It's too cold to go out.
2. He's a great teacher.
3. It figures he'd vote for McGovern. He's from New York.
4. Better dead than Red.
5. Courses like foreign language should be abolished.
6. Everyone is going to die sooner or later.
7. Baseball is boring.
8. Be young at heart, Drink Fizzy Cola.
9. If I were rich, that would be the life!
10. Vegetarians are ruining their health.

Do any of the premises seem based on false or questionable assumptions?

Discuss your findings in class.

different road to get there. Unlike the movement in *deductive* thinking—where we move from the general class to the particular case—in *inductive* reasoning we travel from the particular case to the general category. Whereas deductive reasoning is concerned with the logical "inevitability" and validity of conclusions, inductive inference is concerned with the *probability* and the *reliability* of conclusions. The inductive system of reasoning allows *relative* "truth" and *probable* conclusions.

Maybe we can get a better mental hook on these notions of "relative" and "probable" if we take a look at another brief exchange between John and Bill.

John: I have known a number of water-skiers who were really stupid.

Bill: Why, I was just talking to Mary, your fiancee, and she said she loves to water-ski!

John: Well, that's different! Mary's an exceptional girl!

In this dialogue, "a number of" and "exceptional" are key clues that should have grabbed your attention. In the earlier dialogue, where the *deductive* system was at work, the exchange between John and Bill hinged on a major premise that was *absolute*: *"Everyone* who likes water-skiing is stupid." In the present exchange, where the *inductive* system is at work, John uses as his major, declarative statement (*not* premise) a *generalization* which is both *probable* and *relative* because he has built it up from his observations of a number of (but not *all*) specific cases and used them to draw his generalization about the resultant "group" or category. The fact that the major statement is not absolute permits John, in his final statement, to exclude his fiancee from the generalization by calling her an exception. In this system, John's major declarative generalization is—in a sense—also his *conclusion,* and he can legitimately use his final statement both to "qualify" and reinforce his generalization.

Induction, then, we may describe as *the process of using evidence concerning some members of a class as a basis for making generalizations—probability statements—about other members of that class.* Let's pick a category—say, "People With Fewer Dental Cavities"—and make a trial run on it. Suppose we designate People A, B, C, D, E, and F as members or entities of our category or "exclusive circle," thus:

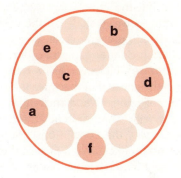

We're on pretty intimate terms with People A, B, C, D, E, and F—intimate enough, at least, to know that they are "People With Fewer Dental Cavities" and that they wouldn't be caught using anything but a dentifrice known as "No-Holes-in-the-Head Toothpaste." About those other people in our circle we know less. The *one* thing we are *sure* of is that these unnamed people use the same miraculous toothpaste used by our friends A, B, C, D, E, and F. "Use the Same Toothpaste" is the property that all of these entities have in common. Whether the unnamed persons have more or fewer cavities is, as they say, open to argument. And that "argument" or line of reasoning runs something like this:

> *Having noted certain common properties ("Use the Same Toothpaste"*
> *and "Fewer Dental Cavities") among these entities (A, B, C, D, E, and F),*
> *we make the inference that these two particular properties are common*
> *to—will be found in—other as-yet-untested members or entities of the cat-*
> *egory group. Having observed entities A, B, C, D, E, and F in the group*
> *and finding that they all have X Trait ("Fewer Dental Cavities"), we infer*
> *that the other, untested members of the category group—because they,*
> *too, have in common with A, B, C, D, E, and F a property or trait labeled*
> *"Use the Same Toothpaste"—will* also *have X Trait "Fewer Dental Cav-*
> *ities." When we reason in this fashion, we are* assuming *that entities A, B,*
> *C, D, E, and F are typical examples* of *all entities in the category or class.*
> *We could—and advertisers often do—carry this assumption one step far-*
> *ther and claim that "People Who Use No-Holes-in-the-Head Toothpaste*
> *Have Fewer Dental Cavities."* [2]

For obvious reasons, this rhetorical use of inductive reasoning is sometimes called "reasoning from example." As in our illustration, an inductive inference is made from a number of examples or specific instances pointing to a conclusion that allows for *probability* while, at the same time, having a fairly high degree of *reliability.*

Deductive and inductive reasoning compared.   In comparing the deductive and the inductive systems of reasoning, you will find that they have some complementary strengths and weaknesses. The deductive method assures validity, or internal consistency, to the development of a proposition or the line of argument: It helps us check that the conclusion we reach is consistent with the premises we started out with. As we've shown, if the proper ingredients (a major and a minor premise at least) are present or can be inferred, and if our premises appear to follow one another in clear and logical order, then our conclusion must follow validly from those premises. However, as we have also pointed out, the deductive form is *restrictive* in the sense that, because the conclusion is immediately implied by the premises, it really doesn't add anything significantly new to them. It merely analyzes or makes specific what is already there or is implied in the premises. Or, to state it another way, the conclusion of a syllogism is already contained within the premises and makes only a *part* of their content explicit. All of this may make for a fairly tight little package, but its *scope* is limited. In short, although the deductive system of reasoning may help us "think straight," it doesn't allow us to take any significant side-trips. When we want to explore ideas or propositions that are new and different, we may find some other way of thinking and reasoning more flexible and useful.

The conclusion of an *inductive* inference, on the other hand, is not contained solely in the instances upon which it is based. The inductive conclusion goes *beyond* the data contained in or suggested by the generalization and is not *restrictive* in the sense that we have used that term. It thus lends itself well to scientific studies, experimentation, and the probing of social issues. At the same time, there is danger that in reasoning from examples we may use too few of them to support the inference we want to make. This will especially be so if the examples we choose are insufficient and too narrow in scope to cover the entire category or class we've used in our generalization. We must use at least a big and wide enough selection so that our listeners can see that they are *typical*. If we don't, they won't go along with our line of reasoning.

A short illustration may help clarify what we mean by "typicality" while, at the same time, demonstrating a pitfall in the inductive system. Suppose we were to say (as an early textbook did) that "Mercury revolves on its axis; so do Venus, the Earth, Mars, Jupiter, Saturn, and Neptune. . . . These are all planets, and therefore all planets revolve on their axes."[2] But these are *not* "all of the planets," and even today there may be still others of which we are not yet aware. This should serve to demonstrate that *induction can never be complete or perfect*. We may always find the exceptional case. As the Scottish philosopher David Hume

Study Probe 2
Locating Examples of Inductive Inference in Contemporary Social Issues

Examine communication materials developed in contemporary discussions of social issues, and single out examples of inductive inference that you find in them. Make a list of specific cases cited in each by the speaker seemingly for the purpose of drawing inductive conclusions. Then ask yourself the following questions:

1. Are the specific cases (in each example) *typical* cases?
2. Are the cited cases *adequate in number*?
3. Are the cited cases *broad enough in scope* to cover the class or set as a whole?
4. How did you determine the *standards* for "typical," "adequate," and "broad enough"?

Compare your answers with those of your classmates, and arrange to explain your findings with others in a small group discussion.

emphasized, "Even if *every* crow we have seen was black, and we believe all crows are black, yet it is possible that the next crow we shall *see* will be white." In sum, the strength of the inductive system of reasoning is that its conclusion goes beyond the generalizable data in making an inference and thus adds something to the proposition or argument, but the weakness of the system is that the inductive conclusion—not being supported by objective "truth" or generally accepted authority—cannot assure necessary validity.

Deductive and inductive reasoning combined. Despite certain weaknesses and shortcomings in both of these systems, as speakers and listeners we can expect to encounter—and use—both of them frequently. Fortunately, because induction and deduction are complementary, we can *combine* them as we try to formulate and put together many of the ideas, beliefs, propositions, lines of reasoning, and other speech substance that we want to talk about in communicative situations. In their combined form, we can use them to analyze and test the strengths of the propositions and arguments that we may hear or wish to advance. Stephen Toulmin, a British mathematician, has developed a contemporary view of an inferential process that combines some of the elements of deduction and induction in a model of the human reasoning process.[3]

The Toulmin Inferential Pattern

According to Toulmin's description in *The Uses of Argument,* we infer from *data* to a *claim,* through the use of a *warrant* or *general proposition.* His plan may be clearer if we substitute the word *evidence* for *data,* and *conclusion* for *claim.* Thus:

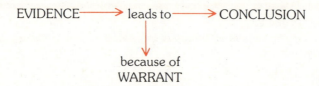

EVIDENCE ⟶ leads to ⟶ CONCLUSION

because of
WARRANT

Toulmin suggests that the warrant or general proposition itself may be given support, called *backing,* and that the conclusion still might not follow if it is countered by an objection, called *rebuttal.* He also recognizes the danger (that we have pre-

Study Probe 3
Anticipating Rebuttal

Read the speech by Virginia Y. Trotter in the Appendix, noting those places or portions where she has foreseen possible refutation and analyzing her attempts to deal with it. Prepare to discuss your observation in class.

viously pointed out) in making a categorized claim or conclusion seem "absolute," and so he includes a *qualifier* for the conclusion. In somewhat more complete form, his model for a line of reasoning (with our changes in terminology) looks like this:

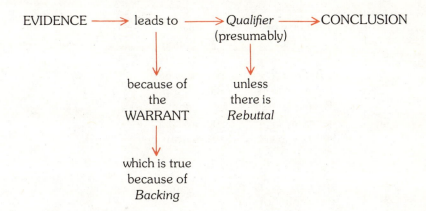

EVIDENCE ⟶ leads to ⟶ *Qualifier* ⟶ CONCLUSION
(presumably)

because of   unless
the   there is
WARRANT   *Rebuttal*

which is true
because of
Backing

In the above, Toulmin's *warrant* represents a generalization or a general proposition which has already been arrived at or accepted. *Evidence* represents a fairly specific item of information. His inferential process attempts to classify within a larger category the specific evidence under the generalization or proposition stated in the warrant. Once this is done, an association is drawn between the evidence and other specific statements, including those made in the conclusion, and also those made under the warrant. This *association* of particulars through the process of categorizing and generalizing is the essence of inference. And, of course, as in all inference-making, there is the necessary overlapping of language and thought. ③④

In the following diagram, Toulmin lays out the procedure by which you can use his inference-pattern to draw the conclusion that "Harry is a British subject."

Study Probe 4
Looking for Backing for a Warrant

Examine the speech by John A. Howard in the Appendix and analyze it for instances in which he has provided some backing for a warrant. Do you accept the backing? If not, why not? In those instances you cite, what kind of backing might you accept? How acceptable is the warrant itself? Be prepared to present either a written or oral report based on your analysis.

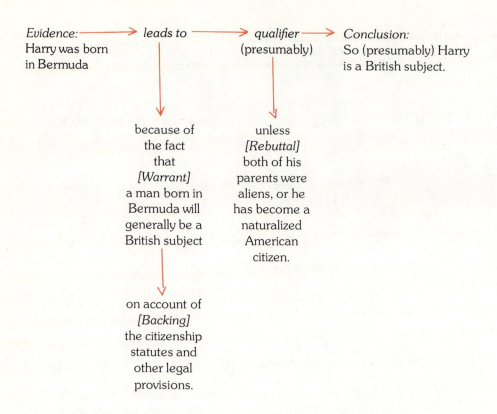

When fully understood, Toulmin's approach is quite flexible and can provide you with further insights into how the inferential process of reasoning works in systematizing speech communication substance. It can help you analyze the assertions and claims you make, showing you how to break apart the elements of a proposition or line of reasoning so that you can inspect the adequacy of each separate part and check its relationships to each of the other parts. Unlike the syllogism, Toulmin's pattern is not "self-contained" and "self-restrictive." With such elements as the *backing* for the warrant, the possible lines of *refutation,* and the *qualifier* to the conclusion, it offers greater opportunities for variations, experimentation, explorations, etc. Of course, probably the best way to understand anything—Toulmin's system included—is to *use* it. Use it to analyze the messages you make and the messages you hear. [5]

SOME COMMON MISUNDERSTANDINGS ABOUT REASONING

In rounding out our consideration of reasoning and thinking there are a couple of common assumptions that we should ponder briefly. The first is the view, held by many, that "logical" reasoning will automatically and inevitably lead to "truth." The second is the supposition that there is a basic and somehow necessary conflict between our "logical/intellectual" nature and our "emotional" nature.

Logic and Truth

Logical reasoning doesn't necessarily lead to truth. Logical thinking, as we pointed out earlier, serves primarily to make our reasoning *consistent,* but it can't guarantee the infallibility or "truth" of our conclusions. Given certain premises, we may find what kinds of conclusions can and cannot follow; but these premises tell us very little about their validity or about the basic perceptions or beliefs from which we are supposed to start thinking and reasoning. The reasoning that I do, for instance, may be rigorously logical; but if the *initial grounds* for my reasoning are false, the inferences I make and conclusions I draw will likewise be false. Or, in another instance, the deluded premises and conclusions of a mentally ill person may be entirely consistent with one another and fit the tests of sound, logical reasoning. Very often, such an individual reasons very well—if not rationally. His problem is a lack of contact with reality—not a faulty manipulation of reality. The categories that he uses as the basis of his reasoning do not accurately represent the nature and ranges of sensory and perceptual experience they are supposed to generalize. It isn't his *system* of reasoning that's flawed; it's the *substance* he uses for it.

Reason and Emotion

Reason and emotion aren't separate entities in human beings, nor are they necessarily in conflict with each other. Over the years, it's true, there have been relatively large numbers of people who have written or spoken about this supposed conflict. A good many of them, especially those who have concerned themselves with the persuasive function of speech communication, have tended to view reason and emotion as distinct, separate, even opposed elements; as a speech contains more of one, it contains less of the other. Quite a few, too, have drawn a distinction between appeals to reason on the one hand and appeals to

Study Probe 5
Applying the Toulmin System to Reasoning in a Speech

a. In the speech by John A. Howard in the Appendix, study paragraphs 7–12 and prepare an analysis of how Dr. Howard has used Toulmin's system in this portion of the address. Give your analysis, in written form, to your instructor.

b. Prepare a similar analysis of the passage included in paragraphs 3–8 of the speech by Virginia Y. Trotter.

emotion on the other. However, when we search through studies and reports of experimentation on the subject, we find little proof of such distinctions and separations.

A more defensible position, it seems to us, is that reason and emotion always occur together—jointly—in any communicative act. On this matter we tend to agree with the view of a number of social psychologists, Martin Scheerer among others. Scheerer maintains:

> In principle, . . . behavior may be conceptualized as being embedded in a cognitive-emotional-motivational matrix in which no true separation is possible. No matter how we slice behavior, the ingredients of motivation-emotion-cognition are present in one order or another. As Adams [another psychologist] succinctly expressed it, "For there is a conative [meaning conscious desire or behavioral tendency] or dynamic component in our most disinterested, scientific, and objective cognition, or we would not make the observation. There is likewise a cognitive [judgmental] component in our blindest lust or rage, or their expressions would not have even the minimum of direction that they seem invariably to have."4

What Scheerer and Adams seem to be saying here is that no communicative interaction can fail to appeal to emotion, to touch upon our feelings. At the same time, no communication in which we participate can fail to involve the arousal and manipulation of language symbols. And, as you must be fully aware by now, the manipulation of language symbols *is* the process of reasoning as we understand it and have tried to explain it in these pages.

One of the factors, we believe, which accounts for the distinctions we make between reason and emotion is that we seem to feel obliged to make our actions appear explainable, reasonable, rational. We are not content to say we are doing something for no particular reason or for no other reason than we want to. So we rationalize frequently, or invent plausible reasons for our actions or conclusions if we can't find probable ones. Most of us at one time or another have, for example, probably reasoned: "Well, I do have a test tomorrow, but the movie would be relaxing. And besides, if I don't know the stuff now, I never will." If you haven't justified a conclusion in some such fashion, you are less susceptible to this human tendency than I suppose.

Correlation of reason and emotion. Not only do emotion and reasoning occur together in any communicative act, but there is also reason to believe that the two are *positively correlated,* that *they work together in a mutual, reciprocal relationship.* Psychologists D. O. Hebb and W. R. Thompson report that:

> Evidence from species comparison suggests that emotional susceptibility increases with intellectual capacity. Man is the most emotional as well as the most rational animal. . . . [Such] correlations between increasing intellect and increasing emotionality would suggest that thought and emotion are intimately, essentially related. There must be doubt concerning

any treatment of emotion as a state or process independent of intellectual processes, and having a separate seat in the nervous system.[5]

In other words, Hebb and Thompson are emphasizing that, between species and within species, emotion and reasoning are inseparably and positively interrelated. From rat to dog to chimpanzee to human (moron to genius), intellectual capacity and emotional capacity increase steadily, and they increase together.

"Oh," you say, "but this conclusion doesn't *seem* to jibe with the human need to appear 'rational'—and with what we can see in everyday life! You don't see intelligent people showing a lot of emotion. They just don't get excited or blow their stacks or lose their cool. So how can you explain the fact that such people are always so calm and 'reasonable' if reason and emotion *aren't* two different things?"

Reasons for emotional control. One explanation, certainly, is that we can and do use our intelligence to *avoid* those situations in which our responses would be openly and extremely emotional. Moreover, as so-called "civilized" persons, we are *conditioned* from infancy onward to "control" (conceal) our emotions. We discover very early in life that in situations invoking fear, anger, despair, great pleasure, excessive excitement, etc., we can reveal *too much* of the self to others. This "gives us away." And, in any case, emotionality often is frowned upon. And so we are conditioned by parents, by peers, and by ourselves to be calm and poised and not to "get upset," not to "lose control," and not to "wear our hearts on our sleeves." So, the more "intelligent" and conditioned we are, the more capable we are of avoiding or at least controlling our emotional behavior. However, when we find ourselves in an emotionally exciting circumstance or when we're thrown unexpectedly and against our will into a highly explosive situation, our response is almost sure to be more "emotional," more visible, and more extreme.

In sum, our capacity for reasoning—since it involves the arousal and manipulation of language symbols—is necessarily and positively connected with our emotional sensitivity. And while reason and emotion (like any other language categories) may be considered separately and specifically in the abstract, when we interact and communicate with others, the two are for all practical purposes joined and working closely together.

To restate briefly our concerns in the preceding pages, we have tried to complete and make more understandable the "picture" of the *flow* of speech communication substance as it continues from human sensation (as originated in Chapter 4) to human reasoning—the essence of this chapter. We have tried also to suggest what happens to the substance as it moves from one phase to the next. If we've succeeded to an acceptable extent, you should now have a clearer comprehension of some of the patterns and problems of systematizing and sequencing the ideas and propositions you want to present to others.

Overall, this should provide you not only with an improved understanding of the "stuff of speech," but it should also sharpen your perceptions and set you to thinking further about the symbolic capacities of language. It should, moreover, help you analyze the rational structuring and inner workings of speech communication messages—both those that you make and those that you hear. In meaningful and lasting ways, this chapter—like those that preceded it—should have enlarged your awareness of *your communicative self*. And the insights and vistas growing out of that awareness should put you a little farther down the road toward becoming a more interesting, more perceptive, and—therefore—more capable communicator.

Suggested Readings

Douglas Ehninger, *Influence, Belief, and Argument* (Glenview, Ill.: Scott, Foresman and Company, 1974). A more basic and elementary presentation of the Toulmin system than the other sources listed here, as well as general introductory materials on evidence and inference.

Douglas Ehninger and Wayne Brockriede, *Decision by Debate* (New York: Dodd, Mead and Company, 1963). A popular argumentation textbook which develops Toulmin's system in a detailed and practical manner.

Harold A. Larrabee, *Reliable Knowledge: Scientific Methods in the Social Studies,* rev. ed. (Boston: Houghton Mifflin Co., 1964). An exceptionally well-integrated, readable, and interesting coverage of the bases and patterns for thinking and inference making.

Stephen E. Toulmin, *The Uses of Argument* (London: Cambridge University Press, 1958). The now classic presentation of Toulmin's layout of the argumentation process.

Reference Notes

[1]Norman L. Munn, *Psychology,* 2nd ed. (Boston: Houghton Mifflin Company, 1951), p. 228.

[2]James M. O'Neill, Craven Laycock, and Robert L. Scales, *Argumentation and Debate* (New York: The Macmillan Company, 1917), p. 121.

[3]Stephen E. Toulmin, *The Uses of Argument* (London: Cambridge University Press, 1958), especially "The Layout of Arguments," pp. 94–195. *Note:* The first two diagrams on pages 104 and 105 are based on Toulmin's scheme; the third is from Toulmin, ibid., p. 105. Also *see* Douglas Ehninger and Wayne Brockriede, *Decision by Debate* (New York: Dodd, Mead & Co., 1963), Chs. 8–9, pp. 98–167.

[4]Martin Scheerer, "Cognitive Theory," *The Handbook of Social Psychology,* 1st ed., ed. Gardner Lindzey (Reading, Mass.: Addison-Wesley Publishing Co., Inc., 1954), v. I, p. 123.

[5]D. O. Hebb and W. R. Thompson, "The Social Significance of Animal Studies," *The Handbook of Social Psychology,* 1st ed., ed. Gardner Lindzey (Reading, Mass.: Addison-Wesley Publishing Co., Inc., 1954), v. II, pp. 553–555.

INTERPERSONAL INTERACTION: SENDING AND RECEIVING MESSAGES

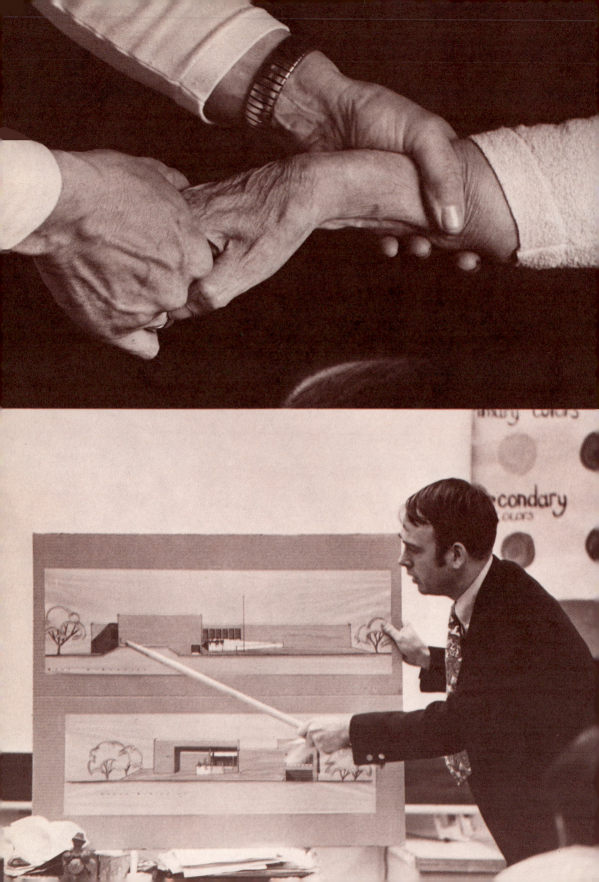

The sending, receiving, and interpreting
of communicative messages are the bases of human
interaction. Messages do not exist in isolation
but are the joint creations of those who
speak and those who listen.
Consisting essentially of "sights" and "sounds,"
they are the ongoing stimuli which bind
together those who engage in speech communication.

W e move now from the intrapersonal to the *interpersonal* dimensions of speech communication. Previously, we noted how we are able *intrapersonally*—within our communicative "self"—to acquire the substance of speech communication and put it into a few useful systems of reasoning and thinking. Now we are concerned with what takes place between our communicative self and one or more other "selves." We will pay particular attention to what goes on (or ought to go on) when we begin to function openly as speaking/listening agents.

Primarily, what we transmit or send out during communicative interaction are *sights* and *sounds*. These are the ongoing stimuli which bind together those who engage in the speech communication process. These sights and sounds are given meaning when they are interpreted as *messages* by other people. And the sending, receiving, and interpreting of messages are the bases of human interaction. In this chapter we will focus especially upon that level of interaction which involves the transmission and reception of information—upon the *exchange of information*—by speaking/listening agents.* Here, we will attempt to define *communication messages* and describe them in terms of their major aspects. We will also be looking, in particular, at those skills which can improve and facilitate the *reception and interpretation of messages,* namely listening and looking. Then, in Chapter 7, we will explore some of the techniques a speaker can use *before interaction* to plan for anticipated response from listeners and for their acceptance of transmitted messages. And, finally, we will examine some of the means by which the speaker can adjust to listeners' feedback *in and during interaction.*

THE SPEECH COMMUNICATION MESSAGE

What is a "message"—basically? How can we most usefully look at "message" as an idea and define it? Often, "message" has been viewed as if it were something that exists apart from the speaking/listening agents—as if it were a separate or discrete element in a communication event. This view of the speech communication message is usually reflected in a model that looks something like this:

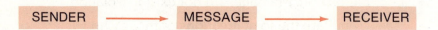

But in the sense that we are using the term here, *message* is *not* a separate element or entity that can somehow be isolated from speaker and listener. *The three are bound together—inseparably.*

Remember, now, that by "message" we are not talking about a document in fixed or written form. As we have emphasized earlier, using the instance of the Gettysburg Address, the written text or manuscript of a speech is merely an inanimate record of a speech event and tells us nothing of the *living interaction* generated by the event itself. The text of a speech shows us, mainly, that a speech event once took place. It is an historical document, much as is a photograph. To better understand the definition of *message* as we are using it, keep in mind, first of all, that *communication messages do not exist apart from communication agents.* Messages are the joint creations of those who speak and those who listen. They are the internal meanings which the transmitted sights and sounds of communication stimulate in the receivers. It is said that beauty is in the eye of the beholder. Similarly, in its final analysis, the communication message is in the mind of the communication agent. [1]

The Japanese drama *Rashomon* provides an illustration of this. In this

---

*By "information" we are referring to *new* data, facts, and knowledge transmitted and received; we are referring to new communicable substance which *reduces uncertainty.*

drama a husband and wife are overtaken in their travels by an outlaw who kills the husband and assaults the wife. The case is heard, and the wife tells her version of the event. The outlaw presents his version. Then, through some happy magic, the husband is brought back from the dead and is able to give his version. All three accounts of the event are different. So, we wonder, what is the truth?

Then another fortunate circumstance occurs. It happens that there was a passerby who was eyewitness to everything. He begins to present his account, and we feel relieved to get at the truth through this objective, disinterested eyewitness. We note that his description differs from all the others. But soon we be-

Study Probe 1
Interpreting Messages Differently

V. I. Lenin delivered this 1917 speech to a crowd in the streets of a Russian city. At the time, an earlier war with Japan and the still continuing First World War had stripped Russia of its resources and its spirit. Many people were starving, but most were searching for jobs, anxious for peace, resentful of the recently deposed tyrannical czar, and impatient for immediate reforms from the new government. The man Lenin calls Kerensky was the country's current leader.

> *Comrades, the revolution is on. The workers' revolution is on, and you are not working. The workers' and peasants' revolution means work, comrades; it does not mean idleness and leisure. That is a bourgeois ideal. The workers' revolution, a workers' government, means work, that all shall work; and here you are not working. You are only talking.*
>
> *Oh, I can understand how you, the people of Russia, having been suppressed so long, should want, now that you have won to power, to talk and to listen to orators. But some day, soon, you—we all— must go to work and do things, act, produce results—food and socialism. And I can understand how you like and trust and put your hope in Kerensky. You want to give him time, a chance, to act. He means well, you say. He means socialism. But, comrades—I tell you Kerensky is an intellectual: he cannot act; he can talk; he cannot act. But you will not believe this yet. You will take time to give him time, and meanwhile, like Kerensky, you will not work. Very well, take your time. But when the hour strikes, when you are ready to go back yourselves to work and you want a government that will go to work and not only think socialism and talk socialism and mean socialism—when you want a government that will do socialism, then—come to the Bolsheviki.* *

You, of course, know the result of this and other speeches by Lenin. Do *you*, however, respond favorably and enthusiastically to this message? What words or ideas in it turn you off? Can you explain why? Discuss the speech in class.

---

gin to see that he, too, brings to the event biases, values, expectations, and beliefs which color even his version. He was outside the event; but as he begins to interpret the sights and sounds that *he* received from it, we can see that—in many ways—he can be no more objective than the others.

We are left with the understanding that we will never know the "truth" of what happened. Even if we ourselves were able to go back in time and witness the event personally, our interpretations of it would probably differ from all the others. Thus we are gradually led to the realization that there is no universal or overriding truth of the event; the truth is what each of the witnesses perceived and interpreted it to be. The meanings and interpretations are *unique* and *internal* for each person who witnessed and interpreted the occurrence.

In like manner, in a speech communication context a single set of transmitted sights and sounds may be interpreted differently and therefore generate different messages—for different receivers. This is why we can say that in communication the message is the creation of the speaking/listening agents and cannot exist apart from them. And because this is so, we *cannot NOT communicate.*[1] Once we are present and involved in a communicative setting, all our behavior—whether intended or not—can be interpreted as *message* by other speaking/listening agents. All behavior can be interpreted, and we cannot *not* behave. As the speaking agent or the initiator of the interaction, we can and must try to select, control, and shape the sights and sounds—the messages—we send out. But once engaged in the communication process, we have no way of completely controlling what the other will receive, nor of restricting the other agent's interpretations of the event and the resultant messages created in his or her mind.

If, for instance, I speak with a certain dialect and my listener interprets that dialect to mean that I have a certain origin or background (whether, in fact, I have it or not), there is little that I can do about *that* message *at that instant.* If I sense that my listener has misinterpreted my dialect, I can of course attempt to "correct" the misinterpretation. But to do this, I must send out *another* message or possibly a *succession* of messages.

ASPECTS OF COMMUNICATIVE MESSAGES

Just what *are* the "sights" and "sounds" which are transmitted, received, and ultimately interpreted as messages in the minds of speaking/listening agents? How can we usefully describe and classify these sensory outputs and intakes so that we can better understand how they serve as the bases for messages thus "created" during interaction? There are at least four aspects that we should consider, and two distinctions that we can usefully draw. One distinction that is frequently made is between the *verbal* and *nonverbal* aspects of a message. Another is between the *content* aspect of the message and the *communicator-relationship* of the speaking/listening agents.

Verbal Aspects of Messages

The *verbal* stimuli in communicative interaction consist of the *words* used (the lexical items) and the *arrangement of those words* (the syntax). The verbal, or language, stimuli can be transmitted by sound alone (as in conversation), or by sight alone (as in a printed newspaper). As we've pointed out from time to time, our language usage is so central to communication that when we think of communicative interaction we often think first and only about language. It's this "and only" that creates the problem here. Certainly the words spoken and their arrangement—the way they are put together—carry vast amounts of potential information from one speaking/listening agent to another. In fact, the complex level at which we are able to use language is one of the big things that defines and characterizes us as human beings. To be sure, language has its limitations, and we shall be considering the effect of these limitations on communicative interaction shortly. Now, however, the point to be made is that there is more to messages than mere words and the way you string them together.

Nonverbal Aspects of Messages

To get depth and fine shades of meaning in our communicative encounters we have to look far beyond the verbal level of information. For instance, the *way* in which we speak a word may add significantly to the information someone will gain from it. You may speak the word NO so that it means DEFINITELY NO. You can say it in such a way that your listener can interpret it as PROBABLY NO. Or MAYBE. Or you can even give it such a finely honed intonation that its "message" comes through as YES. The vocal shadings you add to a spoken word typify what we mean by *nonverbal stimuli*—stimuli that are highly significant in determining the meaning of the message transmitted.

Vocal inflections are, of course, merely one example of nonverbal components or cues which can be interpreted as a part of the total communication message. These interpretable stimuli range from such considerations as the clothing a speaker wears to such situational factors as the seating arrangement of listeners. In fact, so numerous and diverse are these stimuli that some theorists have found it useful to organize the nonverbal aspects of messages into certain general categories. An authority on the subject, Mark L. Knapp, calls attention to five such groupings: (1) body motion, or kinesics, (2) physical characteristics of speaking/listening agents, (3) paralanguage, or vocal shadings, (4) proxemics, or spatial relationships of communicators, and (5) environmental or contextual factors.[2]

1. *Body motion, or kinesics.* This type of nonverbal stimulus includes bodily posture, gesture, and body movement. A quizzical facial expression, a slumping posture, a nervously random shifting of the feet, a very direct eye contact by a speaking/listening agent—all are typical kinesic behaviors which we interpret as a part of the communication message we receive.

2. *Physical characteristics.* Fatness, slimness, baldness, height, facial contours, lameness, dwarfism, femininity, masculinity—any physical feature or trait of a lasting or continuing nature—often will cause us to add nonverbal meaning (whether warranted or not) to messages transmitted by its possessor. In fact, the physical characteristic alone may constitute the entire "message." As we suggested, for instance, when we were talking about ways in which we complete our perceptions, we may evaluate positively a tall and handsome speaker solely on the basis of height or handsomeness.

3. *Paralanguage.* The patterns of vocal inflection we've mentioned are examples of paralanguage. Other vocal stimuli or "paralinguistic" cues that carry nonverbal meaning include loudness, rate of speaking (a drawl, for example), pitch, and timing. Vocalized pauses ("uh" and "er") are frequently interpreted as part of a message (often an unintended part) transmitted by a speaker.

4. *Proxemics.* In this category of nonverbal stimuli we find those aspects of spatial relationships which carry meaning. You may, for instance, be offended when I stand too close to you while we are engaged in conversation because you interpret my adjustment of the spatial distance between us as an intention to "invade your personal territory." In the understanding of intercultural communications, especially, speaking/listening agents need to be particularly sensitive to the proxemics involved. We'll consider this more fully later in the chapter when we talk about *proxemic patterns of interaction* (pages 134–135).

5. *Environmental factors.* This category includes primarily those "physical/sensory" elements of the communicative context which may influence the persons involved in it. The sensory stimuli we receive from the hardness or softness of the furniture, the brightness or dimness of the lighting, the temperature of the room, and even the smells of perfume, stale cigar smoke, etc., are likely to add to the "meaning" of messages transmitted during the communicative event.

Limitations of the Verbal/Nonverbal Distinction

As you can readily see, the verbal-nonverbal differentiation of communication messages has many interesting and useful implications and can help us better understand what goes into the total makeup of a message. At the same time, however, we mustn't overlook the fact that this distinction has at least two disadvantages. Insofar as the verbal part of the distinction is concerned, of course, the category is nicely limited in scope and its boundaries are fairly clear. It covers, as we have noted, only the major language elements of *word choice* and *word arrangement.* The nonverbal category, on the other hand, is used to describe *all stimuli other than language* which can be interpreted as a part of the total makeup of communication messages. Obviously, it has to cover too much. The interpretable range of nonlanguage elements that go into the transmission and reception of communication messages is far too wide to be neatly and simply encompassed in the single "nonverbal" category.

A second difficulty that arises when we try to classify messages as either verbal or nonverbal is the likelihood that we will come to regard the two aspects as being very different and mutually exclusive in function. Actually, however, in almost all speech communication, verbal stimuli and nonverbal stimuli nearly always *occur together*—in combination. And they are *interpreted together* by listening agents who are receiving the message. The internal processing for the two sets of stimuli can be so very similar that we can easily be misled into emphasizing a difference which doesn't make so much of a difference. Knapp calls this difficulty to our attention when he says:

> The term nonverbal *is commonly used to describe all human communication events which transcend spoken or written words. At the same time we should realize that many of these nonverbal events and behaviors are interpreted through verbal symbols. In this sense, then, they are not truly* nonverbal.*

In other words, when thinking about the nonverbal and verbal components of messages, be concerned primarily with the way the two work together in combination. Remember that, for nearly all *practical* purposes, anyway, the verbal and the nonverbal stimuli are an inseparable part of the total message-transmission/message-reception/message-interpretation process. As a listening/looking agent you are almost sure to receive and consider the verbal and the nonverbal in concert and combine them to make meaning. In preparing for and participating in any communicative situation, what is of uppermost importance is that you try to select—to the greatest extent possible—those verbal *and* nonverbal stimuli which will contribute most effectively to the total meaning of your messages. Whether you are trying to transmit messages or provide feedback to them, continue to ask yourself: "Are the verbal and nonverbal stimuli I'm providing *complementary* and *mutually reinforcing?*" If they're not—if they're *contradicting* each other—some quick adjustments and even some entirely new messages are called for.

Limitations of Language

Because language is the one *verbal* component of speech communication messages, it is necessarily a key factor in their formulation, transmission, reception, and interpretation. We need to be especially sensitive, therefore, to the linguistic elements in messages and the ways in which our use of them is likely to affect and limit communicative interaction.[3] During interaction we need to be able to spot the possible limitations of language and strive to overcome or avoid them. Three, in particular, merit attention here: (1) lack of exactitude or specificity in the language code, (2) the static qualities of the "is/are" verbs, and (3) the

---

*Mark L. Knapp. *Nonverbal Communication in Human Interaction*, pp. 20–21. New York: Holt, Rinehart and Winston, Publishers, 1972.

difficulty of using language to transmit information about entirely new sensory experience.

1. *Lack of specificity in the language code.* In Chapter 4 we discussed our "knowing" more than we can "say." We can, for instance, easily and quickly distinguish the face of a friend from a multitude of others, but we really haven't the words to *describe* that difference so that someone else can make that identification easily and quickly. As individuals, each of us can privately "know" many things; but when we communicate that "knowing" to others, we can do it only by means of a language code. However, the language code that each of us must use and understand can never be as specific, individualized, and as accurately descriptive as the actual substance of our perceptions. As a result, any communicating that we do with language symbols has to be carried on at an *abstract* level. And this tends to slow down—and often frustrate—the interactive process. In short, the unavoidable need to carry on communicative interaction at a fairly high level of abstraction is a serious limitation. Whether we are the sender or the receiver of messages, we are constantly confronted with this problem.

2. *The static qualities of the "is/are" verbs.* Another difficulty with language arises from the fact that although speech communication is a highly active and continuously moving process, a few of the much-used words in the language are static and fixed. The statement "This is a wheel" is static and nonprocess, but "The wheel turns" clearly implies movement, process, and continuation. To state this another way, some of the language labels—notably the *to be* verbs—simply do not reflect the notion of *process*.

When I say, "This object is an acorn," my pronouncement has a ring of finality. Unfortunately, language statements often carry this kind of absolute quality when they aren't meant to. If we look at (or for) the object a year hence, we may see—not an acorn—but rather "an acorn *in process*": a tiny oak tree. So "is" the object an acorn or an oak? In keeping with the natural condition of the universe and with communicative interaction in particular, the language we use should always have a tentativeness and "at-this-moment" quality to it. Orville Pence, a former teacher of mine, used to say that the statement "Whatever is, *is*" is not true. He claimed that it is more accurate to say, "Whatever is, is *ising.*"

Although, as the semanticists correctly emphasize, "the word is not the thing," we often react as if "the thing" and "the word" were identical. In fact, because of our fixed and inflexible orientation to language, we frequently *overreact* to these symbolic labels. We can illustrate this point most graphically, perhaps, by noting that many cultural groups and societies have certain words—taboo words—that are "forbidden." In primitive cultures, such words—if uttered at all— often are spoken in fear and trembling or by high priests or medicine men. In our society, some persons can be greatly unnerved by a flip or joking use of the word *cancer,* almost as if saying the word makes the occurrence of the disease more likely. [2]

It may help you offset some of the static orientation you have for language if you keep in mind that we *adapt* to the abstract symbolism of words just as we adapt to the reality of a physical stimuli. In interaction, what's important is that we know when we are adapting to which—and how much. One lump of sugar may taste sweet and pleasant. If we must eat twenty, the last lump may taste terrible. It's the same with words. The first time I hear the expression "Just give me the 'bottom line' " (meaning "Get to the point" or "Just sum it up for me"), I may react favorably to its newness and freshness. After I've heard it twenty times, I've adapted. I've probably closed my ears—and my mind—to it. In the last few years, you may have noticed a similar "adaptation" to certain four-letter words. An epithet that may have been considered quite shocking in the late '60s may well have lost most of its effect by now.

3. *Linguistic inadequacy in communicating about new sensory experience.* Language serves us pretty well when we want to trigger the recall of earlier experiences, to refresh old experiences, or to relate new ideas or concepts to previous experiences. But when we want to use it—*without such reference or association*—to describe or talk (make messages) about a whole, entirely *new* experience, the basic inability of language to transmit or exchange the necessary information soon becomes apparent. How would you explain the color "red" to a person blind from birth? How could you explain with words alone the concept of "snow" to a person who has never seen it?

You could try, of course, to transmit some of the needed information. But very probably and very quickly you would realize that the only effective way that you can describe the "red" or the "snow" experience to others is to translate it into perceptions, categories, and word-labels already experienced and understood by them. In brief, to use language to transmit to others information about new sensory experiences, we must try again and again to relate the "new" to the "old."

If you understand the kinds of language limitations we're surveying, then at the very least you are aware that—to a greater or lesser extent—the mistaken or indiscriminate way we react to many word-symbols significantly inhibits the in-

Study Probe 2
Investigating Taboo Words

Make a list of five or more words you consider to be taboo on some occasions; specify the occasions. In class, compile a master list including the taboo words of you and your classmates. Then try to classify the words into several categories. Are there words which are taboo in politics, in advertising, at funerals, weddings, baseball games, etc.? See how broad a list you can develop. Then try to explain why these words are taboo.

Whenever someone regards a particular word as objectionable but cannot avoid discussing the subject it represents, the person usually substitutes a less offensive, less precise word or phrase in its place. Such substitutes are called *euphemisms*. In class, prepare a list of euphemisms for the taboo words, and discuss in what context each would be appropriate.

teractive process. And if verbal elements in messages literally don't make sense to those who hear them, there can be no real interaction at all.

Relationships Among Communicators

Besides distinguishing, as we have done, between the verbal and non-verbal aspects of communicative messages, we may also distinguish between the interpretations we make about the facts or *idea-substance* of a message and the interpretations we can make about the *relationships among the communicators involved.* These two aspects are, of course, closely related to the "task-related, substantive" dimension and the "affective, feeling" dimension of the self-as-communicator that we identified in Chapter 3 (pages 50–55). They interact to help produce any message we may try to communicate or any interpretation we try to make of it. Every message, therefore, will carry not only some *information* (substantive content) in and about itself, but it will also carry something of the feelings and attitudes generated by the interpersonal *relationships of the communicators.*

In their book, *Pragmatics of Human Communication,* Paul Watzlawick, Janet Beavin, and Don Jackson use the word *metacommunication* to label communication *about* a communication event—that aspect of the message that refers to the relationship between communicative agents. Specifically, they note that every communication "has a content and a relationship aspect such that the latter classifies the former and is therefore a metacommunication."[4]

"Open that door" and "Would you please open the door?" I think you would agree, carry about the same informational content. Note, however, that they also carry feelings about the relationships of the communicators that are very different. In each case the substantive content informs us that the speaker would like the listener to open the door. But tied in with that information is the *metacommunication* that tells us that the relationship between the transmitter and receiver-interpreter is obviously different. In the first message there seems to be more status difference and less concern for tact and politeness than in the second message. These differences provide information about how the speaker views his or her relationship with the other agent in that context.

In short, if we want to analyze and understand a communicative interaction of almost any kind, we're going to have to look pretty closely at both the content aspect and the relationship aspect of the messages being produced by it. Fortunately for us as "working" communicators, the more attention we pay to the clarity and accuracy of our message-substance, the less we'll probably have to worry about the relational aspects—especially if the proper interpersonal relationships are established at the outset. For, as Watzlawick, Beavin, and Jackson take pains to make clear:

> . . . *relationships are only rarely defined deliberately or with full awareness. In fact, it seems that the more spontaneous and "healthy" a relationship, the more the relationship aspect of communication recedes into the background. Conversely, "sick" relationships are characterized by a con-*

stant struggle about the nature of the relationship, with the content aspect of communication becoming less and less important.[5]

Nevertheless, the relationship aspect in communicative messages is continuously significant and must never go unnoticed by either the sender or the receiver.

The *verbal, nonverbal, content,* and *communicator-relationship* aspects of communicative messages—individually and collectively—generate impressive numbers and kinds of stimuli to which we can attach meaning. Working together or in combination, they produce a vast quantity of the "ingredients" we use in message-making and message-receiving. In addition to providing us with useful and necessary visual and auditory stimuli, they are—in a unique sense—the "vehicles" which carry the potential of the ideas and concepts, the feelings and attitudes, and a great many of the less easily classifiable message-inputs which can be sent out, received, and converted by speaking/listening agents into "new" information. They are, in sum, the producers and the facilitators of *information exchange.*

RECEIVING AND INTERPRETING MESSAGES: UNDERLYING ASSUMPTIONS

To know about aspects of messages and what it is that produces the sights and sounds of speech communication is, of course, both useful and necessary. But it isn't enough. It won't help you very much in a practical way unless you can do something specifically about sharpening up the processes you use to *look* at those sights and *listen* to those sounds. If you hope to become a good interactor and communicator, you must first become a good "looker" and a good "listener." You need to be able, first of all, to *receive* and *interpret* communication messages just as clearly, accurately, and fully as possible. Before getting into the specifics of how this can be done, let's look first at four general assumptions:

1. *Message-reception can be improved by training and practice.* Good reception of communicative stimuli can be made habitual. By conscious and consistent effort, as you know, we can change a bad habit or improve a habit that is only relatively good.

2. *Message-reception and message-interpretation can be improved by active participation and personal involvement.* The joint process of listening/ looking is not, as you might at first assume, a passive or automatic thing. You have to *work* at it. To receive the maximum meaning and benefit—the highest impact—from a message, you have to act, react, and interact. You have to make a personal commitment to what is going on; you have to become involved in it, and this obviously requires some effort.

3. *Message-reception and message-interpretation can be improved by understanding and applying the kinds of basic communication principles we are*

talking about in this book. This assumption applies, not too incidentally, to listeners and speakers alike. The more you know about the patterns and practices that occur in communication, the more possibilities and variations you can use to facilitate the exchange of information. Also, with experience, the more realistic you can be in your expectations as to the outcomes of the interaction. Finally, your judgment of what to accept and what to exclude as you try to interpret the messages should become increasingly sensitive and discriminating.

4. *Message-reception and message-interpretation can be improved by developing good habits of listening and looking.* Obviously, you're not likely to contribute very much to the interaction if you don't hear what's being said or see what's going on. Because good habits and sharpened skills in these matters are so basic to productive communication, we need to look pretty closely at them; we need to examine in some depth those specific steps that make good "listening and looking" *habitual.*

GOOD HABITS OF LISTENING AND LOOKING

Much has been written about good listening habits; and *listening,* certainly, is one of the extremely important processes by which we are able to receive and interpret communicative stimuli.[6] Equally important, however, is the process of *seeing* or *looking.* We've already noted the significance of the great numbers of nonvocal and nonverbal stimuli we send out and receive. And we've carefully considered the close interrelation of the nonverbal and verbal aspects of messages. The processes of listening and seeing obviously are complementary and often mutually dependent. And frequently, to attach full and accurate meaning to a message we must look *and* listen—and we must do *both simultaneously.* Therefore, in suggesting what we hope will be some practical aids to improving your interactive skills, we will be viewing the receptive-interpretive processes of listening and looking as *occurring together.*

To develop good habits of listening and looking, we suggest that you: (1) prepare for the communicative situation; (2) focus attention within the communicative context; (3) think about and work with the information you receive; and (4) look for characteristic communicative patterns and variations of them.

Preparing for the Communicative Situation

When you think about the need to prepare for a speech communication situation, don't limit your thinking only to public speaking. All of us are aware, of course, that if we wish or are asked to speak publicly, we must carefully prepare beforehand the message or messages we want to communicate to a comparatively large number of listeners. (The planning and preparation of public speeches is the subject of Chapter 13.) We also know that if we are not the speaker, we must be prepared to do a considerable amount of *listening.* But our suggestion here is intended to go far beyond the public-speaking context and apply to *advance preparation for every communicative interaction* in which you know you will be involved, whether it be dyadic, small group, *or* public, and whether you will be primarily the speaker or the listener, or both.

The employment interview as a detailed illustration.   To illustrate the need for careful preparation of messages and message-making materials, consider the employment interview. We'll begin by assuming that you are the *interviewer*—the employer's representative whose task it is to interview a prospective employee and exchange useful information. To handle your role in this situation you will have to consider the nature of the position-opening. You will have to inform yourself fully *beforehand* as to the attributes and abilities the applicant must have in order to handle the job responsibilities. You will have to determine *in advance* of the actual face-to-face encounter with the interviewee quite specifically the standards of productivity, punctuality, decorum, etc., that you will hold to. Then you must *plan* a series of topics or questions—message-evoking materials—which will elicit the information you need or want.

It is always upsetting, after an interview is over, to think of a question you should have asked, but didn't. Carefully establish in your mind and/or on paper the *order* or *progression* of the topics to be discussed or the questions to be asked. It is usually best to begin with simple questions which the applicant can answer briefly and easily, such as those having to do with biographical data and background. This kind of opening allows both the interviewer and the interviewee to find out a bit about one another and to establish some communicative conventions and patterns before moving on to the interview's main topics of concern.

As you preplan your questions, think them through quite carefully, shaping them so as to ensure that as nearly as possible they will yield the desired information. Vary the *types* of questions you plan to ask. Probably you will have to ask a few questions having yes-or-no answers. Remember, though, that other types of inquiry—notably "follow-up" and "branching" questions—are likely to produce more informative responses. That is, if the interviewee answers a certain question one way, you "follow up" with a certain line of questions. If he or she answers your initial question in another way, you may then elect to "branch" to a different line of follow-up questions. You must anticipate and prepare for both possibilities. As you continue to exchange information, you will want to find out not only about the past experiences of the interviewee; you will surely hope to learn something of her or his future plans, intentions, attitudes, etc. What does this applicant hope to work toward? What short-term objectives? What long-term goals? What financial benefits? What "psychic wages" or self-growth? Using your company's general policies and procedures, you may want to pose hypothetical problems, and then assess the appropriateness of the course of action proposed by the applicant.

Now let's assume for a moment that you are the applicant—the *interviewee*—for a job. Here again, if you wish to be seriously considered for the opening, you must plan in advance. You must be fully prepared to give and to receive meaningful and informative messages. You will have to do a lot of *listening,* of course—concentrated, intelligent, discriminating listening. And also you'll be spending a great deal of time looking and observing. But don't make the common mistake of supposing that because the *interviewer* exercises a somewhat larger measure of control over the interaction that he or she will originate most of the information-seeking questions. There are questions that *you* should be asking, too. Have your list ready, also. Sooner or later, if you stay alert and listen and look with real attention, you'll find your chance to ask them. A few of them, at least. But even if the interviewer does ask all or most of the questions, remember that your *answers* are the central, crucial focus of the "transaction." They can do a great deal to determine the direction and scope of the interview process. In fact, because the interviewer often has more potential control, you—as the interviewee—must plan your answers and message-exchanges even more carefully than for other types of dyadic interaction. ☐3

Frequently I tell graduate students who are planning to be interviewed for college teaching positions to be prepared to answer the question "What courses would you like to teach?" And I urge them to prepare to respond with a one-minute answer, a five-minute answer, and a fifteen-minute answer. My reason for this advice should be obvious: Some applicants, especially those who are people of few words, cannot ordinarily respond for more than a minute or two unless they are fully prepared. They have never learned to amplify and expand upon their answers. Other applicants, particularly those who have never learned to say a thing briefly, are unable to describe their teaching interests in less than half an hour. They have never learned to respond with only the *essence* of an answer; they

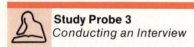

Study Probe 3
Conducting an Interview

Three or four students should volunteer to demonstrate a typical job interview. In advance of the demonstration, the one who will serve as the interviewer should select a job description from a newspaper's want ads and show it to the others (the job applicants).

The interviewer, while keeping in mind the personality traits, experiences, and expertise desirable in a person applying for the job, should prepare a series of questions, first covering biographical data and background, and then covering more substantive issues dealing with the job requirements. The questions should include branching and follow-up questions.

Similarly, the job applicants should anticipate questions and prepare both long and short responses based on the verbal and nonverbal cues of the interviewer. They should prepare specific questions of their own concerning the job requirements, opportunities, etc., as well.

After the interview, the class can evaluate the success of the various participants. Was the interviewer more adept after the first interview? How adept were the applicants?

don't know how to prune out the unnecessary verbiage and details. Almost anyone who has experienced an employment interview is likely to agree that it is a good habit to prepare carefully for an interview and that it is a bad habit to fail to make such preparation.

The small group discussion as an illustration. The same case for thoughtful preplanning and preparation can be made for participation in small group interaction, or group discussion. Often most, if not all, of the group members will merely gather some materials together and head for the meeting. Once the interaction starts, about all that takes place is a random or haphazard fumbling and searching for particular and frequently isolated items of information. The discussers have given no prior thought to the purpose of the interaction, the group goal, the specific and related information that can be productively exchanged, or the agenda and procedures that will affect that exchange.

The point is that an in-progress meeting may not be the best place to ponder about all of the aspects of a problem and to arrive at useful *intrapersonal* ideas and conclusions. All of that should have been done *beforehand!* Careful organization of materials and individual thinking about those materials should occur *prior* to the group meeting. Once there, the members should begin to think about group concerns: *group* organization, *group* goals, *group* solutions, etc. One of the major reasons that small group interaction moves slowly and oftentimes inefficiently is that the participants have not developed the habits of carefully gathering and organizing materials of possible pertinence and of thinking *in advance* about those materials and the possible procedures for relating them. Advance planning for small group interaction will be considered in greater depth in Chapter 11. Here we wish mainly to emphasize that developing good habits in this regard can obviously facilitate communicative interaction and help move the group as a whole toward its objective.

Adding it all up, for *every* speech communication situation—dyadic, small group, or public—in which you engage or intend to take part as either a *speaker* or a *listener* (or both), you should gather and organize your materials and thoughts, anticipate how the interaction may go, and plan possible courses of action which can be taken up and varied as the specifics of the situation may require. The planning should be careful and thorough, and yet flexible so that different alternatives may be pursued according to the particular needs that become apparent as the interaction proceeds. You should always have in mind several possible "private" and "public" agendas that you can follow, and a number of different ways of structuring and presenting your informational messages—and some reservations about why certain of these might work or not work.

All of this ties back, of course, to the claim that we laid out in Chapter 1, namely that the basic pattern of all good speech communication is the face-to-face, person-to-person "conversation." If, as we insisted then, all good speech communication is but an extension of that close personal relationship, then it makes sense to maintain that *thorough preparation* is a prerequisite for achieving that sort of communicative interaction, regardless of the context or the number of people involved.

Focusing Attention Within the Communicative Context

Make it a habit to focus your listening/looking attention on the central point, or crux, of the ongoing interaction. This is easy to say—but hard to do. Our sight, our hearing, our attention must *wander.* This is human nature. We simply can't give constant and full attention to any person, object, or idea for very long. The attention span varies for different people, for different objects, and in different settings. But that span is always limited. We tend to look at a speaker for a few moments, then look away, and—after a time—look back again. Momentarily we may pay careful attention to what the speaker is saying, and then our mind wanders away to something else: to contemplate yesterday's failure, today's dilemma, tomorrow's task. Eventually, we may pull our attention back to what the speaker is saying. But by that time, we will have lost a part of the message—possibly the entire thread or thrust of it.

The habit that we need to develop here, then, is that of drastically *reducing the frequency* of these lapses of attention and *cutting short the interval* of these "drift-offs." In these lapses we tend to think about problems or matters that are quite immediate, pressing, and/or interesting to us. We can to a large extent counter this tendency by *relating the speaker's message to our self-concerns.* By focusing and concentrating upon the crux of the speaker's message, we can try to make it more significant, interesting, and appealing to ourselves as listeners.

"But," you may say, "to make the message 'significant' and 'appealing' is the job of the *speaker!*" And, of course, you are right. *But* if the speaker doesn't or—often—can't do it, then we simply must *listen* and do it for ourselves. If, as we've urged, you've mastered the habit of *preparing* properly for the communicative situation, then what you have to say and what you have to listen to will likely be more important and interesting, and therefore easier to focus upon and follow. And the oftener you can speak *and* listen in a context in which such conditions prevail, the sooner these focusing/concentrating behaviors can become regular speech habits.

Thinking About and Working with the Information You Receive

This is another habit which can help you become better able to focus on the central issue of a message. All too often and in too many communicative situations, we sit back and casually take in only a *part* of the information being transmitted. This is, in essence, the kind of thing we do when we are half-watching a television program at the same time that we are working at a household chore or raiding the refrigerator. When the program has ended, we may remember having watched it, but not much else. We may not feel that we lose very much by this type of partial listening because we "didn't care much about that TV show anyway." But it can lead to bad communication habits. ☐4

Studies have demonstrated that during communicative interaction a listener does have some "free time" available. The usual rate of speaking is appreciably slower than the rate at which we can easily receive and interpret the symbolic materials of spoken language. So, to avoid missing the key or essential information contained in a typical message, we don't have to attend—"look/listen"—continuously to the message-source. Not only is the rate of presentation slower than it needs to be—it is also true that all speech communication has a certain amount of *redundancy* in it. That is, when material is redundant, it carries no "new" information. Ideas are repeated, and phrases that we already know are reiterated, and this repetitiveness permits us to fill in from context some of the significant information we may otherwise miss.

The slower rate at which a message is transmitted and the added redundancy that is almost always inherent in language are necessary, probably, because of the limited attention span we've talked about, and also because of the noise and other communication barriers within the "channel." But whatever the reasons, it is very probable that we have available during speech communication interaction more free time than we actually need for adequate interpretation of the message. What we do with that extra time can be important. It is a good communicative habit to use that time productively.

Broadly speaking, we can think and work more productively with message-information if we (a) relate the information to what we already know, (b) restructure the received message to accord with our own understanding of it, and (c) postpone our evaluation of the message until we've heard all of it.

Relating the received information to what you already know. You'll be able to interpret "new" information better if you can see how it fits with what you already know. Moreover, you will generally find it easier to recall information if

---

Study Probe 4
Determining a Television Viewer's Attention Span

Watch several half-hour television shows and make a chart of the number of commercials in each, the length of time each commercial takes, and the number of minutes between each commercial break. Your findings should provide you with some impression of the number of minutes the average television viewer devotes to the actual content of a show.

To ascertain whether a television viewer notices the content of commercials, watch one of the half-hour shows with another person, and at the conclusion of the program ask the other person what commercials he or she can recall. Don't let that person know beforehand that you plan to do this.

you relate it to your prior knowledge. If you learn some new facts about a person, for example, ask yourself: Do they fit the pattern of what you have thought of the person? Do they fill in missing areas and permit inferences you were unable to make earlier? Do they conflict with any impressions you have had?

You can do much of this interrelating of information and drawing of inferences during actual communicative interaction. Almost always you will find that if you "work" in this way with the information you are receiving *while you are receiving it,* you can make the communicative interaction richer and more productive—and can also improve your communication habits appreciably.

Restructuring the received message into your own words.   As a listener/looker you probably will not get the full meaning of a message unless you are able to see the pattern *behind* the organization of the materials. If the speaker has prepared the message properly, of course, this pattern should be readily apparent and comparatively easy to follow. But if it isn't clear and discernible or is lacking altogether, you'll have to provide it for yourself. In other words, in addition to relating new information to your "earlier" knowledge, often you will find it necessary to reorganize and restructure the received information into a "new" message that somehow makes better sense to you personally.

When you do this, you are—to an extent at least—reducing the message to your comprehension level, reformulating it into a pattern that better fits your understanding, and even silently rephrasing the information into your own words. Furthermore, in translating the speaker's message into terms that are more meaningful to you as a receiver, you become more *involved* with the message and will be better able to remember it. Sometimes, of course, you may need only to mentally rephrase the incoming message. At other times, you will need to go further and restructure and reorganize it in order to understand and recall the information when you need it again.

Actually, what we are recommending here is a process of "mental outlining." In listening to a message and trying to understand it, train yourself to identify and pick out major ideas. Make these the main points in your "mental outline." As main *coordinate points* they should have equal value, or weight, in relation to the whole. They are crucial; they stand out; and, together, they form the "skeleton" of the outline. You must also make clear distinctions between main and subordinate points. *Subordinate points* are lower-level materials which support and develop each of the main points or thematic ideas of the message. Developmental and illustrative materials, although they are often crucial to the fleshing-out of each *separate* main point, are somewhat less significant to the meaning of the message as a whole. That is, if a speaker chooses a weak or inappropriate example to illustrate a main point, as a listener I may reject his choice of supportive material, but I may still want to accept the *main point or idea* in the message.

Postponing evaluation until you've heard all the message.   In listening and looking, your first goal should be to understand the message *as a whole* and the speaker's intention in trying to communicate it to you. Only after you've accomplished that goal should you begin the evaluative process. Many of us try to judge too quickly any *partial* or as-yet-incomplete message sent our way. We tend to discount the remaining, yet-to-be-heard parts of it—particularly if they don't agree with our judgment of the opening statements. We are overly eager to form our conclusions before all the "evidence is in." This kind of premature judging of ideas is an ever-present danger in all speech communication situations; and, as we shall see later, it is especially troublesome in small group interaction.

To develop habits that will enable you to make the best use of your "free time" in communicative interaction, we urge you—as a listening/looking agent— to *put all of the message stimuli you receive into a proper perspective.* This, really, is the essence not only of message-evaluation but also a summation of the advice we have been offering here. Learn neither to *overvalue* nor *undervalue* the verbal and nonverbal elements of the message. Seek a clear understanding of the more important and the less important points in the total message. Especially avoid overvaluing the less crucial points and blowing them up beyond their real importance.

Nor should you let yourself be misled by "first appearances." The physical appearance, clothing, and posture of the other agent may be the first information—the first part of the "message"—you receive in a communicative encounter. These stimuli, however, may not be at all significant to the purposes of the interaction. Because they're the first "information" you receive, however, you'll need to be unusually objective about them. You'll need to postpone your evaluation of what they may mean to the total message and to keep them in proper perspective.

In sum, make it a habit to interpret carefully all messages that you receive, relating the information to your existing knowledge and—where necessary—restructuring and restating it for the sake of optimum clarity. And, finally, make it a habit also to postpone any conscious attempt to evaluate the message until all of its pertinent elements have been fully received, clearly defined and related, and generally understood. Until such time, any evaluation that you make will be incomplete and—very probably—premature.

Looking for Characteristic Patterns and Variations

Whenever people speak in pairs or in small groups, certain norms and implicit rules for interaction emerge and tend to be followed. Another set of good communicative habits, therefore, is to develop a thoroughgoing awareness of these typical patterns, understand the nature of their influence in communicative settings, and adjust to the expectations they generate. As a speaking/listening/ looking agent, you need particularly to be sensitive to *variations* from these expectations, because such variations may, by their very occurrence, reveal crucial message-information regarding the other agent and the interpersonal relationship that will be operative in the interaction.

There are so many interactional patterns and practices which occur frequently in communication contexts that it is impossible to list—much less, discuss—all of them. In fact, because often they are merely implicit or are only "understood" and tacitly agreed to, even the persons who use and follow them don't "spell them out" or describe them specifically. Nevertheless, you'll want to develop habits of recognizing and adjusting to as many of them as you can. So, to help you discover and identify some of the patterns occurring in your own experiences, let's take brief note of three which occur quite often, namely: (a) spatial, or "proxemic," patterns; (b) eye-contact, or "looking," behaviors; and (c) vocal-variety-and-expressiveness patterns. These, as you will note, involve some of the nonverbal aspects of messages that we cited earlier in the chapter. We've chosen them primarily because—to a limited extent at least—you are probably already familiar with them.

Spatial, or proxemic, patterns. Anthropologist Edward T. Hall, a pioneer in the field of proxemics, has written extensively of the study of "personal territory," spatial relationships, and distances maintained by communicative agents. He looked for interaction patterns in the distances which separate and are maintained by persons when they interact. He distinguished among four distances: *intimate*—bodily contact to 18 inches; *casual-personal*—18 inches to 4 feet; *social-consultive*—4 feet to 12 feet; and *public*—12 feet to the maximum carrying distance of the human voice. In other words, if persons are interacting in an "intimate" situation, they probably will either be touching each other or be no more than 18 inches apart. If persons are interacting in a "casual-personal" context, they will be separated by a distance of at least 18 inches, but no more than 48 inches, and so on.[*]

As Edward Hall, John Aiello, and others have noted, each of us has our own "personal space bubble." We don't like to have it threatened, and we grow defensive if we sense intrusion. And we are conditioned in this by such factors as *age, sex,* and *cultural differences.* The older we grow, the more distance we want between ourselves and the other person. When we are quite young, we tend to stand or sit about 12 inches apart. By the time we're 19 or 20 years of age, for most purposes we like to be at least 30 inches away from the other agent. As we reach middle age, we usually want increasingly more—much more—space to "rattle around in."

Aiello has found that ordinarily by the time boys reach the age of 12 years, they don't like to stand close to one another; they will avoid looking at each other; they almost certainly will avoid touching. In contrast, girls are willing to maintain much closer distances, look at each other frequently, and often will touch.[7] In a crowded situation, a group of women will begin to socialize rather quickly; a group of men in a similar situation wil tend to withdraw, become tense, and avoid eye contact unless the spatial separation is about 12 feet. *These prox-*

---

[*]Excerpted from THE SILENT LANGUAGE by Edward T. Hall. Copyright © 1959 by Edward T. Hall. Reprinted by permission of Doubleday & Company, Inc.

emics, or spatial distances, of course, significantly influence the kinds of messages that are transmitted, their substantive and affective content, their interpretation, and the progress of the interaction as such.

Different norms, moreover, exist for different cultures—an aspect that we will consider more fully in Chapter 16. Some foreigners, for instance, typically stand closer together than do Americans in similar contexts. Hall described the case of a foreign statesman who was conversing with an American citizen. The foreigner kept moving closer to establish the distance he considered appropriate. But that distance was too close for the American, so he kept backing away. In the course of the conversation the American continued to retreat across the room, with the foreigner following in close pursuit. Both communicators were of course following the interactive and spatial patterns they had learned in their own cultures. Probably neither was fully aware of the patterns being followed. It is easy to see in this case how conflicting behaviors and expectations could be wrongly interpreted and cause the men—as listening/looking agents—to receive an impaired or incorrect message. The incident also serves to demonstrate how easily a difficulty can arise when any interactive pattern—or variation of it—is significant but is intentionally or unintentionally ignored.

Eye-contact, or looking, behaviors.   This is another category of behavior patterns which characterize communicative interaction and which generate significant expectations in speaking/listening agents. And like the spatial patterns we've mentioned, they have potential variations which can facilitate or impede effective communication. Those who have conducted research in this category have discovered—somewhat surprisingly—that *looking* is associated more with *listening* than with speaking. Suppose you see a picture of two people who are conversing; one is looking at the other, and the second is looking off to the side. In this situation, the chances are strong that the person who is looking away is *speaking,* and the person looking directly at the other is *listening.* This is especially likely to be the case if the listener is a female, for—as some studies have suggested—women use eye contact more during interaction than men do.

Eye contact—depending upon whether it is given or withheld—can be used to gain attention or recognition, to punish or produce anxiety, and to increase or decrease the "psychological" distance between two speaking/listening agents. Most of us know or somehow "sense" that many of these patterns of looking behavior are at work in the communicating we do, but we probably couldn't easily jot off a list of them or readily describe how they are used. Yet if we really want to interact effectively and with confidence, that is exactly what we *ought* to be able to do.

Vocal-variety-and-expressiveness patterns.   This category of interaction patterns, like the spatial and eye-contact patterns, also generates a great many of the nonverbal stimuli that go into the making of communication messages. More often than not, probably, unskilled usage of these particular patterns create a negative impact upon the message-receiver and tend to nullify the interaction.

For instance, when we hear a monotonous oral presentation with little variation in pitch or loudness levels, we interpret this to mean that the speaker is not really involved or deeply concerned with transmitting the verbal elements of the message. Mispronounced or misarticulated words we tend to interpret as revealing information that is disparaging to the education and training of the speaker. A series of vocalized pauses (. . . uh . . . er . . .) and other nonfluencies we take as an indication that this speaker is insecure, or anxiety-ridden, or poorly prepared to communicate with us.

Conversely, we interpret in positive ways the "information" that comes to us from the vocal flexibility and vitality, the articulatory precision, the controlled but projective vocal ranges, and the other orally expressive skills which seem to characterize the competent and practiced communicator. All of these meanings—and more—we may add to the information we gain from listening to a speaker's verbal utterance and from looking at his or her expressive behaviors.

Even this brief examination of but three of the many communicative patterns of interactive behavior—spatial, eye contact, and vocal variety—should serve to demonstrate the vastly significant role such patterns play in formulating, transmitting, and interpreting speech communication messages. Having seen their importance, you would do well to develop habits of communicative awareness that will enable you to recognize what these patterns are, how you and others are us-

Study Probe 5
Observing Nonverbal Communication

Your instructor will ask eight of you to observe—preferably outside of class—the videotape of two people conversing which you prepared for Study Probe 5 in Chapter 1. Then, in class, with the videotape as your reference, each of you should report your findings in one of the following specific areas:

1. *Personal distance.* Were the two speakers at a casual-personal, social-consultive, or public distance apart? (They probably were not intimate.) Why? Did their spacing change throughout the discussion? Why?
2. *Monotony of presentation.* If it occurred, when and why?
3. *Eye contact.* Have a different person observe each of the participants. When did eye contact occur? If the speakers were of opposite sexes, did the woman establish more eye contact than the man?
4. *"Uh's" and "er's."* Again have a different person observe each of the participants. When and why did the "uh's" and "er's" occur?
5. *Facial expression and hand movements.* Again have a different person observe each of the participants. What do the facial expressions and hand movements communicate?

As you observe the tape prior to your class presentation, be sure to take notes, and concentrate on the most significant instances of each area—jotting down approximately when they occur. This kind of preparation will protect the class from the boredom of watching the tape eight times.

ing them, and how you can expect others to respond to them during interaction. At the very least you can begin now to try to identify those patterns and variations which seem to occur with some frequency in your communicative encounters. Then, once you have done this, you can begin to habituate yourself to use them discriminatingly and with conscious intent. [5]

Looking back on this chapter, you'll recall that we've tried to define over a rather broad scale what communicative interaction is and how messages serve as a basis for it. We've singled out for our study and analysis some of the basic, commonly recognized aspects and elements of communication messages, notably the verbal, the nonverbal, the content (substantive or "factual"), and the communicator-relationship ingredients. You've seen a few of the ways in which interaction is impeded or adversely affected by the limitations of our language. You've also reviewed some means for improving your skills in message-reception and message-interpretation. Specifically, these were suggestions to *practice* and *develop* your competence in listening and looking, emphasizing that during interaction you should try to relate the information you hear and see to what you already know, mentally outline and restructure the received information so as to *make it mean something specific and useful to you,* and postpone your evaluation of the message until you've heard, seen, and thought about all of its parts.

Reference Notes

[1]Paul Watzlawick, Janet Beavin, and Don Jackson, *Pragmatics of Human Communication* (New York: W. W. Norton, 1967), pp. 48–51.

[2]Mark L. Knapp, *Nonverbal Communication in Human Interaction* (New York: Holt, Rinehart and Winston, 1972), Chapter 1.

[3]See, for example: Harry L. Weinberg, *Levels of Knowing and Existence* (New York: Harper & Row, Inc., 1959).

[4]Watzlawick et al., *Pragmatics of Human Communication,* p. 54.

[5]Ibid., p. 52.

[6]See, for example: Ralph G. Nichols and Leonard A. Stevens, *Are You Listening?* (New York: McGraw-Hill, 1957). Larry L. Barker, *Listening Behavior* (Englewood Cliffs, N.J.: Prentice-Hall, 1971). Carl Weaver, *Human Listening: Processes and Behavior* (Indianapolis: Bobbs-Merrill, 1972).

[7]As reported in the *Chicago Tribune,* April 17, 1975.

The analysis of listener or audience behavior is
a central concern in all communication. As speakers,
not only must we know the subject matter of our
intended messages, but we must also plan for
anticipated responses from listeners. And during
interaction, we must be able to adapt appropriately
to listener feedback.

In this chapter we are concerned with "what happens" to messages *before* and *during interaction.* What you as the speaker do with and to messages *before the start* of the interaction we will call "message planning" or "feedforward." What you do *during the interaction*—the adjustment you make in response to listeners' reactions—we will refer to as "adaptation to feedback." Here in the beginning, we will provide some specific advice which we hope will prove useful to you as you plan—before the interaction starts—for anticipated responses from your listeners and their possible acceptance of your messages. Later in the chapter we will describe some practical methods for adjusting to listeners' feedback while you are engaged in the process of transmitting your messages to them. Throughout, as in Chapter 6, much of what we have to say will apply to messages of all kinds. Our focus here, however, often will be upon the *persuasive* intent and content of a message. Note, too, that in these pages we will be talking primarily to and about "you and your listeners": a perspective that places you in the role of *the speaking agent.*

As the speaking agent, you must first of all answer the question: *What can I do to gain and sustain the participation of the listening agent?* In a very large sense, we believe, much of the listeners' willingness to participate in the interaction derives from the sensitivity, concern, and respect you show for them. We can't emphasize this point strongly enough: In planning messages for an interactive encounter, you must think *first* in terms of your listeners and prepare your messages—your feedforward—with them in mind.

PLANNING MESSAGES PRIOR TO INTERACTION: FEEDFORWARD

In your advance planning of speech communication messages, you will need to build in an *intentional-message factor* and a *contingency-message factor.* The intentional factor, of course, governs and shapes the message as you intend to transmit it. The contingency factor requires that, *in addition,* you formulate an *alternative* message or sets of messages which you can fall back upon if your intended message appears not to be clear enough, acceptable, or convincing to listeners, judging from their feedback. Usually your intentional message is the one you'd *like* to transmit, the one that—barring unforeseen obstacles or miscalculations—you're pretty sure you *will* transmit. Your contingent message or messages are the "standbys," the ones you *might* or *might not* have to transmit in order to achieve your interactional objective.

To the extent that you can anticipate what you want to happen as well as what could happen in the interaction, you can "feed forward" into your messages the most appropriate verbal, nonverbal, substantive, and communicator-relationship elements. This, in a nutshell, is what message planning is all about—is the kind of thoughtful, analytic foresight that will help infuse the interaction with a clear purpose and strong sense of direction once it gets under way. To do a really good job of planning for both intentional and contingency messages and of building in the necessary feedforward, there are a number of useful, specific steps you will need to take, namely:

1. Identify the values and motives of your potential listeners.
2. Discover—to the greatest extent you can—the *persuadability* of your potential listeners.
3. Aim your message at a specific listener or a small number of specific listeners whom you expect to be involved in the interaction.
4. Analyze the communicative context.
5. Anticipate listeners' expectations.
6. Devise ways of establishing *rapport* with your probable listeners.
7. Adapt the language of your message to the probable listeners and to the context or communicative situation.
8. Discover the "stasis" of your listeners—where they are likely to stand in relation to your proposed message.

You may not need or want to take these steps in the order indicated. Probably, in fact, you will be making some of the necessary analyses, discoveries, and adaptations more or less simultaneously. But all are essential to message planning.

Identifying Listeners' Values and Motives

The analysis of listener or "audience" behavior, a central concern in all communication, has probably received more attention than any other aspect of speech communication.[1] To know and to study the subject matter of an intended message is one task; to know and analyze the nature, inclinations, and biases of other probable participants in the impending speech interaction is quite a different task—and a much more elusive one. And, of course, the larger the number of listening agents, the more complex the task of assessment becomes. Fortunately, there are certain preparations of both a general and a specific nature which you can make.

When preparing to interact with other listening/speaking agents (whether one friend or a thousand strangers), try to ascertain the dominant *values and motives* which will be at work within those persons at the time of the speaking event. Since you will need to make your analysis well ahead of time, often you may have to rely on generalization and speculation. But regardless of how you make it, your appraisal can assist you in two important ways. First, it will almost surely reveal something useful about the nature of the persons you will be facing. You will become more aware of the values to which they cling, of the motives that move them to acceptance or action, of "what makes them tick." Then, this insight will help you predict more accurately the scope and direction of the interaction. You will know what motivations and appeals will move the thinking of your listeners positively toward your objective.

One way to find out about the dominant values and motives of your potential listeners is to look at the kind of *groups* they belong to. With what clubs and other organizations have they affiliated themselves? With what "causes" are they associated? Are they, for instance, predominantly members of a single political party, or a church organization, or a certain social group? Do they come from a particular geographical region? Almost always, the individual identifies with one or more groups or collectives. By identifying with a certain group a person places himself or herself in a category: he belongs to X group; she is one of X. When you identify yourself with a group, you associate yourself with that group and tend to support its collective attitudes, values, and motivations. If you can ascertain the group memberships of your prospective listeners, you can use these associated attitudes, values, and motivations to make more pointed and meaningful messages, and thus facilitate closer interaction.

We can see this "bond" of group-association at work in all communicative aspects of our lives and at all levels of our society. A speaker will wear his Legion cap when addressing an American Legion Convention. He thereby calls attention to the customs of the group and lets his audience know that he, too, is a member of the organization—one of them. A political campaigner almost invariably will wear a hard hat when speaking with a group of construction workers. The idea isn't necessarily to protect his head against falling bricks and debris but to show that he's "with" them—that he's "just one of the boys." Even if the speaking agent *isn't* a member of the organization or group she's talking to, she frequently will try to create a bond of group commonality—a oneness with them—by wearing or carrying a symbol of their profession, trade, or cause. Almost any group can be expected to respond more favorably to one of its own or to one who shows a willingness to be "one" with them, so speakers should feed forward into their messages materials which visibly and verbally emphasize their common bond with their potential listeners.

Discovering the Persuadability of Your Listeners

Another useful means of analyzing the listeners of your potential audience—one frequently encountered in behavioral studies of communication—is to try to relate certain of their characteristics to their probable *persuadability*. By this we mean their *susceptibility or probable responsiveness to persuasive stimuli and messages.* Usually included among these characteristics, or persuasive variables, are (1) self-esteem or ego-involvement with an idea or proposition, (2) hostility and aggressiveness, and (3) sex-related considerations. There are others, of course. But even a quick glance at these three will suggest the potent role that such factors can play in shaping persuasive messages and influencing their acceptance by listeners.

Self-esteem and ego-involvement. Although the findings to date can't be considered conclusive, a number of studies show that certain types of persons will be difficult to influence in a speaker/listener situation.[2] Among these "more-difficult-to-influence" types are (*a*) persons with high self-esteem, (*b*) persons with extreme views, and (*c*) persons with a "vested interest" or strong ego-involvement with the topic or central idea of a message. Your own personal experiences and observations very probably support these findings. After all, people who have much self-confidence and high self-regard are generally confident of the worth of their beliefs and the "rightness" of their biases. Those holding extreme positions and those who are ego-involved in the topic of a message have already made a powerful personal—and, often, public—commitment that would be extremely difficult for them to reverse.

Hostility and aggressiveness. Similar studies have shown that hostile and aggressive personalities are not usually receptive to suggestions or new ideas. Their minds, typically, seem closed to persuasive messages. They tend to hold rigidly and uncompromisingly to their *beliefs* and the *values* they attach to those beliefs. This, in turn, makes it extremely difficult for them to change their *attitudes.* We'll be looking much more closely at this aspect of audience analysis and persuadability when we take up Belief-Evaluation Clusters in Chapter 8.

Sex-related factors.   Men and women seem to differ in the nature and extent of their susceptibility to persuasive messages. Just how much of this susceptibility has been historically and culturally imposed upon women and how much is based on a "difference that *is* a difference" is something that our society is only now trying to discover, but some studies, including my own, suggest that women are easier to influence than are men. I realize that this possible difference may be due in large part to societal norms and the traditional roles that women have been expected to play down through the centuries. These same norms and expectations may also explain why women until very recently seemed less likely to challenge authority figures and institutions. Possibly, too, because of their historic acceptance of authority, women students have been "easier" to teach than men. At least, they seem to follow instructions more closely and complete assignments more carefully. One thing seems sure: Anything that has heretofore been said about the sex-related factors of persuadability must in the future be reexamined, rethought, and—very probably—revised on a day-to-day basis. The emergence of new technologies, new mores, new culture-shaping forces—including the Women's Liberation Movement—make this imperative.

Aiming Your Message at a Specific Listener

The task of audience or listener analysis as we have been describing it up to this point is essentially one of trying to put yourself in other people's shoes: You try to see things through *their* eyes; you try to sense ideas and situations through *their* feelings. You look ahead and ask yourself: "Would *I* respond to my message as I want *them* to respond?" In a word: *Empathize.* Discover all the available, pertinent information about the people who will be receiving and interpreting your intended message. To do this well, you must get to *know* them. Be a "people" person! Get out there and *mingle* with them. Rub elbows. *Look* at them. *Talk* with them. See them as *specific individuals.* [1]

Study Probe 1
Developing Empathy with Listening Agents

As a study of *empathy,* or the ability to place yourself in the position of others and understand their feelings, refer again to the Speech Communication Assessment Scales on pages 57–61. Assume the identity of one of your friends and, using a pencil of a different color from the ones you used two times previously, perform the self-assessment as you believe your friend would do it.

Then ask this friend to take still a different-colored pencil and do the self-assessment.

Carefully compare the two sets of responses. In which areas were you most accurate in predicting your friend's feelings? In which situations were you least accurate? You can further test your empathic abilities by repeating this project with other friends.

No doubt about it—this takes patience, perseverance, and some ingenuity. But if you hope to interact effectively with listeners you must *address your message to a specific listener or group of listeners whom you are aware of and whom you know.* Avoid talking to listeners you can conceive of only in vague and general terms. This applies to *every* communicative situation. Each listener is *different.* Your work with the Self-Assessment Scales in Chapter 3 should have made this fact strikingly apparent. 2

Analyzing the communicative context.   As a speaker you must adapt your message not only to your listeners but also to the *context* or circumstances of the speech event. You must be aware of the various forces which will produce the specific speech situation. What in this context has brought these particular people together at this particular time? Is the situation to be one of *negotiation* where you and your antagonist will try to reach a compromise that will end some impasse between you? Or will the situation require you to be an *arbitrator* and conduct negotiations among others in order to end a disagreement? The problem and the general content of your message may be similar in both instances, but there will be different contextual influences at work in each. Or is the situation likely to be one of *debate,* where you will be contending against another speaker in order to communicate your viewpoint not to your adversary but to a small, select group of evaluative listeners—a panel of judges, perhaps? If so, you must plan your message and marshal your arguments so that they will sway the *listen-*

Study Probe 2
Adapting to an Audience

Pretend you are to deliver a speech arguing for the legalization of marijuana. Though sufficient evidence to support your case may not exist, suppose you can prove:

1.   That marijuana is harmless in small doses.
2.   That it is not psychologically or physically addictive.
3.   That it in no way leads to the use of harmful drugs like heroin.

Write a short statement explaining at least *one* way in which you would adapt your speech for *each* of the following audiences:

1.   A group of students at a major university.
2.   A group of lawyers.
3.   A PTA assembly composed mostly of the parents of high-school students.
4.   A group of policemen.
5.   The United States Congress.

Hand your prepared statements to your instructor. They will be used as a basis for classroom discussion and analysis and/or a written examination of the principles set forth in this chapter.

ers. To try to influence the other speaker in a structured context of this kind will be pointless.

Clearly, the circumstantial aspects of the occasion dictate significant differences in the content, thought-direction, and presentation of a given message. If you're addressing the members of the Rotary Club at a noontime luncheon in the dining room of the local restaurant and you're speaking about your favorite topic, your speech is going to have to be worded and structured differently than the one you presented on the same topic last night when you were addressing the members of the Sunday Evening Club in the church social hall. This will be especially the case if many of the same persons are to be present in both settings.

When you are to be involved in any communicative event—dyadic, small group, or public discourse—find out *beforehand* what else, if anything, is planned for the program: Who else will be involved? What speech "events" will precede and follow the one you're to be engaged in? Will the general atmosphere of the occasion be serious or light? Will you be seated with others around a small table, or will you be speaking to a group from a platform of some kind? If at all possible, make it your practice to inspect the physical facilities and arrangements some time *before* the scheduled interaction is to begin. Inquire about all of the relevant aspects of the occasion, make sure of the intended sequence of events, and find out what usually happens there.

Anticipating Listeners' Expectations

As a speaking agent, you must know what your listeners *expect* of you. This is another crucial aspect of audience analysis and one that is very closely tied into the requirements of the communicative context. Are you, for instance, being called to the specific situation by listeners who are seeking essentially basic information of a straightforward and unbiased nature? If, in such a situation, you urge a certain course of action or "grind an axe" for a cause you support, obviously you'll fail to fulfill your listeners' expectations. Your advocacy and your bias will be out of place, ineffective, and probably downright objectionable. If you are invited to deliver a "give-'em-hell" polemic before a partisan crowd and you accept the invitation, you'd better plan to live up to your audience's expectations and "pour it on."

Will your participation in a given speech interaction be genuinely *desired* by the listeners? Or will your involvement be more a perfunctory or "courtesy" appearance? If your presence there will be merely routine, then to fulfill what's expected of you, you need present only "a few fitting and appropriate remarks." Your hearers would very likely be bored and impatient with a long-winded spiel. If the impending interaction is to be a serious interview, the expectations will naturally be quite different from those generated for an informal chat or a light social conversation. In fact, in almost any communicative situation you can think of, your listeners' expectations must to a significant extent help to shape the message you plan to transmit.

Some pretty harrowing things can happen when the speaker fails to take this into proper account. Once I was asked to speak to a group of women at a meeting sponsored by the American Legion Auxiliary. The person who contacted me, a lively middle-aged woman, told me the group wanted "something light." Imagining her as a typical member of my audience-to-be, I carefully prepared a very light and (in my view) humorous speech on communication problems in marriage. I filled in the whole thing with what I considered funny little remarks about middle-aged marital foul-ups, foibles, and fillips—in a Bob Hope style. I was ready. When I arrived to give the speech, I was greeted by the woman who had contacted me and was ushered into the room set aside for the occasion. As I gazed around at the aged and furrowed faces of my listeners, I felt a sudden, sickly, sinking sensation. I was literally "speechless"—in the awfullest sense of the word! The chairperson, my contact, was the only woman in the room under seventy! The American Legion Auxiliary, it turned out, was producing a series of programs for the residents of one of the local old people's homes. I was faced with a group of sweet, *very* old ladies—most of them *widows*, with a sprinkling of *spinsters*, I later learned. If you can imagine how I suffered trying to improvise a speech in that situation, you can be sure I learned my lesson well. Never again have I agreed to participate in any kind of communicative interaction without first making certain where the event was to take place, at what time, for what purpose, before how large an audience, composed of what kinds of listeners—having what kinds of *expectations.*

One qualification is in order here. Anticipating and analyzing listeners' expectations *doesn't* mean that you should tell them only what they want to hear. One of the interesting things about listeners is that typically they want you as the speaker to be aware of their expectations—but they also expect you to go *beyond* their expectations. They expect to be stimulated, surprised a little, "intellectualized," perhaps, even persuaded. At least they will be curious to see whether or not you *can* persuade them.

Devising Ways to Establish Rapport

Good *rapport,* the empathy that one human being has for another, should be one of your guiding goals as you plan messages and incorporate feedforward. "Having good vibes" describes this feeling of mutual understanding and sympathy. Scientists use the term *sympathetic vibrations* to explain what happens when two tuning forks of equal frequency are held fairly close together. One is set into sympathetic vibration by the sound-wave energy created by the vibration of the other. The necessary condition is that the two "bodies" have identical resonant frequencies.

We can stretch this concept a bit further and say that human beings, too, may have similar "resonant frequencies" in a psychological sense. If two or more individuals having similar psychological frequencies are brought together in a speech communication context, they seem to have a natural tendency to respond favorably to one another. They apparently have many things in common—common backgrounds, beliefs, values, attitudes, experiences, etc. These com-monalities seemingly cause them to respond to stimuli or events in similar fash-ion. In persuasion, one of the consistent findings of behavioral scientists is that people are most significantly influenced by their close friends, associates, and members of their immediate family. Voting behavior of the young citizen, for ex-ample, appears to be determined to a greater extent by the voting behavior of his or her parents than by a political candidate's charisma and election-campaign speeches. Of course, the parent-induced "sympathetic" behavior isn't an in-stantaneous or automatic response. One of the reasons is the offspring's con-stant "close proximation" with the parents and their friends (who probably vote the same ticket). Because of the close association over the years and the re-peated interactions that go on in families, neighborhoods, and working situations, similar "resonant frequencies" are built up in people everywhere. Your job as a message-maker is to discover these frequencies and psychological vibrations and thereby achieve the sympathetic closeness and *rapport* which will put you and your listeners on the same communicative "wavelength." [3]

Adapting the Language of Your Message

There are many different ways, of course, to establish the kind of rapport we've been talking about. One of the important keys to the whole thing is that persons having similar backgrounds are very likely to have similar meanings for *language symbols*. This is because (as we saw in Chapter 4) persons having many experiences in common tend to perceive many of the same stimuli. They tend to develop similar categories for their perceptions, and they are likely to attach the same word-label to many of the categories they hold in common. Individuals en-joying good rapport as a result of having worked closely together in a school,

Study Probe 3
Testing Audience Rapport

Though recognizing that everyone is an individual, a speaker does form some judgments about listeners' attitudes and beliefs on the basis of their physical appearance—their age, dress, hair styles, etc. One way to test the validity of such judgments is to examine yourself. Of course, you can change clothing or hair style daily, but on the basis of what you are wearing and the length and style of your hair *today,* what assumptions do you think a speaker would form about you? What would the speaker expect your attitudes to be about several contem-porary issues?

Discuss your conclusions in class, comparing them to your own self-as-sessment. How closely related are the two? Think carefully and honestly about these questions: Do you ever dress in order to identify with a particular social or political group? Do you share many of that group's beliefs and attitudes?

business, or profession will often "talk a special language." The "jargon" they use greatly abbreviates their messages and, at the same time, strengthens their communicative bond.

Rarely are you likely to find *that* much rapport in the speech communication context. Nevertheless, in making messages, you must try to discover the extent to which such language-bonds *do* exist among your listeners. Fortified by knowledge of how they use and adapt the language, you can feed it forward into your messages in ways designed to tighten the communicative bond and facilitate your listeners' understanding and acceptance of what you are trying to communicate. Within reasonable bounds, you should try to "speak the language" of your listeners. Keep this target constantly in your sights as you plan the *wording* of your messages. Adapt your language to the language of your listeners as you phrase your ideas, propositions, and arguments.

The more perceptive and skillful you become in analyzing your listener(s) or your audience, the greater will be your need for adaptability to and with language. Often you will find that you must interact with a succession of individuals, groups, and public audiences on the same general topic. In speaking with members of the Methodist Women's Club on water pollution, for instance, you may decide to relate your proposition to family life and social values. Later, in talking with members of the Junior Chamber of Commerce, you may decide to relate the same proposition to community life and economic concerns. Obviously, you're going to have to be very *flexible* in wording and phrasing these two messages. You're going to have to "talk a different language" in each instance. You can't hope to be very effective in these two different settings if you try to use identically worded messages. Nor will it be enough to "adjust" the phrasing of a few portions of a speech as you move from one communicative situation to another. The language of the entire message must be tailored—and *retailored*—to fit the beliefs, biases, and values of each succeeding listener or set of listeners. Only in this way will you be able to create the close and sympathetic association and rapport which must exist between communicative agents if there's to be real interaction.

Discovering Where Your Listeners Stand

Not only must you adapt your message to the language "level" of your listeners, but you must also adjust it to what your listeners *know* or *don't know* at the time you will be interacting with them. Classical rhetoricians called this factor "stasis" or the "status of the case." Let's assume that you've ascertained with reasonable accuracy the beliefs, values, attitudes, general background, and key characteristics of your listeners. That's good. *Very* good—but still not enough. You need to know, in addition, *where they now are*—where they stand—in their thinking about the ideas or propositions you intend to transmit to them. At what point in their thinking and believing and knowing will you find them when the interaction begins? At what point in their reasoning process can you most likely catch their consideration? Just where and when can you best "hook" your message onto their collective train of thought?

The importance of stasis for you as a preplanner of speech communication is that if the communicative agents are to be in close association and interacting, *they must see the status of a given case similarly.* No effective communication will occur if you present a message and your listeners don't know enough of what you are talking about to understand your meaning. Nor will any real communication take place if you are belaboring an issue already accepted by the listeners. I once telephoned a life insurance agent, told him I wanted additional insurance, and described the coverage I wanted. When he arrived at my home, he began immediately to try to convince me that I should have more insurance. I explained that I already thought so, that that was why I had called him, and that he could fill out the necessary papers. He continued, despite my protests, to advance arguments of which I was already *convinced.* Time was wasted; there was no "meeting of the minds"; no purposeful interaction took place; I became restless, lost confidence in the salesman, and decided to take my insurance problems elsewhere.

Failing to know the status of your listeners' knowledge can also complicate situations in which you are posing a *problem* in your message or suggesting a *solution.* Sometimes—for instance, when you are interacting with others in regard to social issues—you may find it necessary to demonstrate the *existence* of the problem or the *workability of a particular solution.* If your listener already accepts the existence, focus your message on the solution and don't waste time trying to persuade the listener of something of which he or she already is convinced. On the other hand, don't argue for a specific solution and a new course of action unless your listeners feel that a problem exists.

The thrust of the eight guidelines we've thus far laid out in this chapter is to assist you in your role of speaker-to-be as you try to anticipate your listeners' reactions and plan your messages—both informational and influential. In effect, the greater your knowledge of the other agents, the more intelligently and accurately you ought to be able to predict their receptivity and response. This is why we've been urging—and will continue to urge—you to gather all of the information you can about the other agents who will be involved with you in the communicative context. Without it, you won't have much of a foundation upon which to build the kind of sound interpersonal relationships so needed to generate and sustain productive human interaction.

ADJUSTING MESSAGES TO FEEDBACK DURING INTERACTION

We've been concentrating on the planning a speaking/listening agent can do to develop and adapt messages to other agents before the speech event. Let's turn our attention now to some possible adaptations a speaker can make *during interaction: adjustment to feedback.* *Feedback* we've already defined as the stimuli received from agents who are listening to and looking at the speaker. It's the verbal and/or nonverbal reaction from those who receive communication messages. Our immediate concern here is what you, as the speaking agent, do *in response* to these reactions from your listeners.

If, in your initial steps in planning for a speech communication event, you have carefully anticipated the nature of your prospective audience, have assessed their preferences and priorities, have taken into close account the variables of feedforward, you should feel confident to carry the resultant message into the interactive context itself. You should be ready to take the next important step: *adjusting to the feedback from listeners in and during the communicative transaction.* This step involves an on-the-spot problem which you can detect and solve only with your actual listeners or audience before you. You must correctly interpret other agents' response *while you are speaking,* and you must adapt to that response very quickly. The requisite skill is *adaptive readiness.*

One of the key differences between planning for feedforward and adjusting to feedback is that in the former you are, in effect, predicting *probabilities—* preparing for contingencies which may or may not occur; but in the latter you are facing *immediate actualities.* For feedforward, you can attempt specific preparation; for feedback adjustment you have to rely largely upon general preparation and flexibility. In adjusting to feedback, you must "think on your feet"—and you must think *now.* In planning for feedforward, you are making allowances for what you have good reason to believe *might happen;* in adjusting to feedback, you are making allowances for what *is happening* in and to your listeners. You are obliged to read reactions accurately, devise and assess possible new and unanticipated courses of action, and select the one that seems best to you at that particular instant. This activity might be called "instantaneous feedforward."

Obviously, since you must deal with spur-of-the-moment behavior and decisions, there is no way to design specific procedures to fit the individual case. Nor are there any instructions that can tell you how to make the "best" or even a "good" adjustment to feedback. This points up all the more forcefully the need to prepare your initial messages with the utmost care and thoroughness in accordance with the steps we've previously laid out in this chapter. If you do a conscientious job of planning feedforward, that should help to keep the need for ongoing adjustments to a minimum. In addition, *by interacting with other speaking/listening agents at every opportunity* you can work to develop sound judgment and analytical skills in (1) reading listeners' reactions and responses, (2) reacting to absence of listener feedback, (3) refraining from overreacting to it, and (4) maintaining a balanced view of it.

Reading Your Listeners' Reactions and Responses

If the facial expressions of your listeners reveal puzzlement, you may adjust by restating your point and clarifying it with examples. If your listeners appear bored or sleepy, you may react by interjecting some humorous or novel materials. If your audience is antagonistic or noisily negative, quite probably you may find it helpful to react promptly by voicing a pertinent value generally held by most persons of good will, or by citing some common ground upon which you and your listeners stand.

In this connection, an experience involving Malcolm X provides an example of successful adaptation to audience feedback. When the late Black Muslim leader was speaking in favor of black nationalism to a college audience, he sensed a negative audience reaction to his rate and intensity of delivery. He attempted to adjust to this interpreted feedback by saying, "I'm sorry to be talking so fast, but I haven't much time, and I do have a lot to say." If you hope to be effective as a communicator, you must be sensitive to such listener feedback, must be able to interpret such cues accurately, and must be able to react to them in ways which facilitate positive interaction. Speaker-listener adjustment to feedback can significantly affect both the quantity and quality of the communicative interaction.

Reacting to the Absence of Listener Feedback

When two speaking/listening agents engage in communicative interaction, both of them *influence* and *are influenced*. Both must agree to this joint participation. Erving Goffman appropriately describes this agreement as a "working consensus."[3] By this he means that listeners and speakers must agree—usually implicitly rather than vocally—on whose claims concerning what issues or ideas will be honored at a given moment during the interchange. In its most elemental terms, this means "taking turns" as to who will talk and who will listen next. If there's no such consensus, there can be no real communication. If the listeners supply feedback but the speaker is unable or unwilling to notice and adapt to it, the interaction will be seriously impaired or brought to a complete standstill. Total absence of any feedback to adjust to can produce all kinds of obstacles to human communication.

An early study by social psychologists Harold J. Leavitt and Ronald Mueller suggests the nature and range of some of these obstacles.[4] In the Leavitt-Mueller experiments, a speaker described a geometric pattern to a group of listeners who then tried to draw a reproduction of it. Feedback conditions ranged from "zero" (in which the speaker couldn't see his or her audience and no feedback of any kind was allowed) to "free" (in which the speaker could see the audience and its members were permitted to ask questions and receive answers).

The study found, in essence, that the more complete the feedback between speaker and listeners, the greater the accuracy with which the given information was communicated. Further, free feedback permitted the participants to learn a "mutual language" which appreciably reduced or even eliminated the need for further feedback. Leavitt and Mueller found also that free feedback was accompanied by a high degree of mutual confidence and mutual good feeling among speaking and listening agents, whereas zero feedback caused low confidence and hostility. [4]

At its worst, the inability to respond to communication and feedback from others is a form of mental illness. And even under so-called "normal" day-to-day conditions, failure to provide and receive feedback can do inestimable harm. We can see this quite readily, for instance, in studies of communication conducted in industrial settings.[5] In large organizations one of the major problems is "role ambiguity." Persons with this problem don't quite know where they stand or what's expected of them—just how they fit into the organization as a whole. They may be uncertain about the "task" elements of their job—their specific duties. Or they may feel insecure about the "socio-emotional" elements of their work situation—their interpersonal relationships with management and/or other employees. As you might expect, most of these studies reveal that a frequent cause of role ambiguity is *lack* of communication with or feedback from superiors in the organization. No matter how unsatisfactory the role or job itself may be, ambiguity and uncertainty about it are *even worse.*

The unfortunate effects of zero feedback can, in fact, be observed in all kinds of speech communication settings and situations. Outright heckling or argument is in many ways easier for a speaker to take than listener indifference or no reaction at all. When you are speaking, do everything you can to sense and interpret feedback from your hearers. And try to make them *aware* of this. When you are listening and watching, on the other hand, do what you can—within reason—to provide "readable" reactions. As a speaking/listening agent you must learn to look at your audience, to see the people in it, and to see their reactions. You must come to read reactions as "interest," "approval," "antagonism," "skepticism," "boredom," "polite blank stares," "rejection," etc.

Refraining from Overreacting to Feedback

All feedback mechanisms, it seems—whether mechanical or human—have

---

Study Probe 4
Testing the Absence of Feedback

Try reproducing the Leavitt-Mueller experiment. One class member should stand at the chalkboard with his or her back to the rest of the class. The instructor then will provide another student with a drawing similar to the ones at right, allowing the class but not the person at the chalkboard to view it. The student with the drawing then should instruct the first student how to draw it on the board. The first student, however, cannot look at or ask questions of the second.

Then repeat the experiment with two different students and a different drawing, again concealing the drawing from the student at the board, but this time allowing the two students to view each other and to ask and respond to questions.

The class can then compare the results of the two experiments and determine whether their findings confirm Leavitt and Mueller's.

a tendency to *overreact* to stimuli. A radar-aimed antiaircraft gun programmed to zero in on a swiftly swerving fighter jet tends to develop a momentum that carries it slightly beyond a correct alignment with its target. A prizefighter often tends to overreact to the feinting jab of an opponent and is thereby drawn off guard and off balance. Similarly, in an interactive situation, a speaker will be tempted to overreact and overadjust to listener feedback, thereby losing sight of his or her basic purpose. Listeners—even a small number of them—can create such a strong or noisy response as to cause the speaker to falter, to overcorrect or distort the intended message, or to forget it altogether. Both as a listener and as a speaker, therefore, you must be firmly in command of your material and your emotions—so firmly that you can't be distracted or goaded into *overreacting* to feedback cues of whatever kind.

In a classroom circumstance, one of my students was extremely nervous, almost terrified, at the prospect of speaking to a group (although he seemed to have no problem in handling ordinary one-to-one conversation). In some desperation, he suggested that as an alternative to the more formal speaking assignment he be allowed to read aloud to the class a funny article he had recently found in a magazine. For the sake of at least getting him on his feet, I agreed. The moment came, and he rose with great hesitation and started to read. The first punch line came, and the class laughed. He read on. Came the second punch line, and the class roared. For the first time, the student relaxed and looked at the class. He smiled and read on. They laughed again. It was a metamorphosis.

By the end of the reading, the student "reader" was more at ease than I had ever seen him. He was delighted—and extremely excited—by the feedback he was receiving from his listeners. In fact, he didn't want to turn it off. He didn't want to stop—he really had lost control. Grinning at his listeners, he exclaimed,

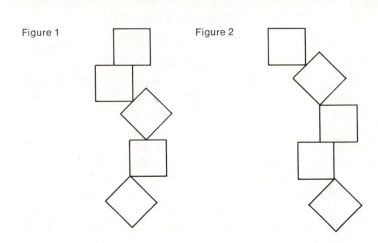

Figure 1   Figure 2

"Well, if you liked that, just listen to *this!*" And he proceeded to tell a crude and decidedly unfunny story, entirely out of context and unrelated to the immediate circumstance. Almost instantly a chill settled over his listeners; and despite the fact that most of them were not oversensitive to the use of four-letter shock words, they didn't laugh at his punch line this time. They didn't even smile. The storyteller had lost them. He had overreacted to their initial feedback.

Overreaction to audience feedback is by no means exclusively a problem for beginning speakers. Experienced orators and seasoned political campaigners are highly susceptible on occasion. Indeed, there are some speakers, as you no doubt have observed, who are so eager to sense from which directions "the winds of change are blowing"—and to react instantaneously to those currents—that their values and goals seem to come more from their listeners than from themselves. Although they may be public figures and supposed "leaders," they are, in fact, "followers"—typical of the other-directed person.

Of all the implications of this reaction/overreaction principle—and we've touched on only a few of them here—you might consider this the most important: *As a speaker-communicator you must strive constantly to maintain control of yourself, and, to the greatest extent possible, of the communicative situation.* Try not to let the feedback and your adjustments to it get out of hand. Keep cool and stay in charge. If you see a frown here or a violent headshake over there, don't let it disturb you unduly. If a heckler tries to bring you to a halt, don't be baited into trying to adapt your message to that person only rather than to the other listeners in the situation. And don't, in your efforts to adjust to feedback, grow defensive and distort your principal purpose. While you must certainly look for feedback and react appropriately to it, try always to *maintain a balanced view* and interpret it in its proper perspective.

Rarely, if ever, will *all* of your listeners react alike or be highly favorable to you as a person and/or to what you are saying. Some will respond negatively, and others not at all. Some of their reactions will be overt and visible; many will not be. What is of continuing importance is that you recognize what it is that your hearers are "saying" to you by their reactive behavior and that you recognize also the potential of that behavior for influencing and being influenced during the communicative process.

In this chapter as a whole we've looked at two significant stages of the message-making process: (1) what should and often does take place *before interaction begins* and (2) what you'd better be prepared to expect—and do—*while the interaction is actually going on.* For the first of these stages we've provided fairly explicit guidelines for the planning and preparation of messages—persuasive messages, in particular. We've noted that in order to plan effectively for anticipated responses from listeners and their possible acceptance of your messages, you will need to (*a*) identify listeners' values and motives, (*b*) discover their persuadability, (*c*) aim your message at a specific listener or listeners whom you know or are at least aware of, (*d*) analyze the communicative context, (*e*) anticipate the expectations of potential listeners, (*f*) devise ways to establish speaker/

listener rapport, (g) adapt the language of your message to your probable listeners and the communicative context, and (h) discover where your hearers stand in relation to your proposed message. Then, for the second stage of message-making we've suggested some potentially useful methods by which you may adjust your messages and your communicative behavior to the feedback provided by other agents with whom you are involved.

Having thus established what we hope is a reasonably clear understanding of informational and persuasive messages and their significance in the interactive process, we're about ready to move in the next chapter to a consideration of principles underlying a somewhat more complex communicative enterprise: problem solving and decision making.

Suggested Readings

Thomas M. Scheidel, *Persuasive Speaking* (Glenview, Ill.: Scott, Foresman and Company, 1967). This paperback book is a concise introduction to influential speech communication. It provides the beginning student with a historical perspective of the subject as well as a contemporary overview.

Winston Brembeck and William Howell, *Persuasion,* 2nd ed. (New York: Prentice-Hall, Inc., in press). The earlier edition (1952) of this textbook has been widely used in courses in persuasion. Beginning students should find the second edition both informative and challenging reading.

Reference Notes

[1] See the early studies in Carl I. Hovland, Irving L. Janis, and Harold H. Kelley, *Communication and Persuasion* (New Haven, Conn.: Yale University Press, 1953), Chapter 5.

[2] William J. McGuire, "The Nature of Attitudes and Attitude Change," *The Handbook of Social Psychology,* 2nd ed., ed. Gardner Lindzey and Elliot Aronson (Reading, Mass.: Addison-Wesley Publishing Co., Inc., 1969), v. III, pp. 247–252.

[3] Erving Goffman, *Behavior in Public Places* (New York: The Free Press, 1963), Chapter 6.

[4] Harold J. Leavitt and Ronald A. H. Mueller, "Some Effects of Feedback on Communication," *Human Relations,* 4 (1951): 401–410.

[5] See "The Social Context of Communication: Introduction" in Dean C. Barnlund, *Interpersonal Communication* (Boston: Houghton Mifflin Company, 1963), especially pp. 164–171. Barnlund's introductions in this book are excellent syntheses of research.

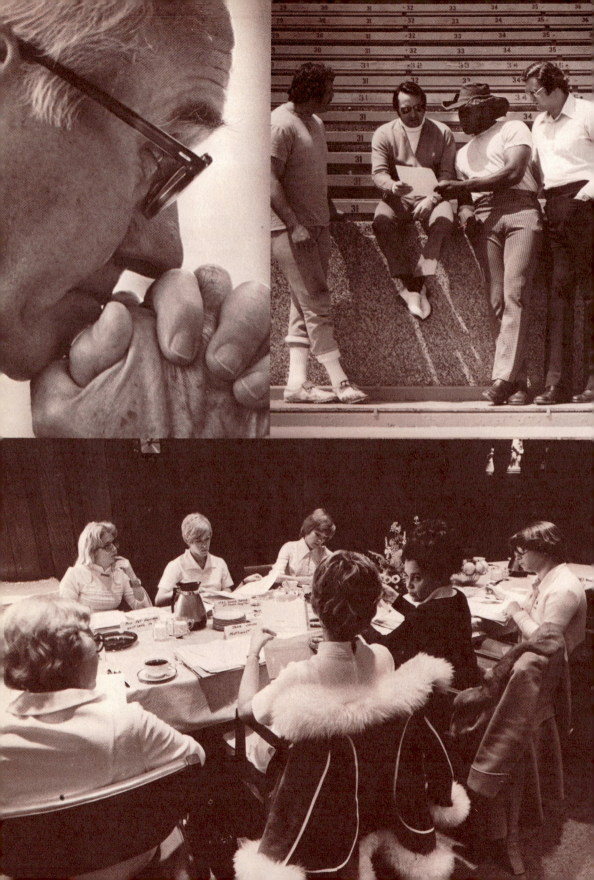

Every phase of the speech communication process involves choices and decisions. In fact, much of speech communication behavior is *decision-making behavior*. The beliefs and the evaluations we attach to those beliefs—our Belief/Evaluation Clusters—powerfully influence the decisions we make both as speakers and listeners.

In preceding chapters we've considered *interaction* as it is effected through and affected by the nature and dynamics of communication messages. And we've noted the functional factors involved in the preparation of those messages to facilitate *information exchange* and to advance *persuasive propositions* designed to influence others. In the present chapter we will focus upon a somewhat higher and more complex level of influential communication and the motivational forces which underlie it: *We will examine communicative interaction as it occurs when people come together for the purpose of solving problems, resolving differences, and/or making decisions.*

PROBLEM SOLVING AND DECISION MAKING

Few problems are solved and few social decisions are made in this world without the use of speech communication. Wherever we go—to the classroom, the lecture hall, the PTA meeting, the political rally, the dining hall, the student center, or the TV set—we are constantly exposed to communicative messages calculated to formulate, firm up, or alter our decisions. *Every phase of the speech communication process, and every setting in which it occurs, involves choices and decisions.* In fact, much of speech communication behavior is *decision-making behavior.* Even before we reach the interaction stage we must do a considerable amount of "deciding." Will I speak? Or will I remain silent? Will I speak to reveal or conceal my true beliefs and motives? What will I say? How should I say it? These typify the kinds of "to-speak-or-not-to-speak" decisions that each of us must make every day.

We know, of course, that carrying our decision making to the point where we are willing to advocate it *orally* is not always a desirable or practical matter. All of us, from moment to moment, *intrapersonally* arrive at decisions of relatively little importance to anyone else—decisions that we don't need to shout from the housetops. We may believe strongly—and even "decide"—that it will rain tomorrow, but we aren't likely to talk passionately or lengthily in support of that decision. However, as we move to the need to solve problems and make decisions about more significant and more crucial matters, we almost certainly *will* want to talk about them—often passionately *and* lengthily. At that point we move into the social and interpersonal arena. Then we become aware rather quickly that decisions on significant social issues usually hinge on *more* than a single and simple proposition. We begin to realize—if we hadn't before—that typically involved in such issues are *numerous* propositions, most of which have numerous *inter-related* elements, *conflictive* aspects, *subpropositions,* and even *counter*-propositions. When we are faced with the need to "decide" on *multiple and complex propositions* of some magnitude, speech communication will be the prominent generative force.

Consider, as examples, some of the issues which have confronted us in recent times. The Report of the National Advisory Commission on Civil Disorders, investigating racial disturbances which occurred in many American cities in 1967, asked three straightforward questions:

> *What happened?*
> *Why did it happen?*
> *What can be done to prevent it from happening again?*[1]

The Warren Commission Report on the assassination of President Kennedy faced the question:

> *Did the bullet which struck Governor Connally of Texas first pass through the body of the President?*[2]

The Club of Rome report, which speculates about the future of our world system, raised the question:

> *What will be the effects of pollution on world ecology if the levels of pollution continue to increase exponentially?*[3]

These questions seem fairly simple and clear. The answers are *not.* The mass of interrelated "multiple and complex" propositions involved in attempting to answer questions of this type are nearly overwhelming. Yet they are typical of the kinds of questions we face from time to time, and rarely do we arrive at absolutely acceptable answers. Obviously, what we need is *a system for the analysis of multiple and complex propositions.* One of our principal intentions in this chapter is to develop such a system. Drawing especially from contemporary behavioral research and decision theory, we'll try to provide a process which can be used both in the analysis and choice of ideas and materials best suited to problem-solving/decision-making interaction. Its utility and advantages should extend also to the assessment of speech communication *effects*—a central concern in Chapter 9.

We'll refer to this "system" as the *Belief-Evaluation Cluster* (BEC) system. The general principle underlying it is that the *beliefs* we hold, the *evaluations* we make of them, and the *intensity* with which we cling to them are central to the speech communication process and are, therefore, central to any problem solving or decision making we may do.

Before moving into a detailed description of this BEC system and its workings, we'd like you to think a bit about the bases for it and the factors involved in its functioning. Your understanding of it and—ultimately—your capability for using it will be enlarged, we believe, by considering (1) *some approaches to problem solving*—the "creative" or "reflective" thinking by which we arrive at possible solutions and (2) by noting the influence exerted upon communicative decision making in particular and influential interaction in general by *(a) human motivation, (b) attitudes and attitude change,* and *(c) value systems.*

GENERAL APPROACHES TO PROBLEM SOLVING

From time to time philosophers, psychologists, and others have evolved patterns which—theoretically at least—are supposed to help us identify problems, locate their probable causes, and sort out possible solutions. To suggest something of the scope and character of such approaches, let's look briefly at *(a)* "creative thinking," *(b)* "reflective thinking," *(c)* inferential patterns, and *(d)* scanning and focusing.

Creative Thinking

The creative thinking pattern of problem solving developed by Graham Wallas proceeds in accordance with the following steps: Step One: *Preparation;* Step Two: *Incubation;* Step Three: *Illumination;* and Step Four: *Verification.*[4] The description of this procedure, involving what some call the "aha phenomenon," has been used in explaining how some scientific discoveries and inventions have been made. According to this explanation, when faced with a problem we first marshal all the available material on the problem and go over it in our mind: the *preparation* step. Next we let the problem "rest" while we turn to some other activity: the *incubation* period. This (it's hoped) is followed sooner or later by the sudden insight or solution: the *illumination!* From the unconscious level of our mind comes the answer we have sought: "Aha!" Then finally we test the insight: the *verification* step.

A number of case studies suggest that such "creative thinking" processes do seem to resemble these steps. One scientist is said to have experienced an important insight while sitting in a bathtub; another while stepping aboard a bus. Maybe you have gained a sudden insight in similar fashion. In attempting to solve a mathematical problem, you may have come to a dead end, given up, and gone on to something else. Then later, when you were engaged in an entirely unrelated activity, the "right" answer suddenly flashed across your mind. ☐1

This is an appealing pattern, and most of us probably try it at times. Unfortunately, in "thinking creatively" for a speech-encounter assignment, many of us demonstrate a considerable enthusiasm for the "incubation" phase of the process, but not much eagerness for "preparation." As the inscription on an ancient Assyrian tablet purportedly reads: "An infertile egg, alas—no matter how long you sit upon it—never hatches a bird that can crow."

Reflective Thinking

A better-known and more widely cited procedure for analyzing problems and discovering solutions is John Dewey's "Steps to Reflective Thinking."[5] Dewey, the noted philosopher and educator, distinguished five phases in his problem-solving sequence:

1. *A felt difficulty.* Something perplexing and puzzling occurs in our experience. Things are unsettled and not right. A new situation occurs for which we have no answer, or perhaps an older "tried and true" solution breaks down and no longer fits the needs. We have a problem.
2. *Location and definition of the difficulty.* Observations are made and data are gathered to make clear just where the difficulty lies and what it is. Different approaches are made so that we may discover fully the nature of our problem.

Study Probe 1
Recalling Instances of the "Illumination" Step

We are all familiar with the illuminating experience of recalling half-forgotten information, but how much experience have you had with the illumination step in *problem solving* or *decision making?* Can you think of any occasions when the answer to a problem you were working on flashed before you? Perhaps it wasn't the answer that suddenly occurred to you, but rather the procedures needed to find the answer. What about decisions you have made for which there was no way of knowing a "best possible" answer? Have such decisions ever come to you in a sudden moment of illumination?

3. *Suggestions of possible solutions.* Alternative hypotheses and potential solutions to the problem are advanced at this stage. These suggested alternatives grow out of the careful analysis made as a result of the second step.
4. *Mental exploration and elaboration of alternative hypothesized solutions.* The meaning and the implications of the various possible solutions are probed. The consequences are investigated. We reason: "If this hypothesis is true, then it follows that . . . ."
5. *Further observation and experimentation.* Here we test by specific and planned observation the proposed hypotheses and their implications in order to accept or reject them. We make a decision.

The series of steps in Dewey's approach may be usefully taken in a problem-solving group discussion—a form of interpersonal interaction we'll be considering in Chapter 11. Note, too, the similarity of Dewey's "reflective thinking" progression to the three essential steps frequently associated with scientific inquiry: (1) *observation* and *description* of phenomena, (2) *explanation* by means of hypothesis and theory, and (3) *testing* of hypotheses and theory. [2]

Using Inferential Patterns

In our probing of approaches to problem solving, we may learn something from the greatest problem solver of them all—Sherlock Holmes:

> *The ideal reasoner . . . would, when he had once been shown a single fact in all its bearing, deduce from it not only all the chain of events which led up to it, but also all of the results which would follow from it. . . . We have not yet grasped the results which reason alone can attain to. Problems may be solved in the study which have baffled all those who have sought a solution by the aid of their senses.* [6]

Study Probe 2
Approximating Dewey's Reflective-Thinking Steps

Dewey developed his five-step approach by having college students write out procedures they followed in solving problems. Try to reconstruct the steps you have taken in working your way through to the solution of some problem. Then compare *your* approach with the Dewey steps. How closely did you approximate his five steps? You could also ask others (friends, members of your family, etc.), less familiar with the Dewey steps, to write out a sequence of the steps *they've* followed. Compare these with Dewey's procedure and with yours. What generalizations do you come to? How closely do you and others follow Dewey's steps? Do the steps covered by you and the others receive fairly equal emphasis? What steps, if any, seem to be omitted most often?

Holmes, you see—when trying to solve a problem—stressed the importance of a background knowledge of facts, careful observation for evidence, and incisive deductive reasoning—a kind of "observational-deducing" approach. His shrewd inferences always followed a specific observation to its implications, and a combining of circumstances into a total integrated view of the matter. But not everyone can become a Sherlock Holmes, and his pattern of problem solving, like those of Wallas and Dewey, cannot ensure "truth" and the "best solution" any more than, say, Aristotle's syllogism.

This is not to say that syllogistic reasoning (pages 98–100) is of no value in problem solving and decision making. But we may find the syllogism rather inflexible and difficult to use in dealing with the "multiple and complex propositions" we encounter daily. If we think for a moment of the origins of such inferential systems, we may understand why this is so. In the early dawning of history, a person's decisions and the consequences of those decisions occurred very close together. In that no-nonsense era a decision was often put to the test immediately. When stalking a voracious lion, the hunter may be allowed only one mistake! The wrong inference could well be the last. As our long-ago ancestors developed the use of language and—with it—abstract thought, decisions and consequences no longer occurred so close together. The syllogistic logic of the Greeks was an attempt, as we've tried to suggest, to provide immediate tests and principles for *abstract* thinking, the consequences of which could not be seen immediately. In our time, its uses seem less appealing and applicable. However, rather than abandon such an inferential approach entirely, it is probably better that—as Toulmin has—we continue to modify and adapt it for our special analytical and communicative purposes.

But Toulmin's inferential system (pages 104–106), even though more flexible and adaptable than Aristotle's, is by no means the final answer in our search for ways to understand human thinking and problem solving. Studies of decision making and game theory point unmistakably toward the fact that *in the actual practice of problem solving, patterns of reasoning vary considerably from person to person.* No two individuals, it seems, will approach a given problem in exactly the same way. In terms of Toulmin's pattern, for example, it's likely that some people will focus more on the evidence than on the warrants. They especially want "just the facts." Other people are more concerned with general principles, and will focus more upon warrants than on what lies behind the warrants. Some are keen to sense possible rebuttal; others appear oblivious to this possibility.

We know also that *not all thinking is done on a conscious level* and that people have, therefore, only a limited ability to govern their own reasoning processes. *Aha phenomenon* is an appropriate label for a sudden insight, but the label doesn't explain *why* we seemingly stumble onto a bright solution. A number of experiments have made it clear that people can develop a rational concept or apply a principle without consciously recognizing the common elements or theoretical relationships involved in a specific instance. From studies of language usage, for example, we know that children who learn to speak a language can use and distinguish proper from improper "grammar" without ever being aware that the language they're using so effortlessly is governed by "rules" of which they seemingly know nothing.[7]

Scanning and Focusing

This approach puts a different emphasis on the problem-solving process. In this view, problem solving comprises a series of patterns, actually, as described by Jerome Bruner, Jacqueline Goodnow, and George Austin in their book, *A Study in Thinking.*[8] These authors use the terms *simultaneous scanning, successive scanning, conservative focusing,* and *focus gambling* to suggest some of the different ways in which different types of persons tend to "look" at a particular problem. In solving a problem, one person may attempt to see the overall picture: He is engaging in *simultaneous scanning.* Another person may try to view the overall picture but look especially for the elements that test the particular hypothesis advanced, one at a time: She is attempting *successive scanning.* Another may focus upon and vary one element of her perception at a time: She is engaging in *conservative focusing* behavior. Still another may narrow his alternatives (as is typical of focusing behavior), but allow more than one element to vary at a time: He is *focus gambling.* Some persons will tend to favor one of these approaches much more than others, and some will take yet other paths. ③

The problem-solving approaches we've just briefly described should be viewed more or less as "ideal" patterns or "models" of how we *may*—and, perhaps, *should*—solve our problems and reach our decisions. But we mustn't confuse them with the way people *do* solve problems and make decisions. Each of them has some serious limitations. For one thing, for these approaches—especially those with inferential patterning—to be consistently accurate and generally applicable, we'd have to assume that the world and everyone in it is "reasonable," that we have conscious control over our thinking, and that we all think

Study Probe 3
Analyzing Your Behavior: Scanning Versus Focusing

Which of these two patterns, *scanning* or *focusing,* is the more typical of your problem-solving behavior? When viewing problems, do you "scan over" the whole situation and permit your attention to be drawn to a few especially noticeable points? Or do you tend to focus on one particular point at a time and resolve it before moving on to another? When making decisions, do you try to envision several alternatives at once and weigh them against one another collectively? Or do you take one alternative at a time, weigh it, and decide upon it before moving on to the next possibility? Or is there some *other* pattern that seems to you to be characteristic of your problem-solving attempts? Do you ever *combine* elements of scanning and focusing in your decision making?

more or less alike. That, I need not emphasize, is *not* the kind of world we live in. These approaches or "systems," like road maps, are helpful for pointing the way and, perhaps, for locating a "destination" or two along the route. If you are a perceptive person, aware of what you are doing, and follow one of the sequences, it may guide and facilitate your search for the solution to your problem. But more than that it very probably cannot do.

FACTORS WHICH INFLUENCE DECISIONS

In problem solving we are largely concerned with pinpointing the problem or difficulty and developing possible alternative solutions. In practical decision making—which comprises the concluding phases of the problem-solution process—we concentrate chiefly upon *choosing the most desirable alternative—making the best choice.* And when we look beyond choice to its underlying causes, we must look closely and deeply at the influences exerted by (*a*) human motivation, (*b*) attitudes and attitude change, and (*c*) value systems.

We'll be concerned now with factors which influence our decisions and which are significant in influencing other people—during interaction—to decide as *we* decide. What happens when we interact with others to analyze "multiple and complex" propositions? We'll try to provide some analytical tools which may help you find answers.

Human Motivation

On the subject of motivation, we are centrally concerned with factors and forces which "cause" us to "decide" as we do. Our needs and our motives are prominent among the factors which affect our actions and decisions: *We act and decide as we do because we have certain needs and wants.*

Psychologists have seen human motivation as the product of primary and secondary motives—a rather useful and usable classification of human striving. *Primary motives,* they say, are those basic physiological needs which must be satisfied if the life of the individual and of the species is to continue. *Secondary motives* are the learned, social needs—the needs we have for functioning effectively and with some satisfaction in our society.

The hierarchy of basic human needs.   Somewhat more detailed and more specifically applicable to our purposes here is the five-level ranking of human needs identified by the social psychologist Abraham H. Maslow.[9] In his theory of motivation, Maslow ranks the five basic categories of needs on an ascending scale in accordance with what might be termed the "persuasive force or power" they exert upon us, or the "priority" given them by the self. The order of these needs, going up the scale, is as follows: (1) *physiological well-being,* (2) *safety and security,* (3) *belongingness and love,* (4) *esteem,* and (5) *self-actualization.*

1.   *The physiological needs* are the "survival" needs that each of us has

A HIERARCHY OF PREPOTENT NEEDS *

SELF-ACTUALIZATION
self-fulfillment: to *be* what one *can* be

ESTEEM NEEDS
self-esteem from achievement, competence, mastery, confidence; reputation, recognition, status

BELONGINGNESS AND LOVE NEEDS
love and affection with family, friends; acceptance and approval by social groups

SAFETY NEEDS security, stability, protection, structure, orderliness, law, predictability, freedom from fear and chaos

PHYSIOLOGICAL NEEDS
food, drink, air, sleep, sex, etc.

for food, water, procreation, and "homeostasis," or balance. These needs—like nourishment, shelter, and sleep—are what we must have for our physiological well-being.

2. Moving upward, on the next level we find the *safety needs*. Human beings desire an orderly, smoothly functioning world in which sudden, unexpected, and potentially dangerous events don't occur often. We need to feel settled and at ease—not threatened and insecure.

---

*Data "Hierarchy of Needs" from MOTIVATION AND PERSONALITY, 2nd edition, by Abraham H. Maslow (Harper & Row, 1970).

3.   Moving to a somewhat higher level, we encounter the needs for love, warmth, and affection—the *need to belong* and *to be loved* by family and friends. These needs reflect our social nature; and, as we emphasized in Chapter 1, they provide one of the major purposes why we bother to speak at all.

4.   At the next level and a little higher up are the *esteem needs*. Each of us must have a measure of self-esteem, self-respect, a reasonably high evaluation of our "self"; and we desire the esteem and respect of *others*. We seek status and reputation; we want to be recognized and appreciated.

5.   And, finally, at the highest level, is something that we've talked about a great deal in this book: the need for *self-actualization*. This is the *self-fulfillment* need: to be the best that we can be—to realize our potential to the fullest.

Maslow's theory holds that these needs form a "hierarchy of prepotency." Essentially, he says, the laws of psychological dynamics dictate that we must proceed from basic to higher need fulfillment. In other words, the *physiological needs come first;* they take precedence over all others. If these basic, "survival" needs are reasonably well satisfied, then we will feel impelled to try to satisfy the higher-level needs—they will "motivate" us to do or want certain things and to behave in certain ways in order to get them. Keep in mind, of course, that this "consecutiveness" is not rigid. Our lower-level needs don't require *complete* satisfaction before the next higher level of needs begins to influence our behavior, to generate motivation for us. But we shouldn't look—either in our own self or in the self of another—for much evidence of self-actualizing behavior unless the lower-level needs have been fairly well fulfilled.

The functional "autonomy" of motives.   We may gain some further insights into motivation by considering what psychologist Gordon Allport describes as their "functional autonomy." By this, Allport means that desires and behaviors which we learn in order to satisfy basic needs may eventually become motivators themselves. They will "function" even if the basic need which originally prompted the behavior or desire and was associated with it has already been fulfilled.[10] For example, early in life your grandfather or your father may have worked hard to provide food and shelter for his family in difficult times. But even after he had provided all of the necessities of life and all the members of his family were assured of the physiological requirements for their comfort and well-being, he continued to work hard. He continued to equate "hard work" with "success." Strenuous effort had become a part of him—had become such a powerful motivator *in its own right*—that he felt driven to it for itself alone long after the *original* need for it had been satisfied. Hard work was no longer a means but an *end;* it had gradually moved over into his category of "values." We will have more to say later about values and value systems and about how they, too, serve as motivators of behavior.

Consistency, cognition balancing, and congruity.   From time to time we have mentioned the need to feel that the world is "in balance" and that consistency prevails in our perceptions and our interrelationships with other persons, places, and things. These psychological and consistency factors provide us with still another basis for understanding motivation:[11] We are motivated to achieve a balance or feeling of harmony among our cognitions.* If anything happens to create a serious imbalance, inconsistency, or "dissonance" among them, then we're motivated to adjust those cognitions to achieve a *new* balance. Using this as a basic premise, three social psychologists—Charles Osgood, George Suci, and Percy Tannenbaum—developed what is termed a *congruity* approach to motivation.[12] Seemingly we are motivated to try to make our perceptions and categories "congruent" with each other and with what we believe to be the "reality" of the matter in question.

To illustrate congruity theory, let's suppose that we hear a speech in which President Ford (whom we will view favorably here) speaks *against* a proposal to increase financial support for higher education (considered here to be a positive concept). According to Osgood, Suci, and Tannenbaum, who conducted many similar experiments, if a speaker we respect (+) speaks against (–) a proposal we favor (+) we will tend to feel that something must be wrong with our evaluation of the speaker, the proposal, or both. We experience *cognitive dissonance* and are therefore motivated to achieve a new balance among our cognitions. To arrive at this new balancing, we might see President Ford somewhat less positively, but we might also see the proposed expenditures for higher education somewhat less positively than before.

Motivation, for the most part, is both necessary and helpful because in its various forms and manifestations it provides the drive and gives shape and direction to our behavior—especially our decision-making behavior. We must recognize, of course, that motivation can be a mixed blessing. Wrongly used, it can make us selfish, overcompetitive, and greedy. Or, the blocking of a goal toward which we have been strongly motivated, coupled with the continuance of its relentless drive, can lead to *frustration*. Frustration, in turn, can lead to aggression or even less desirable behavior such as violence, flight, negativism, defeatism, withdrawal from reality, etc. All such behaviors and outlooks will almost immediately evidence themselves in our speech communications—a special aspect of interaction to which we'll be devoting direct attention in Chapter 12.

Attitudes and Attitude Change

Attitude and *attitude change* are central concepts in any serious consideration of decision making or any other kind of influential interaction. Attitude, as we are thinking of it in this chapter, has two major "parts": a *belief* component and a *value* component. If we want to *analyze* an attitude, somewhere in its struc-

---

*The term *cognitions*, you'll recall, covers all of our knowledge, beliefs, and judgments about ourselves and our environment.

ture we'll encounter these two elements and see evidence of their interaction. If we want to *change* an attitude (a process which some have described as "persuasion"), in some way we must motivate and effect an adjustment of either the belief or the value or both. There are, of course, a number of different views about the structuring of attitudes and how they affect human behavior and communicative decision making. Two of these views, in particular, are relevant to our immediate purpose: *cognition-feeling-response tendencies* and *belief-affects*—or what we might call the "probability" dimension and the "evaluative" dimension of an attitude. Both of these views should help to enlarge our definition and shed additional light on the subject of attitudes as a whole.

Cognition-feeling-response tendencies.   Attitudes, usually, are developed over a period of time and have interrelated elements that can be changed or modified. According to the theories of social psychologists David Krech, Richard Crutchfield, and Edgerton Ballachey, there are *three* rather than two of these interrelated elements: (1) cognitions, (2) feelings, and (3) response tendencies.[13] *Cognitions*—our knowledge, beliefs, and judgments—are similar to the "belief component" that we've referred to. We may believe, for instance, that Georgina is tall, has blonde hair, has a good sense of humor, is loyal to her friends, and fun to be around. These are the *beliefs* we hold about Georgina. *Feelings* are the emotions we connect with an object of our perceptions. We may "feel" pleased to be in Georgina's company; we may "feel" that we like her. These are our *feelings* or emotions toward her. *Response tendencies* are the "action predispositions" or "behavioral readiness" that we associate with an object. This is the way we're *inclined to act* toward somebody, something, or some idea. If we like Georgina (a feeling), we have a tendency to respond favorably toward her: We may seek Georgina's company. If she takes a stand in, say, a small group discussion, our action-tendency is to respond to her—applaud or even speak in support of her position on the matter. These are our *response tendencies* toward her. The three elements—cognitions, feelings, and response tendencies—combine to motivate us to form and maintain our *total attitude* toward Georgina.

Beliefs and affects as attitude dimensions.   According to Martin Fishbein, another authority on attitudes and attitude "measurement," an attitude has two interrelated and *measurable* "dimensions": (1) *belief,* which is the "probability" dimension; and (2) *affect,* which is the "evaluative" dimension. These are not unlike the "cognitions" and the "feelings" components cited by Krech, Crutchfield, and Ballachey. Fishbein's special contribution is his attempt to provide a means of *measuring* his dimensions. To accomplish the measurement, he uses a semantic-differential scale (see facing page):[*]

---

[*]From "A Consideration of Beliefs, Attitudes, and Their Relationship" by Martin Fishbein, in *Current Studies in Social Psychology,* edited by Ivan D. Steiner and Martin Fishbein. Copyright © 1965 by Holt, Rinehart and Winston, Publishers. Reprinted by permission of Holt, Rinehart and Winston, Publishers.

BELIEF SCALE (Probability)
"Fluoride treatments prevent tooth decay."

Likely ⎯⎯   ⎯⎯   ⎯⎯   ⎯⎯   ⎯⎯   ⎯⎯   ⎯⎯ Unlikely

      +3   +2   +1   0   –1   –2   –3

AFFECT SCALE (Evaluation)
"Prevention of tooth decay."

Good ⎯⎯   ⎯⎯   ⎯⎯   ⎯⎯   ⎯⎯   ⎯⎯   ⎯⎯ Bad

      +3   +2   +1   0   –1   –2   –3

If you were responding to the *Belief Scale* as shown above, presumably you would be measuring the *level of probability* (the probability of it's being "true") that you assign to the belief: "Fluoride treatments prevent tooth decay." If you were responding to the *Affect Scale,* you would be attempting to measure the *evaluative level* (in this case, the "goodness" or "badness" level) at which you hold the notion that "prevention of tooth decay" is a worthwhile category or concept. If, for instance, you value highly (+3) the "prevention of tooth decay" and you strongly believe (+3) that "fluoride treatments prevent tooth decay," then your *attitude* toward "fluoride treatments" will be exceedingly strong and quite difficult to change.

    Fishbein maintains, moreover, that each of us has *many* beliefs or "probabilistic" views toward any perception or category-concept of which we are aware. For instance, I believe—at some level of probability—in the existence of an object or category-concept, or whatever; I also believe—at varying levels of probability— that certain elements or characteristics or capabilities are associated with that object. Related to this belief-structure, each of us has *affects* or "evaluative feelings" toward those associated elements. Also, according to Fishbein, *the sum of all the scores on the belief elements multiplied by the scores on their associated affective qualities expresses the individual's total attitude toward the object or concept under consideration.*

    Fishbein's measurement scales are useful because they help us look upon attitudes as being composed of multiple propositions, and his procedure suggests a means for analyzing them. When we look at attitudes from this perspective, we can begin to sense how it might be possible to influence attitude-formation and attitude-change by (a) adding new beliefs or evaluative feelings to your listeners' "attitude systems" or (b) altering the *levels* of their beliefs or feelings. [4]

The relationship of attitude to behavior.   The current literature of behavioral science raises some questions as to what this attitude-behavior relationship is.[14] In the past, it has usually been assumed that there must be a direct relationship between the two—that attitude must be almost synonymous with behavior. In fact, attitudes have been defined by some as "predispositions to behave." Not all students of the subject agree, however; and a few have raised doubts as to whether attitudes do, in fact, predict behavior accurately and adequately.

Perhaps this detailed illustration will demonstrate some of the problems in relating attitude and behavior. Suppose one day that you asked your friend, Georgina St. George, whether she preferred hamburger or steak, and she replied, "Steak." Later, you happen to see Georgina at the meat counter of the local grocery store. She doesn't see you because she's busy looking over all of the meats available. *Then she buys hamburger!* Would you be shocked? Would you think perhaps she had lied to you? Would you say that her attitudes have little to do with her behavior? Probably not, for you would realize that Georgina's earlier and generally favorable response to steak wasn't the sole determiner of her present meat-buying behavior. She may not have enough money to buy steak at the moment, or the available steak may not look very good to her. She might even have had steak at her most recent meal. We might better try to measure Georgina's attitude toward the "buying of steak" at the moment she is making her decision. In short, there are obvious and significant connections between attitudes and behavior, but we must always be very careful to analyze accurately what those connections *are* and how they are likely to affect the decision making we do and that we try to influence others to do.

Value Systems

Up to this point, as we've tried to lay the necessary groundwork for a belief-evaluation system with which to analyze multiple and complex propositions, quite often we've needed to use the terms *value* and *value systems*. From the contexts in which we've used them, their meaning must be fairly clear. It should

Study Probe 4
Listing Belief Statements

Write down as many as possible of the belief statements you hold about each of the following:

1. A school building in which I attend classes or with which I associate myself this term.
2. An instructor I have this term.
3. Our school's grading procedures (A, B, C, or pass/fail, or whatever).

List only *beliefs*. Don't be concerned with differing *strengths* of beliefs. If you believe it—list it. And don't be concerned yet about evaluations. When you've completed your three lists, review each one to see how many different beliefs you've included. Were there any similarities across lists? Did you list both positive and negative beliefs? Compare your lists with those of classmates. Did any of them list beliefs which you share but which you overlooked?

also be reasonably clear by now that values and value systems play an unmistakable role in any decision we make. Value systems are learned, developed throughout our lifetime, and do much to determine our life style. We need, therefore, to understand something of the impact these systems have upon our thinking, how they affect human interrelatedness, and how they may influence communicative decision making. Values, like human needs and motives, have been classified in a variety of different ways. For our purpose here, we can consider two of them as being fairly typical: (a) Eduard Spranger's classification of "value types" of individuals and (b) Jurgen Ruesch's classification of the American value system.

Value types.   Spranger, a German scholar, developed a theory of human behavior in which he maintained that there are certain "types" of individuals—types that can be identified by the *dominant values* held by each. While recognizing that each individual certainly has more than one set of values which influence his or her behavior, Spranger argues that one value system will dominate the behavior engaged in and the choices to be made in any given case. The other values and value systems will become secondary or may even fail to operate at all. These are Spranger's six primary value types:*

1. *Theoretical type*—values the pursuit and discovery of "truth," the "intellectual" life.
2. *Economic type*—values that which is useful, practical, and has material worth.
3. *Aesthetic type*—values form, harmony, beauty.
4. *Social type*—values love, sympathy, spiritual warmth, and sensitivity in relationships with other people.
5. *Political type*—values competition, influence, the potential for exploitive "clout," and personal power.
6. *Religious type*—values unity, wholeness, a sense of universal force and purpose that transcends humankind.

These, Spranger claims, are the value systems that dominate our behaviors and our judgments. The system to which we adhere most strongly and frequently will determine the classification of our "value type." Economic-value type persons, for instance, will want to talk about money, financial manipulation, the country's economy, taxation, and related propositions. Political-value type individuals will usually want to talk about their influence with constituents, what's going on down at City Hall, and competing candidates; and they will enjoy the give-and-take of debating issues and campaigning.

The American value system.   Psychiatrist Jurgen Ruesch, in *Communication: The Social Matrix of Psychiatry*, advances a somewhat different classifi-

---

*From TYPES OF MEN by Eduard Spranger. Translated by Paul J. W. Pigas from the Fifth German Edition. Copyright 1928 by Max Niemeyer Verlag. Reprinted by permission of Max Niemeyer Verlag.

cation of values. He has found, he says, that American values, in particular, show these five emphases: (1) *puritan and pioneer morality,* (2) *equality,* (3) *sociality,* (4) *success,* and (5) *change.* As he states it:

> The American psychology has been described as being governed by the premises of equality, sociality, success, and change, which are thought to be interconnected by the multiple premises of puritan and pioneer morality. These four values, together with the core of moral principles, can be conceived, on the one hand, as pivotal points around which American life revolves, and, on the other, as cornerstones upon which communication is based.[15]

While it is obviously impossible to draw up a specific list of all of the possible value systems held by all persons in this country or elsewhere, these classifications by Spranger and by Ruesch should at least serve to clarify what we mean by a "value system." They should, moreover, suggest the potential power and influence such value systems exert upon human behavior, human relationships, and speech communicative interaction. Because such value systems are deeply ingrained in us from early childhood, they cannot simply be "turned on or off" at will. A strong value system, clearly, will pervade, will persist, and will almost certainly exert considerable influence upon the choices we make and the communicative behavior we use to make these choices known to others. When we engage in a communicative interaction of any kind and for any purpose, others will be quick to spot our values. Values are so central to our thinking, feeling, believing, and forming of attitudes that we can't speak for very long without revealing some of the values which predominate in our value structure. 5

Study Probe 5
Adapting to Value Systems of Others in a Job Interview

Suppose you are applying for a summer sales job in a downtown department store. To obtain the position you must engage in a personal interview with the store manager. Somehow, prior to the interview, you learn that the manager is what Spranger would describe as a "theoretical" value type of person. Plan your interview accordingly, writing a report of sufficient length to describe the approach you would use and the procedure you would follow. As a variation, you might select another member of the class as the store manager, with the two of you role playing the interview for the benefit and suggestions of other class members.

What would be some of the dominant beliefs and evaluations you would expect to find in a "theoretical" type of person? Suggest ways that—during the interview—you would try to adapt to these beliefs and evaluations. Suppose the store manager to be one of the other "types"—*economic, aesthetic, social, political, religious.* Prepare what you believe would be a workable approach and interview plan in that instance.

BELIEF-EVALUATION CLUSTERS:
A SYSTEM FOR ANALYZING SPEECH PROPOSITIONS

So far in this chapter, we have attempted to develop an understanding of some of the general and theoretical approaches to problem solving, as well as the influence on decisions of human motivation, attitude formation and change, and value systems. Building upon this foundation, let's attempt now to develop an understanding of how—in a more specific sense—decisions are made, particularly as this process relates to the process of speech communication. Our basic premise, as we laid it out initially on page 159, is that *BELIEFS (B's) and EVALUATIONS (E's) are central to the speech communication process and are, therefore, central to any decision making that we may do.*

Elements in a Belief-Evaluation Cluster and Their Relationships

As individuals, each of us holds—as we've said—a number of beliefs about and attaches a number of valuations to any category of idea, entity, or activity of which we are aware. The "object" of our belief and evaluation may be a person (our doctor), a place (Timbuctu), an action (snowmobiling), or a proposed action (let's go to the beach). It may be drawn from any time—past, present, or future; it may be real, supposed, or suspected.

For our illustration here let's select *a proposed action* and make some characteristic "belief" statements about it. Most of us probably hold a number of convictions—some positive, some negative—about the taking of birth-control pills. Some typical ones might be:

The Pill is the best scientific approach to keeping national population in check.

The Pill is less costly than having children.

The Pill can eventually solve the problem of urban overcrowding.

The Pill can help to reduce "dependency" taxation.

The Pill can jeopardize the health of those who take it.

The Pill violates the Christian Ethic.

The Pill violates human rights.

The Pill can endanger the capitalistic, producer-consumer system.

Each of us could, of course, attach varying degrees of *value* to each of these *beliefs.* And, faced with making a decision about a policy of birth control, we could place each one in a hierarchical framework: Some beliefs we might hold with complete conviction; others we would probably "believe" with less certainty; still others we would totally *disbelieve* and therefore exclude them from our hierarchy almost entirely. To those beliefs we hold with complete certainty, we might assign, say, a probability level of 1.0; to those about which we hold some doubts we could assign a level of .9; to another, .4; and so on down.

In each of these belief assertions the category of the proposed action, *taking birth-control pills,* is located within a larger category. For example: *The Pill* is an element in the category *Means for population control,* as well as in the category *Dangers to physical well-being,* and so on. When we locate the Pill (attitude-object) within a larger category of concepts (Population Control, Physical Well-Being, etc.), all of the feelings we have for the evaluations we make of the larger category become associated with the smaller category—in this case, the Pill as the attitude-object.

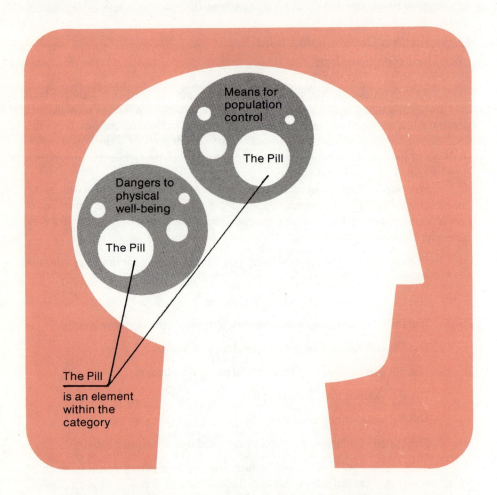

And, of course, the evaluations of (degree of personal feeling) we hold for the concept in the larger category could be rated somewhere within a range between 0 and 1, with 0 representing the lowest possible evaluation and 1 representing the highest possible evaluation. We may, for instance, feel very positive about Population Control (1), but believe that Urban Overcrowding is very undesirable (0). [6]

Belief-Evaluation Clusters in Decision Making

Clearly, any decision we make—or any problem we need to solve in order to make that decision—is going to involve an *aggregate* of all of the beliefs and evaluations we happen to hold in a cluster with reference to the central categorical concept, entity, or activity upon which a communicative interaction is to be focused. In any given case, while we may feel that we are "basing" our decision on a single belief-evaluation, actually we are *ordering our priorities* among *all* of the beliefs and evaluations (B-E's) operating within the total cluster. And in this ordering, our B-E's are conflicting, intersecting, and interacting to produce the decision.

If your listener dislikes "violation of human rights," his or her attitude toward the Pill will be determined in part by the level of belief that the Pill violates such rights, making this belief-level a negative factor in the B-E Cluster. If your listener does not believe that the Pill violates human rights, negative feelings about such violation will not matter. Going further, the individual's level of *belief* that the Pill is a sound, scientific approach to keeping population in check and the

Study Probe 6
Developing and Comparing Belief-Evaluation Clusters

Select one *person* (a parent, friend, or acquaintance) and one *policy decision* (government enforcement of antipollution controls, for example, or gun control, or your school's grading procedures as considered earlier in Study Probe 4, or any similar policy matter), and develop for each the full listing of your relevant Belief-Evaluation Cluster.

Begin by listing all your important beliefs. Then rate the strength of your beliefs on the following scale:

Weakest Possible Belief   *Strongest Possible Belief*

0.00   .10   .20   .30   .40   .50   .60   .70   .80   .90   1.00

Determine next the evaluative component for each of your belief statements and rate your feelings on the following scale:

Lowest Possible Evaluation   *Highest Possible Evaluation*

0.00   .10   .20   .30   .40   .50   .60   .70   .80   .90   1.00

Again—review your BEC for the number of beliefs listed, the range of belief ratings (how many low? medium? high?), as well as the range of evaluation ratings. Compare your BEC's with those of classmates (even on different concepts) and discuss in class some reasons for the similarities and differences which may become apparent.

evaluation of the need to hold down the number of the country's inhabitants will contribute to the total attitude or B-E Cluster. Similar assessments could be made for all of the other elements associated in the cluster. In sum, there is ample evidence that the total cluster of beliefs and evaluations we associate with an entity, object, or concept—combined with the ways in which these associations intersect and interact with one another—are basic to problem solving and decision making.

Assessing the Belief-Evaluation Clusters of others. In the beginning, this associating, clustering, and interaction of beliefs and values goes on inside our minds and assists us toward making our personal decisions. It is largely *intrapersonal.* But when and if we reach the point where we feel impelled to *communicate* these decisions to others and to influence others to "decide" as we have, we must give very serious consideration to what is likely to be going on inside the minds of those others.

Fortunately, there are some reasonably sound assumptions we can make—assumptions that will help us communicate our decisions and the desirability of those decisions to others and influence others to "decide" as we have. We can begin by recognizing that *every other person—*like us—has a unique Belief-Evaluation Cluster for any given attitude-object. This being the case, we can of course expect the elements comprising the cluster in any given instance to vary from individual listener to individual listener.

Typically, there will be some concepts for which a listener will hold many beliefs. For other concepts that same person will hold only a few, if any. Many of the elements in the B-E Cluster of Listener A, for instance, may more or less coincide with those of the speaker. This listener may associate many beliefs and levels of belief with the concept or proposed course of action advocated by the speaking agent; he may "believe" largely as the speaker does.

Listener B, in contrast, may have only a few beliefs about the central idea or proposal. As she approaches the communicative event, she is neither "convinced" nor "unconvinced" of the appropriateness of the advocated position or proposed action. She may be moderately "concerned," but no more than that.

Listener C may have scarcely any beliefs at all about the central concept or the proposed action or the problems therein. Conceivably, the cluster of Listener C's belief-evaluations may in no way resemble those of Listener A, Listener B, or the speaker. Seemingly, he is indifferent to the whole business, and soon may decide only that he doesn't "belong" in this context.

Listener D, on the other hand, is anything but neutral or indifferent. The individual elements in her B-E Cluster may be much the same as those in the speaker's cluster, but the *evaluations* she places upon them may be completely the reverse of those given priority by the speaker. Indeed, some—perhaps many—of Listener D's cluster elements may be such as to interact in a highly conflictive manner with the idea or action advocated by the speaker.

We could proceed in this fashion to describe many different types of listeners, but these four should be enough to suggest the nature and dimensions of your task when, as a communicative agent, you attempt to "analyze" your listeners and formulate procedures for communicatively inducing co-agents to interact positively and productively in the decision-making process. Obviously, in the circumstances we've described, as a communicative agent you must know *the other agent;* you must know *the context;* and you must know—to the greatest extent possible—what is likely to happen when the B-E Clusters of all agents are involved in a communicative interaction.

Interacting with others on the basis of B-E Clusters. Let's look at a few specifics of what *is* likely to happen. In the decision-inducing stage of the communication process particularly, the speaker needs to know as much as possible about how listeners are likely to *feel, react,* and *behave* when confronted with the need to solve a problem or decide on a possible solution. In Chapter 7 (pages 142–144), we discussed some characteristics of listeners which the speaking agent may assess in predicting their response to persuasive messages. Analysis of listeners' Belief-Evaluation Clusters can provide some additional means. In a broad sense, we can reasonably assume that:

1. The more listeners know about a particular, potential attitude-object— the greater their familiarity with it—the more *beliefs* they are likely to have about it.
2. The larger the listeners' experience with the focal attitude-object, the greater the range of their *evaluations* is likely to be.

Just what significance does this hold for you as a speaker? Principally, the analysis of Belief-Evaluation Clusters provides you with a useful system for analyzing multiple and complex propositions—the kind of system we've said that we need to solve problems and reach decisions. When you are speaking for the purpose of influencing others to make a choice or a decision you want them to make, *you must try to change the Belief-Evaluation Clusters of your listeners.* In problem solving or decision making—in fact, in any kind of persuasive interaction—you must in some meaningful way *add to, modify,* or *reorder* the belief/ value structure of the other agents involved.

How, specifically, can you hope to accomplish this? For one thing, you can *supply new information.* Quite possibly, by focusing on this new information you can provide the listener with some new values or new beliefs. These, in turn, may open up some possible paths leading toward favorable interpretation of the new information. As another option, you may try to lead your listeners to *make new evaluations of beliefs presently held.* One usually effective means of accomplishing this is to try to associate your subject or message or proposed action with other and perhaps larger categories that your listeners are known to value highly. You can, for example, tie your premise or proposal in with such larger and generally accepted categories as fairness, productivity, efficiency, thrift, good health, etc. Still another option is to reverse the foregoing procedure by trying to *associate possible objections or unfavorable conditions with categories your listeners are known to dislike, fear, or abhor.* You could, for example, tie your opponent's proposition or premise to high taxes, pollution of the environment, pollution of public morality, highway death tolls, etc. However, there is a strong *ethical* concern here. When you elect this option, you must make every effort to be truthful and objective in attempting to link the position of an antagonist to negative categories of this kind.

The Process Nature of Belief-Evaluation Clusters

The formation of our BEC's is, of course, a *process*. The clusters are in a process of *continuous change*. Belief-Evaluation Clusters not only vary from person to person, but they also change from moment to moment. The beliefs and evaluations which come to our mind at the mention of an idea or category make up our attitude toward that idea or category *at that particular instant.* But, even in a very short span of time, differences in B-E Clusters may develop because one belief or value becomes more important than another or moves to a more central or focal position in the cluster as a whole. As we learn more about a subject or category, or think about it, or talk about it, very likely we will be "infiltrating" our belief-value structures with new and/or different beliefs and values that we attach to those beliefs. We may also be modifying some of the existing ones or even dropping some of them entirely.

The *focal emphasis* we give to the various elements in our belief/value structure and in those of our hearers can be a powerful factor, too, in shaping and directing persuasive interaction. Suppose, by way of illustration, that you are a speaker who is presenting a proposition that you want your listeners to accept. You try to determine—in advance of the encounter if you can—those negative B-E Cluster elements to which your listeners are sensitive. Then you plan and organize your message or messages so that *during the interaction* you dwell on— point out, play up, and otherwise emphasize—these negative elements. In this way you try to make them overshadow and outweigh the positive belief/value elements which your listeners presumably hold but are not "focusing" upon at that particular time. If you succeed in this, you thus manage to shift the focus of the message and of the resultant interaction into an area of greater listener persuadability. Overall, the point we want to nail down here is that because Belief-Evaluation Clusters are always in process, always changing, and constantly shifting to more or less central positions within the structure, the way you handle them with respect to *timing* and *focal emphasis* assumes considerable importance.

ISSUE-ORIENTED INTERACTION: TWO CASE STUDIES

To better understand the nature and diversity of problem-solving and decision-making interaction and to illustrate some of the principles we've been talking about in this chapter, let's take a critical look at two controversies much in the news and in the public mind from time to time; namely:

1. Violence in America.
2. The education of our children.

What makes these topics "controversial," of course, is the fact that each of us holds with some stubbornness and tenacity such a wide-ranging assortment of attitudes, opinions, beliefs, and social-economic-spiritual values (often sprinkled, we may suspect, with only a smattering of genuine information). Inherent in these issues are some deeply perplexing problems. When analyzing and seeking solutions to such problems, reasonably intelligent and well-meaning people will see matters differently.

As we know, when people see implications and solutions differently, they tend to interact "persuasively": They advance arguments (persuasive messages) in support of their individual views. They try to induce listeners to accept the particular "conclusions" or "solutions" they propose. Sometimes, it may appear, there can be no workable solution to a problem nor any real decision on a controversy. Especially is this likely to be the case if we have little or no verifiable information and—to arrive at a decision or conclusion—we must depend heavily on mere conjecture. Not every controversy, you'll probably agree, is susceptible to "settlement."

As you read these two "case studies" or detailed illustrations, think about these things. They have been chosen to demonstrate the point that almost any significant decision must always involve "a systematic analysis of multiple and complex propositions." Above all, we believe they help support the notion that the Belief-Evaluation Cluster system is such a system—and a workable one.

Case Study A: Violence in America

Violence is no stranger to America—or, for that matter—to all humankind. It's been with us since our ancestors lived in caves and tried to fend off saber-toothed tigers with clubs. Ever since, it has run like an unbroken crimson thread through countless conflicts, personal and public, down through history. In recent years, television's preoccupation with and seeming preference for violence have kept it in the public eye. And its widespread recurrence on college campuses in the late 1960's moved it dramatically into the foreground of the public's attention.

Various investigative groups have from time to time attempted to analyze these inclinations to violence and come up with explanations of the causes underlying them. For example, there was the 1967 Report on the National Advisory Commission on Civil Disorders to which we alluded earlier. A somewhat similar study produced the Walker Report on violence occurring during the Democratic National Convention in Chicago in 1968.[16] In the aftermath of that violent series of confrontations, many psychologists, sociologists, educators, news "analysts," and political scientists attempted to answer the question WHY? A careful probing of that question was undertaken, for example, by the Institute for Social Research at the University of Michigan. This study on the attitudes of American males toward violence pertains to the principles of this chapter because it reveals something of the many interrelated beliefs, evaluations, and values which combine in making up those attitudes. You can see some of this pertinence in these concluding statements from the Institute's report:*

1. *. . . violence is widely regarded as instrumental by American men.* (page 243)

2. *. . . almost 50 percent of American men felt that shooting was a good way of handling campus disturbances . . . .* (page 243)

3. *That 20 percent of American men considered it appropriate for the police to kill in these circumstances indicates the ease with which many people will accept violence to maintain order even when force so used is entirely out of proportion to the precipitating incidents.* (page 243)

4. *. . . attitudes toward the use of violence for social control are greatly influenced by the individual's values, particularly his beliefs in retributiveness and self-defense.* (page 243–244)

5. *We believe the facts to be more complex, and to include both affective and instrumental considerations.* (page 244)

6. *More than 90 percent of American men agreed that changes of the kind demanded by students and blacks might be needed.* (page 245)

7. *Among American men as a whole, there is equal agreement that the needed social changes can come about fast enough without the use of violence.* (page 245)

8. *. . . a lack of faith in alternative means of control or change. This doubt is expressed most clearly by black men, half of whom believe change will not come about without some violence . . . .* (page 246)

9. *. . . a fundamental fact of social life—the tendency of any social system to resist change.* (page 246–247)

10. *It seems clear that violence feeds on violence; a violent act tends to evoke a violent response.* (page 247)

11. *The fact that so many Americans define acts of dissent as "violence" in and of themselves speaks to the disrespect and antipathy American men have developed toward the process of change and toward its advocates.* (page 248)

---

*From JUSTIFYING VIOLENCE: ATTITUDES OF AMERICAN MEN by Monica D. Blumenthal et al. Copyright © February 1972, The University of Michigan. Reprinted by permission of the Institute for Social Research of The University of Michigan.

12. . . . *many are convinced that protest is violence* in and of itself. *Moreover, this is not merely a semantic issue. When an action is labeled "violence," the level of police force recommended to control that activity escalates.* (page 249)

13. . . . *relationship between values and attitudes . . . . Retributiveness and the right to self-defense at the expense of another's life account for a substantial part of the variation in attitudes toward violence.* (page 249)

14. *Among men with at least some college education, there is a great deal more consistency among beliefs than there is for Americans in general.* (page 251)

This study on attitudes toward violence suggests that it is an almost universal wish that our domestic affairs should be handled with a minimal use of force. Yet the men sampled did have beliefs supporting the use of violence for social control (Items 1, 2, 3) if certain other beliefs, evaluations, and values were present (4, 9, 13). Many of the persons sampled tended to agree with the proposed social changes (6), but objected to the means to those ends (7). Some believe no other effective means exist (8). This study also demonstrates the significance of language labels. When any act is *defined* as "violence," it takes on all the beliefs and evaluations associated with the category of "acts of violence" (10, 11, 12).

Even the brief excerpts we've cited clearly indicate that before any decision could be reached as to the "Why?" of violence or any other pressing social problem, we'd have to analyze a great many ideas, arguments, and propositions rather than merely one. The short excerpts also serve, we believe, to illustrate and show the workability of the Belief-Evaluation Cluster system. This view is clearly reflected and strongly reinforced by this concluding statement from the Institute's summary:

Social reality is more complex and less consistent, full of simultaneous beliefs in kindness and revenge, professed willingness for social change and distrust for those who advocate it, condemnation of violence and endorsement of violence by police. Such reality is difficult to accept, but its acceptance is necessary. It is necessary and difficult also to give up visions of certainty and instead to think in terms of uncertain and alternative futures, determined by our acts or failures to act.[17]

Case Study B: The Education of Our Children

Education is, if anything, an even bigger and more comprehensive issue (some prefer to call it a "problem") than what to do about violence. In fact, if you follow your daily newspapers and newscasts, you might want to conclude that "violence" is but a *subcategory* within "education." Certainly the education-of-children category is a huge one—so huge that for our purpose here we must limit it to a single small facet or issue-aspect: *Should the philosophy and the environment under which we educate our children be "free," "open," and highly "permissive"?*

As you might expect, even well-informed and well-qualified authorities hold widely divergent views and conflicting opinions on this touchy question. To suggest just *how* divergent and conflicting, we've chosen for this case study a single book, A. S. Neill's controversial *Summerhill,* and quoted statements not from it but *about* it. The statements which follow were expressed by both supporters and critics of Neill's educational views.* As you read them, note in particular that often these "comment-makers" not only are at odds with each other, but they also appear at times to disagree with the very beliefs, values, and attitudes which they hold *within themselves.* You'll have little difficulty, we believe, in seeing their Belief-Evaluation Cluster systems at work in these comments:

—by Ashley Montagu:

Neill holds that no child should be compelled to do anything unless he wants to. This may seem extremely overpermissive to some. Perhaps it is. But what Neill means is that no child should feel compelled, but rather should feel that he wants *to do what is required, that he is acting from internal compulsion. And that is what a good teacher can, in fact, accomplish. Nevertheless, I do think that Neill underemphasizes the importance of learning some things.* (page 53)

Very simply, before anyone can undertake the education of anyone else, be it infant or child or adolescent or adult, he must first be an educated person himself—that is, he must understand the nature of human nature, and he must understand what, at his particular stage of development, the individual in need requires. There are some persons who seem to possess this knowledge almost intuitively. A. S. Neill is undoubtedly one of those persons. (page 58)

—by Louise Bates Ames:

Summerhill is an infuriating book. It infuriated me when I first read it, and it infuriates me today. This is largely because A. S. Neill seems so dreadfully opinionated. Everything for him is black or white. It is also infuriating that though admittedly he has a warm strong feeling of sympathy and even of super-identification with children—especially with bad, rebellious, nonconforming children—he seems to know so little about child behavior. (page 65)

I respect his sincerity—there's nothing phony about him. I respect the consistency of his approach—children should in his opinion have virtually total freedom, and he is prepared to give it to them. I respect his obvious love for children; he really cares what happens to them. I respect the

---

*From SUMMERHILL: FOR AND AGAINST, copyright 1970 Hart Publishing Company, Inc.

fact that he wants to see every child permitted to learn in a manner and in a setting which suits him. I respect the fact that he wants learning to be fun—not a stultifying bore—and be a challenge to the child and not an exercise in memorization. (pages 65–66)

—by Fred M. Hechinger:
Summerhill is not a school but a religion. That is why one can be intrigued by it—can even admire it—without being converted to it. (page 35)

But even if it were not a religion and Neill its prophet and patron saint, Summerhill would not be a school. It is really a family—an ideal family, to be sure, without overly possessive attachments—with an option to learn, but no compulsion to do so. (page 36)

I recommend Summerhill to parents and teachers—but not without misgivings. It is a religion based on love for, and understanding of, children; but it carries with it a religious mysticism that should not be accepted without critical analysis.

There is, in Neill himself, a strange streak of anti-intellectualism, almost a frantic rejection of all academic value judgments. Whatever the child likes, whatever makes him happy, is equal to any other enterprise. Bach equals Elvis Presley.

Neill can get upset about a ruined chisel but refuses to fuss about a book carelessly left in the rain "for books have little value for me." (pages 39–40)

—by John Holt:
Many people will start arguing here about what they call "Permissiveness." The argument is silly and useless. So is the word itself. Like so many pejorative words—"growl words" as a friend of mine calls them—"permissiveness" sticks a two-valued label on a complicated, multi-valued, even multi-dimensioned reality. (page 86)

—by Bruno Bettelheim:
Now why was it particularly easy for Neill's work to be so grossly distorted? I believe because Neill the person and the educator is so much greater a man, so much more deeply human, so much more outstanding a molder of youth, than he is a philosopher or student of psychoanalysis, or a theoretical psychologist. Though all his actions show how deeply attuned he is to the psyche of children, he is often at a loss to explain himself. (page 100)

From these two case studies it should be apparent that, although *specific issues* may change, the *basic social problems* are always with us. We may solve—or think we are solving—an important problem at any given time, but we can be pretty sure we're not solving it for *all* time. The management of violence will always be a problem. The best way to educate our children must change from generation to generation. We can make decisions and act upon them only *in* our time and *for* our time. This realization should create in us more interest in what has transpired in the past, more concern for how our actions today may challenge or frustrate the decision makers of tomorrow, and a greater sensitivity and eagerness regarding our analytical and communicative capabilities to deal with significant social problems now confronting us. [7]

Suggested Readings

Since in this chapter we have proposed some approaches to decision making and have tried to develop some useful analytical procedures, the readings which would probably be of most interest and value are those which offer detailed analyses of problems characterizing contemporary society. The following source may be considered as typical and useful:

Confrontation: Psychology and the Problems of Today, gen. ed., Michael Wertheimer (Glenview, Ill.: Scott, Foresman and Company, 1970). This work presents materials under the following headings, all of which suggest "multiple and complex propositions" for communicatively induced decision making:

1. Identity and Identity Crisis.
2. Conformity, Compliance, and Integrity.
3. Racism and Race Relations.
4. Violence and Aggression.
5. Conflict and Conflict Resolution.
6. Human Control over Human Behavior.
7. Man and Technology.
8. Education, Creativity, and the Student.

Study Probe 7

Assessing Belief-Evaluation Clusters of Others

From the brief excerpts included on pages 182–183, list some of the elements in the Belief-Evaluation Clusters of quoted critics as reflected in their comments about *Summerhill.* If possible, obtain a copy of the book from which these quotations are taken so that you can see and work with the full presentation of each. Some of these critics appear to be generally "for" the educational philosophy of *Summerhill,* and others are "against" it. Contrast the BEC's of persons with opposing points of view. Do they tend to hold differing evaluations about similar belief statements? Bring your written assessments of these matters to class, circulate them, and—afterward—hold a general, informal group discussion in which an attempt is made to form a few meaningful conclusions about the usefulness of the Belief-Evaluation Cluster system.

Also recommended for reading in connection with this chapter are such documents as the *Report of the U.S. National Advisory Commission on Civil Disorders* (Washington, D.C.: U.S. Government Printing Office, March 1, 1968).

Reference Notes

[1]*Report of the U.S. National Advisory Commission on Civil Disorders* (Washington, D.C.: U.S. Government Printing Office, March 1, 1968).

[2]*Report of the Warren Commission on the Assassination of President Kennedy* (New York: The New York Times Company, 1964 Bantam Book edition).

[3]Donella Meadows et al., *The Limits to Growth* (New York: Universe Books, 1972).

[4]Graham Wallas, *The Art of Thought* (New York: Harcourt Brace Jovanovich, Inc., 1926).

[5]John Dewey, *How We Think* (Lexington, Mass.: D. C. Heath Company, 1910).

[6]Sir Arthur Conan Doyle, *The Adventures of Sherlock Holmes* (New York: Popular Library, 1960), pp. 98–99.

[7]See, for example, Bernard Berelson and Gary A. Steiner, *Human Behavior: An Inventory of Scientific Findings* (New York: Harcourt Brace Jovanovich, Inc., 1964), Chapter 5, "Learning and Thinking," pp. 133–237.

[8]Jerome S. Bruner, Jacqueline J. Goodnow, and George A. Austin, *A Study in Thinking* (New York: John Wiley & Sons, Inc., 1956), especially Chapters 4–8.

[9]A. H. Maslow, *Motivation and Personality* (New York: Harper & Row, Publishers, 1954), especially Chapter 5, "A Theory of Human Motivation."

[10]Gordon W. Allport, "The Functional Autonomy of Motives," *American Journal of Psychology,* 50 (1937): 141–156.

[11]See the review in Roger Brown, *Social Psychology* (New York: The Free Press, 1965), Chapter 11.

[12]See Charles E. Osgood, George J. Suci, and Percy H. Tannenbaum, *The Measurement of Meaning* (Urbana, Ill.: University of Illinois Press, 1957), Chapter 5.

[13]David Krech, Richard S. Crutchfield, and Egerton L. Ballachey, *Individual in Society* (New York: McGraw-Hill Book Company, 1962), Chapters 5, 6, and 7.

[14]Leon Festinger, "Behavioral Support for Opinion Change," *Public Opinion Quarterly* 28 (1964): 404–417.

[15]Jurgen Ruesch and Gregory Bateson, *Communication: The Social Matrix of Psychiatry* (New York: W. W. Norton & Company, Inc., 1951), p. 95.

[16]Daniel Walker et al., *Rights in Conflict* (New York: Signet Books, 1968).

[17]Monica Blumenthal et al., *Justifying Violence: Attitudes of American Men* (Ann Arbor: University of Michigan Press, 1972), p. 255.

Chapter 9

THE EFFECTS
OF COMMUNICATIVE
INTERACTION

Information gain, attitude formation, and
attitude change are the basic effects we strive for
when we communicate with others. We may extend
these effects by using *second-level communicators.*
Overall, to achieve a desired effect, we
must be able to alter in some way the *behavior*
and *thought* patterns of our listeners.

In Chapter 2 we pointed out the many reasons why we speak. Now, in a similar manner, we can consider the many *effects* which can follow from communicative interaction. "Why," you might ask, "do we use 'effects' in the *plural* sense? Why not simply 'effect'?" After all, you could argue, a speech event either has an effect or it has not. If you are a speaker seeking contributions to a United Fund, your listeners either contribute or they do not. If you present information about modern art, your listeners either learn or they do not. Purpose and response (effect) either "match" or they don't. But this view, looking as it does from the speaker's specific purpose to the listener's immediate response, is far from complete. If we're to have a comprehensive view of what speech communication can do, we will need to consider several kinds of consequences and possible outcomes *beyond* the effects usually noted.

We are using the term *effects* in this chapter in a rather broad and—at the same time—quite specialized way. Throughout, we will be trying to answer the questions: What is it that we, as speakers, do that *creates* certain "effects"? And, looking at the other side of the coin, what is it that is done to us as listeners that causes us to *experience* certain "effects"? *What "effects" are most frequently and typically brought about by speech communication?* In capsule form, here is a preview of our answers:

1. We learn new information.
2. We experience attitude change through modification of our existing Belief-Evaluation Clusters.
3. We develop "second-level" communicators to extend the range and influence of our messages.
4. We transfer effects to related categories or topics.
5. We influence behavior patterns and thought patterns in others and in ourselves.

Certain of these effects, we might say, are "basic" in that they involve *a direct speaker-to-listener relationship.* Certain others are "extensional" in that they involve third-party or outside *disciples* or *intermediaries* in their accomplishment. And still others involve a "transferral" process. Overall and in the final analysis, of course, all of these "direct" and "less direct" effects work in ways that are often subtle but always powerful to influence *the patterns of our thinking and behaving*—whether as speakers or listeners. This is why we emphasize the "pluralism" of speech communication and the cumulative nature of the processes by which we arrive at those effects.

BASIC EFFECTS OF SPEECH COMMUNICATION

The most readily apparent effects of communicative interaction, it's true, can often be seen by comparing listener responses with the explicit, specific purpose of the speaker. Thus, if your intention as a speaker is to cause your listeners *to act or behave* or *to think* in a certain way, and if the listeners appear to act or behave or to think in that certain way, you have achieved your purpose. You have *created* the desired effect. At the same time, your listeners will have *experienced* certain "basic" effects: (1) *they will have gained new information* and (2) quite possibly *they will have formed new attitudes or changed existent ones through a modification of their Belief-Evaluation Clusters.*

Information Gain

Speech communication will result, quite likely, in the gain of some new information by those who listen. This new information may be unrelated to anything the listener now knows, and may open up a whole new category of meaning. More frequently, however, such information may be taken in by a listener and integrated into *existing* categories of meaning, into *existing* patterns of beliefs and evaluations. That is to say, most of the new information presented by a speaker *adds to what we, as listeners, already know.* It adds to and fills in our presently held categories. In sum, a major effect of speech communication is the addition of new information which we as listeners can integrate into our understanding and with which we can increase and enrich our categories of meaning.

Attitude Formation and Attitude Change

A second and related major effect of speech communication is that as listeners we are influenced to modify and restructure our existing attitudes and views. We are "persuaded" to adjust or realign our Belief-Evaluation Clusters—the system we talked about in Chapter 8 (pages 173–178). As we listen to what the speaker is saying, we may experience changes in certain of our beliefs and move them in the directions advocated by that speaker. A speaker may, for instance, argue for a charitable cause, and our belief level in the value of that cause may increase. Such an increase may, in turn, prompt us to make a financial contribution or sign a pledge card. A speech against birth-control pills may lower our belief level in the safety of that form of birth control and may, therefore, alter our willingness to accept or advocate its use. Because beliefs and evaluations play such significant roles in the effects which speakers create in us as listeners, we might benefit by taking a close second look at the notion of Belief-Evaluation Clusters and how this "clustering" system causes us to experience attitude formation and attitude change. The repetition, we should add, is intentional because this system is so important that we'd like you to be thoroughly familiar with it.

Beliefs and evaluations.   Being human, each of us will have a number of beliefs and evaluations about any entity, activity, or concept of which we are aware. We give these beliefs and values a kind of priority in our thinking, and we make a judgment on that basis. Let's take "San Francisco" as an attitude-object. Any one of us can hold many beliefs about San Francisco. For example:

San Francisco is a city in California.

San Francisco is a large urban complex.

San Francisco has scenic hills and water areas.

San Francisco has available numerous cultural activities.

San Francisco has a moderate climate.

San Francisco has traffic-congestion problems.

San Francisco has air-pollution problems.

Obviously, we could have *varying degrees of belief* in these "attitude statements." Some statements we might hold with absolute certainty, whereas others we could "believe" with less certainty. Still others we might utterly *disbelieve*. Statisticians describe probability as varying between 0 and 1, with 0 meaning no probability of occurrence, and 1 indicating certainty. We could use this scale and say that one belief statement is held with a probability level of 1, another with a level of .50, still another with .10, and so on. In each of the statements listed, the attitude-object or category *San Francisco* is located within a *larger* category: *San Francisco* is an element in the category *Cities in California,* as well as in the category *Cities with moderate climates,* and so on.

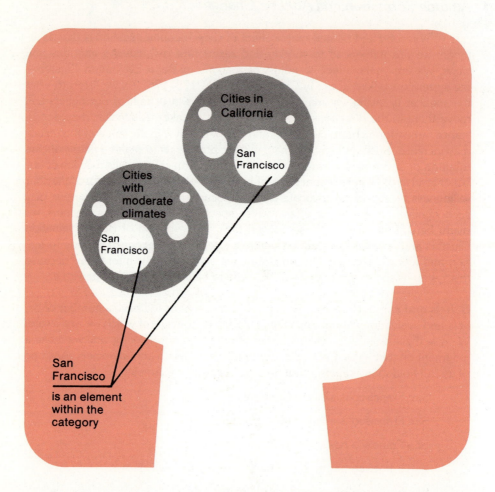

When we locate an attitude-object within a larger category of objects, all of the evaluations and beliefs we attach to that larger category usually become associated with the smaller specific attitude-object. Again, these evaluations could—like the beliefs—be held with varying degrees of tenacity or conviction. We may value highly "cities with moderate climates" (.90), but evaluate "cities with air pollution" very low (.00).

Relationship of B-E Clusters and attitude change. Basically, it's the numbers and kinds of beliefs and evaluations, the way we *combine* them, and the priorities and "rankings" that we give them in our thinking that cause us to cling to an attitude, or to modify it, or to reject it. If, for instance, you dislike "air pollution" (evaluate it negatively), your attitude toward San Francisco will be determined in part by the level of your belief that San Francisco has polluted air, and this combination of evaluation and belief will be a negative factor in your B-E Cluster. If you don't believe that San Francisco has polluted air, your negative evaluation of polluted air won't matter. Similarly, your level of belief that San Francisco is a "large urban complex" and your evaluation of large urban complexes will contribute to your total attitude or B-E Cluster. And so on with all of the other beliefs and evaluations in your "San Francisco" cluster.

Every individual will, of course, have a unique B-E Cluster for any given attitude-object. My BEC's will never be identical with yours. Moreover, we will associate *many* beliefs and values for some of the ideas and concepts we hold; for others we will associate only a *few*. Quite likely, as we learn more about a subject or have more experience with it, we will have more beliefs concerning it and more evaluative reactions toward it. As we hear more about an idea, an entity, a process, or an object—or think about it or talk about it—we will be adding more beliefs and evaluations to the cluster we are forming for it. Almost inevitably *the B-E Cluster that we hold for any given attitude-object must change from time to time.* Even in a short span of time, we will experience different reactions and formulate different judgments and attitudes as certain of our beliefs and/or evaluations become more prominent in our thinking or come into sharper focus. In other words, at any given moment, the beliefs and evaluations which, consciously or unconsciously, come to mind at the mention of an object, concept, or category will comprise our *attitude* toward it *at that moment.*

Using B-E Clusters to effect attitude change.   When we use Belief-Evaluation Clusters in an influential context of this kind we are engaged essentially in a process of *addition* and/or *modification*. As speaking agents we try, first of all, to induce listening agents to *focus* upon certain of the values and beliefs they hold in a particular cluster. Then we try to add *new* information—potential new beliefs and new values—to that cluster. Or we may try to modify the cluster in some way—change the strength and intensity with which certain elements are held. If, as speakers, our focusing effort is accurate and sharp enough, and if our addition and/or reduction are proportionately "right," our listeners may be willing to alter the makeup of the cluster or shift the priorities they've heretofore given certain aspects of it. When and if this happens, we may say that we have influenced these listeners to "change their minds." They have experienced *the effect of attitude change.*

As the speaking agent you have a number of alternative means of creating this effect: (1) you may attempt, as we've said, to *add new belief-propositions to the existing belief systems of your hearers;* (2) you may try to *associate the subject or topic of your message with key categories which you know your listeners value highly, or with categories they dislike;* (3) you may attempt to *change listeners' existing belief levels;* or (4) you may try to *change listeners' existing evaluation levels.* In short, any oral communication directed at influencing other people to accept your idea, viewpoint, or proposition must strive to achieve their acceptance by developing and/or modifying their Belief-Evaluation Cluster systems. [1]

EXTENSIONAL EFFECTS VIA SECOND-LEVEL COMMUNICATORS

In addition to the basic effects we've thus far considered, speech communication almost always produces a good many less immediate and less direct—but nonetheless significant—outcomes and consequences. Often these serve to *extend* one or more of the basic effects or may even go *beyond* them. This is why we refer to them as "extensional" in nature. If you think about these extensional effects for a moment, you'll see that they represent some useful and challenging possibilities for facilitating and improving speech interaction. To achieve them, you'll need to enlist the assistance of some "disciples" or "intermediaries." You'll need to *develop second-level communicators*.

Potentially, any speech-communication setting offers opportunities for the speaker to create second-level communicators. An illustration will help further to define our use of this term. Research on the spread of information originating in the mass media has singled out a group of people who have been labeled *opinion leaders*—a matter to which we'll be devoting more attention in Chapter 15. Frequent and regular users of the mass media—television, radio, magazines, and newspapers—as information sources, these leaders make up a small but concerned group. They take from their sources information about government, current events, the economy, fashions, and advertised products, and proceed to pass

Study Probe 1
Analyzing Your Beliefs

Select an issue or "article of faith" concerning which you hold a quite firm attitude. Samples:

1. *Women should in all respects—sexually, socially, educationally, economically, and occupationally—be the equal of men.*

2. *The death penalty should be abolished.*

Now make a list of the *specific beliefs* which have influenced you to adopt, hold, and defend the attitude which you selected. Rate those beliefs, giving to each a number ranging from .00 (weakest) to 1.00 (strongest) in order to reflect the strength with which you hold them.

Try to formulate a line of persuasion or argument which a speaker might present to move you to reorder the values you've attached to these particular beliefs.

that information along to a larger group of acquaintances. Their acquaintances thus become "second-level *recipients*" who, in turn, pass the information along to others and thereby become "second-level communicators." The majority of these second-level communicators—those who have been surveyed on this matter— seemed to get more of their views from the opinion leaders than from the mass media directly.

In writing about this phenomenon, Elihu Katz describes the process as the "Two-Step Flow of Communication" and makes the point that in many groups these opinion-shapers serve as *intermediaries* between the communicated messages and the other members of the group.[1] The concept of intermediaries as second-level communicators is suggested visually in this simple diagram:

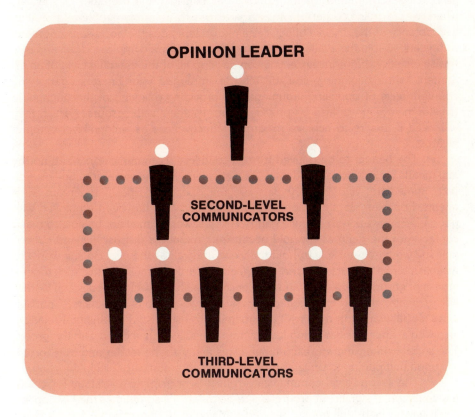

OPINION LEADER

SECOND-LEVEL COMMUNICATORS

THIRD-LEVEL COMMUNICATORS

At one time or another most of us have probably served as second-level communicators. On some occasions, no doubt, we've been "disciples" of an economic or political or educational or religious leader or creed and have "spread the word" to others. On other occasions, very likely we've found ourselves on the communicative firing line between two close friends or relatives and have had to serve as a go-between or intermediary, carrying messages from one to the other to effect a settlement. In the former instances, we may have succeeded in creating a *disciple effect;* in the latter, we were endeavoring to create an *intermediary effect.*

Disciples

Second-level communicators ordinarily can be expected, as we've suggested, to "spread the word" of the initial speaker's viewpoint or proposition to still a *larger* audience. This serves, of course, to extend and reinforce the impact of the message communicated by the initial or "first-level" speaker. And so on down the line to subsequent "levels." In fact, in every speech situation there is the distinct possibility that one or more of our listeners may become a disciple or second-level communicator for us. This has considerable usefulness, especially when we are trying to get our message across to as many people as possible. The potency of the disciple effect, certainly, underscores the good sense of trying to present—within the available time—messages that are complete, clear, and otherwise effective. If, for instance, you can develop all of the essential lines of an argument in the beginning, you will tend to immunize your hearers against the countereffects of opposing arguments. By providing this kind of thoroughgoing development you will also be providing your listeners with resources which they will need if they're to achieve maximum effectiveness as second-level communicators.

The benefit to be derived from second-level communicators need not by any means be indirect or incidental. As a speaker, you may want to plan—as a direct, immediate, and primary part of your specific purpose—to *create* such agents. For example, this approach to communication has been employed with good effect in work with juvenile gangs. A social worker may not be able to make contact with the gang as a whole because its members distrust her and believe that she would be unlikely to hold the views and values they do. So she works to establish direct contact with the *gang leader.* Partly because of the stick-togetherness of groups of this kind and also because a sharp, well-trained social worker will recognize the probable effectiveness of "two persons conversing," an outsider (social worker in this case) can manage to establish a meaningful relationship with a single insider (gang leader) more readily than she can with the group. The social worker, therefore, communicates first with the leader and tries to prevail upon that person to serve as a second-level communicator within the gang.

The second-level communicator effect is not simply a strategy for cheap manipulation. If significant progress is to be made, it's sometimes the best option you'll have. Elijah Muhammad needed a Malcolm X as a recruiter for his Black Muslim movement. Most organizations, in fact, need at least a few especially able adherents or converts to serve as second-level communicators. When you're planning for a communicative interaction, always take time to ask yourself: Whom do I wish my message to reach finally? Who else in the group has the ear of this or that particular listener? Shall my plan be to make a direct, frontal, verbal effort myself? Or will my purpose be better served if I can develop some second-level communicators to carry my message?

Intermediaries

None of us can escape the urgent and frequent need to *communicate across gaps.* And that's what the second-level communicator effect is all about, really. Take the gap between youth and old age. If we work hard at it, we may be able to narrow this gap a little. But the odds are high that we'll never eliminate it. A generation gap, obviously, isn't simply a difference in years. Aristotle (whom you may remember from Chapter 4) put the finger on a good many *psychological differences,* any one of which can create a serious "breakdown" in youth/old age communication. Thomas Hardy, another writer, pictures the dilemma of a person caught in mid-air over the chasm between being "not *young* enough" and "not *old* enough" in this brief passage from *Far from the Madding Crowd:*

> He had just reached the time of life at which "young" is ceasing to be the prefix of "man" in speaking of one. He was at the brightest period of masculine growth, for his intellect and his emotions were clearly separated: he had passed the time during which the influence of youth indiscriminately mingles them in the character of impulse, and he had not yet arrived at the stage wherein they become united again, in the character of prejudice, by influence of a wife and family. In short, he was twenty-eight, and a bachelor.[2]

No doubt Hardy's hero, like many of the rest of us, pondered the problem of how to close the gap between youth impulse and the prejudice of advancing age. And he may have concluded, as we have, that the span isn't likely to be bridged. So the next best thing is to think up ways of communicating *across* it. And that's where second-level communicators can come to the rescue. In crucial situations, they may at least succeed in contributing a sense of empathy and openness. 2

Study Probe 2
Narrowing a Gap in Speech Communication

Using our concept of speech communication as "agents interacting within a context" and our paradigm of two persons conversing, formulate your view of the so-called generation gap. If you see this gap as a communication problem—a breakdown of some kind—try to determine at what point in the process or the relationship the breakdown seems to occur. What obstacles, if any, seem to you to impede or prevent productive oral exchange between your generation and, for example, that of your parents or your teachers?

Prepare a brief statement of four or five specific speech behaviors which, if you were to employ them, might enable you or at least help you narrow or close the generation gap if one does exist.

In addition to—or perhaps instead of—possible breakdowns in speech communication, what other factors do you discern as contributing to the generational barrier?

In addition to helping us narrow a communication gap of some kind, intermediaries often are helpful in pleading our case or putting in a good word for us. In such cases, what we would like to do hinges upon someone else's decision or approval. [3]

There are other times, when, instead of serving as advocates, intermediaries serve as neutral agents for the principals in a potentially disruptive situation. There are numerous conditions under which productive speech interaction can be achieved more quickly and successfully through the intermediation of these so-called neutral speaking/listening agents than through face-to-face confrontation of Agents A and B. You can see this easily, for instance, in the arbitration of labor-management disputes. Points of difference between the principals may loom so large and divisive that when these agents face each other, even their mutual desire for a solution to the problem won't make it happen. Often, two people reaching such an impasse will resort to verbal attacks—even physical assaults—upon each other. When blown up proportionately, this is the kind of communication breakdown that can result in riots and mass violence. In both situations, the verbal and physical action may give the participants some emotional release, but that's about all. Their confrontation at this level isn't going to accomplish much that's constructive and enduring.

Here, as in similar situations where sharp differences and overpowering emotions are likely to develop, the "intermediate" communicators representing the principal parties to the disagreement should come together under the conditions of "two persons conversing." If the intermediaries are truly neutral and willing to work at it, they will be much more likely to come up with a workable solution and one that's acceptable all around. A word of caution, however, is in order. If tension is high, the *number* of intermediaries—of whatever level—should be kept to a minimum. Too many "cooks" may spoil the contextual broth. So, to sum it all up, when you find yourself in a situation where the chances of commu-

Study Probe 3
Using an Intermediary to Gain Approval

Recall an important decision that you have been faced with in your lifetime—one which hinged to a major extent upon the approval or concurrence of someone else, possibly a parent, a wealthy acquaintance, an influential dean, or some similar authority figure. Ideally, this decision should have involved contexts in which you asked (or should have asked) an intermediary to intercede or negotiate for you.

Report the outcome, in writing and/or orally in class, indicating whether you succeeded or failed in obtaining the approval, concurrence, or permission you desired in order to make the decision you *wanted* to make.

If you did not involve a second-level communicator, speculate as to whether and in what possible ways the decision might have "gone" differently if you had done so.

nication conflict are high, think seriously of the possibilities of *indirect* interaction through an intermediary. The effect that can be created in this way may well turn out to be surprisingly positive. The effort, at least, may create good will.

TRANSFERRAL EFFECTS OF SPEECH COMMUNICATION

Effect-transferral by listeners is another common consequence of speech communication, an effect often not anticipated and planned for by speakers. The fact that you categorize a topic or a concept or a belief in a certain way doesn't mean that your listener will categorize it in the same way. Your listener may see it differently or may spot possibilities and make associations that you never thought of. The grass that "grows" hair on a horse "grows" wool on a sheep. A pill that relieves a headache may also ease a backache. We need to remind ourselves, moreover, that *a concept that fits into one category may also fit very well into others.* The point is that you can never be sure that your listeners will think about a topic or a concept in exactly the same way *you're* thinking about it. Suppose you transmit a message designed to convince your hearers that *oysters* have a very high protein content—you want them to change their belief in or evaluation of oysters. Inevitably, whether you wish it or not, what you transmit will cause your listeners to think about and, possibly, re-evaluate things *other* than "high protein content." Your message may, for instance, influence them to evaluate other sea foods in addition to oysters; it may make them speculate about their ability to down raw oysters; it may cause them to wonder about the months in which oysters may safely be eaten; it may even prompt them to yearn for a string of pearls cultured in oysters. Even though they may be convinced, as a result of your message, that oysters do indeed have an unusually high protein content, at the same time they will be transferring some of that influence to other concepts in the oyster category. When a listener's beliefs and values for a given concept or topic rub off on another concept or topic, that listener is *transferring an effect.* Sometimes the person experiencing the effect may be aware of the transfer; often he or she may not be.

Transfer effects often are not immediately visible, nor are they easily predictable. At the time of the communicative exchange, such effects may be submerged and extremely difficult to detect, only to surface later in the form of a noticeably *different* consequence. Some research in which I engaged showed that a speech arguing against federal aid to health and education had significant transfer effects to such related but unmentioned topics as federal aid to farms and federal public-works programs.[3] Obviously, the mention of some categories or topics will generate a great deal more "transfer" than others. Although there is no sure way to prevent *unwanted* transfer effects, you can—by constantly "sharpening" your categories and carefully defining their boundaries—exercise a measure of control over them. Frequently—in the preparation of public messages particularly—you will hear the advice: *Narrow your subject.* The unpredictability of transfer effects is one of the important reasons for this.

EFFECTS OF SPEECH COMMUNICATION
UPON THE SPEAKER

In the give-and-take of the speech communication process, we've been saying all along, both speaker and listener are to be viewed as communicative agents, each interacting with the other, each exerting influence upon the other. The essence of speech interaction is the *mutual adaptation and change* toward the position and understanding of the other. When we are the *speaking* agents, this mutual adaptation and change should in reasonable measure produce these effects: (1) *self-actualization,* (2) *information exchange and information gain,* and (3) meaningful *influence upon the other agent.* These, working together, should produce the all-encompassing effect which we have described as (4) *control of the environment.* Broadly speaking, since the self is both speaker and listener, these four effects may be said to be mutually experienced.

Up to this point, we've been looking upon effects as what "happens" to listening agent. Now let's turn our perspective around and look at a few of the effects which listeners can be said to create in *speakers.* These, mainly, occur during interaction, or as a result of it, and are produced by speaker response to listener feedback, an aspect of interaction which we explored quite fully in Chapter 7.

One of the most important effects created in speakers occurs when—as a result of adjustment to listener feedback—the speaker is influenced to modify his or her ideas, position, or proposition. If listeners continue to reward or otherwise reinforce this modification by *more* feedback, they may succeed eventually in materially altering the speaker's Belief-Evaluation Cluster system. Following an interaction of this lively nature, as a speaker you may be influenced by it to see certain aspects of your subject differently, perhaps as more salient or less salient than before. During the interaction, your listeners have been "conditioning" you to see more positively the materials to which *they* have responded more positively. Or, by their feedback, they may have been prompting you to rethink some of the points in your message which they've doubted or to which they haven't responded as you'd anticipated. The greater the number of listeners providing feedback and the more knowledgeable and respected their views, the greater probably will be the power of this *modification effect* upon the speaker.

If, as the speaking agent, you are aware of the workings of this effect (and you ought always to *try* to be), you can turn it to your advantage in subsequent or related interactions. Suppose, for example, that you're planning a succession of messages—a *campaign* consisting of interviews, small group discussions, and public addresses. You think you know what the key issue or issues are, but you don't know whether your potential listeners will evaluate them as you do. In fact, here in the beginning, you're uncertain as to the *constituency* of the listeners with whom you will be interacting in this series of different communicative settings. So, in planning your "speaking campaign," you decide that in your initial encounters you will advance a fairly large number of ideas and issues. In these early appearances you carefully observe your listeners' reactions to the various points, and you narrow your list to those that listeners responded to most favorably and enthusiastically. Then, in subsequent encounters and speeches you place more and more emphasis upon those points which your hearers—by exercising feedback—have "selected" for you. The effect will motivate you continuously to restructure and rephrase and refine your messages for succeeding circumstances and settings. The conditioning effect which listeners create in speakers isn't limited by any means to a choice of issues or topics. Research studies on "verbal conditioning" have found that a number of speaker behaviors (such as the use of plural nouns and "hostile" verbs and alteration of speech rate), if positively reinforced by listener response, will occur with increasing frequency.[4] This demonstrates again that the speaker is not solely the *influencer* in a speech event; he or she is also the *influenced.*

Another possible effect that a speaker may experience during interaction is a *changed commitment.* This is created not so much by the influence of listeners as by the *act of speaking.* This is a form of "*self*-persuasion." You may have known people who seemed to be talking more to convince themselves than their listeners. By merely talking about an idea, subject, or course of action we may "sell" ourselves on it. A number of experimental studies point to occurrences of this.[5] In an Army study, for instance, soldiers in a public-speaking training course were required to prepare and present speeches favorable to Army life. The results revealed that some "chronic kickers" showed marked improvement in morale. Another study found that subjects could learn the phonetic alphabet more easily if they were required to repeat or rehearse the phonetic sounds aloud rather than simply watch a filmstrip showing the various sound formations. In still another study, a group-discussion procedure involving active participation by all members of the group was found to be more influential than a lecture situation in which the group listened to only one speaker.

From these and similar studies, it seems safe to conclude that active participation in the communication process can influence a speaker to make a changed commitment: to restructure a concept or point of view. The new structure of view, when communicated, may—in turn—create a *self-persuasive* effect. This happens, basically, because the principle of reconstructing an idea can work in two directions. The diagram at the top of the following page is intended to illustrate the way in which the act of communicating a restructured concept may lead to the acceptance of that concept on the part of the speaker.

These, then, are some of the effects to which *speaking agents* are subject. Principally by using the dynamics of feedback, (1) listeners can influence speakers to modify their ideas, positions, and propositions—thereby altering their Belief-Evaluation Clusters; (2) listeners may influence speakers in their "selection" of topics, aspects of topics, approaches, and emphases; (3) listeners may—through verbal and nonverbal "conditioning"—influence the speech and behavioral patterns of speakers. And, finally, (4) through the *act of participating* in a communicative interaction, speakers may influence *themselves* to change a commitment, a concept, a point of view, or a course of action.

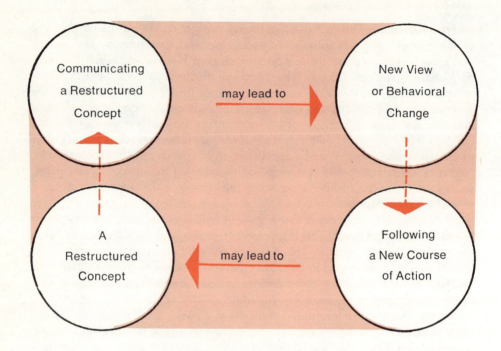

UNDERSTANDING EFFECTS RELATED TO BEHAVIOR AND THOUGHT PATTERNS

As we have seen, one of the most significant effects of speech communication is the influence that the speaker, in one way or another, exerts upon the listener. In fact, as we explained in Chapter 2, since the basic, encompassing *purpose* of the speaking agent is to influence the listening agent, we must conclude that—overall—in order to succeed, the speaker will have to cause the listener to behave and think in a certain way. In other words, as a speaker you won't accomplish your purpose—any purpose—unless you are able to alter and adjust in some way and to some extent the *behavioral patterns* and the *thought patterns* of those to whom you are directing your message. [4]

Vocal/Physical Behavior Patterns

When the physical and vocal patterns of speaking/listening agents are affected, the results are usually immediately apparent, and may extensively influence the interpersonal aspects of communication. When you observe the behaviors of a speaking agent closely, either in class or in your community, you are likely to see some who copy certain of the vocal emphases, gestures, and other bodily movements typically used by television "personalities" and other popular public figures. We tend naturally to emulate those whom we admire.

How does this effect come about? When we observe the ways in which a speaker may modify the bodily and vocal behaviors of others, we see that the factors of *imitation, emulation, assimilation,* and *sensitive discrimination* play an important part. When we identify with other individuals whom we like and respect, we are inclined to take on a few of their gestures, bodily attitudes, and vocal inflections. We may even pick up a few of their pet phrases and try to say them as they do, and we may do this consciously or subconsciously. Many of these vocal-gestural behavior patterns we test out in terms of our self-image and also for their appropriateness and effectiveness with other listeners and watchers. Some of these patterns we soon discard; others we try to adapt and retain as an integral part of our personality and speaking style. Up to a point, this can be beneficial. Listening to good vocal models on radio and in recordings and critically observing skilled speakers on the lecture platform, the stage, the motion picture screen, and the television tube—all can contribute positively to our own speaking style. But by whatever means, subconsciously or by intent, we are continuously being influenced by the vocal and physical behavioral patterns of other agents. And unless they have adopted communicative patterns that are visually or audibly so strange or eccentric as to call unfavorable attention to themselves and interfere with desirable oral interaction, the total *effect* can be positive and beneficial. The important thing is to be able to discriminate between the good and the not-so-good examples we choose to imitate or emulate.

Thinking and Reasoning Patterns

Less immediately discernible usually than the physical/vocal behavior patterns—but more significant probably—are the effects created during interaction upon the agents' *thinking and reasoning* patterns. In their use of such patterns, speakers create—sometimes consciously, sometimes unknowingly—innumerable

Study Probe 4
Recognizing Behavior and Thought Patterns

a. Observe the speech behaviors of people engaging in one-to-several and one-to-many situations. Do you note any eccentric or strange patterns which call unfavorable attention to themselves and which could, conceivably, interfere with effective interaction between or among the speaker and listeners? Make your observations and conclusions the basis of a short written report that you will hand to your instructor.

b. Outline, briefly, one or two of the thought patterns you customarily employ in organizing and expressing your ideas and attitudes to others. To what extent, if any, have you observed the use of such patterning in others: your mother, father, brother, or sister, an uncle, a teacher you've admired, or someone else with whom you have been in comparatively close and frequent contact? Make this analysis the basis of a three-minute oral report that you will present to other members of the class.

and far-reaching effects in the thought-patterning "habits" of listeners. We are not referring here to the propositional substance of a speaker's message, although that may be of much greater immediate importance to both speaker and listeners. What we wish to emphasize is that just as listeners "take on" some of the vocal/gestural behavior patterns of the speaker, they also assimilate—less consciously, but just as surely—some of the *mental-process patterns* of speakers whom they admire and respect.

Attentive listeners may learn not only the substantive content of a communication act, but they may also learn the *form* and *modality* of that act: the way in which the information is organized and structured for presentation. As hearers, if we sense that the speaker's thought-process patterns are useful modes for organizing and giving utterance to our own ideas and thoughts, we will tend to take on these patterns and make them an integral part of our own. If we repeatedly hear a respected authority or much admired person use a particular pattern or thought-structuring, this design will begin to impinge upon our mind. It will begin to impress itself upon our ways of thinking and relating our ideas as we prepare, in turn, to communicate them to others. We will gradually assimilate the pattern into our own idea-making; we will tend eventually to speak with that pattern.

The same factors which are at work when a speaker modifies the physical communicative behaviors of others are also operating to modify their thought-process patterns. Here again we see the influence of *imitation, emulation, assimilation,* and *discriminative choice*. When we emulate thought patterns that are clear, fair, and reasonably objective (no easy task), the results tend to be constructive and desirable. But if we carelessly or indiscriminantly take on faulty, incomplete, or self-deluding ways of producing our reasoning and thinking and communicating it, the possibilities of constructive and genuinely rewarding interaction with others can be impaired. Others are quick to sense that, within broad limits at least, the importance and value we attach to a person, an object, or an idea is strongly reflected in "how we think about it."

To try to catalog anything like a complete list of thought patterns, even for one individual, would obviously be impossible. But in order that you may at least glimpse something of their *complexity* and their *effect* on the communicating we do, we will look briefly at a few that are typical and important; namely: (1) *language-grammar patterns,* (2) *intonational-emotional patterns,* (3) *limited focusing patterns,* (4) *association-with-authority patterns,* and (5) *causative-connective* patterns.

Language-grammar patterns.   Some patterns which can create difficulties in our communicative relationships with others are those involving our use of language and the way we put our word-labels together—their syntactical or grammatical arrangement. In composing a generalized and abstract thought-utterance, for example, we must not mistake the whole for the part or the part for the whole. We cannot, for instance, affirm of the whole that which holds true of one or more of the parts taken separately. We can categorize and pigeonhole only up to a certain point if we wish our statements to have much validity. As we transform our thought patterns into speech, we must remember that a few specific cases or instances cannot "type" all members of a race, a religion, a nationality, an occupation, or a political party.

It's also risky to affirm of an entire entity that which holds true of one or more of the parts when taken separately. Suppose Congress has voted a tax increase, and Mr. X is a congressman. Obviously, we cannot correctly conclude that Congressman X voted for the tax increase. The measure might, in fact, have passed despite his zealous opposition.

Not far removed from this thought pattern is that of the *sweeping, unsupported assertion*. While the abstractive nature of language often compels us to speak in generalities, we must take special care that our statements do not become so broad and so general as to be meaningless. Examine critically the statement, "The true patriot will hold high those democratic ideals that bring pride to the hearts of every American mother." Note in particular the very high level of abstraction in the terms *true, patriot, democratic, ideals, pride,* and *every American mother.* If you try to arrive at essential, criterial subcategories for each, you will quickly realize that the assertion has become so overloaded with the many expansive generalities as to crowd out almost any specific sense or meaningful effect.

Another detrimental pattern for creating and presenting thought-substance involves the centering of listener attention on a *single, special case* and then generalizing from this isolated and often atypical instance. In this manner, the speaker may try to create a desired effect by linking a number of discrete, actually separate, and often unrelated instances together, allowing listeners to infer or suppose a connection among them. By looking only at special cases and *implying* a general conclusion from them, a speaker may impose a kind of mental "gaposis" pattern in the thinking of the listener. This kind of rhetorical card-stacking can, of course, produce inaccurate or biased conclusions. This is a pattern which, unfortunately, most of us probably employ from time to time. We generalize from insufficient evidence, saying in effect: This particular circumstance is true; therefore all of the other possible circumstances must be true, too.

Among the numerous linguistic/syntactic patterns are those of a *transpositional* nature. A speaker, in creating certain effects, will naturally want to use variety, to state a point differently, to "change things around a bit." While this is often desirable, there are pitfalls to be avoided in such patterning. For example, in changing the statement of a proposition from an affirmative to a negative form, we must be careful not to alter or distort our essential meaning. "All university students are eligible for reduced bus fares" can be changed to "No university students are ineligible for reduced bus fares," and our intended meaning will remain more or less intact. But if we change the proposition to "No non-university students are eligible for reduced bus fares," we have obverted or twisted the meaning around.

Intonational-emotional patterns.   Whereas most of the language-grammatical patterns bear centrally upon the *clarity* of communication, many intonational-emotional patterns seem to emerge from what Martin Scheerer calls the "cognitive-emotional-motivational matrix" characteristic of human beings.[6] Quite frequently we are prompted from within to "express our true feelings" about something. Sometimes we feel called upon to do this; more often, probably, we can't avoid doing it. Either way, we may rely heavily upon *emotional coloring* and vocalized accent to pattern and project our meanings. In terms of speaker output, these patterns are often apparent in stressful moments, in situations characterized by aroused feelings. And very often these patterns reveal our true reactions and responses to other agents and certain contexts. By whatever name—accent, intonation, or emphasis—these are patterns which can most frequently impair or impede communicative interaction. These are patterns that creep into the voice despite our best efforts to conceal them.

As we noted in Chapter 6, when we were considering nonverbal aspects of messages, by stressing or accenting a particular word or phrase the speaker can strongly influence the listener's interpretation of a given remark. Consider the Commandment, "Thou shalt not bear false witness against thy neighbor." If emphasis is given the final word, the hearer may interpret the statement to justify bearing false witness against everybody *except* one's neighbor. We need not misquote the words of a source to create an erroneous impression; we need only change the vocal stress to lead a listener to a flawed conclusion.

Earlier we spoke of generalizing from a specific, single case. When we accent our communications emotionally, we may carry the generalization to an even higher level and reduce the essence of the instance to a single word. This is sometimes called a *labeling* or *name-calling* pattern. The label *doting mother* may range in meaning from a kind and loving and generous parent to a thoroughly domineering and tyrannically despicable dowager. The intonational coloring and the context in which the label is used creates the effect, and the pattern works its influence upon both speaker and listener. One derogatory label usually calls forth another from your opponent. And when the substance of a communicative exchange is reduced to a "you're another" level, productive interaction goes out the window.

Limited focusing patterns. Some thought patterns especially narrow and restrict our thinking and reasoning processes. One such pattern is the *either/or dichotomy* or *"two-valued"* orientation. In speaking, as in life, we are frequently faced with a clear-cut choice between two alternatives—and *only* two. We must say either "yes" or "no"; "I will" or "I will not"; "I can" or "I cannot." Even if we can discern a continuum in a given case, we have to assign an arbitrary term to each end of that continuum. Whatever the reasons, we often tend to think in dualities, in opposites: rich *or* poor, fair *or* unfair, clean *or* dirty, black *or* white, tall *or* short, man *or* woman. In many circumstances, obviously, such a pattern is both desirable and necessary.

There are many other circumstances, however, in which it is to our great advantage to discover, consider, and weigh the *multiple choices* available to us before making a final decision or taking a conclusive action. In general, the more knowledge and the more experience we have, the more likely we are to discern viable options. For example, much of the comment and discussion we hear on social issues is presented in a problem-solution pattern. The speaking agent identifies, describes, and amplifies the problem as he or she sees it, and then presents a solution. This pattern is, of course, employed often in public speaking and small group discussion settings. Quite generally, it is a useful one, but one which usually must be structured sequentially and given broad focus if it is to achieve useful results. As we will emphasize in Chapter 11, a number of steps are involved, and we must take time to make the careful analysis needed to identify the problem, locate its symptoms, discern its probable causes, and develop some possible alternative solutions.

However, if we feel hurried, impatient, angry, or fatigued, we may be strongly tempted to bypass some of the required steps. If we yield to this inclination, we limit our focus: We employ an *ellipsis* of the pattern—one which moves too quickly and directly from the "problem" stage to the "solution" stage of the decision-making process, leaving out some of the essential intermediate steps. If we hear "problem," our immediate response-reaction should not be "solution," but rather "analysis," "probable causes," "alternative courses of action," and—finally—"best solution." We're urging against an elliptical pattern of thinking which may, over time, create an impatience or even an intolerance of sound decision making.

The principal point here is that we won't facilitate communication if we pattern our thought-expression on an either/or, take-it-or-leave-it, or all-or-nothing basis. This rules out *compromise*—often an indispensable ingredient of successful and conclusive interaction. In sum, if we hear the disjunctive "either . . . or" with great frequency, our own patterns of thinking may tend to become largely two-valued. We may then fail to detect the subtle and significant shades of difference or degree along a continuum.

Association-with-authority patterns. Although we may assert our independence often and insistently, we are in fact quite *dependent* upon our fellow beings for support, reinforcement, and concurrence. Additionally, the more powerful, influential, and prestigious those beings are, the more likely we are to want to *associate* ourselves, our ideas, and our positions with them. By such association, we hope, some of their power, influence, and prestige will automatically *transfer* itself to us. Generally, too, we are inclined to respect or at least defer to someone who has more wisdom, experience, or special knowledge than we have. As a result, many of our patterns of thinking and speaking are associative and transferential, especially as they may involve an *authority* figure or an authoritative concept.

Authority and deference to it, of course, play major roles in any society. Without them, certainly, we would not have the society we have. At the same time, we may chafe at the constraints they place upon us. A paradox of human nature is that we tend to resent authority—except when it is "on our side." When a personage or an institution or a law or a tradition—in a word, an authority—reflects or concurs with our view of the world, we tend to *invoke* that authority. When, in an interaction with others, we find ourselves faced with the possible acceptance of a decision which we see as going against our preferences or presumed best interests, we look around for help. We try to appeal to a "higher authority." This particular pattern of behavior is, for example, basic to our entire legal system. But all of us have experienced and employed numerous variations of the pattern, from childhood onward. How many times, for instance, have you heard "I'll tell Papa on you!" "Just wait till Mama sees what you've done!" "Call the police!" "I'll take you to court!" Obviously, patterns of associating our beliefs and evaluations and positions with an authority pervades much of human activity, including communication.

Association-with-authority patterns have numerous variations and may work in many directions. Not only is it possible to improve the status of a proposition or elevate a cause by authority-association; it is also possible to *reverse* the effect by using the pattern to assail an opponent's position or to detract from his cause. In almost any political campaign, for instance, there will be situations in which one candidate will denounce the opposing candidate as being "in the Mayor's pocket" or "the Governor's handpicked rubber stamp." This kind of implied guilt-by-reason-of-association pattern is often combined with a pattern of devastating intonational coloring, and we may detect in it also some elements of the labeling and over-generalizing patterns mentioned earlier. In certain circumstances, to damn by association may be justifiable and necessary. Much oftener, we would hope, you will want to employ the association-with-authority patterns in a more positive and discriminative manner.

There is another problem of which we must be aware when invoking authority or employing a pattern of this kind. We might call this the problem of "The Faceless They." *Who* is, in fact, the authority in the following expressions:

They say . . . .

A highly reliable source, who refused to be identified, intimated today that . . . .

According to informed government sources, . . .

The silent majority feels . . . .

When we hear such expressions or such phrases as "The Pepsi Generation" or "peer group" cited as an authority-source, we should be aware of the *identity gap* inherent in those patterns. We should not unwittingly play the game of Follow the Faceless Leader. If we do, we may well come to a point where we see "they" as an authoritative mystique and stop questioning sources.

Obviously, when we associate our communications with an authority-source, either directly or indirectly through testimony or quoted endorsement, we take on certain rhetorical and ethical obligations. Among other concerns, we are obliged to *identify the authority accurately*. If we restate or paraphrase someone's words, at the very least we must present them *correctly, fairly,* and *representatively:* we are not entitled to lift the quotation or the implied concurrence of the authority out of context. Nor, in arguing a case, should we substitute an appeal to an authority for a weighing of the facts at hand.

Causal patterns. From first to last, in an effort to understand the world, we human beings have been fascinated with our origin, our ultimate destination, and the *connections* in between. We try, over the span of a lifetime, to bridge the expanse by continuously asking: *Why?* To *what* can I attribute this occurrence? What is the *cause?* How is *this* related to *that?* It should not be surprising, therefore, that large numbers of our thinking and speaking patterns reflect the search for a *connection* between event and event, between what we presume to be a *cause* and what we suppose to be its *effect.* This chapter itself has, of course, been such a search—a seeking to discover some possible effects generated by asking "What follows from communication?"

Our "causative-connective" patterning reflects the fact that we like to believe that a great many events occur in a so-called "logical" or "explainable" sequence. One happening, supposedly, follows another in a certain natural and almost inevitable order of some kind. Hard at work here is the need to complete our perceptions and balance our cognitions. Of this sequence and order we tend to say—as did the Romans—"*After* it, therefore *because* of it." Actually, of course, the ancients recognized, as do we, that events are rarely if ever so simply and neatly arranged.

The task of making accurate and valid causative-connective associations is extremely difficult. This, as we've said before, is one of the reasons why human beings have devised certain patterns for thinking, reasoning, and communicating about those possible connections. These patterns, in turn, enable us to understand what we must understand if we're to function intelligently. We're entitled, for instance, to expect some kind of discernible connection or relationship (not necessarily a causative one) between the statements or assertions which a speaker makes. If one statement doesn't lead understandably to another or doesn't appear to relate to what has gone before, we say that we can't "follow" his or her reasoning. If a speaker asserts a conclusion that doesn't follow from the premises, we are puzzled by the *non sequitur.* Mr. X may in fact be a good husband, father, churchman, war hero, astronaut, and movie actor. But on the basis of these accomplishments alone—admirable though they may be—we cannot claim that Mr. X will therefore make a good congressman. Nor should we as listeners be led to make that inference or assumption. As we've said, there can be no reasonable guarantee that former events will necessarily cause a future event.

In this section we've observed how communicative interaction works to produce certain effects on the behavioral and thought patterns of listening agents. In particular, we've looked at five that are fairly typical: (1) *language-grammar* patterns, (2) *intonational-emotional* patterns, (3) *limited focusing* patterns, (4) *association-with-authority* patterns, and (5) *causative-connective* patterns. These, we've noted, suggest but a few of the many such patterns created in listeners by speaking agents. Learned and reinforced in our speech interaction with others, they have both advantages and dangers. We should, therefore, try with diligence and discernment to evaluate the *effects* which speech communication can produce in us and in our ways of relating to one another. ⑤

Perhaps we can best conclude this chapter and this part of the text by taking note of the *extent* and *human potential* of effects produced by speech communication. Clearly, acts of communication create numerous effects, most of which have multiple facets and extensions. Some effects, as we've suggested, are intended and planned for; many are unintended and unexpected. Some are immediately or strikingly apparent; a great many others are subtle and become evident only after a passage of time. Some fade fast. Others endure. And much speech communication, as you must surely have concluded from your own experience and observation, seems to have little or no detectable effect at all.

At the same time we have to recognize that an effect may go undetected because many of the overall consequences of communicative interaction extend far beyond the immediate horizon of any observer or analyst. Because *every effect* will almost certainly create others, *every single change* imposed on or within a social system will produce *other changes* in that system. This we might well describe as the "chain reaction" or "cycle" effect of speech communication, involving a vast amount of *new* interaction, some *new* actions, and some *new effects.* This cycle of social/communication effects created by human striving, concern, and speech interaction is evident in the current controversy over the effects of birth control on population control, the effects of automotive necessity on the energy crisis, the effects of the energy crisis on the ecology, the effects of ecology on the desperate shortages of natural resources, and on and on.

Study Probe 5
Recognizing Speaker Influence upon Listeners'
Behavior and Thought Patterns

Read three or four speeches in current issues of *Vital Speeches of the Day, Representative American Speeches,* or other sources suggested by your instructor. Consider speeches touching upon contemporary social problems. Examine the speeches you select and try to identify patterns of thinking and behaving which the makers of these speeches may be trying to create in listeners. Try especially to detect patterns in addition to those we've described. Make a list, including possible patterns of both a positive and a negative nature, and bring it to class.

In a discussion with other members of the class, compare and evaluate several of the lists of patterns. Possibly a "consensus" list should be written on the chalkboard. Do *new* patterns emerge? Are there patterns which appear to be *variations* of those considered in this section of the textbook? Which patterns do you feel tend to exert the strongest influence on *your* thinking and behavior?

In energizing social changes of magnitude and urgency, speech communication can and does produce significant and far-reaching effects. The history of this country—indeed the whole history of the human race—dramatically attests to this. So, even though spoken interchange must often seem limited and transitory, it unquestionably serves as a sharp cutting edge for forces seeking social action and change. It can serve either as a first and necessary move or as an added impetus to forces already on the move. If we desire to engage knowledgeably in any kind of interaction—of whatever magnitude—we are obliged to weigh the actual and potential consequences of our speech behaviors. We are obligated to respond to those consequences sensitively and sensibly.

Suggested Readings

William J. McGuire, "The Nature of Attitudes and Attitude Change," *Handbook of Social Psychology,* 2nd ed., ed. Gardner Lindzey and Elliot Aronson (Reading, Mass.: Addison-Wesley Publishing Co., Inc., 1969), vol. III, pp. 136–314. This general source has been cited often in this textbook; and McGuire's chapter, in particular, has much that is important to know about speech communication effects.

George A. Borden, Richard B. Gregg, and Theodore G. Grove, *Speech Behavior and Human Interaction* (Englewood Cliffs, N.J.: Prentice-Hall, Inc., 1969). This work affords significant materials dealing with speech communication effects as they are found in the intrapersonal, interpersonal, and public communication contexts.

Martin Fishbein and Icek Ajzen, *Belief, Attitude, Intention and Behavior* (Reading, Mass.: Addison-Wesley Publishing Co., Inc., 1975). This excellent new source provides an introduction to theory and research concerning the formation and changing of beliefs, attitudes, intentions, and behaviors.

Reference Notes

[1] A convenient discussion of Katz' theory of second-level communicators is included in Walter Weiss, "Effects of the Mass Media of Communication," *The Handbook of Social Psychology,* 2nd ed., ed. Gardner Lindzey and Elliot Aronson (Reading, Mass.: Addison-Wesley Publishing Co., Inc., 1969), vol. V, especially pp. 142–143 and 169–172.

[2] Thomas Hardy, *Far from the Madding Crowd* (New York: The New American Library, Inc., 1960), p. 15.

[3] Thomas M. Scheidel, "An Exploratory Study of the Relationships Between Certain Organismic Variables and Response to a Persuasive Speech," unpublished Ph.D. dissertation (University of Washington, 1958).

[4] Leonard Krasner, "Studies of the Conditioning of Verbal Behavior," *Psychological Bulletin,* 55 (1958): 148–170.

[5]William J. McGuire, "The Nature of Attitudes and Attitude Change," *The Handbook of Social Psychology,* 2nd ed., ed. Gardner Lindzey and Elliot Aronson (Reading, Mass.: Addison-Wesley Publishing Co., Inc., 1969), vol. III, pp. 238–240.

[6]Martin Scheerer, "Cognitive Theory," *The Handbook of Social Psychology,* 1st ed., ed. Gardner Lindzey (Reading, Mass.: Addison-Wesley Publishing Co., Inc., 1954), vol. I, p. 123.

INTERPERSONAL
CONTEXTS
OF SPEECH
COMMUNICATION

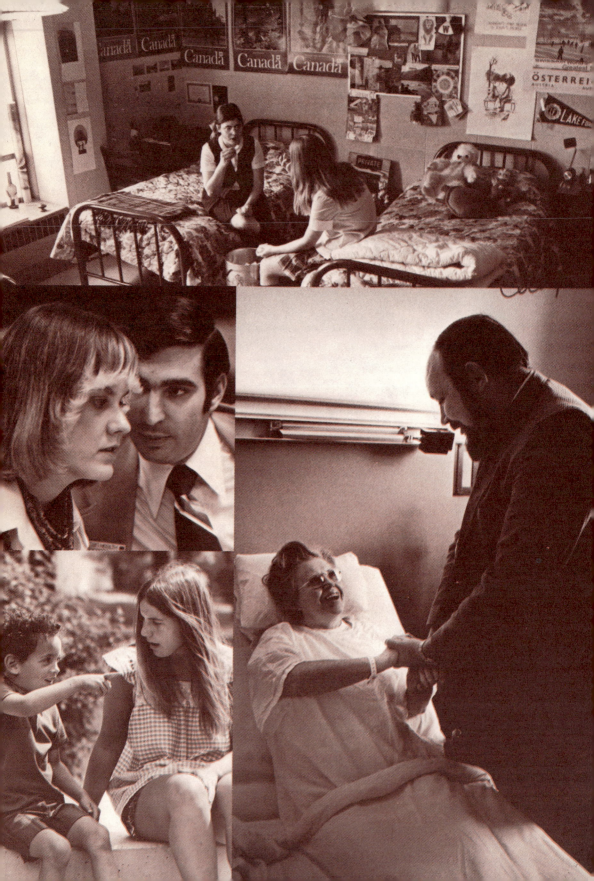

Chapter 10

DYADIC COMMUNICATION

Interacting with another person is the
most frequent form of speech communication—
and potentially the most productive. To achieve
a successful relationship, both agents should
be aware of each other's needs and of what the
context calls for. Both should actively strive
to improve the quality of interaction.

The image of *two persons conversing* was presented in Chapter 1 as a general model for speech communication. The two-person, or dyadic, situation contains all of the essential elements of the speech communication process, and the principles applicable in that setting should apply as well to every other communication form and setting. Two-person interpersonal communication is the most frequent form of direct speech involvement. As we noted earlier, even in a small group discussion interaction occurs most often between two participants. And it is two-person communication that allows for the most direct interaction and involvement.

In Chapters 6 through 9 we introduced the basic principles for interacting effectively in dyadic and other forms of speech communication. We stressed the necessity for understanding the communication agents and the context, and for achieving interaction by the appropriate concerns for feedforward and feedback. We return now to the topic of two persons conversing in order to amplify some of the general principles from earlier chapters and to suggest additional, specific ways for achieving interaction in the two-person setting.

We must recognize at the beginning that in some instances full communicative interaction between two persons may be unattainable. One agent, or both, may refuse to meet the other, or one or both may withdraw totally from the context. However, such cases may still not be entirely hopeless. An intermediary, or second-level communicator (X), may be enlisted to intercede between non-interacting agents (A) and (B), so that two-person interaction occurs between A and X, and then between X and B. It is even possible that the intermediary X may be able eventually to induce agents A and B to resume direct interaction. [1]

Rarely are the channels between communication agents completely open. In extraordinary circumstances (a natural catastrophe such as an earthquake, or a man-made catastrophe such as an urban riot), an individual may have communicative channels fully opened to receive as many informative cues as possible. In such events "uncertainty" is the prevailing mood. In strange environments (travel in foreign countries) we may be more open than usual in pursuing friendships, once the acquaintanceship is initiated. As we strive to achieve empathy with foreign acquaintances, we may try harder than with people of our own culture to interpret and respond appropriately to the sometimes unfamiliar verbal and non-verbal messages they send out. (In this regard, See Chapter 16, "Intercultural Communication.") Children typically maintain open channels; and until or unless they are taught that strangers may be dangerous, they will talk with almost anyone. [2]

In ordinary dyadic situations, neither extreme of completely closed or completely opened channels is usual. Most often the available channels will be only *partially* open because of the demands of the particular situation, status differences between agents, personality characteristics of the agents, and other dissimilarities. In this chapter we will avoid the extremes and consider only those cases in which speaking/listening agents are willing at least to entertain possibilities for interaction and are open to mutual efforts in that direction.

Study Probe 1
*Examining the Role of the Intermediary
in Interpersonal Communication*

a. Describe any experience you have had with the use of an intermediary in dealing with another person—perhaps the arrangement of a blind date or an agreement to purchase something "through a friend who can get a better price." Cite some of the values and problems evident in your experience.

b. Outline a serious argument which could be presented for both sides of the proposition that marriages should be arranged by matchmakers rather than the couple involved. In what ways would a matchmaker be similar to an arbitrator in a labor-management dispute? How would a matchmaker differ from a marriage counselor? Would different values be taken into account?

INTERPERSONAL SPEECH AS PATTERNED COMMUNICATION

When two acquaintances meet one another on the street, they invariably exchange a few routine remarks in passing. A casual observer might say that they are simply following social custom—that their conversation is a standard greeting ritual and nothing more. The content of what is said in such an exchange means little. The frequently asked question "How are you?" does not really call for—or even want—a full answer.

As with other human rituals, the behavior in a greeting ritual is obviously patterned and very predictable. After all, we learn communicative rituals early in life and play them over with little variation thousands of times. But to conclude that communication rituals are casual, routine, and unimportant would be a mistake. On the contrary, such rituals can have *considerable significance*. The significance of these learned patterns for interaction is not in their content, but in the fact that they occur—in the fact that the ritual is performed, and performed according to "rules" or expectations. These rituals can tell us much about the relationship between the speaking/listening agents. [3]

Much of our dyadic communication operates according to unstated but well-accepted rules. These rules, and the resulting behavioral patterns, are learned much as are the rules for grammar: We tend to follow the specific rule of grammar even though we may not be able to describe or state it explicitly. This is probably because we internalized rules of this order by constant practice and imitation of others when we were very young—long before they were taught to us in school.

One rule of dyadic communication is that we "take turns" when speaking. One person speaks, then the other, and so on. If one person were to speak all the time, some communication might occur; but obviously the act could not be called a conversation. We also learn, as a rule, about how *long* such a ritualistic communication should be—about how much interaction time is appropriate. The duration of the greeting ritual must be fitting for the agents interacting within the given circumstance or context. Although we cannot know exactly how much is "too brief" or "too much" time, we do develop a feeling for such matters. If the

---

Study Probe 2
Exploring the Openness of Communication Channels

Describe some emergency situations which you have encountered. How receptive were you and the other speaking/listening agents to communicative stimuli at those times? What were the chief channels of communication that you used? Can you recall and describe other situations—not emergencies—in which the channels of communication were similarly open? Can you remember your first meeting with a club or organization at which you were a "foreigner" and all the others present were members who were well acquainted with each other? These experiences can be similar to travel to a foreign country.

exchange is unusually brief, it may signify something about a changing relationship between agents. If, on the other hand, one agent who has had only a nodding acquaintance with a second agent stops to talk for an extended period of time, the breaking of the pattern may signify an overture for closer friendship. Whenever one agent violates the rules or does not meet the expectations of a situation, the deviation from the norm will likely be interpreted by the other agent as a statement about their relationship. One may break an expected pattern of communication, but not without implicitly calling for a restructuring of the situation. Any change from expected communication patterns can be interpreted as being meaningful and significant. [4]

Virginia Satir, along with many other scholars, has suggested that any communication from an individual has two levels: the *denotative* level—the literal content; and the *metacommunicative* level—a comment on the literal content, as well as on the relationship between the communicative agents.[1] This concept is described as a *metacommunication.* Suppose, for example, that one person—while smiling—directs an insulting comment to another. The smile is metacommunication. It says that the literal comment can be ignored because the remark is not intended seriously. The smile also says that the relationship between the agents is such that bantering of this type is permissible.

Communication rituals evolve, and they eventually define our behavioral norms. They embody prescribed patterns of what is "normal" and what can be expected. Following the pattern of a communication ritual becomes somewhat akin to following the rules of a card game. Rules and procedures become settled first. If we know and follow the "rules," everyone else who knows what the "rules" are also knows what's going on. If we violate the "rules," those familiar with the accepted patterns become perplexed. Communication rituals maintain order and

Study Probe 3
Studying a Greeting Ritual

Consider the following communicative exchange:

John: Hi.
Bill: Hi. How are you?
John: Great. And you?
Bill: Just fine.
John: Good. See you around.
Bill: Right. So long.

Would you judge this conversation to be typical of that which might occur during a brief encounter between friends? Do you perceive anything in an exchange of this kind other than a typical greeting ritual? Explain. We discussed earlier (Chapter 6, pages 124–125) the "content" and "relationship" components of communicative messages. Apart from the content, what is the "relationship" message in the exchange above?

allow for efficiency in communication as long as they are accepted by the participants. If they are followed, the communicative interaction can proceed—the game can be played out. But if they are rejected or broken by either party, then the interpersonal relationship and the context must be restructured or terminated. This is what we mean when we say people have "agreed to disagree."

In sum, *one factor contributing to efficient and effective interaction is the mutual acceptance of unstated rules for communicative conduct.* The mutual following of such rules can most often be observed in patterned, relatively predictable, and reliable behavior in communication contexts. In such situations, the expectations of one agent about behaviors of the other agent tend to be confirmed, and a ground for trust and further interaction is possible. Let us turn now to practices which speaking/listening agents can follow to understand the expectations of others with whom they communicate.

DETERMINING WHAT THE CONTEXT CALLS FOR

A communicative agent should seek first to discover the demands of the specific context in which the communication takes place. What does the situation require? We might begin by listing some of the possible contexts in which two persons converse and the demands these contexts impose upon communicators.

Examples of Dyadic Contexts

The following are a few examples of contexts in which two persons may converse.

1. *Loving relationship.* The individuals may proclaim trust, affection, and concern for one another—for example, husband and wife.

Study Probe 4
Identifying Communication Patterns

What are some other patterns and rules that you follow when speaking with another person? How far apart do you stand or sit? Do you orient yourselves face-to-face? Do you each speak an equal amount of the time? Do you observe different patterns and rules with different people? You might follow up this analysis by reading Erving Goffman's *Interaction Ritual* (Garden City, N.Y.: Doubleday & Company, Inc., Anchor Books, 1967).

Identify three communicative patterns you dare not break with a close friend lest he or she think "there's something wrong." Explain why this is so. (For example, are there some persons with whom you must always "joke around," and others with whom you must be more serious?)

2. *Therapeutic association.* One agent may attempt to help the other resolve a personal crisis or emotional difficulty—for example, a doctor and patient, or a counselor and client.

3. *Social conversation.* Two persons may exchange views, reinforce one another's beliefs and evaluations, or engage in "grooming" talk—for example, two close friends.

4. *Becoming acquainted.* Strangers may meet and interact while getting to know one another—for example, new neighbors.

5. *Instruction.* One agent may hope to enlighten the other by presenting evidence, facts, and/or acceptable new beliefs—for example, professor and student.

6. *Interview.* One speaking/listening agent may assess the qualifications of another for a certain task—for example, personnel director and prospective employee.

7. *Bargaining.* The agents may try to negotiate a difference in position and resolve a conflict between themselves—for example, agents in a labor-management contract dispute.

8. *Persuasion.* One agent may attempt to change the Belief-Evaluation Clusters of the other—for example, insurance salesperson and customer.

9. *Combat.* The agents may engage in verbal battling in the hope of destroying each other's position—often while aiming at the persuasion of a third party who is observing the encounter—for example, opponents in a political debate.

10. *Coercion.* One agent may attempt to force compliance of the other by the use of threats—for example, armed kidnapper and captive.

This brief listing will illustrate the wide range of experiences which can be subsumed under the heading of *interpersonal communication.* For each of the many possible contexts in which two persons converse, we should have some guide as to what is expected—what the rules are—what will facilitate interaction.

Assessing Dyadic Communication Situations

The Assessment Scales provided below are similar in some respects to those you completed in Chapter 3 (pages 57–61). They are designed to help you assess your reactions in the ten interpersonal communication contexts just described. Mark the scales just as you did those in Chapter 3. First, try to imagine yourself in the situation described in the title. Then, for each of the three listed responses (a, b, c) circle the number (7, 6, 5, 4, 3, 2, 1) in the response-continuum range which best describes how you think you would feel in the designated situation.

If, for example, the descriptive term at the left end of the scale (pleasant) *describes your feelings completely,* then circle the number 7; if the descriptive term at the right end of the scale (not pleasant) describes your feelings most accurately, circle the number 1. If one of the terms *describes your feelings fairly well,* but not completely, then circle the number 6 or 2, one range position away from the term. If one of the terms *describes your feelings only somewhat,* but better than does the other term, then circle the number 5 or 3, two scale positions away from the appropriate term. If neither term at the ends of the response-continuum scale seems appropriate, or if both terms *describe your feelings equally,* then circle the number 4.

Using two colored pencils, respond *twice* to the scales given here. First, complete each scale according to *how you believe you would feel* in the given contexts. Then complete the scales according to *how you believe the other person in that context would feel.* Compare the two sets of reactions or predictions. Then compare your scales with those of your classmates.

DYADIC COMMUNICATION-SITUATION ASSESSMENT SCALES

1. COMMUNICATING IN A LOVING RELATIONSHIP

a.	pleasant	7	6	5	4	3	2	1	not pleasant
b.	informative	7	6	5	4	3	2	1	not informative
c.	self-fulfilling	7	6	5	4	3	2	1	not self-fulfilling

2. COMMUNICATING IN A THERAPEUTIC SETTING

a.	pleasant	7	6	5	4	3	2	1	not pleasant
b.	informative	7	6	5	4	3	2	1	not informative
c.	self-fulfilling	7	6	5	4	3	2	1	not self-fulfilling

3. COMMUNICATING IN A SOCIAL CONVERSATION

a.	pleasant	7	6	5	4	3	2	1	not pleasant
b.	informative	7	6	5	4	3	2	1	not informative
c.	self-fulfilling	7	6	5	4	3	2	1	not self-fulfilling

4. COMMUNICATING WHILE BECOMING ACQUAINTED

a.	pleasant	7	6	5	4	3	2	1	not pleasant
b.	informative	7	6	5	4	3	2	1	not informative
c.	self-fulfilling	7	6	5	4	3	2	1	not self-fulfilling

5. COMMUNICATING IN AN INSTRUCTIONAL SETTING

a.	pleasant	7	6	5	4	3	2	1	not pleasant
b.	informative	7	6	5	4	3	2	1	not informative
c.	self-fulfilling	7	6	5	4	3	2	1	not self-fulfilling

6. COMMUNICATING IN AN INTERVIEW SETTING

a.	pleasant	7	6	5	4	3	2	1	not pleasant
b.	informative	7	6	5	4	3	2	1	not informative
c.	self-fulfilling	7	6	5	4	3	2	1	not self-fulfilling

7. COMMUNICATING IN A BARGAINING SETTING

a.	pleasant	7	6	5	4	3	2	1	not pleasant
b.	informative	7	6	5	4	3	2	1	not informative
c.	self-fulfilling	7	6	5	4	3	2	1	not self-fulfilling

8. COMMUNICATING IN A PERSUASIVE SETTING

a.	pleasant	7	6	5	4	3	2	1	not pleasant
b.	informative	7	6	5	4	3	2	1	not informative
c.	self-fulfilling	7	6	5	4	3	2	1	not self-fulfilling

9. COMMUNICATING IN A COMBATIVE SETTING

a.	pleasant	7	6	5	4	3	2	1	not pleasant
b.	informative	7	6	5	4	3	2	1	not informative
c.	self-fulfilling	7	6	5	4	3	2	1	not self-fulfilling

10. COMMUNICATING IN A COERCIVE SETTING

a.	pleasant	7	6	5	4	3	2	1	not pleasant
b.	informative	7	6	5	4	3	2	1	not informative
c.	self-fulfilling	7	6	5	4	3	2	1	not self-fulfilling

Questions for Analyzing Communication Contexts

The behaviors expected of you in such situations as those you have just considered will vary along several dimensions; and you can determine what those expectations are, in part, by answering such questions as the five which follow.

Does the context call for cooperation or conflict?* In the Assessment Scales, the ten dyadic communication contexts have been presented in an order starting with those requiring the most cooperation and concluding with those likely to produce the most conflict. 5

The question we are considering is easy to answer in the contrasting cases. Conflict is not a typical, expected behavior in a loving relationship, nor is cooperation typical of a coercive context. Of course, some contexts may call for a measure of *both* cooperation and conflict. In an interview, for example, the agents may—at one and the same time—have cooperative desires and conflicting interests. You must assess carefully the degree of cooperation and/or conflict expected in a given setting, for you will be more successful as a communicative agent if you employ behaviors that are generally expected in that setting (unless, of course, you wish to attempt a restructuring of the entire situation).

However, we should be alert to the possibility that behaviors may turn out to be entirely *unexpected*. There may be instances in debates, for example, in which one agent's behavior is more appropriate for a bargaining context—consisting of an attempt to compromise on the issue. The other agent may refuse to restructure the combative situation, catch the opponent off balance, and make the position of the opponent appear weaker. We will suggest later in this chapter a procedure for safely initiating changes such as this.

Does the context call for symmetrical or complementary behaviors? Paul Watzlawick, Janet Beavin, and Don Jackson, in their *Pragmatics of Human Communication,* suggest that all communicative interchanges are either symmetrical or complementary, depending on whether they are based on equality or difference.[2] Symmetrical behavior, they say, means that the agents behave

---

*In Chapter 12, "Managing Conflict in Interaction," this particular aspect of human interaction is explored in depth.

Study Probe 5
Analyzing Cooperation and Conflict in Communication Contexts

Would you agree with our rank ordering of communication contexts in the Assessment Scales as moving away from cooperation and toward conflict? If not, what modifications would you make in the order? In your judgment, what level of cooperation and what level of conflict exist in Contexts 5 and 6?

similarly—from the same motives, and toward the same ends. Complementary behaviors appear in situations in which the behaviors, motives, and aims of the agents differ. Yet, differing behaviors need not indicate conflict. The behavior of one may fill out or complete the behavior of the other. Hence, it is "complementary." Communicative behaviors of two agents may be termed complementary if their actions mutually supply each other's lack. 6

A loving relationship is symmetrical: The agents act alike, for the same reasons, and for the same ends. In conflict situations, the agents may also act much alike, for the same reasons, and for the same ends. So the conflict setting may also involve symmetrical behaviors. Therapeutic and instructional contexts, on the other hand, are more likely to involve complementary behaviors. The behaviors of the agents in these settings differ from one another, but mesh together in accomplishing the agents' shared goals. The Cooperation/Conflict and the Symmetrical/Complementary behavioral dimensions of interpersonal communication are not perfectly correlated. The rank ordering of our contexts on these two dimensions would not be identical.

Briefly, then, in answering the question, "Does the context call for symmetrical or complementary behavior?" you must ask whether the context calls for you to "mirror" the behaviors of the other agent (symmetrical behavior) or whether your behaviors should be the counterpart of the behaviors of the other agent (complementary behavior).

Does the context call for the presenting of self or the sharing of self? Some research scholars have distinguished between "presentational encounters" and "sharing encounters."[3] In "presenting" yourself, you would attempt to project (or "present") an image of your own choosing, and to protect yourself. In "sharing" the self, your goal would be an openness and an overlapping of your "self-system" with that of the agent with whom you wish to interact. These scholars believe that self-sharing relationships are continually being developed during sustained conversations.

In *The Presentation of Self in Everyday Life*, Erving Goffman views human interaction as though it were action in the sense of the theatre. He discusses

Study Probe 6
Comparing Behavioral Dimensions

Rank order the ten dyadic communication situations according to whether they call for symmetrical or complementary behaviors. Compare this ordering with that you found acceptable for the Cooperation/Conflict continuum in Study Probe 5.

Consider the classroom settings in which you are interacting this term. In what ways are your behaviors and the behaviors of your instructors symmetrical and/or complementary?

the actions of an agent as being "on stage" and "off stage." He suggests that a waitress, for example, is "on stage" when waiting on customers, and "off stage" when in the kitchen picking up orders.[4] She may be quite natural and open (sharing) with the kitchen employees, but may wear a "smiling" mask when presenting her image to the customers. As a communication agent, you must determine in every setting what type of image and how much image-projection is expected of you.

Does the context call for movement toward, against, or away from the other agent?   Psychiatrist Karen Horney classifies dyadic interpersonal relations as indicating movement by each agent toward, against, or away from the other agent.[5] Movement *toward* shows affiliative and affectionate desires; movement *against* reveals combative tendencies; and movement *away* indicates a desire not to be involved with and influenced by the other. "I like you," "Let's fight," and "I'm sorry, but I don't want to get involved" are verbal illustrations of these three directions in which interpersonal interaction may move.

In a loving relationship, the expected movement would be toward; in combat, the movement would be against. What of the instruction and interview contexts? Possibly the movements in the latter settings could be either toward or against, but more probably there would be an ambivalence or balancing caused by tendencies toward and tendencies against. In any of the contexts we have discussed, the relationship could deteriorate for one reason or another so that one or both agents would decide to move away and withdraw from the interaction.

Does the context call for a continuing or temporary association?   Referring again to our ten dyadic communication situations in the Assessment Scales, those that we found at or near the "loving relationship" end of the continuum would tend to be continuing relationships also, while those at the opposite end would tend to be more temporary and short-lived.

In your work with the Assessment Scales, you have no doubt observed that we have placed at the left-hand ends of the scales descriptive terms which suggest the more favorable or "positive" conditions in a communicative relationship; and at the opposite ends we have positioned the less favorable or "negative" conditions. Quite probably, too, you have observed that continuing relationships seem generally to be associated with the factors at the positive ends: pleasant, informative, self-fulfilling. A wide range of research studies—especially those based on observations and reports having to do with gaming settings, community-conflict situations, and international relations—support the validity of such an association and conclusion.[6] From this research, it appears that, with extended interaction, one agent tends to reciprocate the actions of the other, and both come to behave similarly. Of course, we must be wary of drawing causal inference and stating that continuing relationships *cause* harmonious relationships. It might be the other way around. If such relationships do indeed exist, their harmoniousness may be so satisfying and rewarding that they cause continuing relationships. Or, possibly, both conditions may derive from some other common cause. We do find, however, that continuous relationships and harmonious relationships are positively correlated. And this in itself should be sufficient reason for anyone who desires either condition to strive for both.

We have been insisting that when you are a communicative agent, you should always seek to determine the contextual demands and—from them—the expectations the other agent will have about the communicative interaction. But how shall you do that? For one thing, you can try to concentrate your efforts upon finding useful answers to the five questions which you can ask about the context. These will assist you in determining what patterns of behavior will be expected of you, specifically:

1. Does this particular context appear to call for *cooperation* or *conflict?*
2. Does the context appear to call for *symmetrical* or *complementary behaviors?*
3. Does the context appear to call for *self-presentation* or *self-sharing?*
4. Does the context seem to call for movement *toward, against,* or *away from* the other agent?
5. Does the context appear to call for a *continuing* association or only a *temporary* one?

In a dyadic relationship, you should know that if you meet the expectations of the other agent, you will be seen by that person as "playing according to the rules," and the interaction can proceed as is normal in that specific type of context. If, on the other hand, you "break the rules" and *deviate* greatly from the other's expectations, then the normal relationship will be violated and must undergo significant restructuring. Unfortunately, you can never be sure of the outcome of such a restructuring. The consequence of such a period of uncertainty

Study Probe 7
Learning to Use Gradual Reciprocal Increments

a. For each of the five major questions considered for speech contexts and summarized in the text, discuss with another person some specific ways in which communication agents desiring to improve a particular interpersonal relationship could attempt to do so by gradual reciprocal increments. Compare your conclusions with others who will be discussing the same procedure and problem.
b. Together with a classmate, role play the following situation (or devise one of your own), using gradual reciprocal increments to improve the conflictive nature of the context. Before the experiment begins, expand on each agent's role so that the discussion will be as realistic as possible.
    Situation: A college administrator meets with the leader of a group of students to discuss the students' concerns for a greater voice in policy-making decisions, curriculum changes, hiring and firing of faculty members, etc.

and even chaos could eventually, of course, be a more honest and productive relationship. On the other hand, the outcome could be the utter destruction of the relationship. In either case, the stakes may be very high, and you or the other agent—or both of you—could prefer not to take the necessary risk.

Clearly, what we need is a helpful means for changing the interpersonal relationship for the better *within the existing context.* And there is such a means.

CHANGING THE NATURE OF A CONTEXT: GRADUAL RECIPROCAL INCREMENTS

As you are aware, one of the central and continuing themes of this textbook has been that speech communication is a dynamic, ongoing process, a process which is constantly undergoing change and development. Within such a process, we believe, *a carefully guided change* in interpersonal, communicative relationships is possible. This change, we think, can be effected by means of what might be described as *gradual reciprocal increments.*[7] By following such a give-and-take, reciprocal arrangement, an agent can effect controlled change and improvement in an interpersonal relationship.

Simply put, *this incremental procedure calls for a series of small changes gradually initiated by one agent and reciprocated by the other.* You, as the first agent, must begin by modifying—by a small amount at least—your attitudinal, communicative behavior (perhaps becoming more cooperative, or more self-sharing), making sure that you modify it enough so that it may be easily detected by the other agent. You then wait to see if your movement is reciprocated. If it is, you may make another small attitudinal/behavioral change in the same direction, wait for reciprocation, and—if it does appear—continue to repeat the procedure. If, following your initial effort, your partner chooses not to reciprocate or elects to change to a different relationship, you stand to lose very little. The risk taken with your first small change is not great. [7]

If handled with care and genuine concern, a change by means of gradual reciprocal increments can help avoid the confusion of a drastically altered relationship and can, at the same time, pave the way for a more mutually satisfying and useful relationship between agents. [8]

Study Probe 8
Applying Gradual Reciprocal Increments
to a Personal Problem

In an interpersonal relationship in which you may now be having trouble communicating, attempt to modify the situation using gradual reciprocal increments. Then prepare a written report describing your efforts in some detail and indicating the extent to which they appeared to be reciprocated and successful.

DEFINING STATUS AND ROLE POSITIONS

In the preceding pages we have been concerned with determining some of the contextual requirements of interpersonal communication. We asked what particular situations require and what expected behaviors derive from those requirements. Here, our purpose will be to ascertain what the status and role positions of *another* agent require and to examine the behavioral expectations created by *those* requirements. From the standpoint of the communicative agents, our present concern is closely related to the earlier one and in some ways overlaps it, for the other speaking/listening agent is—as we know—always a part of the total, interactive context.

Status Positions

Status can be thought of as *a collection of rights and duties assigned to and expected of an individual.* Differences in ability, position, control over others, age, and wealth are some of the elements which may create status differences between agents. Other status differences often are decreed by social organizations and social conventions. For example, most organizations have an assigned hierarchy of leadership which establishes status differences within and sometimes outside the organization. In groups without prescribed order, such status differences usually develop as time passes.

Status levels, whether formally or informally created, are always somewhat like the "pecking order" among animals: to be operative, the ordering must be accepted by all the parties involved. Such acceptance is clearly evident in a number of research studies of the effects of status upon communication in small groups. These studies have found that, quite without regard for the actual situation itself, perception of status differences alone will lead to changed behaviors.[8]

Status differences are often revealed by the manner in which one individual addresses another. If two men address one another as "George" and "Mr. Brown," we recognize their status differences immediately. As you know, in many languages a distinction is made between a formal and an informal word for the person "you"; one "you-word" is far more formal than an alternative "you-word." In languages where this is the case, status differences are revealed when two agents address one another with different forms of *you.* [9]

Study Probe 9
Identifying Status Differences

Refer again to the ten dyadic contexts we employed in the Assessment Scales earlier in this chapter. In the most typical instances of each context, specify the status differences that usually exist between the agents involved. Under what circumstances might the hierarchical order change? In what ways would the status differences between the persons affect their communication?

We expect persons of high status to make more *pivotal* comments, to initiate more interaction, and to control and direct interaction. This does not mean, of course, that they necessarily talk more; they may or they may not. Persons of lower status are expected generally to show deference in their communicative behavior—regardless of how much or how often they speak. These expectations would apply to what is said, how it is said, and when it is said. [10]

Role Positions

Whenever two agents interact, each one will be playing or acting out some kind of role. A *role*, as we define it here, *is a unified pattern of behavior that reveals only a part of an individual's total nature.* Psychiatrist Carl Jung has pointed out that we can never meet another person with the totality of our personality. We can never, in fact, have all the facets of our personality even under our own control at one time. In a particular social context we develop—or at least "present"—only specific *parts* of our personality, according to the communication context and the other agent with whom we are trying to interact. An individual is a child to his parents, a student to his teacher, an employee to his job supervisor. Jung wrote of these roles as the *personae,* a Latin word meaning "masks."[9] A

Study Probe 10
Exploring Status Differences

a. We usually associate higher status with persons who occupy space in the front of a group, room, or at the head of a table. What are some other physical, nonverbal factors you associate with high status? Consider physical appearance, speaking mannerisms, dress, and voice.

b. Using the two floor-plan diagrams of the business office shown below, arrange a desk, chair, table, three side chairs, and two file cabinets so as to (1) maximize and (2) minimize status differences between the occupant and a visitor.

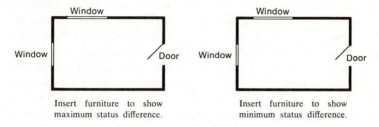

Insert furniture to show maximum status difference.

Insert furniture to show minimum status difference.

c. Role play each of the following situations twice—once in the office arranged for maximum status difference, then again in the office arranged for minimum status difference: (1) executive interviewing prospective employee, and (2) executive meeting with his counterpart from another division to review progress on an important project.

role that we play or a mask that we wear in a given situation will depend largely upon and reveal something of our relationship with the other communicator. As with status differences, if the agents mutually understand and accept the masks being presented, they can proceed with the interaction.

Although status and role differences may exist, it is nevertheless possible to achieve effective interaction. To do so, you will of course have to strive for sensitivity to the *needs* of the other agent. And you cannot hope to achieve this sensitivity unless you have some way of predicting what those needs are likely to be.

Considering the Needs of the Other Agent

William Schutz has presented a useful analysis of three interpersonal needs.[10] In developing this threefold system of needs, Schutz contends that each of us has a:

1. *Need for inclusion.* The need to establish and maintain a psychologically satisfactory interaction and association with others. The need to be "in" and involved. The need for esteem in the eyes of the other agent.
2. *Need for control.* The need to establish and maintain a degree of control and power over the other agent. The need to feel personally competent and responsible.
3. *Need for affection.* The need to establish and maintain a relationship of love and affection with another. The need to be close to another. The need to feel that the self is lovable.

In every instance, as a communicative agent desiring to develop sensitivity you should consider these needs of the other agent and how the satisfaction of these needs relates to that person's status and roles. While you cannot always do what is necessary and appropriate to fulfill these satisfactions, by being aware of them you will at least better understand what impels the other person to think and behave in a certain way.

Eric Berne's analysis of complementary and crossed transactions relates to the point we are making here. In *Games People Play*,[11] Berne observed that in every social setting an individual exhibits the ego states of Parent, Adult, or Child. (Berne distinguished *ego states* from *roles*, but that distinction is not pertinent to this point.) He argued that communication can proceed smoothly as long as transactions between the agents are complementary. If, for example, two adults address each other as adult-to-adult, they can interact on that basis. If Bob addresses Laura as child-to-parent and she reciprocates by addressing him as parent-to-child, they will also have established a *complementary transaction.* But if Bob tries to approach Laura as child-to-parent while she is looking for an adult-to-adult relationship, they have fallen into a *crossed transaction* which will surely create misunderstandings. Each will be sending messages which violate the other's expectations. If they can become aware of their uncomplementary roles, they may be able to adjust them; but if they continue in this crossed transaction, their communication will be impaired, or even impossible. ⊞11

Whether you view your co-communicator's needs as Schutz suggests or see your role relations as Berne proposes, as a communicating agent you are sensitizing yourself to the status and role differences of your "other" and to what this human relationship demands. Again, because of the patterned and role-like nature of communication and the efficiency which can result from following accepted patterns for interaction, you may attempt to choose the role and status positions you will exhibit during interpersonal interaction, and will try to assess the positions you anticipate your colleague will exhibit. Your next task is to compare the expectations of the two agents, yourself and your "other," to see whether they are in harmony. If so, the interaction may proceed. If not, you should probably seek a better balancing, if that is at all possible. One means of striving for such a balance is by using the *Gradual Reciprocal Increments* which we have previously discussed (page 225). In addition, as we shall outline in the ensuing section, there are some other procedures which may be profitably pursued by agents who seek improved interaction.

SEEKING MUTUALITY AND BASES FOR INTERACTION

Alienation is commonly used to describe the feelings of remoteness being experienced by significant numbers of individuals in our contemporary society. The frequency with which the word is heard suggests that many of us may have lost our grasp on the fundamental touchstones of social interaction. Family and church play a less central role in our time than in previous eras. Often, increasing technology and population are singled out as factors which have diminished our potential and our significance as individual human beings. Today, many of us are searching seriously for new and better roadways to group identification and community awareness. What possible actions in the interpersonal context may help to mend and heal these feelings of alienation? On the following pages we suggest several additional procedures as meaningful and practical approaches to improving interpersonal interaction.

Study Probe 11
Evaluating Communication Transactions

Refer to the Speech Communication Self-Assessment Scales which you completed in Chapter 3, pages 57–61. Using Berne's concept of complementary or crossed transactions, analyze your interaction in each of those contexts. Note any specific ways in which this analysis helps explain the anxieties and frustrations you may have experienced in certain of those settings. File a written report of your analysis with your instructor.

Seek a wide range of communication experiences.   One means by which communicative agents can better prepare themselves for successful speech communication interaction is to gain experience in as many differing communication settings and with as many different individuals as possible. The more varied the situations we encounter and learn to adjust to, the more flexible we should be in adapting to still newer situations. The more we tend to confine our interaction to a single group of similar people in the same setting and with the same purpose, the greater will be our difficulties in facing new and different situations. [12]

Our counsel to you as a student of speech communication is that you should not close off near-at-hand opportunities for speech interaction. Too many students, for example, search for materials for assigned papers only in libraries, and neglect to interview professors and others who may be experts on the subject and who may be easily accessible on campus. Don't overlook such an opportunity to widen the scope of your interpersonal speaking experiences. Some citizens, both old and young, complain about the actions of the city council, but they only talk *about* members of the council—rather than *to* them. Aside from the limited effects which "talking about" can induce, you will be missing a chance to take direct action and widen your communicative contacts—an opportunity which any alert person ought always to cultivate.

Search for possible common ground.   The character of each individual, as we have seen, has many facets. These facets often prompt individuals to clash with one another on certain limited levels and to interact as antagonists. Quite possibly, however, if both would pause to think, they would realize that in their many-faceted characters they *could* find certain similarities and points in common—likenesses which could serve to establish a common ground and produce positive, productive interaction. Unavoidably, you will find it necessary from time to time to interact with others on matters of dispute. In such circumstances, begin by trying to search out *mutuality* and lines of *commonality*. As a strategy for interpersonal relations, almost invariably you will find it easier to interact with another in controversial matters if you make a real effort to find common ground.

 Study Probe 12
*Assessing the Heterogeneity / Similarity Ranges
of Other Agents*

List all—or most of—the persons with whom you have talked in dyadic settings for periods of longer than five minutes during the past week. What is the range of ages, occupations, beliefs, values, and experiences of the persons on your list? Would you say these persons, as a group, are heterogeneous and varied, or are they generally like one another? What do they have in common? Develop a simple, concise "analysis chart" of your findings and be prepared to discuss it with other members of the class and/or to hand it to your instructor as the basis of a possible private interview with him or her at a later date.

Kim Giffin and Bobby Patton describe a technique used by R. D. DuBois in promoting better relations among representatives from disparate groups.[12] Instead of having these persons come together and talk about intergroup differences and conflicts, DuBois had them talk about their most pleasant childhood memories. (A contemporary instance of this practice might involve representatives from industry and labor unions.) What appears to happen is that, after a time, members of these essentially different groups find that many of their childhood happinesses, feelings, and experiences were similar. This gives the participants a common ground.

Some might argue that a discussion of pleasant childhood memories is time-consuming and irrelevant to the problem. These objections must be taken into consideration. Yet, as we pointed out in Chapter 2, there are many reasons why we communicate. Before the basic communicative purpose can be effectively pursued, it may be necessary for the persons involved to prepare the psychological climate with techniques such as those suggested here.

Maintain continuing involvement with the other agent. A communication agent should strive to sustain interaction and involvement with the other agent over as long a period as is practical and appropriate for their mutual purposes. In our discussion of continuing contexts (pages 39–42), we pointed out that those settings that maintain the mutual association of the agents tend to have certain positive ends. Those communicators who interact frequently tend to like one another better, and gradually become more alike in their beliefs, evaluations, and values.

Practice active affirmation in interaction. Consider the following pair of statements:

a. My pet is a dog.
b. My pet is not a dog.

The initial statement is an *affirmation*. The second statement is a *negation*. Aside from this obvious distinction, there are other significant differences between them. The first statement informs us (1) that the speaker has a pet and (2) that the pet is a dog. This short assertion carries a great amount of information. It eliminates any uncertainty we may have had regarding the question of whether or not the speaker has a pet. But the statement also reduces uncertainty among many more possibilities. The second statement leaves us in doubt. If the speaker has a pet, it could be any one of dozens of possible pets. The first statement reduces the possibilities by all but one when it informs us specifically that the pet is a dog. Information theorists define information as a "reduction of uncertainty." By that definition, the first statement is much more informative. In contrast, the second statement is not nearly as informative. We may infer from the statement that the individual has a pet, but we have no idea what it may be. Of the dozens of possibilities, the statement eliminates only one. The second statement reduces much less uncertainty than the first, and is a great deal less informative.

This example reveals the nature of affirmation and its advantages over negation. Affirm a policy and we know what you support. Negate a policy and we may have no idea what you stand for. And *you* may not either. There are some who speak at length about repression in our society, in the present structures in university education, and elsewhere. Often these speakers list at length what they *don't* like. But some of them are suddenly inarticulate when they are asked what they want—what they *do* like. Quite frequently the only "constructive" suggestion they make is to "get rid of the old system." But this apparent inability or unwillingness to speak positively and informatively can only frustrate the other agent and does little to promote productive interaction. For *lack* of information, the very pattern of communication heightens rather than reduces conflict between agents.

The type of analysis we have offered for *affirmation versus negation* is applicable also for the *active-versus-passive* dimensions of behavior. Activity, like affirmation, carries a large amount of information. Passivity, on the other hand, leaves us uncertain as to just what the other person stands for. 13

What we have said, certainly, should not be interpreted to mean that you ought never to oppose programs or never play passive roles. What we do wish to emphasize is we can be most helpful to the other agent if we decide what actions we *do* advocate and support and then speak *for* those positions. We owe it to any other agent with whom we interact to have thought sufficiently about the subject under discussion to have formulated a clear and specific position to advance, advocate, or support.

Strive for supportive rather than defensive interaction. In a study based on observations of small group discussions in various contexts, Jack R. Gibb distinguished between communication behaviors typical of *supportive* climates and

Study Probe 13
*Making Interpersonal Speech Active
and Affirmative in Interviews*

Select a classmate as a partner and, together, work out two hypothetical job interviews. Alternate in your role playing between the positions of *interviewer* and *interviewee*. In one instance, as interviewee, simply respond impromptu—"off the cuff"—to the statements put to you by the interviewer.

In another instance, before participating in the interview, plan carefully a summary of your abilities, experience, qualifications, and interests. In particular, review pages 126–129 in Chapter 6 where we explored the interviewer-interviewee relationship. Make tape recordings of the interviews so that later you can make a careful analysis of the interaction.

In preparing a report on your analysis, indicate—among other things—in which of the two instances your speech behaviors were more active and affirmative.

of *defensive* climates in interpersonal interaction.[13] Gibb's classification system contrasts six pairs of behaviors, as follows:

	Supportive		*Defensive*
1.	Description	vs.	Evaluation
2.	Problem orientation	vs.	Control
3.	Spontaneity	vs.	Strategy
4.	Empathy	vs.	Neutrality
5.	Equality	vs.	Superiority
6.	Provisionalism	vs.	Certainty

Gibb's system suggests (Item 1) that remarks which are descriptive and neutral in connotation will tend to be supportive, whereas comments that are highly evaluative in connotation may cause the other agent to become defensive. Similarly, attempts to control the other *agent* will create defensiveness, whereas an orientation in which attempts are made to control the *problem* will be supportive (Item 2). Note that in Item 3 Gibb proposes that stratagems intended to manipulate will cause defensiveness, whereas open, spontaneous discussion will be supportive. In some respects, this third pair of terms can create misunderstanding. We must not infer from Gibb's study that spontaneity is always "good" or that careful planning is "bad." The difference should be seen as one of manipulative strategy in contrast to open and honest discussion. It is not a difference between careful planning and unplanned remarks made on "the spur of the moment." [14]

Neutral comments directed toward the other agent, according to Gibb, might be interpreted as signifying a lack of concern and lack of desire for involvement, whereas empathic remarks show a sensitivity toward the other person and the ability to see the matter from his or her view (Item 4). Furthermore, if

---

 Study Probe 14
Differentiating Supportive and Defensive
Communication in Interpersonal Contexts

Join another classmate in developing a series of role-playing conversations. Build your experiment in two different contexts: (1) *a social conversation context,* and (2) *a bargaining-and-negotiating context,* with you and your partner performing and then exchanging roles for each context. Vary your role playing in each of these contexts so that in one instance you use "supportive" behaviors and in another you employ "defensive" behaviors. Again, if possible, tape record your conversations for later analysis. Prepare a report describing the results, concentrating on the differences among the various communicative climates arising from the alternating contexts and contrasting behaviors.

your comments show that you consider the other as an equal rather than as an inferior, you are clearly being more supportive (Item 4). And finally (Item 5), statements that are absolute and uncompromising may create a defensive response, whereas a provisional or tentative approach will be likely to evoke a more supportive response.

We have suggested in this chapter that dyadic speech communication is patterned. To achieve the highest levels of interaction, as a communicative agent you should be aware generally of the usefulness of following and occasionally reshaping the expectations deriving from these patterns. You will do well always to be sensitive to the demands of the communication context in which you find yourself. Working sensitively with the other agent, you should strive to determine the status and role relations between the two of you. With this knowledge in mind, together you should seek the closest possible interaction. An efficient principle in this quest is the modification of behavior by *gradual reciprocal increments*. In seeking bases for interpersonal interaction, we've emphasized, each of you should seek *empathy, affinity,* and *harmony* with the other. The behaviors suggested throughout this chapter are all intended as means to those ends.

Suggested Readings

Erving Goffman, *The Presentation of Self in Everyday Life* (Garden City, N.Y.: Doubleday & Company, Inc., Anchor Books, 1959). In this paperback the individual is seen as playing roles and presenting himself in all his speech communication interactions.

Paul Watzlawick, Janet Beavin, and Don Jackson, *Pragmatics of Human Communication* (New York: W. W. Norton & Company, Inc., 1967). This work presents interesting material about patterns and problems in communication interaction.

Kim Giffin and Bobby R. Patton, eds., *Basic Readings in Interpersonal Communication* (New York: Harper & Row, Publishers, 1971). This paperback contains interesting selections from varied sources relating to interpersonal communication. It permits the reader to sample widely and follow up on those references he or she finds most interesting.

Reference Notes

[1]Virginia Satir, *Conjoint Family Therapy,* rev. ed. (Palo Alto, Calif.: Science & Behavior Books, Inc., 1967).

[2]Paul Watzlawick, Janet Beavin, and Don Jackson, *Pragmatics of Human Communication* (New York: W. W. Norton & Company, Inc., 1967), pp. 67–71.

[3]J. Watson and R. Potter, "An Analytic Unit for the Study of Interaction," *Human Relations* 14 (1961): 245–263.

[4]Erving Goffman, *The Presentation of Self in Everyday Life* (Garden City, N.Y.: Doubleday & Company, Inc., Anchor Books, 1959).

[5]Karen Horney, *Our Inner Conflicts* (New York: W. W. Norton & Company, Inc., 1945).

[6]Kenneth W. Terhune, "The Effects of Personality in Cooperation and Conflict," in *The Structure of Conflict,* ed. Paul Swingle (New York: Academic Press, Inc., 1970).

[7]David Braybrooke and Charles E. Lindblom, *A Strategy of Decision* (New York: The Free Press, 1963), especially Chapters 5 and 6.

[8]Floyd L. Ruch and Philip G. Zimbardo, *Psychology and Life,* 8th ed. (Glenview, Ill.: Scott, Foresman and Company, 1971), pp. 105–106.

[9]See the summary of Jung's views in Ira Progoff, *Jung's Psychology and Its Social Meaning* (New York: Grove Press, Inc., 1955), especially Chapter 3.

[10]William C. Schutz, *FIRO: A Three-Dimensional Theory of Interpersonal Behavior* (New York: Holt, Rinehart & Winston, Inc., 1960).

[11]Eric Berne, *Games People Play* (New York: Grove Press, Inc., 1964), especially pp. 29–34.

[12]Kim Giffin and Bobby R. Patton, *Fundamentals of Interpersonal Communication* (New York: Harper & Row, Publishers, 1971), pp. 183–184.

[13]Jack R. Gibb, "Defensive Communication," *The Journal of Communication* 11 (1961): 141–148.

Chapter 11

SMALL GROUP COMMUNICATION

For small group interaction to be *effective*
and productive, each participant must understand
and assume responsibility for the group's goal—
its substantive *task function*—and for maintaining
healthy, objective attitudes by all concerned—
the *social-emotional* function. All participants
should share the *leadership role*.

The small, communicating group pervades every level of modern society. Most organizations, ranging from whole societies, governments, giant business concerns, and educational systems, to local civic clubs, activity groups, and often families, rely on small group interaction for their existence and maintenance. While some persons may shy away from speech making to larger audiences (even at their own personal loss), it is nearly impossible for any of us to avoid participation in small group communication. This context for communicative interaction, therefore, deserves careful attention.

THE USEFULNESS OF SMALL GROUP DISCUSSION

As a means for problem solving, decision making, and information sharing, as well as for mutual support and personal growth among members, communication in the small group setting offers many advantages which an individual acting alone or which two people interacting will not have available. Let's examine the purposes, advantages, and disadvantages of small group discussion.

Purposes of Group Communication

As we've indicated, the small group discussion setting can serve a wide range of purposes. It is used very extensively for *problem solving* and *decision making*. An organization is faced with a problem which must be solved and the need for some course of action. A small group of individuals come together to discuss the situation and arrive at the best solution to their common problem. Such a group can meet at the highest or the lowest levels of the organization. The problem may be profoundly significant or of lesser importance. Yet the communication problems at both levels may be much alike. Most of our emphasis in this chapter will be upon this decision-making function of group discussion.

Another important purpose of group communication is *information sharing*. Sometimes a group does not have as its goal the determining and implementing of policy. Or it may not be qualified or authorized to make decisions. Or, having that authority, the group may prefer or desire to achieve a different goal. For example, subcommittees in the League of Women Voters are frequently formed to survey problems and assemble and organize pertinent information. The information is usually intended for distribution to League members before the group acts as a body to formulate a decision. The task within the subcommittee, then, is to gather and share information. In a slightly different way a meeting of a Great Books group has the primary purpose of information sharing and intellectual stimulation. However, since information sharing through group effort also occurs as one of the phases of problem-solving discussions, our emphasis upon problem solving will ensure coverage of the way in which information is shared within other small groups.

A further purpose of group communication can be to provide *mutual support* and *personal growth* for the participants. For example, group therapy is now widely practiced.[1] Organizations such as Alcoholics Anonymous serve the primary function of providing mutual support to their members. It is also true, however, that while some group meetings emphasize this goal in their activity, *every* group discussion contributes somewhat to this end. Although it may not be so pronounced, mutual support among participants is a function and, ideally, a result of *every* decision-making discussion. We can therefore treat supporting functions of groups as we consider the major functions of problem-solving groups.

Advantages of Group Communication

Why bother with communication in groups? Why not let single individuals, at every level within an organization, make all policy decisions?

Research studies have shown a number of ways in which group decision making can be superior to that of individuals.[2] First, the group can usually assemble more resource material than any one person can. If the task in any way permits a division of labor, then the group will collect more information. Group processes are also superior in that random errors can be eliminated as the data of a number of individuals are pooled. One person may get sidetracked because of a simple mistake, or fail to see an obvious alternative solution. A group of people can correct these temporary oversights of individuals.

Professor Dean Barnlund compared decision making by individuals, by group-majority rule, and by group discussion. His study revealed that discussion was significantly better.[3] He found that membership in the discussion group produced a higher level of interest in the successful completion of the task. Group members knew their views were being weighed by others and were more careful and deliberate in their thinking. Group members also recognized a wider range of issues inherent in the topic than did individuals working alone. The studies further revealed that the competition among the private prejudices of the group members resulted, finally, in a more objective view of the problem.

Group work is also beneficial because it provides social motivation and rewards. People often seem to enjoy working together in groups and are stimulated by that setting. Any researcher using groups for a study is always aware of what is called the "Hawthorne effect," so termed because of some early studies in industrial settings of the Western Electric Company plant by that name. The most important finding of these studies was that when persons perceived themselves as members of a special group working on a special task, their morale improved and their productivity increased.[4]

Another related advantage of group work is the *increased commitment* which the individual feels to the group's decision. Some studies have indicated that if individuals have participated in and have been able to express their views during decision making by a group, they will then be more committed to the group's final decision, even if it does not represent their own or their original view. Other studies show that participation in group discussion of a topic is more likely than individual reflection to produce behavioral changes. In these cases, the public commitment to a course of action and the feeling of having had a fair hearing probably contribute to the result noted.[5]

Disadvantages of Group Communication

Group problem solving is not all profit, however; there is some cost. Before discussing these "costs," you will probably find it useful to probe some of your personal experiences and try to recall some of the deficiencies and drawbacks which may have frustrated various discussion groups.

The major limitation of group discussion is that it takes so much time. *Time* must be available, and well used, if the full benefits of this form of communication are to be realized. There are problems and cases for which there is not adequate time for group processes to be employed. A second limitation has to do with the nature of the participants—namely *people*. All the human weaknesses and problems characteristic of human communication will be apparent in group discussion. A number of these will be discussed later in this chapter. When we participate in group discussion we must be prepared for these limitations and be tolerant of them. In most instances involving social problems, the benefits to be gained from this form of communication far outweigh the disadvantages. [1]

CONCEPTS OF LEADERSHIP

For years the topic of leadership has been a dominant concern in the theory, research, and teaching about group communication. Let's look at this concept rather closely for a moment, and organize our application of communicative principles around it.

Early studies of leadership attempted to determine the underlying *traits* of leaders. The idea was to identify leaders, to see what they had in common, and to ascertain how they differed from non-leaders. Measurements of intelligence, information, and even height and weight were sought. Some positive findings did appear from these studies, but on the whole they were disappointing. The findings of one study seemed to contradict the conclusions of another. Eventually the trait-index approach to leadership analysis largely faded away.[6]

Another hope has been to learn about leadership by looking for general leadership *styles*. Some early studies compared "autocratic," "democratic," and "laissez-faire" styles of leadership. In the "autocratic" approach the leader remains aloof from the group and dictates procedures. In the "democratic" situation the leader takes an active role in guiding the group's activity, but allows the group to determine policies through discussion. In the "laissez-faire" style the leader plays a passive and aloof role, available only if called upon. Generally in these studies the "democratic" style has proved superior.[7] Rarely, however, is leadership in real life so stereotyped and consistent.

Psychologist Floyd Ruch summarizes some of this research with the general observation that:

> . . . it has been found that leaders in most situations are distinguished by three important characteristics: their awareness of group attitudes (social perception), their ability in abstract thinking, and their good emotional adjustment. Personal popularity may also play a part.[8]

Study Probe 1
Examining Some Impediments to Group Progress

Consider again three groups in which you have recently participated. What problems were most apparent in your experience with each group? Attempt to categorize these problems (1) as being related to the task or goals of the group, or (2) as being primarily social-emotional in nature. Can you make any generalizations about the relation between the purpose of a group and the factors which hindered or impeded its work?

Ruch also observes that *good leaders and good followers have much in common.* This point begins to get to the heart of the matter.

Robert Bales has suggested that leadership is not a one-dimensional concept. His studies indicate that there is "task" leadership in which a person focuses upon the work or task confronting the group and guides the discussion toward the goal. There is also a "social-emotional" leadership which functions primarily to prevent conflicts, resolve tensions, and promote group unity.[9]

Many studies on leadership end with "it all depends. . . ." It all depends on the situation, the persons involved, the topic, the setting. One person may emerge as a "leader" in certain cases, but not in others. In any discussion, one individual may "lead" at one time, but not at another. And one person may lead primarily on task matters, whereas another may lead mainly on social-emotional matters. [2]

Leadership should not be viewed as a static concept. We should not search for the leader or the act of leadership. Rather, we should consider *leadership functions: the actions which influence group members in positive ways toward the achievement of their group goal.* Any one, or all, of the members in group discussion can serve as leaders. Some will lead at certain times and in certain ways. At other times and in still other ways, others may lead. *Leadership occurs whenever an individual expresses a comment that exerts a positive influence on the group's interaction.* Any person doing this is fulfilling a leadership role and serving a leadership function.

But you may say that a person is often assigned—by a teacher or an executive—to be "the leader." In reality, however, that person is assigned to serve as *chairperson,* as coordinator and guide for the discussion. He or she will, it is to be hoped, lead at certain times and in some ways during the discussion. But so should all the other participants. We expect a chairperson to serve as *guide* during the meeting; but we hope every participant will serve, along with the chairperson, in fulfilling the necessary and helpful leadership functions. This is the kind of shared leadership that makes groups function most productively.

Study Probe 2
Analyzing Yourself in a Leadership Role

Recall your association with task groups in which you have served in a position of leadership. Describe your performance in terms of "style." Would you characterize your behavior as "autocratic," "democratic," or "laissez-faire"? Would you categorize your leadership functions as primarily oriented toward the group's *task* or toward the *social-emotional needs* of the group and its participants? In which leadership roles have you felt most comfortable? most successful? Verify your analysis by asking a friend, who was a member of one of the groups for which you served as leader, to answer these same questions about you.

With this concept of the nature of leadership in mind, let's look at the essential principles for effective speaking in the small group communication setting. Whether you're acting as assigned chairperson or as discussion participant, you will need to observe some practical guidelines in planning for task functions and for social-emotional functions in group communication.

PLANNING FOR TASK FUNCTIONS

Let's first consider the discussion *task*. What is essential in order to accomplish the group's goal? What steps should be followed? We will suggest here one possible means of developing thought and talk in a small group decision-making discussion. We will attempt to cover fully the decision-making interaction, although occasionally we will comment on discussion forms having more limited goals. Whatever has bearing upon the larger case should also fit the limited one.

Choosing the Problem-Solving Sequence

Assume that the members of a small group are given a problem to discuss, and are asked to arrive at the best possible solution. How can they proceed most effectively from problem to solution? There are *a number of alternative approaches* that could be taken.

The group could, for example, consider an "incrementalist" strategy, related in some ways to the Gradual Reciprocal Increments procedure we described in Chapter 10.[10] The Incrementalist approach is based upon the view that most groups are composed of individuals who do not have the necessary personal capabilities, or the time, or significant agreement on basic underlying values, to follow the more rigorous and traditional Reflective-Thinking process.

The Incrementalist approach is *problem*-centered rather than *goal*-centered. It focuses closely on the problem and seeks immediate remedial steps, rather than reflecting on the problem and developing a long-range comprehensive set of goals and procedures needed to reach those goals. So this approach is said to move *away from* the immediate problem rather than to move *toward* a distant goal. Suppose, for example, there is a problem of inadequate parking on a college campus. An "incrementalist" would tend to search for a quick way to provide a few more parking spaces. A "reflective thinker" would be inclined to study the larger problem and come up with a comprehensive plan for campus transportation. The interests of the "reflective thinker" would go far beyond parking spaces.

The Incrementalist approach also suggests that all actions are to be taken in small or incremental steps away from the status quo (present policies and practices). According to the incrementalists, there is little "risk" involved in taking these small steps. If a mistake is made, it is easy enough to return to the starting point. This strategy asks only that the participants agree to the proposed action and not that they share underlying reasons for that action. The Incrementalist approach can sometimes be helpful as a means for changing and improving inter-personal relationships, and every group decision maker should be aware of its possibilities. Yet, at the same time, it could be argued that this method permits "muddling" along and drifting into even more dangerous problem situations.

The "mixed-scanning" approach of Amitai Etzioni is another possible strategy for solving problems.[11] This strategy tries to combine some elements of the more traditional approaches with Incrementalism. It asks the participants to scan generally over the problem situation, eliminating alternative courses of actions which have "crippling objections": means for implementation-of-solution are not available; proposed solution violates moral code of participants; proposed solution is not "politically" feasible, etc. Those alternatives surviving the initial scanning are then scanned again in greater detail. More are eliminated, and those remaining are scanned again until only one remains. This approach also requires that continuous scanning and evaluation be carried on as the proposed solution is enacted. This procedure, too, has merits which decision makers may wish to consider.

The major decision-making procedure to be considered here, however, is the more commonly used Reflective Thinking Sequence derived from John Dewey's description of the steps in thinking (Chapter 8, pages 160–161) and adapted by others through the years. The procedure we are suggesting here is rigorous in that it demands a high level of effective interpersonal communication—more, perhaps, than some of the other approaches. Yet we believe that it is potentially the most effective problem-solving system.

The Reflective Thinking or Problem-Solving Sequence is composed of the five steps listed below. In following this sequence, the group progresses through the five steps, completing each step to the satisfaction of the majority of the group members before moving on to the next, and building one step upon the other; thus:

1. Analyze the problem (symptoms).
2. Determine causes.
3. Establish standards for judgment.
4. Consider possible actions.
5. Settle on the best solution.

1. Analyze and detect symptoms of the problem.   The first step calls for an analysis of the problem—a diagnosis of the symptoms. How do we know that we have a problem? We usually become aware of a problem because we can see its *symptoms,* the *signs* of a problem. How do we know that we are physically ill? We have a headache, feel weak, and have an above-normal temperature which can be easily measured. These are symptoms or signs of illness. How do we know that we have a water-pollution problem? Because a beach is condemned as physically unsafe for swimming; fish and fowl die and can no longer live in and on the water; plant growth spreads throughout the underwater area. All these events are definite and real, and they are easy to observe, measure, and count. These observable, measurable phenomena are the symptoms or signs of a problem.

The first step, then, in a problem-solving discussion should be to consider and assess the symptoms or signs of the problem. If there are no symptoms, there is little use in further discussion; if there are symptoms, the group should *list and evaluate them.* Just what has happened and what is happening? How widespread is the problem? How significant is it? Do the symptoms matter—can we live with them? The group should also attempt to assess the *trends* of the symptoms. Is the scope or size of the symptoms increasing? If we do nothing about the symptoms, will they simply fade away? Are any present attempts being made to meet the problem? If so, what are they, and what effects are they having upon the symptoms? What actions, if any, have been taken to reduce the symptoms, and what are the current trends? In this first step the group should present, consider, evaluate, and come to some clear conclusions about the evidence indicating symptoms or signs of a problem. The point here is for *all* communicative agents to come to the fullest possible understanding of the observable effects of the problem and their probable consequences if the problem is not solved.

2. *Determine the causes of the problem.*   The second step, and a most crucial one, is for the group to ascertain the causes of the problem. This is a very difficult step and a stumbling block to the solution of many human social dilemmas. Much of the difficulty lies in our analysis of causation and in the confusions pointed out in Chapter 9 (see page 207). We must realize first that the *symptoms of a problem are not usually the causes of the problem.* Symptoms are observable effects, or results, or signs. Causes are usually complex and often not observable, but they are the forces that produce the problem.

The headache lets us know we have a problem. But the headache results from our having "a cold"; the headache does not cause the cold. An unseen virus is the cause of the problem. So how do we treat a cold? Sometimes we take aspirin and in a few days the cold is gone. But it is important for us to realize what we have done here: We have followed a course of action to eliminate a symptom temporarily. We have done nothing about the cause. If our body did not wage the real battle against the cause, we could take aspirins continually and never be rid of the affliction. ③

Just as anyone who is suffering from a cold must bear in mind the differ-

Study Probe 3
*Distinguishing Between Symptoms and Causes
of a Problem*

Discuss several contemporary issues with your classmates in small group settings. In each case try to distinguish between the *symptoms* of the problem and the *causes* of the problem. For example, you might consider: (1) the rising crime rates, (2) pollution of the environment, and (3) diminished U.S. prestige abroad.

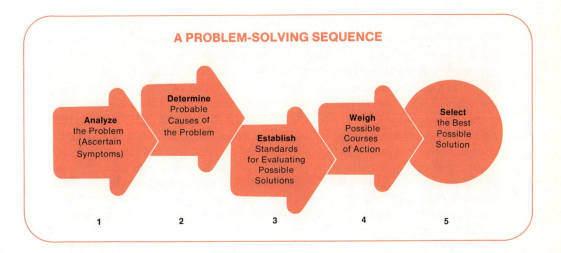

A PROBLEM-SOLVING SEQUENCE

Analyze the Problem (Ascertain Symptoms)

Determine Probable Causes of the Problem

Establish Standards for Evaluating Possible Solutions

Weigh Possible Courses of Action

Select the Best Possible Solution

1   2   3   4   5

ence between the symptoms and the causes of the illness, so a discussion group must distinguish with equal clarity between symptoms and causes, and know which is going to be treated. Social ills, unlike physical disorders, have no intrinsic defenses or mechanisms to search out and eliminate the cause of the problem. They require intervention from "outside." If the problems are to be "cured," intensified group efforts will be necessary. Too often, in dealing with social problems, we make the "mistake of the common cold": We attempt to eliminate problems by treating symptoms only. Most often this is unsuccessful. Even if we eliminate a symptom but allow the cause to remain unchecked, that cause can produce other symptoms. At times it may be necessary to treat the symptoms of social problems, as in instances of public-welfare payments and wars. To effect genuine and lasting improvement, however, we must search out and treat the causes. Consider an environmental problem. Dead fish and a condemned beach are, as we have said, symptoms and not causes. We may continue to restock streams and clean up beaches regularly; but if the water remains polluted, the fish will continue to die and the beaches will be periodically unsafe. A wiser course would be to seek the cause and try to eliminate the pollutants.

There are understandable reasons why individuals and groups tend to attack symptoms only. Causes are elusive because they are most often unseen, even unseeable. Frequently they are psychological rather than physical. Usually they are complex. Usually they can be viewed not only as causes of certain effects but also as effects of even more remote causes. They are often multifaceted, so that they have a different appearance if viewed from different angles. Consider another example. Why is Person X a criminal? One may view him and his situation from an external standpoint and attribute his criminal behavior to an undesirable childhood environment, a broken home, erratic discipline, and so on. Another look, taken from inside, may suggest that his criminality is due to feelings of rejection, a lack of love, and so on. A different view, still from inside, will suggest that a chromosome abnormality is really the cause. All views yield answers that agree that the man is a criminal, and they agree on what he has done. But the understandings of the causes differ widely. This example might shed some light on the tendency—which all of us exhibit—to treat only the symptoms of problems. It is a far simpler course of action.

In the cause-determination phase of group problem solving, you and your colleagues in discussion must consider alternative points of view from which problems (signified by symptoms) can be inspected and their causes discovered. You must realize that framing causes is like setting the boundaries of a concept prior to verbal labeling. The boundaries must be arbitrarily established by your group. In all of this you should be guided by an awareness of your goal, and you should choose an approach to the examination of causes which will facilitate the remainder of the discussion. If a broader social view of the causes rather than a narrower psychological perspective will make it easier to arrive at a workable solution, then you should use the former.

After proposing, considering, and weighing the causes as they see them, members of a discussion group should eventually arrive at a list of causes *with some judgments as to their relative strengths*. Which are the primary causes, which the secondary? Which causes must be treated if any progress is to be made? Which are less crucial? These are decisions group members must make at this stage in their efforts, or else they cannot know what to solve.

3. Establish standards for evaluation of possible solutions.   As their third step, the discussion participants need to decide on the standards by which they will judge possible solutions. Consider an analogy. If you planned to buy a car, you would not merely walk into an automobile agency and say, "I want to buy one of your cars"—period. If your mind were no better settled than this remark suggests, you would have to consider every automobile the dealer had, or buy whatever he offered you. The chances of your purchase being a "good" one *for you* would be limited. Your actual practice would be to determine in advance *standards* for your selection. You would arrive at the dealer's showroom knowing you were interested in a certain model, a certain size, a certain price range, and so on. No doubt you would have additional requirements—engine horsepower, trunk space, gas mileage, ease of maintenance, and possibly more. You would give such information to a salesman who would then select from all possible choices only those that fit the standards you have established. Time would not be wasted in considering unacceptable choices. This is the efficient way to proceed, unless you're just "window shopping" and don't mind impulse buying. Most social problems, however, are far too important for us to proceed in any such "window-shopping" manner. As we've emphasized, time limitations are always a big factor in group decision making, so everything possible should be done to keep the work of the group orderly and efficient. By establishing definite standards for an acceptable solution, we greatly improve efficiency. But groups often omit this step unknowingly, and move directly from causes to solution, if not from problem to solution.

If it is to function efficiently and with genuine understanding of what it is doing, a problem-solving group needs to pause after completing its view of the problem (symptoms and causes) to take stock of what kinds of answers are even *worthy* of consideration. Is there really *need* for solutions at all? If there is, then *just what* needs solving and what does not? What *special requirements* must be met? What *limits* choices among solutions? These are among the questions participants in problem solving need to ask themselves before rushing headlong in search of answers.

One of the most practical standards any acceptable solution will have to meet is that it must fit within the limits of your resources—financial, personpower, etc. To toy hopefully with a $1000 solution if your group can raise only $100 wastes time and effort and is foolish. To speculate about the merits of a solution that will require the work of more people than you have available to work is equally wasteful and frustrating. There are other kinds of "standards" that also need to be explored. *Which* causes should you or can you attack? In what order? Or to what degree would a solution be acceptable if it could only reduce symptoms? And if symptoms are to be reduced, which ones and in what order? Only after considering such questions as these about the "standards" that acceptable solutions have to meet are the participants in a discussion prepared to move to consideration of possible courses of action. ⁴

4.   *Consider possible courses of action.*   As a fourth step in problem solving, your group should locate and consider the possible courses of action available to you within the limits of your established standards. Initially, you can assemble a listing of all possible solutions which you and your colleagues have found or developed, including only those which *fit the major, limiting standards.* Once this list has been assembled in as complete a form as possible, you and the other participants can focus upon each possibility in turn and judge it against the full set of standards, as well as against each of the alternative solutions in your list. Probably, few proposed solutions will attack the specific causes of your problem and meet the established standards for judgment to your complete satisfac-

---

Study Probe 4
Establishing and Applying Evaluative Criteria

Plan to meet with a small group of classmates for two sessions. At the first session select something to be judged, and determine the standards by which this "something" could be evaluated. Be specific, and try to consider all of the ramifications of the criteria you are establishing. At the second session, apply these standards to something specific, and make a judgment accordingly. For example, you could set up standards for judging political speeches, television commercials, summer jobs, or restaurants; then subsequently, you could evaluate a particular speech, a televised commercial, a summer job, or a restaurant by using the stated criteria as your basis for judgment.

tion. You will usually find it necessary, therefore, to make *comparative* judgments and compromises. In this way you can determine the relative effectiveness of the proposals, or perhaps alter and combine plans to make them more satisfactory. 5

In evaluating the proposed solutions, members of a discussion group must do more than weigh one solution against another and against the standards. Each solution must also be considered in terms of its *consequences*. Where would this proposal lead? What side effects might it produce, and how would we like those side effects? As we emphasized in Chapter 9, most changes introduced in a system will have far-reaching effects, and those effects should be predicted and assessed. Perhaps an example will help to clarify this step of the sequence. As we battle the causes of disease and mortality, we increase population, with its attendant effects. So, in a way, the widespread use of penicillin and other "miracle drugs" is a remote cause of water-pollution and city-parking problems. Some ramifications, perhaps less dramatic, are inherent in many solutions you will deal with. Some solutions may effectively counter the cause of a problem, but they may have so many undesirable side effects as to be impractical and unwise.

During this—the fourth—phase in problem solving, then, a group lists possible solutions, considers their probable consequences, and judges them against the standards for evaluation. With this knowledge clear to everyone, group members are then ready to make a decision as to the "best" action or solution.

5. *Select the best possible solution.* In the fifth and final step in problem solving, the group endeavors to settle upon the best possible solution—the original and climactic objective and one which follows quite naturally from the work of the fourth step. The best possible solution may be among those proposed earlier, or it may be made up of parts or combinations of several proposed solutions. It may have long-range as well as short-range components. The solution may entail the steps for its own implementation and later reevaluation.

As a general rule, if the group elects to employ the Problem-Solving Sequence, each of the five steps should be completed in turn. As we have emphasized, a group should stay with each of the consecutive phases of the sequence

Study Probe 5
Brainstorming

In a small group setting, choose a problem for consideration by the group, and then try to "brainstorm" for possible courses of action or solutions to the problem. Bear in mind the following guidelines to be heeded in this technique: (1) Present as many different possibilities as you can. (2) Do not expand or develop any suggestion when it is made; just note it and move on. (3) Do not criticize any idea which is suggested, or any person suggesting an idea. See how many possible solutions the group can list in ten minutes.

until all questions related to that phase have been defined, determined, and/or resolved; only then should the participants move on to the next phase. Each step should be built upon the preceding stages. The causes should be causes of the problem discussed. The standards for evaluation should fit the ascertainable causes. The possible solutions considered should conform to the standards selected. *The entire process should demonstrate coherence and progress from problem to final solution.* If followed carefully, this sequence can do much to provide order and efficiency in group decision making. In applying this sequence, however, the participants must be flexible. The proposed steps may have to be modified in some cases. This system must *serve* the discussants rather than master them.

Wording the Discussion Question

With the general problem-solving sequence in mind, we can turn now to the *chronology* of planning for the discussion task functions. The first task is to decide upon the *wording* of the problem-solving question. The framing of a discussable question must be considered carefully because the way a question is phrased usually provides some direction for its answer. The group members have to *see* clearly, and *agree on,* both the point of discussion and terms of the discussion. Without this prior agreement, the discussion may not "get off the ground." Susanne Langer presents one such case.[12] Suppose one person asks the question, "Who created the earth?" and another person replies, "No one created it!" Langer says the second person has not really answered the question at all; he has *rejected* the question. This can happen in discussions of social problems. A group may meet to answer the question, "How can we best improve our mathematics program in X Junior High School?" Suppose one or more participants begin by saying, "We don't see anything wrong with the program." These participants are rejecting the question. A comment such as this could start an argument that is really apart from the question itself. The question *assumes* the improvement is necessary, desirable, and possible. Only participants who are willing to make these assumptions can profitably discuss the question. Perhaps the members of the group should discuss first whether there is anything wrong with the present program.

Not everyone, of course, will always agree that problems exist; not every participant will accept every question. Nor should they. We are simply suggesting that everyone should begin with a mutual basic assumption—should "start off on the same foot." If one person comes prepared to suggest new programs and another is set only to defend the present system, there will be difficulties. Remember the "status of the question." If the "status" is not similar for all participants, the discussion cannot begin smoothly. It is the function of phrasing discussion questions to identify the "status" at which *this* group can and will begin the problem-solving process. *A good discussion question must be so framed that the participants will agree with the assumptions inherent in it.* The question must ask for precisely the kinds of answers which all participants are seeking.

A discussion question should be stated in interrogative form, simple and clearly put; and the meaning of essential terms should be agreed upon by the participants. If, for instance, a discussion is to focus on water pollution, *what* we want to know about it must be clearly asked and the meaning of the terms must be settled before attention is turned to analyzing "the problem."

Beyond these requirements, a problem-solving question should call for the entire Problem-Solving Sequence. "What should constitute our foreign-aid program to Country X?" asks for consideration of symptoms, causes, standards, possible actions, and solution. If we were to ask the question "What is wrong with our foreign-aid program to Country X?" a simple listing of the ills of the present program would probably suffice as an answer. This question in no way asks for a solution. "What has caused the pollution in Lake X?" does not call for a solution. If you desire only a listing of problems, or difficulties, or causes, you may ask a question leading to such a listing. But *if you want a solution, you should ask for it.*

A good problem-solving discussion question will usually limit the scope of the topic, but not limit the consideration of potential solutions. "How can we best improve our educational system?" is much too broad. It could at least be narrowed to "How can we best improve our educational system in the United States?" Better still might be "How can we best improve our secondary education system in Madison?" or "How can we best improve our mathematics program in X Junior High School?"

Most discussion groups attempt to answer questions that are too broad. There are several reasons why the consideration of very broad questions is inadvisable. The problems, in these instances, are often seen as too complex; sufficient materials are not readily available for a thorough and satisfactory analysis, and the discussion tends to be carried on at such a general level as to be of little value. The topic should be qualified and limited in scope to a subject-area that the group can conceivably cover. As with our education problem, questions usually can be limited to certain levels, to certain geographical locations, or to specific subjects.

On the other hand, the wording of discussion questions should not arbitrarily rule out the consideration of any possible *solution.* A topic should be open to the evaluation of all possible solutions. For this reason it is never good practice to frame a problem-solving discussion question that can be answered with "yes" or "no." "Should this state legalize abortion?" is a question that can be discussed, but it is not a problem-solving question. It proposes a specific course of action and asks, "Do we want this particular solution—yes or no?" It is a question that could well occur in the latter steps of the Problem-Solving Sequence, when the group is evaluating several alternative courses of action and attempting to arrive at an overall solution. It could occur under problem-solving questions such as "How can we best meet the problem of overpopulation?" But, in itself, it is a question that begins with one possible solution to be evaluated rather than a problem to be solved. Under the topic of "birth control," abortion could be evaluated in conjunction with many other possible solutions. Ideally, the interplay and joint evaluation of several possible solutions will lead to a better answer.

In sum, it is usually desirable for problem-solving questions to be simply and clearly stated, to call for the consideration of all the steps of the Problem-Solving Sequence, to limit the scope of the topic, and not to restrict the solutions which the group may consider. The assumptions underlying the question should be agreed upon or tacitly accepted by all the participants before the group proceeds to consider the problem. 6

Preparing Materials and Agenda

Whether you serve as the assigned chairperson or as a participant in a group discussion, you will need to know the topic well. Every group member should assemble as much material as possible on all aspects of the problem. As a participant you will probably have to refer to your research materials during the discussion. Therefore, those materials should be abstracted or copied on note cards, organized for easy reference, and brought to the meeting. This is simply a precaution against becoming confused about the facts or your own ideas during the give-and-take of discussion in a group.

The *agenda* for a meeting is the order of topics to be considered. These topics should be coordinate and related to one another. During the discussion, the participants will take up these topics in the sequence suggested by the agenda. Included in it, of course, are those topics that must be covered if the group is to answer the discussion question. For a problem-solving question, the agenda most often will be the five steps of the Problem-Solving Sequence adapted to the proposed content of the discussion.

A group should settle on its general agenda as early as possible, preferably before the first working session. This will enable the participants then to use the items in it as reference points for research on the topic for the ordering of their materials. This will be true even if the task is not one of problem solving. If a book-review group is planning a discussion, it will likely be more effective if a ten-

Study Probe 6
Evaluating Problem-Solving Discussion Questions

Evaluate the suitability of the following six questions for problem-solving discussions:

1. In what ways would more government planning help?
2. What steps, if any, should be taken to end tensions in the Middle East?
3. How can we best cope with increasing technology?
4. How can we best improve the mathematics program in X High School?
5. Should student automobiles be prohibited on campus?
6. What are the problems with drugs?

In instances where you feel the example is not a good problem-solving discussion question, modify it so that it becomes acceptable.

tative agenda is determined before the participants begin preparing. For problem-solving questions, a participant can safely use the steps of the sequence as headings for the organization of research materials. [7]

As we have previously suggested, the chairperson has additional responsibilities for task functions and must plan for them. If you are to be the chairperson, you should prepare your outline for the agenda, listing the main headings and subordinate points which must be taken up. You should plan a *series of questions* that you can pose to ensure that the group will keep moving along from step to step in the agenda. You may anticipate some points where *transitional remarks* must be made and at which *summaries* might be helpful. You should attempt to gauge very roughly how much *time* can be allotted to each step so that you can keep the group moving toward the goal. You should give some thought to procedures for *ending the discussion*. Is a final summary enough? Must there be a written report? Is any follow-up meeting or other action needed?

At the outset of the meeting, before the main discussion begins, the chairperson and participants ought to *agree on goals and procedure or agenda*. Often, groups tend to omit or overlook this step; instead, they "take off" in several directions at once. It is much simpler and certainly more efficient to spend a few moments to review and agree on the agenda and procedure before moving to explore the problem posed in the discussion question.

Necessary Attitudes for Task Functions

Task functions, or goal-related speech behaviors, also have an attitudinal component. No task should be pursued without *motivation* and *feeling*. What are some of the desirable *attitudes* which contribute to effective group work on a

Study Probe 7
Preparing and Following an Agenda

With the other members of your class, try the following group experiment. Agree on a problem-solving discussion question to be considered. Then divide the class into groups of five or six persons each. Let each group set up a different agenda.

The following lists suggest kinds of agendas that various groups might use in consideration of the question.

Group 1
{
a. Symptoms
b. Causes
c. Evaluative criteria
d. Possible solutions
e. Best solution
}

task? We suggest that the discussion participant should (1) *be goal oriented,* (2) *show a sense of inquiry,* (3) *be a good listener,* (4) *be patient,* and (5) *be willing to share leadership functions.*

Being goal oriented.   If group members keep in mind their immediate task, the time available, and their ultimate goal, their solution will probably be found sooner and be of greater usefulness. Of course, goal-oriented discussion is hard work. It is much easier to ramble aimlessly in a "bull-session" manner. If the group does go astray, the chairperson or any one of the participants can attempt to get it back on the track by presenting a summary of the group's progress up to the point of the digression, and then by asking a question to get the discussion moving again—away from the tangent and in a more productive direction.

Showing a sense of inquiry.   A second desirable attitude is a sense of *inquiry.* We may assume that, before the discussion begins, all group members have certain beliefs and evaluations about the topic. This is only natural. But the task will be made easier if the participants are open to new and additional information, to the opinions of others, and if they desire to learn more about the topic. In fact, without this sense of inquiry, the group can settle nothing. Asking appropriate *questions,* a subject we considered in some detail in Chapter 6 (pages 127–128), is essential for such inquiry.

We may note also that the question is a helpful way of raising an objection. Suppose someone says something with which you disagree. If you say, "Well, I don't agree with that," you only create a conflict. The other person has no idea *why* you disagree. Suppose you say, "I don't agree with that because . . . ." In this case, he does know your grounds for disagreement; but in your first five words you are flatly inviting a clash. It may be better to ask, "What about the

---

	a.	Survey of the facts
Group 2	b.	Possible solutions
	c.	Criteria for judging
	d.	Best solution

| | a. | Possible solutions (by "brainstorming") |
| Group 3 | b. | Best solution |

Following the discussion, each group should report its progress to the class as a whole. Compare the solutions arrived at by the various groups. In what ways did each group's agenda influence the end result of the discussion?

chances that . . . ?" and proceed to phrase the essence of the objection in question form. This calls upon the other person to answer your objection without your having introduced any personal conflict into the issue. Then, too, if you ask a question, you are calling for an answer; and you yourself may be more interested in the answer than in declaring your disagreement. Clearly, the manner in which an issue is raised will influence the matter of the answer. Task functions motivated by and revealing a desire for inquiry will usually be more productive. *But the motives must be positive.* If the question form is used out of a sense of manipulative strategy and not a sense of inquiry, the positive effect may be lost.

Being a good listener. Another necessary attitude for effective task-functioning is the intention of being a *good listener.* Good listening consists of attending carefully to what others say, understanding the meaning, and being able to rephrase it to their satisfaction. Descriptive studies, you may recall, have pointed out that a time differential exists between our usual listening rate and our thinking rate. Although a speaker normally will utter 125–150 words per minute, most of us are able to listen to oral communication if it comes to us three times that fast without losing much comprehension. As we pointed out in Chapter 6 (page 131), this is due, in part, to a natural redundancy in our speech. Thoughts are repeated, and standard phrases are used. Many elements in any spoken message could be omitted without greatly reducing comprehension.

Because of this rate differential and redundancy, as a discussion participant you will necessarily spend much of your time in listening. How, then, will you use that time? *A good listener will use this time to reflect on messages, rephrase them, and associate them with other related elements in order to understand and evaluate them.* Accordingly, it is a useful exercise occasionally to ask another, "Are you saying . . . ?" or "Is your point that . . . ?" See if you can state another person's point in *your* language to the other person's satisfaction. Thus, you will be checking on your own "spare-time" thinking. Try this when you seem to be in disagreement with another. If you can do this successfully, you are probably doing a good job of listening, and you will certainly be engaging in the clarification of ideas for yourself and others. *Another aid to listening and memory is the taking of notes.* During a discussion, all group members—and especially the chairperson—should periodically make notes of the major lines of development and accomplishment that might be especially helpful for recall later in the discussion.

Being patient. Another helpful attitude for task functions is *patience.* As we have stressed, the most efficient procedure in problem solving is to take up points one at a time and resolve each before moving to the next point. However, some participants have little patience. Once a problem is mentioned, and before it or its causes or anything else has been discussed, the impatient participant will offer a solution. Such comments offered prematurely can frequently do more harm than good to group progress. As we pointed out in Chapter 9 (pages 205–206), the natural human impulse is to meet every problem head-on with a quick solution, but good group discussants must try to curb this impulse. You must be patient enough to assist others in understanding the issues as you see them; and, further, you must be patient enough to take the time to understand their positions with reference to those issues.

Sharing leadership functions.   A final desirable attitude is a willingness to share leadership functions with all group members. It is especially important that an assigned chairperson not be so jealous of this position that he or she tries to dominate the group-guidance chores. A chairperson should encourage other group members to assist with all task functions—and they should cooperate. It should not always be the responsibility of the chairperson to make internal summaries, or to ask the questions that get the group back on the right track, or to note that the group must soon move on to the next topic. *Everyone* should be ready to do these things when they are needed. Concern for the task shows goal orientation. As we discussed earlier in this chapter, every group member should be motivated by this attitude, and it should be apparent as all shoulder the responsibilities for the group's task functions.

A Sample Case for Discussion

Some of the problems of task-oriented groups may be seen more easily, perhaps, in an example. On the first day in a discussion class, I often assign four or five members of the class to discuss a "sample case"—without any advanced warning or preparation. No chairperson is designated. The purpose is to see how the discussion "naturally" progresses, to note what weaknesses are most common, and to single out some of the points on which we must concentrate when we attempt to interact in a small group context. What follows is a transcript of actual—and typical—student comments about the case. Remember that the participants have not been informed of the activity in advance, have made no preparation, and are given no instruction other than to arrive at a group decision on the question. *All* members of the class, however, are given the following information about what we might call "The Bill and Jan Case":

It is Christmas vacation time at college, and Bill and Jan are planning to talk again to their parents about marriage plans. They are hoping to be married in June. They have gone steady for the past three months since meeting early this fall. Bill is twenty years old and in his third year in engineering—a five-year program. He has slightly better than a B average. He must attend at least one summer session to finish on schedule in two and one-half years. Jan is nineteen, a sophomore in history, with nearly an A average. She has considered graduate school because of encouragement by two of her professors.

About 80 percent of their college expenses thus far have been paid by their parents. Bill and Jan have made up the other 20 percent by work during summers, he for a construction company and she typing in an office. Jan's parents oppose their marriage so soon. Bill's parents say they are willing to go along and would continue to give the couple the same support they now give Bill.

What do you believe the couple should do about marriage plans?

(The discussion usually begins after several moments of awkward silence.)

Bob: Well, I don't think they should be married so soon.   **(1)**

Paul: It's not a good idea to rely so much on parents for money. They may become psychologically dependent on them, too.   **(2)**

Kay: Well, I don't know.   **(3)**

Bob: She could become pregnant. Then where would they be?   **(4)**

Paul: Right.   **(5)**

Dan: They are very young. How old—or how mature—should one be before he gets married?   **(6)**

Kay: Well, it all depends.   **(7)**

Sue: Won't they just be frustrated if they don't get married? It could interfere with their studies.   **(8)**

Paul: I just don't believe in taking money from parents. When people get married, they should be independent. Or at least nearly independent.   **(9)**

Kay: What will happen to Jan's plans for graduate school?   **(10)**

Sue: Still, it's their business. I don't see why they can't do whatever they like. Who are we to tell them what to do?   **(11)**

Dan: Maybe we should look at the other side—why should they get married?   **(12)**

(and so on)

This portion of a discussion, typical of this situation, reveals a number of problems: Bob's opening comment is a common one. The discussion begins with a personal, immediate, and unqualified answer to the group question. It is as if the speaker intends to end the discussion rather than begin it. There are also many comments, such as 3 and 7 by Kay, which offer very little to the group. They are just statements of personal perplexity. One major difficulty is revealed in comment 11 by Sue. These group members have not *discussed* their purpose or goal. Comment 11 really asks whether there should *be* a discussion; the reason for the discussion is not clear. Why is the group meeting? Why are they taking up the question? Are they to give advice or not? If comment 11 has a point, then the discussion has not. But this would not be the case had the group begun by considering whether they had a discussable problem.

Rarely does the group begin by making any procedural plans for these impromptu discussions. Only occasionally does a group member suggest an agenda which could be followed, or suggest that the group might pick a chairperson to guide the interaction. As a result, these experimental discussions usually drift aimlessly, touching on many points but settling few. There are periodic comments, such as 2 and 9 by Paul, which raise issues basic to the central question. But they are never systematically considered by all group members at one time, and they are not resolved. Seldom does one discussant build on or react to the comments of another.

In sum, these initial "class demonstration" discussions usually lack just about every attitudinal quality we have specified for accomplishing task functions. Rarely is a clear procedural pattern agreed upon and followed. There is no organized and complete consideration of standards for judgment. Yet in the basic information I give the class about "The Bill and Jan Case," there are many points that could be important in weighing a final decision. What about the ages of the couple? Their continuing their education? Parental support? Chances of the unexpected, such as Jan's becoming pregnant or Bill being injured or ill? True, some of these points are mentioned in hit-or-miss fashion during the quoted discussion, but none is examined for its significance or its bearing on a final decision. The many possible alternative courses of action are seldom mentioned. The question is usually treated as if it were: "To marry in June—yes or no?" But several other possibilities could readily be taken into account: The couple could be married later this summer, or next summer, or the next—when both have their college degrees. The consequences and likely results from following a specific solution are seldom pursued. For any decision that would affect our lives as importantly as this one, we should want all reasonable solutions to be considered quite fully. But in this type of demonstration discussion, the many different possibilities are infrequently listed and weighed against carefully derived standards for judging. There is little of the problem-solving sequence, and there are few of the suggested task-function attitudes apparent in these discussions. Fortunately, once the task functions of discussion have been examined in class and practiced during the semester, there is usually noticeable improvement.

Our example is a fair representation of what you and your colleagues are likely to do with a group task unless you turn your minds sharply toward *methods* of discussing a topic. Whenever several people sit down together, the invitation to wandering, desultory conversation is strong. Some degree of self-discipline in communication is needed even in one-to-one discourse, as we showed earlier; and both self-discipline and group-discipline become more and more important as the numbers of communicative agents are increased. This is why we have urged that you learn and generally follow the stages of the Problem-Solving Sequence. Not only does the sequence present an efficient way of proceeding; but also, if it is agreed upon and followed by a group, it helps keep digressive, chaotic talk to a minimum. 8

Additional Task Techniques

There are a few additional approaches which group members may sometimes employ to assist their task functioning. Let's examine a few of them briefly. We described the brainstorming procedure in Study Probe 5, and you had an opportunity to gain some experience with it at that time. The objective of this technique is to bring out more ideas and suggestions from the group members than would ordinarily be forthcoming. Participants in brainstorming sessions are asked to offer as many suggestions as possible, no matter how "far out" some of them may appear to be. Because no immediate evaluation of any suggestion is permitted, the participants tend to feel freer in voicing their ideas. Brainstorming can occasionally be a useful procedure to help along a group experiencing some difficulties with task efforts. As a group participant you should consider recommending its use from time to time.

Another possible approach is the Nominal Group technique, which could be labeled a "silent" form of brainstorming.[13] This procedure begins by having members of the group remain *silent* while they list (write out) ideas or answers appropriate to the question immediately before them. The "silent listing" is fol-

---

 Study Probe 8
Analyzing Discussion Participation—Personal Interaction

Observe a small group discussion, and tally each comment made by each participant. Using a chart like the one below, indicate to whom each comment is made. Distinguish between comments made to other individuals and those addressed to the group as a whole.

Person Making Comment	Person to Whom Comment Is Directed						Total Comments
	A	B	C	D	E	Group	
A	—						
B		—					
C			—				
D				—			
E					—		

Who made the most comments? Who made the fewest comments? Who most often addressed the group as a whole? Can you identify cliques by finding persons who speak most often to one another? In your opinion who was the task leader, and who was the social-emotional leader? Compare their profiles on the chart. What other pertinent information can be gleaned from this kind of analysis?

lowed by a general "open listing" of all participants' suggestions on a flip chart or chalkboard. Following this, there is "silent voting" to derive a ranked list of the most important items that have emerged by the listing process. Here again, the purpose of this technique is to generate a larger number of ideas and suggestions than would be likely to occur with normal interactive procedures. It also helps to equalize the input potential and the voting powers of the participants.

And, finally, we should take note of the Delphi process, which can be used by some groups to facilitate the decision-making task. This is a procedure which can be employed when group members are too numerous or are physically too far apart to assemble for a face-to-face interaction. With the Delphi approach, *a series of questionnaires with continuously monitored feedback* is used to develop a kind of "absentee" or "proxy" interaction. It also serves to develop a *growing, cumulative consensus* among participants who because of physical or other practical considerations are unable to be present for the more conventional forms of group communication.

Each of these various approaches which we've described briefly—brainstorming, Nominal Group, and Delphi—can on occasion be useful and effective for groups with certain kinds of problems.

Study Probe 8 (continued)
Analyzing Discussion Participation—Nature of Comments

Observe a small task group, and analyze their discussion-participation according to the types of comments which are made by the members. Using a chart like the one below, tally and categorize each comment made by each participant.

Type of comment / Person	Initiating new ideas	Clarifying ideas	Substantiating ideas	Developing ideas	Summarizing ideas	Agreeing	Disagreeing	Asking questions	Making procedural comments
A									
B									
C									
D									
E									

Which participant would you judge to be the task leader and which the social-emotional leader of the group? Compare their profiles. What other conclusions can you draw from an analysis of this kind?

PLANNING FOR SOCIAL-EMOTIONAL FUNCTIONS

While the discussion task provides the purpose and the goal for a problem-solving discussion group, task functions are not the only important acts in group process. There are also certain significant non-task functions which involve *social-emotional* behaviors and which are needed to produce maximally effective interaction within groups.

The Scope and Value of Non-Task Functions

Research studies have found that fewer than half of the comments in discussion are strictly essential to the task. Much of the time is (usefully, in most cases) taken up with exploratory comments, comments affirming agreement among participants, comments elaborating and clarifying ideas already before the group, humorous comments, and so on.[14] Clearly, such social-emotional behaviors also play a major role in group discussion. It may well be that these functions contribute to or even are essential to the accomplishment of task functions. My own research into the discussion process suggests that the movement toward the final solution is not a steady, uniform, linear development. Rather, *the development of an idea seems to occur in phases:* Participants carry an idea forward for a time; then there is a pause, followed by more forward movement, followed by another period of pausing. These recurring "plateaus" are characteristically occupied by social-emotional comments. They are intervals during which groups consolidate their gains, relax for a moment, and confirm mutual agreement and support.

These are times, also, when speech communication serves purposes (as identified in Chapter 2, pages 26–47) other than the basic communicative purposes of informing and influencing others.

Probably, many of the values and satisfactions derived from group work are the results of social-emotional functions. Task efforts can provide the solution

---

Study Probe 9
*Understanding Small Group Interaction
Through Role Playing*

Conduct the following role-playing experiment in class. The instructor will choose some issues for discussion by four- or five-member groups. School grading policies or dormitory problems are two possible topics. One member of the group will act as chairperson. One or two other members of the group should play a special "problem role" (for example, a domineering advocate, a joker, a reluctant participant, a person who wants to rush to a solution); but the chairperson and the other participants in the experiment should not be aware of these "special roles." As the discussion proceeds, observe how the chairperson and other members of the group react to and resolve the problems that arise.

to problems, but social-emotional responses are probably responsible for much of the group spirit and rapport, the solidarity, and the group loyalty to the solution that are often observed in small discussion groups. The increased likelihood for behavioral change might very well find its motivation in social-emotional activity.

Social-emotional functions—like task functions—should, of course, be the concern of *every* group member. As with task functions, better results can usually be attained if all group members are responsible for and contribute to these efforts. The "strength in numbers" comes from united action. If most group members work together on both task and social-emotional leadership functions, the chances for productive group meetings are much improved. Therefore, if we hope to be effective in small group communication (or in any other context of oral interaction), we must learn as much as possible about the other agents who will be involved and about the communicative situation. We should try to anticipate the communication problems that may develop during the meetings. Beyond the general aim of contributing to the establishment of a pleasant, relaxed, lively atmosphere for the occasion, all participants should also aim to cope with the inherent difficulties. Just as we plan beforehand for speech making and for discussion task functions, so should we plan in advance to meet social-emotional communication problems. 9

Communication Problems in Small Group Discussion

There are, of course, many communication problems which may arise during a small group meeting. Let's look at some of the more frequently occurring problems and try to develop some suggestions for handling them. Specifically, we'll consider (1) *the withdrawing or reluctant participant,* (2) *the too-talkative participant,* (3) *participant defensiveness,* (4) *tendency to conformity,* and (5) *interpersonal conflict.*

Conduct this experiment several times, with different issues, different groups, and different "special roles." Each time this role-playing experiment in small group interaction is conducted, analyze the discussion on the basis of the personal interaction between the group members and of the kinds of comments each member contributes. Pay special attention to the skill shown by the group members in handling the "problem participants." Note also how successful the members were in their consideration of the issue chosen for discussion.

Use the charts in Study Probe 8 as guides in formulating your answers concerning each experiment. Provide your instructor with your written evaluation of the effectiveness and/or ineffectiveness of each discussion group.

The reluctant participant. A group needs all of its resources and cannot afford to let a member sit silently if that person has something to offer. If one or two members of the group are saying very little, what should a chairperson or the other participants do? Often, the advice given is that the chairperson or some other participant ask the "non-talker" a direct question in order to get him or her involved. However, often such persons are somewhat shy and are driven even deeper into their shells by direct questions. A better approach, perhaps, is to *begin by asking yourself why this person is withdrawing.* Coming up with an answer for this question underscores the need for knowledge of the other agents and for planning the encounter with them in mind. Perhaps the "silent" or non-talking person is failing to interact because he or she knows nothing about the topic and hasn't made much effort in preparation. If that's the case, about all you can do is pleasantly *invite* participation, but don't insist on it. Sometimes you have to recognize that the best contribution such a person can make to the group (and if only ill-prepared persons could realize this) may be to sit quietly.

On the other hand, as one who is involved in the interaction you may know that a quiet colleague *does* have a contribution to make, but is shy. If possible, you should talk to this individual before the meeting and make opportunities for other group members to do likewise. This will make it easier for him or her to speak up during the interaction. Try to find out what aspects of the problem interest "reluctant" participants most, or on which topics they have the most information. Then during the meeting attempt to involve them primarily in the discussion of those topics. If you are chairperson and can make the seating arrangements, be sure shy or withdrawing participants aren't given a chance to isolate themselves on the periphery of the group. If they are allowed to sit where they like, they probably will seek out that location. Place them in seats near the center of the group, or elsewhere so you can see them easily and direct talk toward them. This at least will provide some insurance that those who are reluctant to talk won't be excluded from the group for "geographical" reasons alone. Moreover, once discussion is under way—especially on those topics you know to be of most interest to these non-talkers—you may ask these timid or withdrawn members an *indirect* rather than a direct question. Say, for instance, "Does anyone have information about . . . ?" and look at the individual who hasn't become involved in the interaction. This puts some pressure upon the person, but not as much as if you were to ask, for instance, "Do you know anything about this, Ann?"

Repeatedly, we have stressed the importance of getting all participants in a group discussion involved early in the meeting. As a matter of principle, we should know *why* a certain person may be withdrawing from the group discussion and meet the problem on its own terms. Whether you are chairperson or a participant, if a potentially valuable group member is not contributing to the discussion, the situation deserves countering efforts on your part.

The too-talkative participant. Another difficulty (and, on the surface, opposite from the former) is the group member who wants to talk *too much* and *too frequently.* Not all participants normally speak for an equal amount of time. Some naturally talk more than others. By the label "too-talkative participant" we mean that person whose talk exceeds the normally expected quantity, and thereby calls undue or excessive attention to himself or herself and prevents the normal participation of others. Here again, begin by asking yourself a question: Why is this person talking so *much?* If you have met the individual prior to the discussion meeting, you may have some insight into his or her personality. Perhaps the garrulous participant has an especially strong background on this topic and has made extraordinary efforts in preparation. If so, you may decide that his or her talking so much is really helpful for the group efforts, and you may elect to take no countermeasures.

Unfortunately, there are other reasons why people talk too much. Some are verbose and avoid one word where two will do. For this person you might occasionally interrupt with "Your position, then, is . . ." and proceed to provide a concise summary. Be ready to draw in other members, too. If the talkative participant agrees with your summary, you can move on to another person, having seemingly "closed" the long talker's point. Some people talk simply to hear themselves. You may need to interrupt these people occasionally. Or you may redirect attention by comments such as "We haven't heard from X about this," or "I wonder if anyone else has a comment on this point?" Again, there is the device of asking a general question and *looking* at some person other than the "talker" for an answer. If you know the too-talkative person well enough, and have established good rapport with him or her, you might even be able to be more pointed in turning off the flow of words. The values of knowing your fellow discussants, as we've emphasized, can be considerable. If you are responsible for the seating arrangements, you may place too-talkative discussants *away* from the center of the group, nearer the periphery. If you are chairperson, place them in such a way that your glances won't encourage them unintentionally. Obviously, it would be tactless and probably pointless to try to silence anyone, but reasonable attempts to limit the comments of some can contribute to group achievement.

Participant defensiveness. Few normal people enjoy criticism and rejection, and for this reason the actions of group members sometimes betray caution and conservatism due to fear of taking a public stand and thus subjecting themselves to possible rejection. If discussants feel that their ideas are rejected by a group, they may react either (1) by withdrawing from the discussion and offering fewer ideas, or (2) by becoming openly antagonistic and negative. One of the best ways of countering this tendency is to try to keep personalities out of the discussion as much as possible. *Ideas should be separated from persons.* Once an idea is presented for consideration, it is better to label it the *group's* idea than to identify it "Joe's idea." Then if the idea is later rejected, it will not be so necessary for any one member to feel personally rejected.

Another procedure for limiting defensiveness is the process we have called "brainstorming." Here the group tries to present as many different ideas on a topic as possible. Criticism is ruled out when the ideas are presented. The more ideas presented and the wider their range, the better. All group activity could profit from a little of the spirit of brainstorming. All participants should try to make it easy for the others to offer suggestions without fears of immediate and undue criticism or ridicule. Even when "brainstorming" ends and the group returns to evaluating, any limits on ideas presented should derive from considerations of the task and not from social-emotional concerns.

Conformative tendency. Another communication problem in discussion work is the *tendency to conformity.* In a classic study, Solomon E. Asch found that about one third of his subjects would conform in their judgment of the lengths of drawn lines even when their own perceptions differed from the stated majority opinion.[15] Similar conformity is sometimes observed in discussion groups. People become tired, or impatient, or less concerned, and so are "willing to go along" uncritically even with doubtful views that are advanced in groups. However, conformity or indifference of this sort should be guarded against. Sometimes, when the moment arrives for a transition from one agenda topic to another, the chairperson may summarize by saying, "Well, we seem to have agreed that . . ." and the participants may all indicate their concurrence. However, if you have listened to the discussion and know that the summary statement doesn't accurately describe what really happened, or that it could hardly be acceptable to all in view of the discussion, you should ask *why* there is no challenge to the summary. If you suspect that some members of the group are going along out of frustration or desperation, you may want to seek the reasons for those feelings. Genuine settlement of issues can only be accomplished by open discussion. Bypassing issues only delays the trouble. Of course, if the main reason for undue conformity by participants is fatigue, perhaps the time has come to adjourn the meeting.

Conformity has its value and, to some degree, is essential to productive group work. In any game one must be willing to conform to certain rules. In group discussion, as we have emphasized, individuals must conform to the norms and goals and procedures decided upon by the group. They must also conform to certain expectations about group conduct. But if members begin pointlessly conforming and become willing to go along with anything, then the communication process has broken down, and this problem must be confronted. The difficulty itself should be raised and discussed.

Interpersonal conflict. A certain amount of clash and conflict between ideas and points of view is almost inevitable in the group communication process. Sometimes these conflicts represent differences of opinion which must be settled before a group can move on. At other times they may reveal genuine personality conflicts or significant differences in the basic value systems of the participants. Our next chapter will deal in detail with such conflicts.

When such conflict arises, all group members should be aware of it and should promptly attempt to assess its cause. As we have seen, it is always wise to keep the interplay of ideas as objective as possible. This can be done if you use

questions to probe the conflict of views. You and your colleagues need to understand fully each other's positions. "Are you saying that . . . ?" "Is it your view that . . . ?"
"What about the problem that . . . ?" Look first to see where the conflict rests. Is it
merely a *semantic difference*—similar positions being stated in different words?
Or is there a *difference in sources or materials* that leads to the conflicting views?
If so, the sources of materials can be compared. In all cases it is wise to keep
ideas and personalities separated. Ideas, language, sources, and even values can
be dissected without danger to group productiveness, but personalities cannot.

Sometimes a group has a genuine, full-blown personality conflict in its
midst. In these cases, above all, try to remain calm and try—to the extent that
may be possible—to keep the antagonists from interacting too directly and too
emotionally with one another. If you are the chairperson, seat them in such a way
that it is difficult for them to challenge each other *directly*. Keep emphasizing the
group task and goal so that these important matters remain uppermost in the
minds of everyone. Let the ideas of the pair in conflict interact *through you* rather
than directly. This is like stepping between two people who are fighting—but with
much less danger of being hurt yourself. Remember that in trying to "manage" a
conflict problem—as with any other communication difficulty—your practice
should be to search for what lies *behind* or *beneath* it and to do whatever you
can do to alleviate the trouble without hindering the forward progress of the
group's interaction. You will almost certainly be able to understand what lies at
the roots of conflict and, perhaps, how to handle it more capably after you've
studied *interpersonal conflict management,* our major concern in the chapter that
follows.

Suggested Readings

Robert F. Bales, *Personality and Interpersonal Behavior* (New York: Holt, Rinehart &
Winston, Inc., 1970). This important work brings together the research of twenty
years by Professor Bales and his colleagues. It presents his latest revision of Interaction Process Analysis, a procedure for the study of small group interaction
comments. It also presents detailed studies of types of group participants—their
personality characteristics, their contributions and behaviors in groups, their personal values.

Marvin E. Shaw, *Group Dynamics: The Psychology of Small Group Behavior* (New York:
McGraw-Hill Book Company, 1971). This current textbook summarizes the psychological sources in which small group research is available. The treatment covers the nature and origin of groups. Findings relevant to the physical environment, the personal environment, the social environment, and the task
environment of groups are presented.

Irvin D. Yalom, *The Theory and Practice of Group Psychotherapy* (New York: Basic Books, Inc., Publishers, 1970). This source provides another approach to small groups. While our interest has not been on the goal of therapy in group interaction, Yalom's work is interesting reading, and it provides texture to our special interests by overlapping in some places and contrasting in others.

Reference Notes

[1]Irvin D. Yalom, *The Theory and Practice of Group Psychotherapy* (New York: Basic Books, Inc., Publishers, 1970). See Suggested Readings above. See also Morton A. Lieberman, Irvin D. Yalom, and Matthew B. Miles, *Encounter Groups: First Facts* (New York: Basic Books, 1973).

[2]Marvin E. Shaw, *Group Dynamics: The Psychology of Small Group Behavior* (New York: McGraw-Hill Book Company, 1971), pp. 59–67.

[3]Dean C. Barnlund, "A Comparative Study of Individual, Majority, and Group Judgment," *Journal of Abnormal and Social Psychology,* 58 (1959): 55–60.

[4]F. J. Roethlisberger and W. J. Dickson, *Management and the Worker* (Cambridge, Mass.: Harvard University Press, 1939).

[5]Floyd L. Ruch and Philip G. Zimbardo, *Psychology and Life,* 8th ed. (Glenview, Ill.: Scott, Foresman and Company, 1971), pp. 492–493.

[6]Cecil A. Gibb, "Leadership," in *The Handbook of Social Psychology,* 2nd ed., ed. Gardner Lindzey and Elliot Aronson (Reading, Mass.: Addison-Wesley Publishing Co., Inc., 1969), v. IV, pp. 205–282.

[7]Marvin E. Shaw, *Group Dynamics: The Psychology of Small Group Behavior* (New York: McGraw-Hill Book Company, 1971), pp. 270–274.

[8]Floyd L. Ruch, *Psychology and Life,* 7th ed. (Glenview, Ill.: Scott, Foresman and Company, 1967), p. 566.

[9]Robert F. Bales, "In Conference," in *Basic Readings in Interpersonal Communication,* ed. Kim Giffin and Bobby R. Patton *New York: Harper & Row, Publishers, 1971), pp. 418–431.

[10]David Braybrooke and Charles E. Lindblom, *A Strategy of Decision* (New York: The Free Press, 1963), especially Chapters 5 and 6.

[11]Amitai Etzioni, *The Active Society* (New York: The Free Press, 1958), especially Chapters 11 and 12.

[12]Susanne K. Langer, *Philosophy in a New Key* (New York: The New American Library, Inc., 1942), p. 15.

[13]The best available description of the Nominal Group technique, as well as the Delphi process, is by Andre L. Delbecq, Andrew H. Van de Ven, and David H. Gustafson in *Group Techniques for Program Planning* (Glenview, Ill.: Scott, Foresman and Company, 1975).

[14]Thomas M. Scheidel and Laura Crowell, "Idea Development in Small Discussion Groups," *Quarterly Journal of Speech*, 50 (1964): 140–145.

[15]Solomon E. Asch, "Effects of Group Pressure Upon the Modification and Distortion of Judgments," *Groups, Leadership, and Men,* ed. H. Guetzkow (Pittsburgh: Carnegie Press Publishers, 1951), pp. 177–190.

MANAGING CONFLICT IN INTERACTION

by Brian R. Betz

Department of Communication, Indiana University Northwest

Conflict is an inevitable ingredient of human
interaction. It may be productive or
counterproductive, depending on how it is managed
and used. Properly managed, conflict can be
a constructive force in increasing our energies,
sharpening our awareness of situations,
and stirring up our creativity in problem solving.

In Chapter 2 we emphasized that one of the major purposes of speech communication is to establish *social contact* in order to achieve human understanding and cooperation. In Chapters 10 and 11 we laid out procedures for achieving that purpose in two important interpersonal communication contexts: dyadic and small group. Experience, however, tells us that our social contact frequently leads to misunderstanding, strife, and conflict. We are all too aware of the problems arising between parents and children, wives and husbands, students and teachers, management and labor—the list could go on and on. Obviously, therefore, in any consideration of speech communication and human interaction, *conflict* must be a crucial concern. In this chapter we'll attempt to develop an orientation to the problems of interpersonal conflict so that we may better understand what it is, how it works, and how we can live more satisfactorily and successfully in a personal and social world electric with tension and turmoil. Although we'll deal primarily with conflict in dyadic situations, our observations may also be applied to conflicts within and between much larger groups.

269

PRELIMINARY OBSERVATIONS ON THE STUDY OF CONFLICT

We find wide disagreement among theorists over how we are to define *conflict.* Is it the same thing as "competition," "fighting," "hostility," "aggression," or "stress"? Shall we define it in terms of its function, its effects, the participants, or the situations? Or in terms of all of these things? Rather than trying to formulate some neat definitions easily pocketed in the memory, we shall first examine one theorist's view of the conflict process to identify certain characteristics of conflict situations and then work toward a tentative model for the study of conflict.

A Model for Studying Conflict

The "characteristics" of conflict are, perhaps, most clearly evident in the analysis by Louis R. Pondy.[1] He views conflict as a dynamic process involving a relationship between two or more individuals in a sequence of five stages:

1. *The antecedent conditions.* This stage represents the basic cause or issue over which the conflict arises—for example, incompatible goals, scarcity of resources, desire for autonomy.
2. *The perception of conflict conditions.* In this stage, the involved individuals become aware of the incompatibility of their relationship with each other. What was latent as an "antecedent condition" now becomes exposed.
3. *The affective impact of conflict.* The third stage recognizes the emotional consequences resulting from the perceived conflict—for example, tensions, stress, anxiety, hostility, etc.
4. *The manifest conflict behavior.* In the fourth stage, the conflict becomes visible in various expressive behaviors ranging from mild disagreement to open warfare.
5. *The conflict aftermath.* If the conflict episode is actually resolved to the satisfaction of all of the participants, then a foundation is laid for productive cooperation. On the other hand, if the incompatibility and antagonism are not resolved, but only suppressed, then the original antecedent conditions of Stage 1 will still be present in the relationship, and we can expect new eruptions of conflict.

If we think about Pondy's analysis for a moment, we will find inherent in his sequence a number of key characteristics useful in describing human conflict: (1) *dynamic* —conflict is a dynamic process having interrelating stages of behavior; (2) *relational* —conflict is the "product" of an interaction in which at least two parties endeavor to "relate" to each other, but with considerable difficulty; (3) *contextual* —conflict, like any other interaction, occurs within a limited social, psychological context or "place"; (4) *perceptual* —through their perceptions the involved parties become aware, to a greater or less degree, of the incompatible goals, resources, and ego-involvement which lie at the root of the conflict; and (5) *disruptive* —as the conflict episode evolves, the accustomed patterns of order and harmony within the individual or group are broken or at least thrown into a serious "imbalance."

Our model for the study of conflict begins with the dynamic structure set forth by Pondy and takes into account to a greater or less degree all of the characteristics we have identified as belonging to conflict situations. Although this model necessarily oversimplifies the complicated nature of the conflict process, it does provide a useful structure for our considerations.*

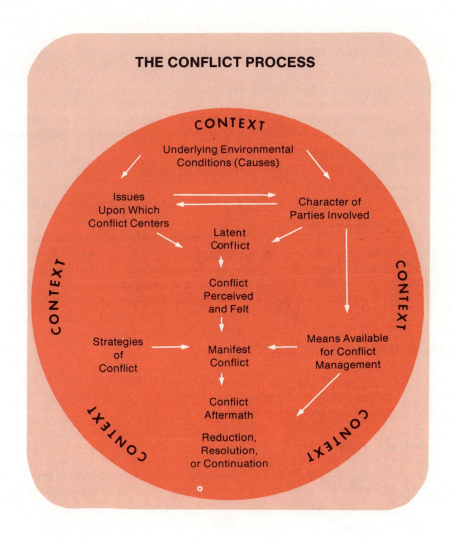

THE CONFLICT PROCESS

CONTEXT

Underlying Environmental Conditions (Causes)

Issues Upon Which Conflict Centers

Character of Parties Involved

Latent Conflict

Conflict Perceived and Felt

CONTEXT

CONTEXT

Strategies of Conflict

Manifest Conflict

Means Available for Conflict Management

Conflict Aftermath

Reduction, Resolution, or Continuation

CONTEXT

CONTEXT

---

*Diagram adapted from Louis R. Pondy, "Organizational Conflict: Concepts and Models," *Administrative Science Quarterly* 12 (1967), p. 306, and Alan C. Filley, *Interpersonal Conflict Reduction* (Glenview, Ill.: Scott, Foresman and Company, 1975), p. 8.

Basic Assumptions Regarding Interpersonal Conflict

Before we go any farther in our consideration of conflict, let's take a moment to lay out the chief assumptions on which this chapter is based:

1. Conflict is an inevitable and necessary part of human growth—either for the individual or for a group.
2. Conflict can be productive if we meet the challenge it offers but counterproductive if we allow it to overwhelm us.
3. The term *conflict* can have many meanings, and conflict can arise from many causes and assume a variety of forms.
4. The nature of the communication process itself gives rise to conflict.
5. Our style of language can increase or decrease the number and severity of conflict situations.
6. Conflict management, like all communication, is an art which demands that we be skillful communicators, that we be able to analyze the scene accurately, and that we choose the appropriate means to deal with the problem.
7. Not all conflict can be solved, but *every* conflict situation can be *managed* in such a way that it can be lived with.

Finally, we must keep in mind that the *intra*personal conflicts going on within each of us may give rise to and influence many of the *inter*personal conflicts in which we take part. Our success in dealing with interpersonal conflicts may depend in large measure on our ability to cope with our own internal conflicts. Although this chapter will be concerned primarily with conflict between two or more parties, we shall not lose sight of the close relationships between those conflicts and the internal conflicts that may accompany them.

THE NATURE OF INTERPERSONAL CONFLICT

To understand more fully the nature of conflict, let's consider *(a)* causes, *(b)* issues, *(c)* perception of the issues, *(d)* contexts in which conflict takes place, and *(e)* factors that determine its intensity.

Causes of Conflict

The cause of all conflict may ultimately be found in the very purpose of our existence. This, as we explained in Chapter 2, is our search for self-identity and self-fulfillment. In our consideration of Maslow's hierarchy of human needs in Chapter 8 we pointed out the dynamics of this need pattern as it impels us forward in our search for self-actualization. Inevitably, this search will produce conflicts within ourselves and with others.

If these assumptions are valid, then we can condense all of the causes of human conflict into two basic categories: (1) *a deprivation of need* or (2) *an im-*

pingement of territory. Self-fulfillment requires that our emerging needs be satisfied. To do this we must establish for ourselves a physical or psychological territory, the locus of our self-identity. Since every society has only limited resources for the satisfaction of individual needs and a limited amount of territory, all of us discover from time to time that in trying to satisfy our needs we deprive others of their needs or they deprive us of ours. We find that our territory is being violated or that we are violating someone else's territory. In every such instance we have a potential cause of conflict.

With this broad view of *conflict causality* in mind, we can now consider some specific causes of conflict present in our everyday experience. We use *causes* here to refer not to the issues over which two or more parties could come into conflict but to the underlying social and psychological conditions that nurture conflict. We shall be concerned with the causes both of interpersonal conflicts and of the intrapersonal conflicts which contribute to conflicts between people.

As Americans, we place a high value on aggressive behavior. Coaches, parents, friends—all remind us that we have to win, that we must "get ahead." Winning or "getting ahead" frequently demands that we deprive others of their needs or impinge on their territory.

Because our American society is relatively open and democratic, it lacks many of the stabilizing traditions common in other societies around the world. In an open society there are no hard and fast norms which tell us how we are to lead our lives as wives and husbands, parents and children, and all the other social roles. The normless society may give us freedom of choice, but it also deprives us of familiar models upon which to pattern our lives. In the process of shaping our life's expectancies, we experience a multitude of conflicts. Our maturity grows in the soil of conflict. In the "land of opportunity" we face a marketplace for highly competitive, highly contradictory values and life styles. Not only are the values many, but they are rapidly changing. Faced with this gallery of values, we find choices difficult, and conflict inevitable.

Because our society is made up of many cultural groups, each with its own set of values and interests, we are faced with the cultural differences which create what sociologist Everett V. Stonequist has called the "Marginal Man"—"poised in psychological uncertainty between two (or more) social worlds, reflecting in his soul the discords and harmonies, repulsions and attractions of these worlds, one of which is often 'dominant' over the other; within which membership is implicitly if not explicitly based upon birth or ancestry (race or nationality); and where exclusion removes the individual from a system of group relations."[2] In Chapter 16 we will deal in detail with some of the specific problems arising from cross-cultural communication. We mention cultural differences here as another instance of value patterns linking communication and conflict.

Both for practical advantages, as in business or government, and for psychological support, most of us need to be part of groups that share our interests. Group membership may help us cope with many of the conflicts we encounter, but it may also lead us into conflicts involving incompatible social roles, conformity, and the demands of group allegiance.

Frequently we experience incompatibility between two social roles we are called on to play. The resulting conflict makes it difficult, or even impossible, to perform either role adequately. The stress can be extreme. The conflict between the roles of housewife and career woman is but one example of this type of frustrating incompatibility.

You will remember our mention in Chapter 11 of conformity as a factor influencing group decision making. As a source of conflict, conformity can force us to act in ways that violate our personal values, and can create an inner stress with a variety of disruptive effects.

The allegiance we feel as members of a *group* may at times demand behavior which runs counter to our *personal* values. We are faced with a dilemma which forces us either to do violence to our integrity or to endanger our relationship with the group. We solve such situations by weighing the value group membership holds for us against our commitment to our personal values. John Dean, former White House counsel, was faced with this type of conflict as he found himself caught between his loyalties to the Presidential staff and to what he considered his duty in revealing details of the Watergate case.

The example of John Dean illustrates one of the many ways in which interpersonal and intrapersonal conflicts interact. John Dean's open dispute with other White House aides grew in large part from his attempts to deal with his own conscience. Psychologist Gordon W. Allport has called conscience "the knifeedge that all our values press upon us whenever we are acting, or have acted, contrary to these values."[3] Conscience need not be considered exclusively as a religious phenomenon, but rather as the rational judgment we use to measure the harmony between our behavior and our values, whatever they are. The guilt we feel over a disharmony between behavior and values creates the conflict. And as the psychiatric profession will attest, guilt conflicts are the root of much mental illness in our society today.

Social psychoanalyst Erich Fromm offers a useful distinction between the mature and the immature conscience. The immature conscience is rooted in fear and admiration for a father figure whose approval we seek and whose rejection we fear. Characterized by unquestioning acceptance and childish dependence, this type of conscience is developed at the expense of our own integrity. Under the direction of an immature conscience, we have no internalized values, merely the dictates of an authority figure who makes our decisions for us. On the other hand, the mature conscience—Fromm also refers to it as the "humanistic conscience"—reflects our judgment of our effectiveness as human beings. *"Conscience,"* he concludes, *"is thus a re-action of ourselves to ourselves."*[4] As an expression of our self-interest and integrity, the humanistic conscience voices our loving care for ourselves.

In each of us lives a little of Walter Mitty. We nurture myths and fantasies, feeding our mistakes of yesterday and today on the dreams of tomorrow. Psychoanalyst Rollo May suggests that a myth is "man's way of expressing the quintessence of his experience—his way of seeing his life, his self-image and his relations to the world of his fellow man and of nature. . . ." Every myth, he says, carries "an element of ultimate meaning which illuminates but reaches beyond each individual man's concrete experience."[5] Conflict arises from the gap between what we are now and what our dreams of tomorrow promise us, and this conflict will affect our dealings with other people and the ways we handle interpersonal conflicts.

Issues Upon Which Interpersonal Conflict Centers

Out of the social and psychological climate we have briefly discussed in the previous section arise the issues which can bring two or more people into conflict. To analyze a conflict accurately, we must understand the types of issues bringing the parties into conflict. As the issues vary, the strategies and dynamics will vary accordingly. These strategies and dynamics can be expected to center upon such issues as: *goals and means, values, control of resources, testing of relationships, assumptions and beliefs,* and *propriety.*

Goals and means. For the individual or for a group beginning a task, the first question is "Where are we going?" and the follow-up: "How will we get there?" Since rarely are goals and means so obvious that we can see no alternatives, the struggle to answer these two fundamental questions presents us with a perennial source of conflict.

Values. As humans we possess a constant need to compare and place an evaluation on the people, things, and situations around us. Social psychiatrist Jurgen Ruesch notes that value is a "device which renders incomparable things commensurable."[6] He also says that it is a "device by which closely similar things can be differentiated." Values, as we noted in Chapter 8, enable us to rank things and thus create an order of preference in our lives. Since assigning values to things is such an intensely personal matter, the patterns of values within society will vary as persons vary. Problems over family budget or federal spending witness to the tensions value can trigger. Because values are so much a matter of personal preference, the ego-involvement greatly complicates conflict resolution.

Control of resources. We do not have to labor the point that in every society there is only a limited supply of money, goods, property, jobs, etc. Because our survival and security depend on some degree of control of basic resources and because they are in limited supply, we frequently experience the stress and frustration of competition in satisfying our needs. In some instances the conflict may be primarily intrapersonal, but in far more cases we control resources at the expense of others' needs or by impinging on their territory. Conflict over resource control tends to trigger exercises of power, search for status, or validation of roles.

Relationships. Issues revolving around relationships may be occasions for role testing or pursuit of ambitions. Often when the quality of a relationship is not precisely understood by the participants, conflict will be enacted to define the relationship more clearly. Child-parent conflicts, especially where adolescents are involved, are many times efforts by a parent to reinforce an established role or by the child to forge a new role.

Assumptions and beliefs.   Our entire world of "reality" is based upon an intricate system of assumptions and beliefs about what is and what is not, what is good and bad, what should and should not be. These systems give order, structure, expectation, meaning, and security to our lives. In the same way that our value systems are highly relative to us as individuals, so are our systems of assumptions. Thus, we can expect the same problem of ego-involvement which we find in value-centered issues.

Propriety.   Taste, style, preference—all contribute to our personal sense of propriety—of what goes with what. This sense of propriety grows out of our assumptions, values, expectations, and past experiences; and it governs many of the practical, often unconscious, choices by which we establish our life styles. Here again we find an issue with strong ego-identification. Although we have heard the Latin phrase quoted to us: *"De gustibus non est disputandum—*You can't argue about taste"—as a matter of experience we know that people *do* argue very much about matters of taste. Like value, propriety cannot be proved, only assumed. Also like value, propriety-centered conflicts demand of the participants a high degree of motivation toward resolution.

Perception of the Issues

It is quite possible for two parties to be in conflict with one another and yet not understand the issues that divide them. Social psychologist Morton Deutsch suggests that conflict be distinguished in terms of the parties' perception of the issues involved. The classification he suggests hinges on the relationship between the *objective* state of incompatibility and the state of incompatibility *as perceived by the conflicting parties.* Deutsch distinguishes the following six types:[*]

1. *Veridical* (an accurately perceived conflict). Here an objective basis of conflict exists, and the parties involved accurately perceive it. Mutually exclusive goals aimed at limited resources make reconciliation through shared results impossible. A man and wife, for example, have only one car. The wife has scheduled a golf match at precisely the same time that her husband has scheduled a tennis game. The one car is the only available transportation to either the golf or tennis game, and the two locations are on opposite sides of town. This type of conflict is quite difficult to resolve without generating resentment, since to satisfy one party the other party must sacrifice completely his or her immediate satisfaction. Any kind of resolution will demand willingness from both parties to set mu-

[*]Morton Deutsch. THE RESOLUTION OF CONFLICT, CONSTRUCTIVE AND DESTRUCTIVE PROCESSES. New Haven: Yale University Press, 1973. Pp. 11–15.

tually agreed upon priorities and decide accordingly, or to employ a third-party device, acceptable to both parties, to make a binding decision. As priorities, the couple might decide according to who needs the diversion more or who had the most recent chance to "get out." A third-party device could be the flip of a coin or writing to "Dear Abby."

2. *Contingent.* In this type of conflict, the parties involved perceive themselves in a "veridical" or true conflict, when actually their problem can be arranged to their mutual satisfaction. In the case mentioned above, if the wife or husband could arrange to get a ride from a friend while the other took the car, both would be able to carry out their plans. If, however, having the car would become the real issue rather than simply having the afternoon's recreation, then the contingency of the conflict would disappear and a secondary veridical conflict would exist.

3. *Displaced.* This type of conflict exists at two levels, each level having its own issues. At the manifest level—the talking level—the conflict interaction takes place. This is, however, only symbolic of a deeper, more vital conflict which, for some reason, the parties cannot openly discuss. A husband who feels rejected because of the quality of his sexual relations with his wife may not be able to confront her with the problem, and instead he displaces his unexpressed conflict over their sexual relations with an argument over the wife's spending habits. Thus, we can refer to the *manifest* level at which the talking takes place and the *suppressed* level where the acute distress is felt. Frequently, the frustration experienced over the suppressed conflict generates an emotional response totally out of proportion to the issues involved in the manifest conflict. This seeming overreaction to the manifest issues may be confusing to the individual who is unaware that the other party is experiencing a *displaced* conflict.

Any resolution of this type of conflict must begin by bringing the suppressed conflict issues out in the open and talking about them. Then the conflict can be approached as any manifest conflict with its own characteristics.

4. *Misattributed.* In this situation, the wrong parties are in conflict over the wrong issues. Social strategies of "scapegoating" or "divide and conquer" typically result in misattributed conflicts. The fear and hatred incited against the Jews by the Nazis during World War II is such an example. Or there is the case of workers who during depressed economic periods divide themselves along racial or ethnic lines in an effort to find someone to blame for their problems. Misattributed conflict tends to stem from anxiety, frustration, ignorance, and a sense of helplessness. Those involved strike out at whoever is nearest and most vulnerable, and here we have the classic example of the pecking order.

5. *Latent.* In this type of conflict, although no conflict exists, all the ingredients for open conflict are present. For various reasons—displacement, repression, misattribution, or simple unawareness—the individual does not experience the conflict. The latent conflict can erupt into an open conflict when and if the proper focus is placed on the issues and on the relationship of the parties in-

volved. If, for example, workers in a certain industry are being exploited but are unable to voice their grievances, the conflict remains latent. This was the situation among the coal miners before safety laws were enacted. Effective leadership organized the miners, giving them a sense of possibility for improving their conditions. With the miners' heightened awareness of issues and strengthened group solidarity, the latent conflict among them exploded into open conflict. We may add, as a corollary, that the longer the conflict remains latent, the more severe will the eruption be when and if it takes place.

6. *Pseudo.* In this type of conflict, because of a misunderstanding of behavior and motives, no objective basis for conflict exists. All of us have been in what we thought was a hostile encounter, when suddenly we became aware: "Oh, *that's* what you mean! If I'd known, we wouldn't have had to fight." While there may be no objective basis for conflict, the conflict itself is real because it is perceived as real. And it can certainly be as damaging as any "real" conflict. What is necessary in handling pseudo conflict is to eliminate misunderstanding—this presupposes that the misunderstanding is recognized—and to allow the parties involved to sense the actual harmony that exists.

Contexts Surrounding
Interpersonal Conflict

Conflict is always contextual. It must take place in a physical, psychological, and social setting that influences its development and outcome. In analyzing a conflict, then, we must take into account not only the issues in dispute but also the context which affects the ways the parties react to the issues. In particular, we are interested in four key aspects of the context. First, we want to know about *the character of the parties involved.* The parties to a conflict will certainly have personality traits which, although not at issue, contribute to the atmosphere in which the conflict is waged. Second, we must inquire into *the relationship which the parties had with each other prior to the outbreak of the conflict.* Third and fourth, we are concerned about the *social environment* in which the parties meet and the *audiences interested in the conflict,* for these will obviously affect the way the conflict is carried out.

To analyze a conflict situation more precisely, we can ask several questions regarding each of these four areas of context.[7]

1. The characteristics of the parties in conflict.
   a. What are their values, goals, and motivations?
   b. What physical, intellectual, and social capabilities do they have for waging and resolving the conflict?
   c. What are their beliefs about conflict?
   d. What degree of credibility, openness, and honesty does each possess?
   e. How capable is each of violence or retaliation?

2. The prior relationship between the parties.
   a. What degree of personal closeness existed?
   b. What does each believe about the other and expect from the other based on their prior relationship?
   c. How does each party assess the other's view of him or her?
   d. Does the prior relationship make communication easier or more difficult for the parties?

3. The social environment within which the conflict takes place.
   a. Does the climate inhibit or stimulate the show of hostility?
   b. Does it encourage or discourage resolution of the conflict?

4. The interested audiences to the conflict.
   a. What is their relationship to the parties in conflict? To each other?
   b. What are the characteristics of the audiences?
   c. What interest do they have in the conflict? In its outcome?

Factors Determining the Intensity of the Conflict

The conflict will be more intense and the stress placed on the participants more severe: (1) the longer the conflict continues; (2) the more vital the disputed issues are to the participants; (3) the greater the intensity of frustration experienced by the participants; (4) the greater the strength of the opposing forces and the more equal the forces are; (5) the more unfamiliar the participants are with the issues; (6) the less competent the participants feel—either correctly or incorrectly—in coping with the conflict situation; (7) the greater the ego-involvement; and (8) the lower the stress tolerance of the participants.[8] [1]

Study Probe 1
Analyzing Your Own Interpersonal Conflicts

During the next week keep a log of two or three interpersonal situations in which you are experiencing conflict. For each of these situations write out answers to the following questions:

1. What are the issues involved?
2. What underlying causes may have given rise to the conflict?
3. What matters of *context* affect your strategies in the conflict and the ways in which you can go about resolving the differences between you and the other party?

At the end of the week-long interval, try to determine whether or not the insights of this analysis have made your conflicts more manageable. Write a short report on the results of this experience and hand it to your instructor at a time he or she may specify.

CONSEQUENCES OF CONFLICT

Conflict, considered without regard to its ultimate consequences, tends to have the following general, psychological effects: (1) ego-defenses increase; (2) anxiety increases; (3) proneness to hostility and aggressiveness appears; (4) outlook becomes less flexible and values more entrenched; (5) perception tends to become distorted; and (6) physical and psychological energies increase.

Although most of the effects just enumerated (and, indeed, the word *conflict* itself) may sound negative to most readers of this text, not all social and psychological theorists view it in that way. It is true that such writers as George A. Lundberg, Elton Mayo, and Talcott Parsons view conflict as a *malfunction* counterproductive for society. In their opinion, society functions best when it is stable, harmonious, and integral—without conflict. On the other hand, writers like Charles H. Cooley, Lewis Coser, Karen Horney, and Georg Simmel find a constructive value in conflict—although they would readily admit that conflict can in certain circumstances be destructive to the individual or society.

Beneficial Effects of Conflict

In this chapter we shall assume that conflict is both necessary and fundamentally beneficial. To support this belief we offer the following reasons:

1. Conflict keeps the person or group alert and prevents stagnation.
2. Conflict requires review of personal and social institutions and procedures and thereby promotes healthy change.
3. Conflict helps refine self-identity by testing and assessing the self.
4. Conflict occasions the airing of issues and problems, thus creating the opportunity for solutions.
5. Conflict can restructure relationships, making them more appropriate.
6. Conflict can foster greater group cohesion.
7. Conflict can help the person or group analyze goals and the appropriateness of the present means of achieving them.
8. Conflict can stimulate creativity.

As a further contribution to the argument that properly managed conflict can be a constructive force, let us consider the following two statements. Sociologist Charles H. Cooley writes:

> Conflict, of some sort, is the life of society, and progress emerges from a struggle in which individual, class, or institution seeks to realize its own ideas of good.[9]

And psychoanalyst Karen Horney, speaking from her years as a therapist, states:

> To experience conflicts knowingly, though it may be distressing, can be an invaluable asset. The more we face our own conflicts and seek out our own solutions, the more inner freedom and strength we will gain. Only

> when we are willing to bear the brunt can we approximate the ideal of
> being the captain of our ship.[10]

As a constructive motivation, conflict increases our energies, sharpens our awareness of situations, stirs our creativity in problem solving, and—as an overall effect—steps up our efficiency. This is the psychic reaction of many athletes who perform best when they face their most challenging moments.

On the other hand, prolonged and unresolved conflicts have precisely the opposite consequences. As Karen Horney remarks: "Living with unresolved conflicts involves primarily a devastating *waste of human energies,* occasioned not only by the conflicts themselves but by all the devious attempts to remove them."[11]

Detrimental Effects of Conflict

In discussing the psychological effects of conflict, we must distinguish between manageable conflict and conflict allowed to become prolonged and unresolved. All conflict tends to produce frustration, stress, and tension. If we use conflict to motivate us into heightened awareness and more efficient operation, it can be highly productive. If, however, we are unable to resolve the conflict and it continues, the effects may be devastating.

Beyond the buildup of frustration, stress, and tension present in all conflict, prolonged conflict heightens our sense of vulnerability. Our lack of success in coping makes us more depressed, indecisive, and anxious. Faced with our procrastination and ineffectiveness, we feel guilty and we attempt to quiet our guilt by resorting to "busy work." The longer the stress goes on, the weaker becomes our self-assurance. A growing self-doubt forces us to compensate; and, in doing so, we become more egocentric, hypersensitive, irritable, and physically exhausted. Our usual ease in decision making, our confidence, our appreciation of our own dependability and sincerity—all begin to wane. We become less creative, and we find it difficult to think objectively. Our judgment becomes polarized by a defensive pattern of "me against them." Our flexibility in adapting to changing scenes decreases, and ultimately we find that our thinking processes have become disorganized, fragmented, and ineffectual.

All these destructive consequences of unmanaged conflict accentuate and perpetuate themselves in a vicious cycle. If this conflict is allowed to run its full course, the whole psychological system eventually breaks down. Such a breakdown need not happen, however; and in the following section we will discuss ways of managing conflict to prevent such psychological damage.

CONFLICT MANAGEMENT

There is probably no more important task which faces us as persons and as a society than the handling of our conflicts. Our success or failure will measure the quality of our psychological, economic, social, and political lives.

We need not labor the point that conflict is inevitable in even the most successful relationships—in marriage, friendship, business, or whatever. Our purpose in this final section of the chapter is to provide an orientation that will help us to handle our conflicts more effectively. Although we will consider "norms," we want to avoid giving the impression that conflicts can be handled by manipulating a variety of handy formulae. Human living cannot be directed with a slide rule—there is no science of living a human existence, only an art. Like every art, human living must proceed from valid principles and assumptions; it must be practiced with careful attention to the details and differences of the immediate moment; and, finally, the results of our art must be evaluated to see precisely how faithful we have been to our principles and to the demands of the present moment.

Describing Goals in Managing Conflict

The first question we should ask in approaching a task is what the goals of the task are as we see them. The question of terminology is crucial, for how we describe our goals determines what kind of means we choose in approaching the goals, what expectations of success we hold out to ourselves, and what kinds of resources we will enlist in carrying out our task. Here we use the term *conflict management* in the generic sense, designating all forms of dealing with conflict situations. Using this term, we can discuss various situations under one broad category, and thus we can establish comprehensive principles applicable to a wide spectrum of conflict episodes.

Conflict reduction. Because of the nature of the issues, the parties involved, or the setting, some conflict situations can at best be managed by the parties' accepting a less severe level of frustration, stress, and tension. In such cases, there is no "true" solution to the conflict. If the parties involved choose to continue to interact, they must be satisfied to live with an acceptable degree of conflict simply because—given their commitment to the relationship—it is unavoidable. Many job situations are managed through such reduction of conflict. Because of compensating factors, such as salary, prestige, or power, the individual may choose to endure conflict conditions. The decision to function within the context of a reduced conflict is practical under the following conditions: (1) that the rewards of remaining in the conflict situation are greater than the rewards of abandoning the situation; (2) that the stress elements of the conflict can be lessened to the point that we can live with them productively; (3) that the parties can enjoy compensations outside the conflict situation; and (4) that we retain a sense of essential self-direction and do not feel trapped in an unavoidable situation.

Conflict resolution. Conflicts can be resolved in several ways with varying degrees of satisfaction: *withdrawal, temporary solution,* or *permanent solution.*

1. *Withdrawal.* In this type of resolution, either or both parties simply disengage themselves from the area of conflict. Having judged that the situation

can't be reconciled to the satisfaction of both parties, the parties abandon their pursuit of the goals which occasioned the conflict and establish new goals. If two business partners can't resolve their differences about the goals of their company, they may decide to dissolve the partnership.

2. *Temporary solution.* Here we have a situation in which the issues of conflict have returned to an amiable and cooperative relationship. However, due to the psychological makeup of the parties or the nature of the issues in question, there is every likelihood that the conflict will erupt later. Displaced conflicts are typically solved on a temporary basis. The manifest conflict is reconciled, but the suppressed conflict remains latent and later triggers another manifest conflict. Likewise, when superficial issues are mistaken for fundamental issues and only the symptoms are remedied, we have a temporary solution.

3. *Permanent solution.* We may consider a solution permanent which has the following characteristics: *(a)* the parties feel that their needs are sufficiently satisfied; *(b)* they have accepted without rancor whatever losses they may have sustained; *(c)* the relationship of the parties has been relieved of hostilities; *(d)* there is no practical expectation that the former conflict will erupt again. The permanence of the solution may derive from the equity of the settlement, as in the case of heirs who expect and receive equal shares of an estate. Or it may also be the result of resignation to the inevitable, as in the case of the drama student who goes to New York seeking a career and, after enough unsuccessful auditions, judges that he or she has no future in the professional theater and returns home. This withdrawal becomes a permanent solution to the conflict.

Attitudes Toward Goals

The way we approach a goal and the kind of satisfaction we demand of that goal determine to a great extent the probable success we will have in managing conflict. We may take a *win-lose* attitude, a *lose-lose* attitude, or a *win-win* attitude.

Win-lose attitude. This attitude forces us to approach conflict as a situation in which one party wins—achieves her objectives or satisfies her needs—and the other party loses—has his objectives stymied or his needs frustrated. A poker game is a simple example of a truly win-lose situation. The winner's gains always come from the losers' losses. We cannot afford, however, to project the poker situation into our lives. Even in poker the losers can always salvage some gain by recognizing that they were able to socialize for the evening. To be a "good loser" we must be willing and able to lose. The win-lose attitude we are describing here is the result of a too narrow focus on one goal to the exclusion of all other benefits. It reflects an insecurity, defensive rigidity, egocentrism, and hostility which fosters a need to put down or destroy the other party. If we box ourselves in with this attitude where someone must always "pay" or be hurt, then any lasting conflict solution becomes impossible.

Lose-lose attitude.   In some conflicts the parties involved feel backed into a corner with no room for relief or satisfaction of needs. This attitude says, "If I can't have it, neither can you!" An example is the husband who very reluctantly goes with his wife to a party only because she "makes him go." Feeling that he has "lost" and she has "won," the husband spends the entire evening making a fool of himself to embarrass his wife and to turn her winning into losing. In this highly egocentric scene, both husband and wife come home defeated, frustrated, and hostile toward each other.

Win-win attitude.   Here the parties involved are able to see in the conflict the possibility of shared gain. In such an integrative approach, the resolution of the situation becomes the means of mutual satisfaction. All the parties face the problem with a strong commitment to finding a resolution and they play down any desire they may feel to satisfy their own egos at the price of another's defeat. Thus the teacher who finds conflict with her students over the date for an upcoming test can listen to the students' reasons for postponing the test. By adjusting the date so that the students have longer preparation time, she can satisfy their needs for more effective learning—which is also her own need—and still allow herself sufficient time to grade the tests equitably, which satisfies the students' needs. Having time to do the grading without rushing also permits her to maintain her professional standards.

Some Procedural Approaches to Conflict Management

Four processes, in particular, have some positive possibilities for us when we are trying to reach resolution of a conflict: (1) *problem solving through discussion,* (2) *negotiation and bargaining,* (3) *binding third-party arbitration,* and (4) *maintaining the status quo* as long as possible—or the "organizational answer" to conflict.

Problem solving through discussion.   When the stress and disruption of conflict arise, the involved parties can sit down and jointly discuss the issues and problem areas in order to find a solution. By approaching the situation primarily as a problem to be solved, the parties have less ego-investment and can more readily avoid ascribing a win-lose or lose-lose character to the interaction. Obviously, the more effective the parties are as communicators, the more effective will be their discussion and the less acute the stress of the conflict. Later in this chapter, we will discuss more thoroughly some relevant procedures to implement conflict reduction through problem-solving discussion.

Negotiation and bargaining.   John W. Keltner, an experienced negotiator, offers a useful distinction between negotiation and bargaining. *Negotiation,* he says, refers to that "process of discussion between representatives of two or more groups that leads to the settlement of differences or the making of an agreement over matters of mutual concern. Negotiation is not involved in judicial decision-making, in arbitration, or in unilateral decision-making. In fact, true negotiations are impossible unless both parties are restrained from unilateral decision-making."[12] *Bargaining,* on the other hand, according to Keltner, refers to situations "characterized by argument, persuasion, threats, proposals, and counterproposals between two parties as they seek to win concessions from each other in return for favors granted." The differences between negotiation and bargaining center around the heightened stress and threat inherent in bargaining contrasted with the sharing of goals and interests which are part of the less hostile atmosphere of the negotiating scene.

Binding third-party arbitration. In situations where the discussion, negotiation, or bargaining has been stymied and the parties are deadlocked, a third party may have to be consulted to make a decision that will resolve the conflict. Thus when neighbors cannot reach an agreement over property lines, they take their case to a civil court where a judge hands down a decision. Labor-management disputes are frequently settled by a federal arbitration board whose decision is binding on both parties. Binding arbitration takes the decision-making process completely out of the hands of the participants; and, for that reason, the parties may find difficulty in accepting the decision. Obviously, the arbitration must be acceptable to both parties if the solution is to have any effect on the conflict. Like revolution, binding arbitration should be employed only when all other means of reaching a solution have been exhausted. This type of settlement short-circuits the interaction of the two parties and may permit the deeper issues of conflict to fester beneath the surface while the more immediate and, perhaps, superficial issues are reconciled.

The "organizational approach" to conflict resolution. Psychologist Daniel Katz has described a strategy commonly used by our society in dealing with conflicts.* Representing a kind of "folk-wisdom" approach aimed at maintaining the *status quo* as long as possible, the process moves slowly and (one suspects) somewhat reluctantly through three phases. In the first phase, whatever the problems—racial tensions, salary disputes, or marriage conflicts—we assume that the system we're working with is basically good and that the cause of the problem is inefficiency. Presupposing this, we can solve the problem simply by doing better what we're doing now. If trying to increase efficiency within the present system is not the answer, then we move to the second phase: We set up some kind of outside supporting machinery to make the system do what it cannot do on its own. This typical "institutional solution" we see exemplified in blue-ribbon commissions appointed to study crime, in coordinators appointed to coordinate present coordinators, or in "Let's form a committee to look into this problem."

If neither increased efficiency nor outside supporting machinery succeeds

*From "Approaches in Managing Conflict," in CONFLICT MANAGEMENT IN ORGANIZATIONS by Daniel Katz. Ann Arbor, Mich.: The Foundation for Research on Human Behavior, 1961. Pp. 12–16. Used by permission of The Foundation for Research on Human Behavior.

in eliminating the conflict, then—says Katz—we move into the third and final phase: We try to change the structure of the institution to lessen the built-in conflict. Only at this final phase does the institution come to grips with the causes of the conflict. The flaws in this institutional procedure result from the inertia and resistance to change that are built into almost every organization. We mention this approach to conflict management here not to endorse it but, rather, to alert us to its prevalence and its weaknesses.

Psychological Responses to Conflict

In the conflict situation we inevitably feel the need to protect our self-structure as the stress of the conflict tightens around us. From psychological research we know there are internal mechanisms which we automatically and unconsciously use in defending ourselves. None of these actually changes our situation, but they do help us deal with the anxiety we feel. They include *denial, rationalization, compensation, regression,* and *integration.*

Denial. In the case of latent conflict, which we discussed earlier, we may try to put the very existence of a conflict totally out of our minds by refusing to face the facts of our situation. Many alcoholics refuse to acknowledge that they have the disease of alcoholism, and not until they are able to admit the existence of their problem can they hope to manage their conflict.

Rationalization. This process, which we all use from time to time, allows us to justify our behavior to ourselves and to others by attributing acceptable motives to it. If we want something badly enough, we usually have no problem finding "good" reasons to spend the money even though it will throw our budget out of balance. Rationalization, like denial, creates only a temporary quieting of the conflict because the consequences of the rationalized decision may trigger more conflict.

Compensation. When the conflict scene becomes too stressful, we may resort to compensation. This involves rejecting the goals or rewards expected from the present conflict and substituting other goals not part of the conflict. In this situation we avoid the conflict and substitute an alternative which can give us some satisfaction. The success of compensation will depend upon the degree of satisfaction the alternative goal is able to offer. Compensation, as a conflict-reducing mechanism, represents a form of compromise.

Regression. In situations in which we feel inadequate in coping with conflict, we may attempt to retreat from the present into the past. Again this is an avoidance strategy, similar in some respects to denial. Through imagination and fantasy we hope to make the present conflict go away. Psychiatrist Bruno Bettelheim describes the regression of prisoners at the Nazi concentration camps of Dachau and Buchenwald who "lived like children, only in the immediate present. . . . They were boastful, telling tales about what they had accomplished in their former lives."[13]

Integration. This approach accepts the present conflict situation, and through insight seeks to change what can be changed, to accept what cannot be changed, and to integrate life within that framework.

Preliminary Conditions Necessary for Resolution of Conflict

If we are to succeed in reconciling a conflict, we must have certain attitudes clearly in mind. *First,* both parties must see the value and necessity of resolving the conflict. If either party derives satisfaction from the conflict itself, then any attempt at management will work counter to his needs, and he will be highly uncooperative in the problem-solving interaction. *Second,* both parties must be willing and able to make changes. If in a conflict over property, for example, the party occupying the property needs the property to survive, obviously there can be no flexibility on her part. *Third,* any win-lose mentality should be discarded because such an attitude can only strengthen hostility. *Fourth,* each party should at the outset of the discussion reveal what each considers to be maximum needs or conditions. *Fifth,* both parties must accept the fact that any resolution will never result in their complete satisfaction.

Since the style of our communication is a product of our style of thought, in conflict management we need to remind ourselves of the *attitudes* which will contribute most effectively to the dialogue. Among the attitudes which can help us deal constructively with conflict are these:[14]

1. *Tentativeness*—avoid absolute verdicts.
2. *Acceptance of differences*—maintain your own standards and values without demanding that others support and live by them.
3. *Loyalties*—stay within a flexible yet discriminating frame.
4. *Sense of humor*—be able to laugh at yourself and your scene.
5. *Task orientation*—direct all your efforts to reconciling the conflict.
6. *Willingness to seek common ground and share benefits.*
7. *Agreeing to disagree* when necessary.
8. *Openness and compassion*—remember that there are other sides to issues.

Selective Perception: Organizing Our Awareness of the Conflict

From our earlier consideration of sensation and perception (Chapter 4), we know that the whole of our "real" world is the product of our selective perception which gives meaning, stability, and expectation to our lives. It gives us a defense against threatening situations, reinforces our values and beliefs, and in general permits us to see what we need and want to see.

Understanding the process of selective perception is crucial if we are to deal effectively with conflict. Selective perception tends to assign positive and negative stereotypes to the participants in a conflict. These stereotypes of "good guys" and "bad guys" trigger a cycle which is self-perpetuating and self-fulfilling. We can structure this very nonproductive behavior process in the following model:

1. We begin by perceiving the other party as an aggressor and hostile to us.

2. We become defensive and withdraw from contact with that party.

3. As a result of our withdrawal, communication between us is reduced.

4. As communication is reduced, common understanding of each other's attitudes and goals diminishes, and we grow farther apart.

5. With the diminishing of common understanding, our suspicion grows, so that we interpret the other party's behavior as increasingly hostile.

THE NONPRODUCTIVE BEHAVIOR CYCLE IN CONFLICT

Besides perpetuating and increasing our hostility toward the other party, our selective perception reinforces the following attitudes which make conflict management more difficult: (1) *"It's OK for ME, but not for YOU."* Adopting this double standard of behavior blinds us to our own faults and drives our opponents into a corner, where we very conveniently find him or her guilty. (2) *"It's all YOUR fault!"* Here we saddle the other party with all the blame by setting up a neat polarity of good and bad—and we, of course, are always on the good side. (3) *"It's not ME!"* and *"It's not ME either!"* When neither side of a conflict can admit any responsibility for the conflict, we have a situation of universal righteousness. While this attitude avoids any direct finger-pointing at the other party, it also violates the almost universal principle that in any conflict both parties are to some degree contributing to the problem. [2]

The Language of Conflict

As we have stressed throughout this chapter, conflict makes us feel aggressive and defensive. All too often the style of our communication betrays a need to wound or destroy the opposition and to reinforce and protect ourselves. When we foster this type of attitude, we are projecting to the other person a strong sense of rejection—"I don't like you. You threaten me. We can't talk!"

When we are under conflict stress, our style of communication tends to take on the following characteristics which make the conflict destructive rather than constructive: (1) we use value statements, making them sound like facts; (2) we express our values in very simplistic right-and-wrong terms, leaving no room in the middle for the grey areas of "maybe"; (3) we try to defend ourselves by using emotive name-calling to put the other party in his or her place; (4) we employ a rigid, this-or-nothing framework for our expectancies; (5) we use sweeping generalizations to avoid a concise awareness of the scene and to keep our opponent at a distance; (6) we indulge in a much more intrapersonal dialogue within ourselves as we attempt to gain better control over the scene by monitoring our own feelings more closely; (7) we tend to overreact and to express our overreaction verbally and nonverbally.[15]

Study Probe 2
Selectively Perceiving the Bases of Conflict

Choose an individual whom you feel you dislike and who generates conflict for you. Rate this person on a scale of 1 to 10 in the following categories: (*a*) trustworthiness, (*b*) truthfulness, (*c*) openness, (*d*) values he or she shares with you, (*e*) willingness to accept differences, and (*f*) integrity. Determine as accurately as you can on what concrete evidence you base these ratings. How valid are your own ratings? What function has selective perception served in your ratings?

When we allow the threat, anxiety, and stress of conflict to guide our communication style, we are very neatly closing all the channels of dialogue and making understanding between ourselves and the other party impossible. And, of course, we are also shutting out any possibility of constructive conflict resolution.

Too often in talking about language and communication we project the idea that language is in some way disfranchised from people. We must not lose sight of the fact that language is really a "people" process. For that reason we cannot lay down rigid rules for language usage in conflict situations; rather, we must try to develop positive attitudes toward each other, using the kind of talk that reflects openness and sincerity and that nourishes common understanding.

We should be interested in creating an atmosphere which encourages dialogue. To accomplish this, we must bring to the oral interaction the kind of language competence which says, in effect, "We *want* this transaction to succeed and, therefore, we are willing to work within the following *guidelines*":

1. Accept the other party as a person, even though we may disagree with many of his or her values and beliefs.
2. Be convinced that we have enough in common to make communication possible.
3. Focus on the problem which is to be dealt with. Avoid threats, name-calling, ego-involvement.
4. Be descriptive, using nonjudgmental terms, and avoiding the strongly emotion-laden words.
5. Choose the specific rather than the general focus.
6. Discuss the issues that are most open to change rather than those which offer little hope of alteration.
7. Foster spontaneity by giving feedback when it is appropriate and at the time it is called for. This avoids the confusion that results when we react now to something that happened in an earlier encounter. The other party may possibly misinterpret our behavior.
8. As nearly as possible fit our words to our experience of reality. Remember, reality is what things do to us and for us.
9. When we respond to persons or situations, we should make sure that the other party or parties accurately interpret our meaning.
10. Project an expectancy of success and acceptance. [3]

The Problem-Solving Approach to Conflict Management

Earlier, you will recall, we considered briefly four procedural approaches to conflict management: *problem solving through discussion, negotiation and bargaining, binding third-party arbitration,* and *maintaining the status quo.* Each of these procedures, as we noted, has its own particular merits and advantages, depending upon the nature of the conflict, the attitudes of the persons involved, and the goals each seeks. Here we will take a detailed look at one of these procedures, not because it is necessarily superior to the others, but because—since it follows closely John Dewey's five steps in problem solving that we talked about in Chapter 11—all of us are probably more familiar with it.[16] In addition, we feel, by applying Dewey's method to the problem of conflict resolution, we can see quite clearly some of the dynamics, the give and take necessary to produce positive, constructive results.

Step One. Analyzing and detecting symptoms of the conflict. Conflict is the result of the dynamics of human interaction. Searching for the symptoms that overlay the causes, we can question these specific areas: (a) the quality of the relationship between the parties; (b) the way in which the parties define the problem; and (c) the quality of the situation in which the conflict takes place. In the first of these areas we discover, as precisely as possible, how both parties see themselves and each other, and how they perceive the conflict scene. In many situations, the tension between the parties exists principally because neither party clearly understands the other, and perhaps does not fully understand his or her own feelings about the problem.

Here are some questions we can ask: What was the relationship between you and the other party before the conflict erupted? How has it changed? How would you describe your behavior as it contributes to the conflict? The behavior of the other party? How do you think the other party would describe his or her own behavior as it contributes to the conflict? How would he or she describe your behavior? How do you experience the problem and how would you describe it? How do you think the other party experiences and describes the problem? How broad are the dimensions of the conflict as you see them? As the other party sees them? What are the areas of disagreement existing between you? Areas of

---

Study Probe 3

Analyzing Communication for Conflictive Language

Select a speech from *Vital Speeches of the Day* or similar source which supports one side of a controversial topic such as abortion, women's liberation, or gun-control legislation. If you are unable to locate a speech that suits your purpose, select an article from a newspaper or a magazine. Read the speech or article, looking for the following elements of language which tend to accentuate the conflict: (a) value statements used as if they were facts, (b) name-calling, (c) over-generalizations, (d) simplistic right-wrong orientations, and (e) use of this-or-nothing framework in proposing a solution.

When you've completed your note-taking and analysis, rewrite those sections of the speech or article which you feel aggravate the conflict, trying as you do so to lessen possible hostility and to facilitate agreement. Take additional notes on the kinds of mental adjustments you have to make in order to rewrite the material. Be prepared to report orally or in writing on the insights you've gained.

common understanding? How vulnerable do you feel in the conflict situation? How vulnerable do you think the other party feels?

Step Two. Determining causes of the conflict.

The success of any problem-solving endeavor will depend on how accurately the causes of the problem are diagnosed. As we said earlier, the symptoms of a problem are not usually the causes of the problem. Because symptoms are more apparent and can be more immediately dealt with than the causes, we may be tempted to deal with the problem only at the symptomatic level and ignore the fundamental question of where the real causes lie. Obviously, this step is the most crucial; but it is also the most difficult, since all of us tend to suppress motives and issues into our unconscious. When we use denial, rationalization, or fantasy in dealing with conflict, reaching a permanent solution becomes almost impossible. And for this reason, many of our conflicts are solved only temporarily or not solved at all.

The questions we need to ask in connection with this second step are: What incident or circumstance triggered the conflict? What are the key issues aggravating this conflict? What behavior do you find unacceptable in the other person? What behavior does the other person find unacceptable in you?

Step Three. Establishing standards for evaluating possible solutions.

In this third step we are setting up the framework for the solution. Basing our criteria on what we already know about the symptoms and the causes of the problem, we are now in a position to concentrate on the kinds of solutions available.

We should know: What kind of flexibility in choosing a solution do you feel you possess? What kind of flexibility does the other party possess? How strong is your need to solve the problem? How strong is the other party's need? How do your needs for maximum satisfaction compare with the maximum needs

Study Probe 4
Assisting Others to Resolve Problems and Reduce Conflict

Read the following letter written to newspaper columnist Ann Landers by a "wavering" reader:*

DEAR ANN LANDERS: I am a Baptist. My fiance is Lutheran. Mike's parents have money. My mother is a widow and lives on a limited income. Mike's folks are putting on the wedding and reception. Both will be in their church.

As the time grows near, I become more and more depressed. My religion means a lot to me. Mike says his religion means a lot to him, too. We have talked it over several times, but it always ends up the same way—a stalemate.

We are both 22 and very much in love—at least I thought we were. Now I'm not so sure. What does this sound like to you?

Signed: WAVERING

of the other party? How free do you feel in accepting less than maximum satisfaction? How free is the other party? What, if any, common goals do the two of you share? What would be the minimum action each of you would have to undertake to begin to solve the problem?

Step Four. Outlining possible courses of action.   At this point, the two parties should sit down and list for themselves the various options which are available to them in seeking a solution to their problem.

We will need to know: How does each of you see the results of each possible solution in terms of personal satisfaction? What degree of effort and sacrifice will be involved in working out each possible solution? What solution do you see as the most workable? What solution does the other party favor? How can the two of you mutually consider your preferred solutions and choose one solution which the two of you feel will offer the most promise?

Step Five. Selecting the best possible solution.   This fifth and final step follows as the logical sequence of the previous steps. The two of you have thought your way through the maze of alternatives and have at last arrived at a plan which seems to hold out hope for making the conflict manageable. Now your task is to put it into action. 4

As every set of blueprints represents only an abstraction that demands careful translation into concrete living, so a program of conflict resolution will demand a sensitive implementation. Each step of the implementation must be monitored to see if what you had anticipated is actually taking place. If the results you had anticipated are not forthcoming, then your plan must be rethought—you

---

Based on what you have learned about conflict and conflict management in this chapter, carefully write out a set of recommendations and step-by-step actions designed to assist "Wavering" and her fiance Mike in resolving their problem and avoiding serious conflict. If you can foresee no hope for a positive solution, explain your reasons for arriving at this conclusion and offer a set of steps aimed at managing the negative outcome that you foresee.

Bring your written recommendations to class, hand them to the instructor, and be well prepared to role play for the other members of the class one of three key persons in the dilemma: (a) "Wavering," (b) Mike, or (c) the mediator between them—as your instructor may designate.

*Ann Landers Column, Friday, June 27, 1975. Reprinted by permission of Ann Landers, Field Newspaper Syndicate, and the Chicago Sun-Times.

must review the earlier steps. You may have misread yourself or the other party. Whatever the miscalculation may have been, as long as the two of you are interacting, the dynamics of the situation can still be changed.

Our purpose in this chapter has been to provide an orientation to those particular communication problems which are a part of interpersonal conflict. We have advanced the view that conflict is an inevitable and—potentially—productive force at work in human affairs. Communication designed to reduce conflict is— like all of living—an *art* demanding an understanding of basic principles, a sensitive application of those principles to concrete situations, and a valid appraisal of our effectiveness as communicative artists. In considering some of the causes, types, conditions, issues, effects, and functional values of conflict, we have tried to establish a reasonably broad framework within which to tailor our sensitivity to the needs, possibilities, and outcomes of conflict situations. What we have had to say in this chapter is firmly based on the belief that we can grow in our proficiency to handle conflict to the extent that we can free our creative powers of awareness and sharpen our insight. Although we can never hope to find a world free of conflict, we can try to free our world of the destructive conflict patterns that too often haunt it.

Suggested Readings

Lewis Coser, *The Functions of Social Conflict* (New York: The Free Press, 1956). Although you may find this book rather heavy reading, it's well worth the effort since it provides a full synopsis of conflict theory.

Morton Deutsch, *The Resolution of Conflict: Constructive and Destructive Processes* (New Haven: Yale University Press, 1973). Here you will find a collection of theoretical essays and research papers which are quite technical at times but which offer a wide-ranging perspective on conflict theory.

Alan C. Filley, *Interpersonal Conflict Resolution* (Glenview, Ill.: Scott, Foresman and Company, 1975). This very helpful paperback text offers a direct and concise overview of the theory and strategy of conflict reduction.

Fred E. Jandt, ed., *Conflict Resolution Through Communication* (New York: Harper & Row, Publisher, Inc., 1973). This collection of essays presents a good overview of conflict resolution theory from a variety of viewpoints.

Reference Notes

[1]Louis R. Pondy, "Organizational Conflict: Concepts and Models," *Administrative Science Quarterly* 12 (1967): 298–306.

[2]Everett V. Stonequist, *The Marginal Man: A Study in Personality and Culture Conflict* (New York: Charles Scribner's Sons, 1937), p. 8.

[3]Gordon W. Allport, *The Individual and His Religion* (New York: Macmillan, Inc., 1962), p. 90.

[4]Erich Fromm, *Man for Himself* (New York: Holt, Rinehart and Winston, Inc., 1947), p. 159.

[5]Rollo May, "Introduction: The Significance of Symbols," in *Symbolism in Religion and Literature,* ed. Rollo May (New York: George Braziller, Inc., 1960), p. 34.

[6]Jurgen Ruesch and Gregory Bateson, *Communication: The Social Matrix of Psychiatry* (New York: W. W. Norton & Co., Inc., 1951), p. 45.

[7]Morton Deutsch, *The Resolution of Conflict, Constructive and Destructive Processes* (New Haven, Conn.: Yale University Press, 1973), pp. 5–7.

[8]James C. Coleman, *Personality Dynamics and Effective Behavior* (Glenview, Ill.: Scott, Foresman and Company, 1960), p. 163.

[9]Charles H. Cooley, *Social Organization* (New York: Charles Scribner's Sons, 1909), p. 199.

[10]Karen Horney, *Our Inner Conflicts* (New York: W. W. Norton & Co., Inc., 1945), p. 27.

[11]Ibid., p. 155.

[12]John W. Keltner, *Elements of Interpersonal Communication* (Belmont, Calif.: Wadsworth Publishing Co., Inc., 1973), pp. 235–236.

[13]Bruno Bettelheim, "Individual and Mass Behavior in Extreme Situations," *Journal of Abnormal and Social Psychology* 38 (1943):445–446.

[14]Our list of constructive attitudes incorporates material from Gordon W. Allport, *Personality and Social Encounter, Selected Essays* (Boston: Beacon Press, 1960), pp. 177–178.

[15]The section entitled "The Language of Conflict" has material incorporated from Alan C. Filley, *Interpersonal Conflict Resolution* (Glenview, Ill.: Scott, Foresman and Company, 1975), pp. 34–47.

[16]The section entitled "The Problem-Solving Approach to Conflict Management" has material incorporated from David W. Johnson, *Reaching Out, Interpersonal Effectiveness and Self-Actualization* (Englewood Cliffs, N.J.: Prentice-Hall, Inc., 1972), pp. 203–219.

PUBLIC CONTEXTS
OF
SPEECH
COMMUNICATION

SPEECH PLANNING AND PREPARATION

Before delivering a more or less formal,
uninterrupted speech to a comparatively large
group of listeners, carefully plan and organize
what you want to say. Do all you can
to adapt the message to the audience,
to make the material as appealing as possible,
and to counteract undesirable effects.

In this chapter and the one which follows we shall be concerned with that type of communication which occurs when *a single agent uses sustained discourse to address a more or less sizable audience.* Occasions requiring this form of communication are numerous. Individuals may be asked to speak at PTA meetings or to present their views to a civic or professional organization. While a public meeting is in progress, a member of the audience often is called upon to voice an opinion or to supply information. Each such occasion requires one communicator to achieve effective interaction with many others.

All of the general principles of productive interaction which we have considered in the previous chapters are applicable also to the public, one-to-many speaking situation. For the speaker to select a realistic goal, establish credibility, maintain a working relationship with others in the interaction, and observe whatever customs or traditions may prevail is as necessary in public contexts as it is in dyadic or small group communication. Moreover, the basic principles of message-planning and of feedback apply here just as they do in the one-to-one and the group settings. What makes the one-to-many speaking situation unique are the special tasks which, as a rule, must be undertaken when *preparing* for it and the special problems which are involved in *presenting* a more or less formal, uninterrupted message or flow of messages to a comparatively large group of listeners. Accordingly, we shall consider here the basic "guidelines" and procedures entailed in speech planning and preparation. Then—in Chapter 14—we will look at those principles and behaviors that will be useful to you as you begin to practice your speech and present it to an audience.

To facilitate and make more practical our work in speech planning and preparation, we've included in the Appendix of this textbook two sample or "model" speeches. The first of these, "The New Furies," was presented by John A. Howard as a commencement address at The Prairie School, Racine, Wisconsin, on June 6, 1974. The second, "Women in Leadership and Decision Making," was delivered by Virginia Y. Trotter to The Academic Woman Conference, Kansas State University, Manhattan, Kansas, on February 15, 1975. From time to time throughout our considerations of public communication interaction, we'll be drawing upon certain of the materials and characteristics of these sample speeches to illustrate a concept, to explain a procedure, or to identify a particularly useful application of a principle or a point.

In addition to their illustrative function, these sample speeches are—we believe—well planned and carefully prepared to gain and hold attention, stimulate thought, and accomplish quickly identifiable speaker purposes. They also include a wealth of well-chosen speech-communication "substance." Three qualities, in particular, make these speeches worthy of your close study and analysis. First of all, rather than being a "showcase address" made to exhibit the speaker's skill or virtuosity, each is *a genuine piece of earnest communication* aimed at winning an audience response to a significant idea. Second, each speech is *the work of a single mind,* not the product of a ghost writer or of a group of close advisers. And, third, *the organization and style* of both speeches, as well as their "message-content," raise them well above the average and, therefore, set a desirable and achievable standard which each of us can beneficially strive to attain.

PLANNING THE SPEECH

Suggestions made in Chapter 3 concerning self-assessment and in Chapters 4 and 5 on acquiring and organizing speech substance or materials are especially pertinent when you are planning a public speech. You should always think carefully about your own strong points and your limitations as a speaker, and you should also gather *more material* than you will actually be able to use when you're speaking. If you collect just the minimum amount necessary to carry the central idea and purpose of your message through to its anticipated conclusion, you will have so narrowed your range of choices that you can't select for your supportive materials the *best* example, the *most telling* statistic, or the *strongest* testimony. You will have no alternate or contingency materials to fall back upon if you have in any way misjudged your audience or the communication circumstance. This is what is likely to happen to you if you read only *one* article in preparation for the public speech event, or if you consult merely *one* authority or source. If you limit yourself in this way, you can do little more than "parrot" the views of somebody else. Your listeners (especially those who have read the same article) will quickly downgrade you as a mere marionette, bereft of originality and incapable of exhibiting those qualities of integrity, understanding, and judgment upon which effective public communication so largely depends.

A second reason for gathering more material than you may actually be able to use in a public speech is that you will often need to *make rapid adjustments to the feedback you are receiving from relatively large numbers of listeners simultaneously.* Suppose, for instance, that as you proceed, your listeners appear puzzled or behave in such a way as to "tell" you that they are not accepting an idea that you consider highly important. What can you do? Probably very little *if* you are inadequately prepared, have given little or no thought to feedforward, or have neglected to gather and assimilate an *over*-abundance of relevant information. But if you have accumulated an ample store of facts and insights upon which you can draw *while you are presenting the speech,* you can respond to the situation by citing additional examples, introducing a different explanation, or referring to a fresh body of statistical data. In these and similarly supportive ways, you can often save a point that otherwise would have been lost on your listeners, and turn your speech as a whole from a failure into at least a modest success.

Selecting or Adapting a Subject

When the subject on which you are to speak is left to your own discretion, in addition to considering your own interests and enthusiasms—what you yourself would like to talk about—consider also the *interests and needs of your listeners* and the *occasion* on which the speech is to be presented. If the attention of your audience is to be held and successful interaction achieved, people must see some reason for listening to what you have to say. Does your topic concern their health or physical well-being? Does it contribute to their financial security or professional advancement? Does it touch on their hobbies or leisure-time pursuits? Does it make a difference to the community in which they live? To their roles as taxpayers and citizens? To the happiness of their families, friends, and associates? If a subject does not meet these or similar requirements, discard it. If you try to speak about it, very probably you will be wasting the listeners' time as well as your own.

Finally, in selecting a subject, consider its appropriateness to *the occasion* on which the speech is to be delivered. Are you speaking at a high-school graduation, the meeting of a local service club, before a group of retired persons, as part of a convention program or memorial service? How much time will be available? What may precede or follow your remarks? These are typical of the circumstances and conditions which should be taken into account when you are deciding on a subject and trying to determine the breadth or depth of its development.

Besides those situations in which you are merely asked to address a certain group and are free to select your own topic, the chances are strong that you will also encounter situations in which you are asked to speak on a subject known to lie in your particular area of experience or expertise. Thus a lawyer may be asked to talk on recent changes in the state's criminal code, an engineer on plans for a new municipal water-treatment plant, or a teacher or school principal to explain the guidelines which are followed in assigning grades or otherwise evaluating student work. Obviously, in each of these cases the subject is too large or complicated to handle adequately in a ten- or fifteen-minute talk. Therefore, you will need to select from everything that might be said only those aspects of the problem which are most likely to be of interest and concern to your listeners. In addition, you will need to handle these matters in a way that best accords with their present knowledge and educational background.

In making such adaptations, principles similar to those outlined above will prove useful. Talk about those facets of the subject which touch your audience directly. Select materials or take points of view that can be adequately dealt with in the time available. Do not try to tell all you know about the subject or to hurry over so many different facts and ideas that no one of them will have a chance to sink in fully. In speech making, as in many other things, it is always better to do a few things well than to do many things poorly.

Excellent examples of selecting a subject suitable to the audience and occasion are provided by the sample speeches in the Appendix. The three "self-deceptions" to which John A. Howard points in his address carry advice of special pertinence to young persons about to embark on college or work careers, but also have relevance for parents and other older people in the audience. Moreover, the commencement occasion makes this kind of inspirational subject highly appropriate. Finally, Dr. Howard's topic, though an important one, is narrow enough to be handled adequately in a short period of time, and thus to fit well into a commencement program.

Since Virginia Trotter's speech was delivered at a conference for academic women, it was natural for her to select as her subject some aspect of the contemporary woman's movement. Beyond this, however, she adapted her remarks to her listeners even more closely by dwelling on the role of women in the educational system and pointing out what they themselves might do to improve the situation. Thus the speech as a whole takes the form of a strong challenge to the listeners and emphasizes their opportunities to effect the desired changes.

Analyzing the Audience and the Occasion

In considering the various factors which should be taken into account in selecting your subject, you already have begun the second of the important tasks involved in speech planning and preparation—analyzing the listeners and the occasion. The importance of such an analysis and the considerations it should entail were pointed out in Chapter 7 as a part of the discussion of message planning and feedforward. To what occupational, social, or religious groups do your listeners belong? From what geographical region do they come? What is their predominant age? Their sex? Are they well educated or poorly educated? What values are they likely to hold? To what kinds of motivational appeals will they tend to respond? How much do they already know about the subject you are hoping to talk about? What do they expect of you as a speaker?

An analysis of this kind is pertinent in any type of communicative interchange, whether it involves two persons, a small group, or an audience of thousands. In the one-to-many situation, however, it takes on added importance from the fact that *the speaker's discourse must, as a rule, be more carefully and fully planned in advance.* Moreover, the larger the number of persons involved, the more difficult it becomes to make accurate judgments of the listeners' interests, values, and attitudes. For this reason, as the speaker you must take the utmost care in assessing the demographic and psychological characteristics of the persons to whom you will be addressing your speech. And you must also give careful thought to the physical/psychological context in which you will be presenting it. A piece of advice, venerable with age, is that a speaker's preparation time should be divided equally between a study of the subject to be discussed and an analysis of the listeners to whom the subject is to be presented. Essentially, this is still a sound directive which every public communicator will do well to heed.

Determining the General and Specific Purpose

As we have already learned, we speak for many different purposes: to assert our self-existence, to reveal or conceal a self-image, to find self-satisfaction, to exchange information, to influence others to think and believe as we do, and to diminish tensions between ourselves and others. Any one of these purposes may, from time to time, motivate us to engage in the one-to-many communicative situation. Usually, however, when we "make a speech"—as distinguished from participating in a dyadic conversation or a group discussion—we do so because we have what is sometimes described as a *contextually oriented* aim or goal. That is, we speak because the nature of the situation and the expectations of the potential listeners within it require that we try to entertain, inform, persuade, inspire, or actuate our audience.

These communicative aims—*entertainment, information, persuasion, inspiration,* and *actuation*—constitute what are commonly referred to as the *general purposes* which public speeches may serve. Although it may have a *number* of objectives or purposes, almost inevitably every public speech will have one of these general purposes as its *principal* goal. And one of your first and most important tasks as the speaker is to determine at the very outset—before you begin the actual planning and preparation of your message—just what this is. Failure to do so almost certainly will cause you to produce a speech that lacks a clear focus and that will therefore be difficult for your listeners to follow.

But besides having a *general* purpose or overriding goal, *every* speech you make must also have a sharply defined *specific* purpose. What is it, *specifically,* that you wish your message or messages to accomplish? What *specific* premise, proposition, principle, point, or idea do you want your listeners to understand and accept? To what *particular* belief or course of action do you wish to move them? Whether or not you are able to identify and label your general communicative intent, your speech planning and preparation will be aimless, random, diffuse, and—very probably—frustrating in the extreme if you fail to know and communicate to your hearers *why* you are speaking to them. Being able to determine and to state your specific purpose briefly, clearly, and pointedly is one of the most significant—and often the most difficult—jobs confronting you as a public speaker.

Once chosen, your specific purpose should be *written out* as concisely and as directly as possible—preferably in a single, simple sentence. Write it at the top of a blank sheet of paper. Then, as you accumulate ideas for your speech, jot them down on this same sheet. For each idea, your specific purpose should serve as a standard against which you can measure its relevance and its comparative value and strength.

A sample speech outline showing the general and the specific purpose may be found on pages 316–317.

Here are three other examples which indicate the difference between the general purpose and the specific purpose of a public speech, and show how these two purposes are related:

General Purpose: To inform.
Specific Purpose: To inform the audience of the procedures involved in filing a claim against the United States Postal Service.

General Purpose: To persuade.
Specific Purpose: To persuade the audience that marijuana is not a habit-forming drug.

Study Probe 1
Identifying General and Specific Purposes of Public Messages

Select a number of items from current daily newspapers, and determine the *general* and *specific* purpose of each. Which of these items or "messages" are primarily concerned with *providing information?* Which seek to *influence belief or action?* Which seem to be designed principally *to entertain?* Can you find any items that appear to have *inspiration* as their overriding goal? Is the *specific* purpose of each of the items stated explicitly? If not, state it for yourself, write it out in each instance, and be prepared to hand this analysis—along with your selected "message" items—to your instructor.

General Purpose: To actuate.
Specific Purpose: To get the listeners to volunteer to conduct a door-to-door canvass for the Heart Fund. 1

ORGANIZING THE PUBLIC SPEECH

Once you have determined your general and specific purposes and have assembled ample developmental/supportive materials, you are ready to begin organizing your "speech substance" accordingly. Organizing means that you *select, arrange,* and *develop* in simple, clear, and seemingly natural order the ideas and information you wish to present to your audience in order to accomplish your communicative purpose. Like *every* good composition, a speech should have three major divisions or parts: an *introduction,* a *body,* and a *conclusion.* Unless there are special reasons for not doing so, it is usually a good idea to think first about the organization of the body. After its contents and structure are determined, you will be in a better position to decide on a suitable introduction and conclusion.

Selecting and Wording the Main Heads

Begin work on the body of your speech by determining the major ideas, or "main heads," you wish it to contain and deciding how these "heads" may be most effectively worded. To determine the main heads, ask yourself: "What do I need to *explain* or *prove* in order to accomplish my specific purpose? What facts or concepts, if grasped by my listeners, will automatically cause them to understand the procedure, theory, or relationship I am trying to make clear? What proofs and appeals will most easily and persuasively lead them to accept the proposition I am setting forth?" The ideas and claims which meet these tests—which support your specific purpose most closely and directly—will constitute the major heads of the speech.

Except in unusual circumstances, these *principal ideas should be severely restricted in number.* In a five- or ten-minute speech it may not be possible to make more than one or two ideas clear or to prove more than one or two contentions. Even in longer speeches you may need to limit yourself to three or four major ideas. Too many points developed too briefly are difficult for an audience to remember or are likely to be supported so weakly that they are not accepted as valid.

When you are satisfied that you have selected the strongest or most illuminating ideas you can, write your specific purpose on a fresh sheet of paper and set these major heads down beneath it. Re-examine your specific purpose in terms of this list. Ask yourself: "If these main heads were adequately supported and developed with the necessary facts and explanations, would the specific purpose of my speech be accomplished? Have I omitted any head necessary to achieving this end? Have I listed more heads than are necessary?" Unless you are able to answer these and similar questions to your full satisfaction, keep adjusting the list until it meets the tests of pertinence and economy outlined above. [2]

After you have listed and tested the main heads of your speech plan, determine how you can best word them in order to communicate your ideas clearly and forcefully. In doing this keep in mind that the major heads as well as the specific purpose of the speech itself always should be worded as clearly and succinctly as possible, since long and vague statements are difficult for the listeners to comprehend and remember. Often it will prove helpful to state the heads in a series of parallel phrases, in order to emphasize the coordination and equal weighting of the various points. For example, in a speech on types of taxation you might frame the heads as follows:

> Income tax—the tax on what we *earn.*
> Sales tax—the tax on what we *buy.*
> Property tax—the tax on what we *own.*
> And so on.

Whatever pattern you follow, however, make sure that, in addition to stating those ideas in your speech that most directly and strongly support your specific purpose, the major heads you choose also are clearly and effectively worded.

Observe how clearly the major heads stand out in John A. Howard's speech, "The New Furies," reprinted in the Appendix. Each new head is identified by a number (First, Second, Third), and is given a brief and clear statement. Thus the speaker leaves no doubt in the audience's mind that he has concluded one major idea and is beginning on another. In addition, by keeping the major heads few in number (three), he makes it easy for the listeners to carry away with them the principal points he wants them to remember.

Arranging the Main Heads

After the major heads have been chosen and worded to your satisfaction, they must be arranged into a suitable *pattern* or *sequence.* The patterns which

Study Probe 2
Analyzing a Speech "Manuscript" for Its Major Headings

Read John A. Howard's speech, "The Three Furies," in the Appendix. Then, when you have succeeded in identifying the major points or heads intended by the speechmaker, write them out—in "outline" form—on a clean sheet of paper. In the lower portion of this sheet (and on a second one if you need it) comment briefly on how well the major heads of the model speech meet the tests of pertinence and economy we've mentioned in this chapter. Be prepared to hand the results to your instructor.

are perhaps most frequently used by speakers and which you might well consider as you come to organize your speech are five in number:

> The chronological pattern
> The spatial pattern
> The causal pattern
> The problem-solution pattern
> The topical pattern

This list, of course, is not exhaustive. Nor are the items included necessarily mutually exclusive. Often they can be combined in various ways, the chronological pattern, for instance, being used to describe the history of a famous building and the spatial pattern then employed to explain how it has been remodeled for current use. Considered individually, however, the five patterns are distinct in nature and function.

Chronological pattern. This pattern follows a *time* sequence, listing first those events or actions which occurred first and then mentioning in order the various happenings that succeeded them. By employing a time sequence a speaker can show the audience a developing problem in its consecutive stages or can help listeners understand a historical situation that otherwise might be quite confusing.

Spatial pattern. Occasionally the significant relationships among the main heads of a speech can best be made clear by arranging them according to spatial criteria. For example, in discussing election results, you might review first the returns from the Northeast, and then from the South, Middlewest, and West. In explaining how a product is assembled, you might make the process clear by following the product through the plant along the assembly line.

Causal pattern. When using the causal pattern, the main heads of a speech are related as cause-to-effect or effect-to-cause. Thus you might first point to unfavorable crop yields and poor marketing conditions and then show how farm income has dropped. Or, reversing the process, first mention the drop in farm income and then attribute this decrease to crop failures and unstable market prices.

Problem-solution pattern. Frequently it proves desirable to arrange the major heads of a speech by first describing a problem that exists and then advancing a program to solve it. When speaking on child abuse, for example, you might begin by calling the listeners' attention to the extent and seriousness of the problem and follow this by proposing a federal statute designed to eliminate the evil.

A possible variation on the strict problem-solution pattern of development is illustrated in the model speech by Virginia Y. Trotter. After outlining the problem by referring to the various ways in which the position of women today compares unfavorably with that of men, Ms. Trotter does not offer a detailed solution herself. Instead, she reviews briefly the progress made by women in the field of education, and challenges her women listeners to extend this progress further by changing their own attitudes and using their imaginations to develop a new image for their sex. Thus, strictly speaking, her speech may be said to consist of a problem and a *challenge* rather than a problem and solution in the usual sense.

Topical pattern.   Still another arrangement for organizing the major heads of a speech is known as the topical pattern. When employing this pattern, you look for the *parts or divisions into which a subject naturally falls,* and employ these to provide a structure for the speech. Following this pattern, a speech on our national government might be divided into discussions of the *executive* branch, the *legislative* branch, and the *judicial* branch. A speech on chess could be divided into the *opening moves, mid-game moves,* and *closing moves.* 3

Most important in giving a pattern to the main headings of a speech is that you choose some arrangement which fits your subject and which contributes directly to the achieving of your specific purpose. This, at the same time, will facilitate your listeners' understanding. The five patterns we've mentioned can be helpful because they are all *usual* ways of thinking about things and so are keyed to improve audience understanding. Through long conditioning, people in our culture have come to think in terms of temporal, spatial, causal, problem-solution, and topical relationships. At this moment, for example, you probably are wearing a watch, and there is probably a larger clock in the room. Within the last hour you quite likely have looked at one of them to check the time. Clocks direct much of our activity—often to the extent that we become their servants rather than their masters. Consider also how often we think in spatial terms—going uptown, turning left, traveling north. At other times, our thinking is dominated by causes and effects. Given an occurrence, we asked what brought it about. Shown a new development, we wonder what effects it will produce. As we emphasized in Chapter 9 (pages 201–208), many of these habits and patterns of thought are basic to us. If we were computers, we would say they are "wired in."

Study Probe 3
Evaluating the Main Heads of a Speech

Examine critically the major heads in one of the two model speeches in the Appendix. Write them out as the maker of the speech apparently intended. Then write your answers to the following questions: (1) What is there about the wording of these heads that helps to make them clear and easy to remember? (2) In what pattern are they arranged? (3) How well does this pattern fit (a) the *subject* of the speech, (b) the *purpose* of the speech, and (c) the kind of *audience* to whom it seems to have been addressed? Be prepared to discuss your answers in class and to hand your written analysis to the instructor if it is asked for.

This is why you as a speaker assist your hearers to listen and to remember when you structure your messages in one of these ways.

Choosing Developmental Materials

When you have determined your specific purpose and properly phrased and patterned the main heads of your speech, you will be ready to move on to the next step: filling out the main heads with *developmental materials.* No aspect of speech preparation is more important than this one. If the ideas contained in the main heads are to make an impression on the listeners, they must be *explained, emphasized, clarified,* and *made pertinent.* Sometimes they also must be *substantiated* or *proved.*

Six types of materials are useful in this regard. They are:

Definitions
Examples
Comparisons and contrasts
Narratives
Testimony
Quantitative data

Definitions. Often a speaker will need to introduce a new term or concept to an audience or will want to use an old term in a new and unfamiliar sense. When this is the case, it is important that the term or concept be defined so there will be no uncertainty about its meaning—about what is included in it and what is excluded from it.

Although a formal logical definition requires that the item to be defined first be placed in a general class or *genus* and then differentiated from other members of that class (An apple is a *fruit [genus]* that is *red* and *round* and *juicy [differentia]*), you may not always need to use such stringent methods of definition. You may, for instance, clarify what something means by pointing to an actual example of it ("If you will recall the Methodist Church on First Street you will understand what I mean by English Gothic architecture") or by telling what it is not ("By 'socialism' I do not mean 'communism,' a form of government which in principle denies the right of private ownership. On the contrary, I mean . . ."). At times a number of methods may be combined. The important thing is that the listeners have as clear an understanding as possible of what is in your mind when you use a certain word or phrase and that they see how the concept thus expressed relates to the major heads and to the specific purpose of the speech. [4]

Examples. Examples are probably the most widely used type of developmental material. As specific, elaborated instances of actual or hypothetical cases, they are useful in illustrating a general rule or principle or in giving listeners an idea of a prevailing condition or state of affairs. When the instance cited is a typical one or when it is used in combination with a number of parallel cases, an example also may furnish proof of a claim. When planning a speech, collect as many examples as possible of the conditions you want to describe, or assemble a number of examples that support a claim you wish to make. Then choose for the speech itself those examples which best fit the subject on which you are speaking and the concerns of the audience you are addressing.

Comparisons and contrasts. Often it is useful to develop an idea by comparing or contrasting it with something the audience already is familiar with. Thus you might explain the game of rugby by comparing or contrasting it with football, or tell how to perform a new and strange task by comparing it with an old one. In addition to serving as a means of explanation, carefully employed comparisons and contrasts may also help prove a claim. When used for this purpose, however, it is essential that the items brought into comparison be closely similar or that those set in contrast be markedly different.

Comparisons designed to serve as proofs sometimes are referred to as *analogies,* and are divided into two classes, *literal analogies* and *figurative analogies.* Literal analogies compare phenomena belonging to the same class of things—animals with animals, people with people, inanimate objects with inanimate objects. Figurative analogies, on the other hand, "cross the species line" and compare things that fall into different classes or categories.

Using literal analogies you might, for example, argue that since stricter driver's license examinations have reduced the number of fatal accidents in State A, they also would do so in neighboring State B, or that since publicly supported television in Great Britain results in a higher level of program quality, publicly supported television would have the same effect in the United States. Comparisons of the action of the heart to that of a suction pump or the brain to a giant telephone switchboard would, on the other hand, constitute figurative analogies. As a rule, figurative analogies provide less strong and convincing proof than literal ones. Under certain circumstances, however, the items brought into

Study Probe 4
Exploring Definitions

Define each of these terms, first by *genus* and *differentia,* and then by example:

bigot	entertainment
sexism	responsibility
insecurity	diplomacy
love	life

On what types of communicative occasions might you choose to define these terms by the first of the above methods, and on what types of occasions would you be more likely to use the second?

comparison, though belonging to different classes, may be so similar in nature that the resulting figurative analogy has proof value.

Narratives.   Rather than citing an example or drawing a comparison or contrast, a speaker may at times use *a story* or narrative to develop a point. This method of development, when well used, has the advantage of lending to an idea the interest values of tales and stories, with their elements of suspense and climax. A carefully chosen narrative also may enable a speaker to illustrate a point in an indirect way, thus *implying* rather than openly asserting a controversial claim or proposal. Under authoritarian or oppressive forms of government, for instance, criticisms of the system often are couched in humorous stories. Narratives may take the form of *anecdotes* as well as of more extended tales. An anecdote is a brief story, humorous or serious, which usually deals with true-to-life characters. Another common form of narrative is the *fable,* a fictitious story using animals or imaginary persons as characters. Still another form of narrative is the *parable*—a fictitious illustrative story from which a moral is drawn.

Beginning students of speech tend to overlook narratives in favor of examples and literal comparisons as methods of development. As you weigh the major heads you plan to present in a speech and search for the best means of explaining or supporting these points, consider whether in some cases a narrative in the form of a story, anecdote, fable, or parable might not communicate your idea most effectively. Remember, however, that a good narrative must be sufficiently worked out so that the elements of *suspense* and *characterization* are fully evident. If treated too briefly, it has no higher interest or dramatic value than a simple example.

Testimony.   Much of what we know and believe has come to us on the "say-so" of others. There are such great limits to what we can learn through direct, personal experience that we have to rely on what others can tell us. Moreover, as we demonstrated in Chapter 9 (pages 205–207), association-with-authority patterns carry considerable persuasive weight with both listeners and speakers. Speakers, no less than other individuals, depend upon this resource. They seek and cite expert opinions so that their own statements will seem more authoritative; or they quote them simply because another person has said so very well what they themselves wish to say. The most important consideration to be kept in mind when using testimony is that the person or persons cited be recognized as *authorities* by the audience. If this is not the case, the speaker should digress for a moment to make clear why the opinion or recommendation quoted deserves attention. In addition, the best authorities are those which are recognized to be relatively *unbiased* on the matter at issue. Not only do audiences suspect statements that reflect someone's personal bias; they may also suspect the motives of a speaker who quotes such statements. [5]

Quantitative data.   Numerical or statistical data in their various forms can be extremely useful both as a means of *explanation* and as a source of *proof.*

Every speaker should understand at least in an elementary way the forms such data may take and should be able to use them. As means of explanation, statistics are perhaps most often used to develop a precise description of a state of affairs or to compare two or more phenomena. Although in either case clarity and accuracy are desirable, the second—making comparisons—requires that additional cautions be kept in mind. Are the situations being compared really comparable? Were similar methods used in gathering the two sets of data, and were similar standards set up to evaluate them? Were the data gathered at approximately the same time? Were the items selected for study defined in the same way? Unless there is assurance that these and similar questions can be answered in the affirmative, the comparison which the statistics draw will be of little value.

When statistics are used for proof, rather than simply as a means of explanation, all of the preceding conditions continue to hold and, in addition, certain other cautions should be observed. Do the figures provided cover a sufficiently long period of time to establish a definite trend, or do they only reflect a temporary and passing state of affairs? Do quantities expressed in terms of averages, means, medians, and the like cover up significant differences in the data thus summarized? Do the statistics come from a reliable source? Were they gathered under carefully controlled conditions and analyzed by applying the appropriate statistical techniques? Considerations of this sort are important not only in determining the intrinsic worth of the data itself, but also in assuring the audience's ready acceptance of the information.

Besides making sure that the figures are reliable, the speaker who uses statistics to develop or support a point must do *everything* possible to aid the hearers in understanding the *meaning* and *significance* of the data reported. Large masses of figures presented in detail usually tend to confuse an audience

Study Probe 5
Evaluating Sources of Testimony

Make a list of the persons whose testimony you would accept on the following topics:

> energy crisis
> malpractice insurance
> trends in the business cycle
> our Far Eastern policy
> marijuana
> the future of professional baseball

For each person on your list, jot down the credentials—positions they hold, experiences they have had, etc.—which cause you to regard them as expert sources of testimony. Compare your list with those of classmates and discuss your reasons for including particular individuals.

rather than enlighten it. Very large numbers—figures in the billions or trillions—are difficult for an audience to grasp unless such numbers are accompanied by explanatory comparisons. Figures "tossed off" too rapidly may leave no impression at all.

When presenting bodies of statistical data, therefore, keep certain guidelines in mind. Do not cite more figures than are necessary to explain or prove your point. Whenever you can do so without sacrificing accuracy too greatly, use round rather than exact numbers; say "nearly two and a half billion" rather than "two billion, four hundred million, four hundred and fifty thousand." Support your oral presentation with charts, graphs, or columns of figures presented visually. Speak slowly and with frequent pauses to let the hearers grasp the full meaning and significance of what you say.

Provided they are fairly and effectively used, statistics constitute one of the speaker's most important means of developing ideas. The problem is to learn how to select them properly and to communicate them effectively. The speech in the Appendix by Virginia Y. Trotter is well worth studying as an example of how statistics and testimony may be used to support a speaker's claims or to make ideas more concrete and compelling.

Definitions, examples, comparisons and contrasts, narratives, testimony, and *quantitative data*—these, then, are the developmental materials that "flesh out" and support the skeleton provided by the main heads of your speech and become the substance or body of it. 6

The Introduction of a Speech

When you have finished planning for the body of the speech, you should next consider how to *introduce* the message you have developed. The introduction, though necessarily shorter than the body, is no less important and should be worked out with care. The introduction of a speech has three basic functions:

1. To catch attention and arouse interest in the topic.
2. To relate the topic to the concerns of the listeners.
3. To provide a bridge to the body of the speech.

Study Probe 6
Using Developmental Materials in a Public Speech

Prepare and present to the class a three-minute speech in which you explain or attempt to prove *a single point*. Use at least three types of developmental/supportive materials. At the conclusion of your presentation, conduct a lively, informal interchange with the other members of the class, encouraging them to criticize your use of these materials in explaining or proving the point at issue.

Catching attention and arousing interest.   The opening words of a speech should be chosen with a view to catching the attention of the listeners and awakening their interest in the topic to be discussed. To accomplish this, you may tell an anecdote, ask a provocative question, make an interest-arousing statement, or perhaps read a startling quotation.

Whatever method you use, however, remember that there is a difference between simply gaining attention and directing that attention to the subject at hand. In a recent class in public speaking, a student whipped out a bell from beneath her jacket and suddenly rang it. Another student secretly lighted a firecracker behind the lectern. In neither case did the action have any relation to the topic of the speech that followed; therefore, the actions detracted from rather than helped the speakers achieve their purpose. Instead of focusing audience attention *on the subject* to be discussed, these speakers unwisely did things that split attention *away from the subject* and centered it on their own strange behaviors.

Relating the topic to the concerns of the listeners.   After you have caught the initial attention of your listeners, it is usually a good idea to introduce a few sentences in which you show why the topic of your speech should be of concern to them. Why should they *care* about the situation or problem you plan to discuss? What do they have to *gain* from understanding what you say or from doing as you propose? How does your topic touch upon their beliefs and values? At the outset, many—perhaps most—audiences tend to be reserved or apathetic. Unless this apathy is counteracted, they will not be apt to listen to your ideas with attention or to react as you desire.

Providing a bridge to the body of the speech.   The final task of a good introduction is to provide a bridge to the body of the speech—to lay the groundwork for what is to follow. This may involve giving your listeners *a brief preview* of the points you expect to cover or stating *the position that you are going to take* on the problem at issue. At other times, you may find it necessary to *define one or more crucial terms* or to *refer to the sources* from which you will draw your information. In any case, you must be sure to tie the introduction of your speech to the body of your speech by means of a smooth *transition* that gives sense and direction to the succeeding discussion. The introduction which stands as an independent unit isolated from the remainder of the speech is of no more use to you or your listeners than the introduction which fails to catch their attention and arouse their interest.

The Conclusion of a Speech

The purpose of a good speech conclusion is twofold: (1) to reinforce your specific purpose and the leading ideas of your speech and (2) to bring your message or messages as a whole to an appropriate and satisfying close. As a general rule, therefore, in ending your speech you should:

1. Summarize the main points of your speech.

2. Appeal strongly for your listeners' acceptance of the ideas you've advanced or the action you've proposed.

3. Induce in your listeners a sense of climax or finality—by your words and your manner indicate that your speech has been rounded out and brought to a natural and logical conclusion.

Always consider the possibility of returning in your conclusion to an idea or allusion made at the beginning of your speech. 7

OUTLINING THE SPEECH

After the structure of the speech has been set and the developmental materials selected and arranged, the whole should be reduced to a carefully constructed outline. Such an outline serves both as a check on the organization and content of the speech as planned and as an aid to fixing these elements firmly in your mind.

Types of Outlines

In common practice, two different types of outlines are recognized—the complete sentence outline and the single word or "catch phrase" outline. As its name implies, the complete sentence outline consists of formally framed sentences written as they might be used during the actual presentation of the speech. The single word or "catch phrase" outline, on the other hand, is made up of individual words or short phrases designed to jog the speaker's memory about the ideas to be presented.

Study Probe 7
Evaluating Speech Introductions and Conclusions

a. Identify the elements in the introduction and the conclusion of one of the model speeches in the Appendix. What methods are used in the introduction to catch attention and arouse interest? Does a smooth and natural "bridge" carry the listener from the introduction into the body of the speech? What method or methods are used in the conclusion to bring the speech to a close? Do they do so successfully?

b. Find in the magazine *Vital Speeches of the Day* two speeches in which still different methods are used to develop the introduction and conclusion. Report your findings to the class, including in your report an evaluation of the methods employed.

Sometimes these two methods may be combined, so that the main heads of the speech appear in the outline as complete sentences and the developmental materials are represented by single words or short phrases. Such an arrangement, many speakers believe, enables them to be certain of expressing their leading ideas in the precise form they desire, but also leaves them free to adapt their developmental materials to situations which may arise during the presentation of the speech.

Principles of Outlining

Under normal circumstances the main heads of your speech as previously selected, arranged, and worded will constitute the major points in your outline, with the developmental materials standing in a subordinate relationship to them. In good outline form, these major points should be positioned nearer the left-hand margin of the page and the developmental materials deeply indented. In addition, the parts or divisions of the speech—the introduction, body, and conclusion—should be clearly indicated. Thus, when put into final form, your speech outline might look something like this:

MR. DRIVER, DIG DEEP

General Purpose: To inform.

Specific Purpose: To explain to the audience why still higher gasoline prices are in prospect.

Introduction

I. According to some of the best authorities, the day of $1.75 a gallon gasoline is not far off.
    A. This means that as drivers we will have "to dig into our pockets" far more deeply than we have to date.
    B. Why has this unhappy situation come about?

Body

II. Present and prospective increases in the cost of gasoline are chiefly the result of four factors.
    A. Artificial price fixing on the part of the major oil-producing nations (OPEC).
        1. First fixed early in 1974.
            a. Price set at more than $10 a barrel.
            b. Production restricted so as to maintain this price.
        2. Price policy reaffirmed several times since.
            a. In a meeting at Vienna early in 1975.
            b. In a meeting in Algiers later the same year.

  3. Still higher prices threatened.
      a. Shah of Iran has declared the price will go up if the Western nations do not control inflation.
      b. The Oil Minister of Saudi Arabia says his nation will restrict production to maintain price level.
  4. All attempts to break the OPEC cartel have failed.
 B. Continued use of the automobile as a major form of transportation.
  1. More people are driving cars today than ever before.
  2. The "craze" for smaller, gas-saving cars is passing.
  3. There is strong pressure to abolish the 55-mile-an-hour speed limit.
 C. The determination of our government to restrict oil imports.
  1. Such restriction is needed to protect our balance of payments.
      a. Two out of every five barrels of oil we use come from foreign wells.
      b. Billions of dollars leave the country every year to pay for this oil.
  2. Restricting imports will raise price of gasoline ten cents or more a gallon.
 D. Developing new sources of domestic oil is a risky and expensive process.
  1. It may be necessary to dig many wells before finding one that produces oil.
  2. It is necessary to go to the expense of digging deeper and in less favorable locations.

Conclusion

III. These four factors—artificial price-fixing, continued use of automobiles, government restriction on oil imports, risk and expense of developing new domestic sources of oil—working in combination, will undoubtedly continue to push the price of gasoline ever higher in years to come.
  1. There is little that consumers individually or collectively can do to combat them.
  2. Drivers of cars must, therefore, be prepared "to dig into their pockets" even more deeply than they are today.

   In this outline not only have the developmental materials been arranged under the main heads to which they apply, but two other principles of good outlining also have been observed: (1) *each unit in the outline is limited to one and only one idea,* and (2) *a consistent set of symbols has been used throughout.* Both of these principles are important. If two or three ideas are run together under one symbol, the relationships they bear to one another and to the other ideas in the outline will not stand out clearly. If one set of symbols is used to develop one of the main heads and other sets of symbols are indiscriminately applied to the others, you probably will have a good deal more difficulty in fixing the various points in your mind and also will be more apt to become confused as you stand before the audience.

Your outline, like the speech it represents, should be developed gradually through a series of stages. First rough out the points you wish to cover and the order in which it seems best to consider them. Then fit the developmental materials under each head, checking to make certain that they apply to the point under which they are placed and not to some other. With this much done, think again about the *order* in which your major ideas are arranged. Is the order logical? Does it fit the subject and purpose of your speech? Will it help the audience grasp your main points and see the relationships that exist between them? Is it followed consistently throughout the body of the talk? If not, is the reason for varying the order made clear? Check the *developmental materials* also. Do they in each case fall beneath the point they are designed to support? Are they in each case the strongest or most telling materials you could select? Are they arranged in the most effective way?

The chances are that as you study your rough outline you will want to make a number of changes in the way you order your materials and also perhaps in the materials themselves. Only after you are satisfied that you have the best content possible and have arranged it in the most effective way should you write up the outline in its final form. 8

MAKING YOUR MESSAGE MORE APPEALING

The "message" of your speech—the body of facts and ideas you wish the listeners to understand or accept—will be embodied in your main heads and in the materials you use for their development. These factors alone, however, will not ensure that your listeners will attend to your ideas or endorse the plans or proposals you advance. In addition to having a solid and well-organized content, a successful speech also must hold the audience's interest and must—as we

Study Probe 8
Learning to Make Outlines

Following the principles of good outlining set forth in the preceding section, each member of the class should make detailed outlines of three speeches printed in *Vital Speeches of the Day* or some other convenient source. (The same speeches should be outlined by all students.) Exchange these outlines among yourselves to ascertain how closely you agree on where the body of the speech begins and ends, what the main heads are, and how the developmental materials are subordinated to the main heads. With this phase of the Probe completed, select the "best" of the three speeches you've analyzed, outline it in accordance with the form described in this chapter, and hand the written result to your instructor.

explained in Chapter 8—motivate the listeners to respond as the speaker desires. The "elements of interest" and the "motive appeals" we are now to consider are directed toward these ends, and may, therefore, be thought of as devices designed to "facilitate" the acceptance of the speaker's message.

Elements of Interest

As you know from your own experience, not all people find the same things equally interesting. Some are avid followers of the sports pages; others never glance at this section of their daily papers. Some are absorbed in science, others in literature and the arts, and still others in politics and current affairs. However much individuals may differ in these and similar respects, they still tend to have their interest aroused by a more or less common set of circumstances or conditions. They are, as a rule, more interested in those *events or states of affairs that affect them personally* than in happenings that are remote from them in time and place. They are more interested in *the new and unusual* than in the ordinary and commonplace, in *reports about actual persons or occurrences* than in abstract ideas or vague generalized statements, and in *events of unknown or uncertain,* rather than certain, outcome. Finally, with few exceptions, people tend to have their interest aroused by *humor.*

Because of these common tendencies, it is possible to draw up with a fair degree of accuracy what have previously been referred to as "elements of interest"—those particular ideas or subjects which—other things being equal—cause listeners to find a speech more interesting than it might otherwise be. For our purposes, such a list may include the following five elements:

1. The relevant
2. The novel
3. The concrete
4. The uncertain
5. The humorous

When planning and preparing a speech, always consider carefully how one or more of these elements may make your message more attractive. Develop your ideas in such a way that they are *relevant* to your listeners; show how the information you are giving or the proposal you are advocating affects them personally. Bring forth fresh and *novel* facts and conceptions rather than old and timeworn ones; open up new and previously unexplored vistas of thought. Present specific data and *concrete* instances and cases rather than talking in general terms. Frequently the most effective speech is the one that is most tightly packed with references to the listeners' own *sensory experiences*—to what they themselves have seen, heard, touched, or tasted. In organizing your speech, take account also of the interest that can be aroused by the unknown or *uncertain.* Introduce a measure of *suspense* about the solution you intend to offer for an existing problem; build up your ideas in *climactic order;* inject a sense of *conflict* by bringing alternative views into opposition and showing how one would necessarily exclude the other. Whenever appropriate, illustrate your points with *humorous* phrases or anecdotes. Use these to give the audience relief from an extended discussion of complex or technical matters and also to put your leading ideas into a form that is more likely to be remembered after the speech is over.

As was pointed out earlier, the introduction of a speech has as one of its principal purposes to catch the attention of the listeners and to arouse their concern for the subject at hand. A speaker should not, however, make the mistake of thinking that the interest gained by a good introduction will remain at a high level throughout the remainder of the speech. More often than not, listeners begin to tire, their attention wanders, or their interest wanes. Therefore, all parts of the speech should be developed with a concern for maintaining the interest of the audience. This advice pertains to the body and conclusion of the speech, no less than to the introduction.

Motive Appeals

As we remarked earlier, the members of an audience may understand clearly the proposal or plan of action outlined in your speech and yet not be moved to endorse that proposal or to behave as you desire. This, more often than not, is because they do not see why doing so will be to their advantage. In order to overcome this obstacle to the responses you are seeking, you must *show how the belief or action in question will contribute to the satisfaction of one or more underlying human desires or motives.* Admittedly, however, the subject of motivation is complex, and many questions concerning it remain unanswered. Motivation, you'll recall, was an aspect of message-making that we explored in Chapter 8 (pages 164–167). Because motivation is so crucial to the response listeners make to your message, we believe the subject merits your close review of those earlier pages and also a brief reexamination here.

Theories of Motivation

In broad terms, as we've noted, psychologists seem to look upon human motivation as the product of *primary* and *secondary* drives or needs. Maslow, you'll remember, lists five basic human needs: (1) *physiological well-being,* (2) *safety and security,* (3) *belongingness and love,* (4) *esteem,* and (5) *self-actualization.*[1] By placing these needs on various levels, he emphasizes their relative importance in the life of the individual. Not until the basic physiological needs are satisfied will the socially acquired "secondary" drives take over as motivators. Moreover, among our socially acquired needs, some demand a fairly large measure of satisfaction before others will come into play. Maslow recognizes, of course, that the hierarchy he has proposed is not applicable to all persons in all circumstances. In general, however, the order he proposes seems a useful and productive way for the public speaker to look at the springs of human action.

A second aspect of motives and motivation that we looked at was their "functional autonomy," a principle developed by Gordon Allport, a Harvard psychologist.[2] According to his view, behaviors and desires originally learned in order to satisfy physiological and safety needs may eventually become motivators themselves, even in the absence of the basic and originally associated need. A way of life developed to meet an essential physiological need *itself* becomes a need or a motive.

And, finally, a third view of motivation that we examined arises from "consistency theories": In our behaviors we are motivated principally by a desire to achieve *a balance or harmony among our cognitions.* An example of this type of motivation is the "congruity" approach developed by Charles Osgood, George Suci, and Percy Tannenbaum.[3] Briefly, this theory holds that a disapproved idea (one we dislike or distrust) advanced by a speaker whom we admire will take on new "credibility," whereas an approved idea (one that we "like") advanced by a source of whom we are critical will lose credibility or credence. Faced with a situation in which, as listeners, we have one opinion of an idea or point of view and a *different* opinion or estimation of the speaker who advances it, we adjust our evaluations so as to bring these discrepancies into congruence.

All three of these theories provide interpretations of human behavior which the public speaker must take into careful consideration when planning a speech. Without entering into the continuing argument about which theory comes nearer to stating the whole truth of the matter, the speaker would do well at least to consider the various stages or levels in Maslow's "hierarchy" when selecting his or her appeals, and should be aware that patterns of behavior which now seem to have little purpose often are, as Allport suggests, deeply rooted in underlying physiological needs. The speaker should also recognize that, in an effort to achieve "consistency" or "congruity" among opposing values, listeners tend to depreciate or discount views expressed by a source held in low esteem and to look more favorably upon distasteful or unpopular ideas when these come from a highly esteemed writer or "authority." 9

Study Probe 9
Discovering Motives and Motive Appeals

a. Recall as objectively as you can one of your actions of the past few days—your decision to buy a new article of clothing, to cut a class, or to write a letter to the editor; or your behavior toward a friend or associate. Can you identify the underlying need or motive that caused you to engage in the particular behavior? Were you aware of your motive at the time you behaved as you did? Were you perhaps led to act because you were subjected to an appeal to that motive?

b. Find in the popular magazines at least three advertisements which contain appeals addressed to one or more motives. Report your results orally, displaying the advertisements to the class as you do so.

See if other members of the class agree with you concerning the motive or motives employed. Are they able to find in the advertisements elements of motivation you missed?

An example of strong but subtle audience motivation may be seen in John A. Howard's speech. Throughout, Dr. Howard bolsters his case by skillfully appealing to his listeners' sense of social or communal responsibility, and then in closing he focuses more specifically on their own desires for personal achievement and self-actualization. In the speech by Ms. Trotter, by contrast, the motivation is much stronger and more obvious and is directed more steadily toward the single goal of self-actualization. Indeed, her entire speech may be looked upon as a call to women to actualize their potentialities and thus to take their full and rightful place not only in the educational system but in all areas of society.

COUNTERACTING UNDESIRABLE
SPEECH COMMUNICATION EFFECTS

When your aim as a speaker is to influence the beliefs of your listeners or to cause them to act in a particular way, besides considering the aspects of speech planning and preparation we've considered thus far, you should also recognize and take steps to counteract certain undesirable effects your speech may produce.

Recognizing Unwanted Consequences

Many speeches, especially those intended to alter the opinions of the audience, may produce effects quite contrary to the speaker's design. These negative effects include (1) the *boomerang effect,* (2) the *regression effect,* (3) the *sleeper effect,* and (4) the *focusing effect.*

The boomerang effect.   There always is a danger that a speech effort may backfire. Its impact may be such as to move the listeners in a direction almost exactly the *reverse* of what the speaker intends. In almost every speech-research study, investigators have found a few audience members whose beliefs and evaluations change in a direction opposite from that advocated by the speaker. Seemingly, these listeners are somehow offended or perhaps alienated by the speech, and so they react negatively. The speaker not only fails to influence them toward the position he or she is advocating, but—worse—causes them to move in a counter direction, away from the very position they are being urged to adopt. The causes of this kind of "boomerang" reaction are not clear, but the reaction itself is common enough to warrant some speculation.

Suppose that a speaker argues against a position that you, a listener, support. His or her speaking may have little or no effect upon you; you may be completely unmoved. Your beliefs and the evaluations relative to the subject remain essentially what they were before the speech began. But suppose that a college administrator, in arguing against the ability of college students to make their own academic decisions, speaks against your position in a manner that you consider unfair or untruthful. You may then react *negatively* and be prompted to favor your own "side" of the issue even more strongly than you did originally. This "retroversive" response-effect is very human and understandable: Our reaction, generally, to people who treat us unfairly or who lie to us is markedly negative and personal. Any evidence of insincerity or dubious motive which you attribute to a speaker may produce a boomerang effect.

The regression effect. With the passage of time following a speaker's presentation of a message, audience attitudes tend to move back toward the positions the hearers held before listening to the speech. The memory of the speaker's point becomes blurred, and the impact of the message fades. Thus a position strongly endorsed by listeners during the speech or immediately thereafter may within a few days or weeks be abandoned or held much less strongly. Note, for instance, the way in which the public's concern for "the ecological urgency" originally soared. Scores of speakers addressed themselves to the subject; some scientists made dire predictions concerning the ultimate destruction of our environment; radio stations issued urgent messages; television producers presented documentaries urging that drastic actions be taken. And we all enthusiastically agreed. Now, however, competent observers have noted a drop in the level of public concern; they see it reverting—and perhaps rather quickly—to a level approaching apathy. [10]

Sleeper effect. Another finding from research studies which bears significantly upon the speaker's efforts to modify listener belief or behavior has been labeled the "sleeper effect." This phrase names the phenomenon wherein *a source*

Study Probe 10
Recalling a Regression Effect

Recall a speech, editorial, or article which you encountered some days or weeks ago and which caused you to change your mind on a matter important to you— the fitness of a certain person to hold public office, an aspect of our domestic or foreign policy, etc. Then describe as well as you can: (1) your position on this matter *before* you were exposed to the speech, editorial, or article; (2) your position *immediately after* being exposed to it; (3) how you feel about the matter *today.*

Is your position still as strong as it was immediately after exposure to the message? If so, what was it about the message that made such a lasting impression on you? If your position now is less strong, how do you account for this fact? Have you been exposed to counter-messages? Have some of the ideas and arguments that originally made such a strong impression on you come to seem weak or fallacious? Or has the original impression just faded and worn off as time has passed? Develop a detailed set of notes which you can hand to your instructor prior to a more or less formal, five-person discussion in which "consensus" answers to the foregoing questions are formulated.

and a message become dissociated as time passes, and the influence of the source tends to be separated from the influence of the message.

As we've previously pointed out, experimentation supports the view that a speaker's prestige or lack of it will add to or diminish the persuasive influence a message exerts. A high-prestige source will be more influential than a low-prestige source if both present identical ideas and arguments. However, an examination of the *long-term* effects of persuasive messages has led to some surprises. Research has shown that the positive or negative effects of the source upon the listeners' reception of the message may disappear as time passes. Thus when a high-prestige source speaks in support of a given position, audience attitudes—initially swayed toward the view presented by the source—may later revert to the position held prior to the speech. Or, conversely, when a low-prestige source presents a public speech, the immediate reaction may be less pronounced than the reaction as measured some weeks in the future. In each instance, a plausible explanation of the change in attitude is that over a period of time the negative effect exercised by the low-prestige speaker wears off, while, on the other hand, the audience no longer so strongly associates the high-prestige speaker with the point of view he or she presents.

Focusing effect. We have all seen photographs in which some subjects are in focus while others blur into the background. The subjects in focus are the ones that gain our attention. When looking out of a window, we can focus either on the window glass itself or on some object beyond it. In the first case we may notice scratches and bits of dirt on the window glass, whereas a distant tree is blurred. Or we can focus on the distant tree and see it clearly, in which case we no longer are aware of the scratches on the windowpane. The fact that we cannot focus on both objects simultaneously has an important analog or "parallel" in the study of speech communication. In a speech setting, the listener always will focus on and hence will tend to emphasize certain elements at the expense of others. Let us examine this phenomenon more fully.

As we saw in our analysis of the Belief-Evaluation Cluster system in Chapter 8, every listener comes to a speech setting with a more or less fully developed set of beliefs and evaluations. These beliefs and evaluations are held with different degrees of salience or prominence. Together, they constitute the listener's original *attitude* or *predisposition* toward the topic. As the message is presented, however, the listener's attention will, in all probability, be channeled in *new* directions. The speaker will emphasize certain points and ignore or skim over others. As a result, a particular focus or pattern of emphasis will be established.

If the speaker is performing successfully and is commanding the attention of the listener, while the speech continues this pattern will be maintained. *Later,* however, when the speech is over and the listener returns to his or her usual environment, the focus established by the speech will tend either to persist or to fade. Sometimes the focus established by the speaker will be so sharp that even after a long period of time its outlines remain in the listener's mind. On other occasions, the habitual and comfortable thought configurations the listener held prior to hearing the speech will again take over. The focus established by the speech will be replaced by the focus which he or she held prior to being exposed to the message.

Because the focusing process operates in this way, it not only is partially responsible for the effects which may immediately follow a communication event, but it also partially explains the regressive reaction noted above. *What we are focusing on at a given moment will be most influential in determining our behavioral response at that moment.* 11

Compensating for Undesirable Effects

Just as the nature and causes of the boomerang, regression, sleeper, and focusing effects are not yet fully understood, the research into methods for *preventing* or *minimizing* these effects is not yet far advanced. It does appear, however, that to some extent they may be guarded against by *immunization* and *campaigning*.

Immunization.   By "immunization" we mean giving full attention to the side of the issue which the speaker does *not* favor—presenting facts and arguments opposed to the position advocated as well as facts and arguments which support it. This is the reasoning behind the use of the immunization technique: If a speaker presents only one side of an issue, he or she may achieve the immediate response desired. But suppose that after a period of time members of the audience are exposed to a *different* speaker, one who brings up an *opposing viewpoint.*

Thus confronted, they may be swayed in the direction advocated by this

Study Probe 11
Focusing the Attention and Interest of Listeners

From your own experiences and observations draw four or five elements, devices, or factors which you, as a communicating agent, might employ to "focus" the attention and interest of other agents. Examples:

1. Amount of time speaker devotes to the topic.
2. Vocal emphasis.
3. Visual emphasis through gestures, etc.
4. Repetition or restatement of an idea.

Why do you think that these factors would have a focusing effect? Is it possible to rank them in terms of their probable importance or effectiveness? With the other members of the class participating, conduct an informal group discussion in which you attempt to summarize (on the chalkboard, preferably) those factors or devices which apparently are used most frequently by student speakers to focus listeners' attention and interest.

second speaker. If, however, the original speaker, in first addressing them, mentions and successfully refutes the major opposing arguments, his listeners will tend to be "immunized" against these appeals and, therefore, more likely to remain unswayed by them. Because objections to the proposed belief or action have been given full consideration in the original presentation, their sting has been removed and their effect blunted well in advance.

Admittedly such immunization will not always work. And even if it does, it won't guarantee against later reversals in audience attitude. Moreover, under the best of circumstances, a caution must be observed. If your listeners are not very knowledgeable and discriminative, to set forth more than one side of an issue may be confusing and therefore dangerous to your case. Even under these circumstances, however, the possibility of immunizing your audience by exposing them to contrary arguments is always an option that should be considered. 12

Campaigning.   Very early in life we become aware of the power of *repetition* in achieving our purposes. As children, we didn't ask for a piece of candy only once; we asked and kept on asking until we got it or else concluded that our plea was utterly hopeless. Skilled speakers also know the value of reiterating the essential points of a message, as well as repeating the message itself at a number of different times or places—in effect, of carrying on a *campaign* on the message's behalf. By engaging in such practices, speakers are merely borrowing a leaf from the book constantly resorted to by advertisers and sales promotion experts.

As a means of combating the *regression* and *sleeper* effects, *campaigning* on behalf of a message may often prove most helpful. There is, however, a danger in "pushing" a message so hard or repeating it so often that the listeners become satiated and the *boomerang* response sets in. Just as in the case of any technique of rhetoric or persuasion, therefore, campaigning needs to be carried on with judgment and restraint.

Study Probe 12
Immunizing Listeners Against Opposing Arguments

Select a current issue or problem in which you are interested and on which you have well-defined beliefs. Develop four or five good *arguments in support of your position* on this issue. Then work out four or five *counter-arguments* which might be used to immunize the listeners against future objections.

Hand a written summary of your pro and con arguments to your instructor, and be prepared to discuss the advantages, disadvantages, and dangers in such a procedure. Might not the counter-arguments be so strong that they—rather than the constructive arguments for your position—persuade the listeners? Explain how you will guard against this danger.

MAKING A FINAL CHECK OF YOUR SPEECH PLAN

Let's assume that, following the numerous suggestions and cautions mentioned above, you now have before you a complete and carefully drawn outline of the speech you propose to present. As a last step in the preparation process, it always is a good idea to check over this outline, with a view to three different but related matters: the *organization or structure* of the speech, the *developmental materials,* and the *ties or transitions* by which one point is related to another.

Organization or Structure

So far as the organization or structure of the speech is concerned, ask yourself the following questions:

1. Do I have a discrete and clearly defined introduction and conclusion, and do these parts or divisions of my speech discharge economically and effectively the functions they are designed to serve?

2. Do the main heads in the body of my speech divide up the subject in a reasonable and natural way? Do they cover all aspects of the topic? Do they represent the really significant points that I wish to make—the points which I wish my listeners to remember in future days and weeks? Are they few enough in number so they will be remembered easily?

3. Are the main heads of the speech arranged in a logical and easy-to-follow order? Does each one grow naturally out of the point that precedes it? Is the order I am employing—chronological, spatial, or whatever it may be—the one best adapted to the subject I am discussing and to the interests and attitudes of the audience I am addressing?

4. Are the heads of my speech essentially co-equal in scope and importance, or does one of them seem trivial or out of place when put alongside the others? Would each of the heads, if understood or endorsed, lead immediately to an understanding or acceptance of my specific purpose?

Developmental Materials

In checking over the developmental materials you have selected to support the main heads, ask these questions:

1. Is each head adequately supported by developmental materials? Are the points which require explanation made clear? Are the points which require proofs firmly established?

2. Are the developmental materials used of good quality? Do they come from reputable sources? Are they up to date?

3. Do the materials used as proof meet the tests of logical adequacy and audience acceptability? Are the statistics free of fallacies? Do the quotations or testimony employed as evidence come from authoritative sources? Have enough examples or comparisons been introduced to establish the point in question?

4. Are the developmental materials reasonably varied in nature? Are examples, comparisons, statistics, and the rest interwoven into a pleasing and varied pattern? Or is one type of material used to the practical exclusion of the others?

5. Are the developmental materials in each case properly placed under the head they are designed to support? Would the listener who understood them immediately understand the head the materials are used to clarify? Would the listener who accepted them automatically be obliged to endorse the contention the materials are intended to prove?

Ties or Transitions

Finally, check the ties or transitions by which the major heads of your speech are held together and by which the developmental materials are related to the major heads. Ask:

1. Am I doing everything possible to make it easy for my listeners to follow my line of thought? Am I showing them, through the use of appropriate transitional phrases, how one point relates to another? Am I forecasting my intended arguments by briefly indicating them early in the course of my speech? Or if this does not seem appropriate, am I providing occasional summaries which remind the audience of the road that has been covered and of the matters that still remain to be considered?

2. Do the transitions I have planned accurately express the sort of relationship I wish to convey—an extension of an idea presently being considered, opposition between ideas, subordination of one point to another, etc.? In short, have I used such words and phrases as "Moreover," "On the other hand," "Therefore," and "For example" correctly?

3. Are the transitions I have supplied varied enough stylistically so as not to become boring or call unfavorable attention to themselves by being repeated over and over? Do they, no less than other aspects of my speech, show some originality in conception and at least a minimum of grace in expression?

As the foregoing pages make evident, the process of planning and preparing a speech for public presentation is by no means a short or easy one. An appropriate subject must be chosen or an assigned subject narrowed and focused in a way that will be appropriate to the audience and occasion. A general purpose must be selected; and within the area thus delimited, a specific purpose must be carefully framed. The major heads or ideas that support the specific purpose must be determined and given clear expression. Interesting and authoritative developmental materials must be gathered and arranged. The speech must be supplied with a suitable introduction and conclusion. Ideas that will interest the audience and appeals that will motivate them to believe or to act must be woven into the body of the speech. Attention must be paid to certain undesirable or retroversive effects which appeals may have, and plans for counteracting these must be laid. Finally, an outline which accurately reflects all of this planning must be set down and used as a base for checking the organization or structure of the speech, the adequacy of the developmental materials, and ties or transitions by which the speech is held together. This is the blueprint for the detailed, ongoing, uninterrupted, public message that you will now begin to *practice* in order to ready it and yourself for *presentation* to your audience—the area of concentration in the chapter which follows.

Suggested Readings

There are many excellent textbooks where the interested student can find more detailed treatments of public speech preparation. The following are highly recommended:

Alan H. Monroe and Douglas Ehninger, *Principles and Types of Speech Communication,* 7th ed. (Glenview, Ill.: Scott, Foresman and Company, 1974), especially Chapters 7–12 and 14–16.

John F. Wilson and Carroll C. Arnold, *Public Speaking as a Liberal Art,* 3rd ed. (Boston: Allyn and Bacon, Inc., 1974), especially Chapters 4–8.

Reference Notes

[1]A. H. Maslow, *Motivation and Personality* (New York: Harper & Row, Publishers, 1954), especially Chapter 5, "A Theory of Human Motivation."

[2]Gordon W. Allport, "The Functional Autonomy of Motives," *American Journal of Psychology* 50 (1937):141–156.

[3]See Charles E. Osgood, George J. Suci, and Percy H. Tannenbaum, *The Measurement of Meaning* (Urbana, Ill.: University of Illinois Press, 1957), Chapter 5.

Chapter 14

SPEECH PRACTICE
AND
PRESENTATION

Every speech is something like a symphony
with higher and lower moments,
recurring but differently developed themes,
calculated simultaneously to give and
to require audience involvement. In order to
orchestrate these moments, practice orally
and present public speeches frequently.

Before reading this chapter, we urge you to review Chapters 6 and 7, especially those sections concerned with verbal and nonverbal messages (pages 119–121) and adapting communication messages to listener feedback *during* interaction (pages 149–154). The principles and processes we examined there are basic to understanding and interacting with listeners in public speech communication settings.

With a completed, reviewed, and evaluated outline of your speech before you and armed with the self-assurance that comes from "knowing your stuff" insofar as message content and form are concerned, you are ready to move into the second phase of your preparation for a one-to-many speech occasion: You are ready to practice your speech for presentation to an audience.

PRACTICING TO COMMUNICATE ORALLY

When we practice our *speech delivery skills,* what we are doing—among other things—is trying to sort out and assimilate desirable vocal, gestural, and "physical control" patterns. We are trying to discover and settle upon what is for

331

us individually the best way to "say and do" a speech. Typically, we first experiment with various ways of expressing and transmitting our message. Then we select what we feel works best; we rehearse it and repeat it; we assimilate it—make it an integral part of our thinking and behavior, thereby putting it on an "habitual" level before we face our listeners.

Working Out Patterns of Presentation

In specific steps, we believe, these are the essential process-components of practicing for a public presentation of a speech:

1. *Identifying* potentially effective vocal/gestural behavior patterns.
2. *Experimenting* with these patterns to determine their probable usefulness and appropriateness for the coming speech event.
3. *Selecting* those patterns which are most suitable.
4. *Integrating* such patterns with the "flow" and intent of message content.
5. *Repeating* them until the desired degree of pattern/content has been achieved.

Begin your practice by *standing up* and delivering your speech *aloud,* from your outline, in an empty room. Too many beginning "practicers" merely sit at a desk and mumble their way through the speech. This is like practicing a tennis stroke while you're seated in a chair. It misses the whole "feeling" of the activity. You should try to practice your speech in conditions that are as nearly like the actual situation as possible. You can't expect to feel comfortable speaking out before an audience if your only practice has been to mumble to yourself.

In the early stages of practice you should try to "talk through" your entire speech aloud several times without stopping. Referring to the outline when necessary, begin to set the *sequence* of main ideas and developmental materials firmly in your mind. When we have listened a number of times to a long-playing record that contains several selections, we can anticipate which one will come next. You should develop the same kind of anticipation for the sequence of ideas in your speech, and *oral practice* is one of the most effective ways to do this.

Consider also whether you will use notes when presenting the speech, and, if so, what kind they will be. You might use a full-speech manuscript or decide to speak from an outline. Most likely, however, you will depend on a few notes which contain in an abbreviated form the leading ideas you wish to advance, together with a summary of the developmental materials that support them. These notes may be put on 3 x 5 or 4 x 6 cards, or on half-sheets of 8½ x 11 paper. The smaller the space you allow for such notes, however, without making them difficult to read, the more easily you will be able to handle them while speaking. As a speaker, you ought to use whatever type of notes is most helpful to you. The important point is that they contain the essential information in easy-to-read form. Moreover, you should use such aids sparingly and only to the extent that they are absolutely necessary to enable you to move through your planned remarks without awkward hesitations or digressions. If you have practiced thoroughly, usually you will need to refer to your notes only infrequently when passing from one point to another or when presenting a mass of detailed data.

The chief objection to the use of notes in formal speaking is that ordinarily they are badly used. Given a manuscript, most speakers stare at it and read it word by word with all the liveliness they would have if reading a long list of names from a telephone directory. There also are speakers who, throughout their speeches, stare down at their notes even when they know perfectly well what they wish to say, thereby losing all communicative contact with their audience. As a speaker, you should keep your notes at hand for *emergency purposes only* and should address your listeners—not your note cards. When practicing, strive to free yourself from them as soon as possible. The less you need to look at your notes, the more you can study your listeners and note the feedback signals they are giving you.

"Well, then," you may ask, "if I hope to reproduce faithfully the materials I plan to present and am to do so while maintaining close physical or eye contact with my listeners, should I memorize my speech?" Many persons would quickly answer, "By no means!" To leap to such a conclusion, however, would be to overlook the useful fact that there are many different forms or degrees of "memorizing." Probably no one should memorize a speech *word for word.* Not only would such a practice be wasteful of the speaker's time, but the chances are strong that it would result in an artificial and noncommunicative kind of delivery. Many successful speakers do, however, memorize *portions* of their speeches—the first few and the last few sentences, and possibly the transitional phrases they plan to employ. They also may memorize the ways in which they wish to state their major heads, so as to be sure that these will come across to the audience in a clear and easy-to-remember fashion. The remainder of the message, on the other hand, is presented *extemporaneously* with words as they've evolved from previous practice and as they occur to the speaker as he or she stands before the audience. By this combination of memorized and extemporaneous presentation, the speaker may be helped over the rough spots without sacrificing the spontaneity and close audience contact upon which effective communication depends. [1]

Making Language Vital

The period during which a speech is being practiced aloud is, of course, the ideal time to consider and experiment with the language that is to be employed in presenting it. In this connection, we've already stressed the importance of stating the main heads as clearly as possible and in a way that will cause them to remain in the listeners' minds. What we are concerned with now is the words or language used in the speech as a whole. Here the guidelines you should observe may be summed up in three brief imperatives: *Be clear, be appropriate, be vivid!*

Be clear. Clarity of language increases the likelihood that the intent of your message will become immediately obvious to your listeners. Clarity is achieved by choosing words and expressions that convey your ideas in such a way as to require the minimum of "translation" by listening agents. In order to achieve clarity, *use concrete and specific terms* rather than abstract and general ones. *Use familiar words.* If unfamiliar technical language or jargon must be employed, it should be defined or explained as you use it. Also keep your sentences fairly brief, though you should avoid overcondensation. A single "yes" is sometimes not enough to provide listeners with a full answer to a question. If it is not, we have an instance of brevity but not clarity.

Be appropriate. A second important quality of language is appropriateness. *The language you use must be appropriate to you as speaker, to the audience, to the context, and to the subject.* As we emphasized in Chapter 6, you shouldn't use the same language in all situations. Some occasions are more formal than others. Some audiences expect elegance in speech. Others appreciate a down-to-earth—even an earthy—approach. A good exercise is to practice a speech with one type of audience and occasion in mind, and then practice it later for a different hypothetical context and a different group of listeners. This kind of exercise can help you develop a variety of stylistic approaches to a subject and in this way increase your total fund of verbal resources. As you gain command over a wider range of speaking styles, you also will gain the ability to adapt to a wider range of speaking situations.

Be vivid. To be effective, *language must be vivid*—lively, intense, sharp, and colorful. There are so many devices for making a speech vivid that you'll find it

---

 Study Probe 1
Using Outlines and Notes

a. Select a subject for an informative or persuasive speech and, following the instructions set forth in Chapter 13, draw up an outline for this speech. Also prepare a set of notes which you plan to use in presenting it. Hand the outline and notes in to the instructor for detailed criticisms. Then revise the outline and notes as suggested; and, by practicing the speech aloud, prepare to deliver it in class. Hand the final, revised outline to the instructor as you get up to speak. Your notes, of course, may be used during the presentation itself.

b. Interview someone in the community who is known as an effective public speaker—a professor, minister, business person, city official. Find out how this individual goes about preparing his or her speeches. Does this speaker always draw up an outline? What sort of notes does he or she use? What general advice about speech preparation and presentation does this individual have? Report your findings to the class.

difficult to select only a few. You'll be forced to omit a great many other possibilities. Yet because vividness is so important, we must consider at least some of the means which we may use to vivify our communications. Among the most useful from the standpoint of the public speaker are: *metaphor, hyperbole, irony, the rhetorical question, antithesis,* and *parallel and balanced phrases.*

In the *metaphor,* a word or phrase that literally denotes one object or concept is applied to another for the purpose of suggesting a *likeness* or *similarity.* For example, in a lecture on the "Blues" as a musical form, Leonard Bernstein said that the improvising jazz player uses a popular song "as a kind of dummy to hang his notes on. He dresses it up in his own way, and it comes out an original." By means of the "dummy" metaphor, Bernstein was able to present a *visual* image of what the musician actually does melodically. The use of metaphor can easily add this quality of visualization and concreteness to an otherwise abstract thought. At the grave of his brother, Robert G. Ingersoll visualized and softened the concept of a premature death by this means:

> Yet, after all, it may be best, just in the happiest, sunniest hour of all the voyage, while eager winds are kissing every sail, to dash against the unseen rock, and in an instant hear the billows roar above a sunken ship. For, whether in midsea or 'mong the breakers of the farther shore, a wreck at last must mark the end of each and all. And every life, no matter if its every hour is rich with love and every moment jeweled with a joy, will, at its close, become a tragedy as sad and deep and dark as can be woven of the warp and woof of mystery and death.[1]

Another device often used to add vividness to language is *hyperbole,* an obvious and deliberate exaggeration. "Candidates in this election are up against the battle of their lives." "Her genius outshone all the rest—dazzling in its impact and brilliance." These are typical examples. These statements claim more than is really meant; we grasp the emphasis intended from the exaggeration itself. But you must be wary of hyperbole. Consider the sports announcer who labels every minor mishap in a game "a tragedy," and almost every play "a momentous play," "the greatest pass in history!" When overused, hyperbole soon becomes dull—and often incongruous—losing its ability to clarify, emphasize, or vivify.

A speaker also may vivify ideas by using *irony*—a figure of speech in which the intended meaning is contrary to the words uttered. The incongruity between the words and the vocal inflection in Mark Antony's "For Brutus is an honorable man" reveals heavy irony when read aloud. Irony is a resource that often allows a speaker to use humor as a cutting edge with persuasive effect. And the contrast between what is really meant and the literal words gives vividness and liveliness to the ironic image. Don't, however, confuse irony with sarcasm—a dangerous "cutting edge" when inexpertly used.

Rhetorical questions create audience involvement and enliven style by calling for implicit audience responses. William Wirt's account of Patrick Henry's speech to the Virginia House of Burgesses contains this series of questions:

> *But when shall we be stronger?*
> *Shall we gather strength by irresolution and inaction?*
> *Why stand we here idle?*
> *What is it that gentlemen wish?*
> *Is life so dear, and peace so sweet, as to be purchased at the price of*
>   *chains and slavery?*

Can you imagine an audience unmoved by such questioning?

Sometimes a speaker may make use of *antithesis,* by bringing opposites together verbally. The clashing of cognitions makes the point and lends vividness to what is said. All of us are acquainted with the statement, "Ask not what your country can do for you, but what you can do for your country." Although its real origins are clouded in time, some of the memorable quality of this line comes from the balanced rhythms of the clauses, but much of it comes from the *opposed* sentiments that are expressed.

Finally, a widely used and effective vivifying device, *parallel and balanced phrases,* is evident in the antithesis just quoted. Parallels and balanced phrases may occur in main headings or in developmental material, together or separated in a speech, with similarity in whole or only in part. You already know many instances of this device: "The *length* of life, the *breadth* of life, the *height* of life." "I *came,* I *saw,* I *conquered.*"

Metaphor, hyperbole, irony, the rhetorical question, antithesis, and *parallel and balanced phrases*—these are merely a few of the resources you may draw upon to add vividness to your language. Used correctly, these vivifiers will help dramatize your points and thereby alert your listeners to the important issues in your speech.

Working to Improve Your Oral Style

We have just reviewed some of the things that can be done to make language usage effective. Now *how* can you, as a public speaker, incorporate this knowledge into your own speech habits and style so as to ensure that such usage will become almost automatic? It will require effort. You should probably start with an assessment of your own spoken language. You also must *begin to pay more attention to how you speak; you must listen to yourself.* This will be difficult, for our speaking style soon becomes habitual, and we use words and patterns of words without being conscious of them. You should attempt to judge how ample and varied your spoken expression is *now.* Do you often struggle to find the right word—and then give up? Do you overuse any expressions so that they become distracting to a listener? The language of some speakers is sprinkled with expressions such as "you know," "you see," "and so," and similar overworked phrases. To such speakers, these are "fillers"; to listeners, they become grating repetitions.

The most helpful, positive aid to language improvement probably results from careful reading and analysis of *models of good language.* Try to read good speeches such as those available in the collections of famous speakers. Above all, read some of these models *aloud* so that the sound and the sense of the language will combine in your consciousness. Oral language is meant to be heard, and you need to *hear* it in order to receive full influence from it. Moreover, reading aloud can be of great general benefit to any student of speech. For comparison, you ought to listen to yourself on tape recordings in order to evaluate and refine your own oral language.

How the qualities of clarity, appropriateness, and vividness combine to produce an effective oral style may be seen by examining the speech by Dr. John A. Howard, "The Three Furies," in the Appendix of this book. Throughout this speech, simple words are combined into relatively short and direct statements of the speaker's ideas. In addition, without sacrificing the dignity naturally appropriate to the occasion, Dr. Howard maintains a lively and conversational pattern of expression that does much to vivify his ideas and to hold audience interest. In the speech by Virginia Y. Trotter (see Appendix), notice how the words *seesaw* and *escalator* are used figuratively to make vivid the notion that competition between the sexes will hinder rather than promote women's progress toward full equality. [2]

PRESENTING THE SPEECH

The Greek orator Demosthenes once was asked what is the most important element in speaking, and he quickly replied, "Delivery." When asked what is second most important, he again replied, "Delivery." And third most important— "Delivery." Cicero agreed: "Delivery, I say, has the sole and supreme power in oratory."[2] While the factors that make up speech are probably too interrelated to allow any such rank ordering to be very meaningful, there can be little question that a well-delivered speech has a much greater chance of being effective. *Delivery is, therefore, a factor you should pay special attention to when presenting speeches.* As with language and style, you should attempt to hear and visualize

Study Probe 2
Learning to Adapt and Enliven Style

a. Select a suitable speech from *Vital Speeches of the Day* or some other available source, and rewrite it as *you* would present it to an audience of junior-high-school students. That is, in addition to expressing the ideas of the speech in a way that would make them comprehensible to persons of this age and educational level, state the ideas as *you yourself* would state them, thus giving the speech your own "personal idiom."

b. Find a speech whose language seems to you especially striking or vivid, and either orally or in writing—as your instructor may require—point out the methods which were employed to achieve this effect.

yourself in the role of speaker and should work, among your other goals, for improved speech presentation.

Delivery, as a speech concept, involves the auditory and visual "channels" through which symbols are transmitted during the speech act. A speaker's delivery makes up the sights and sounds of communication insofar as the listeners are concerned, and it is from these sights and sounds that they infer and interpret meanings. In the ensuing pages we will concern ourselves with the auditory and visual channels employed in oral communication, providing some analyses of and suggestions regarding each. We also will devote attention to some useful things which a speaker can do to improve speech-delivery skills.

Auditory Factors

Auditory stimuli are what the listener hears. The essential dimensions of these stimuli are pitch, intensity or loudness, rate, and quality. *Pitch* is the perception of the frequency of the transmitted sound waves. The greater the frequency of cycles per second, the higher the pitch. Some studies have shown that speaking which is judged effective is associated not so much with a certain pitch level (a high-pitched voice or a low-pitched voice) but with *variety* in pitch. We have all heard speakers who drone along in a monotone. Nothing stands out in their speeches, and the total effect induces uneasiness or sleep. All of our experiences indicate that such speech tends to diminish listeners' comprehension and retention of what is said. Variety in pitch level is, therefore, something you should strive for if you don't already have it naturally. And, of course, the vocal variations must be meaningful. Emphasis in intensity always should correspond with emphasis in thought.

Loudness is the perception of *vocal intensity*. Some speakers speak so softly they can hardly be heard; other speakers shout their entire speeches, seeking in this way to give emphasis to what they say. But if *every* thought is accentuated through loudness, no single idea stands out from the others, and nothing is emphasized. Sometimes by dropping the voice and presenting a point in a low and calm manner, a speaker can give it emphasis simply because of the *change* in the strength of the stimulus. *Vocal contrast* is imperative in making a succession of ideas stand out—each from the other.

Speech rate has to do with timing and pace. Words on a printed page stand more or less equidistant from one another, and follow along uniformly. This is not true in oral discourse. What appear as words on paper are combined in utterance, so oral pace becomes a matter of spacing "bursts" of sound that are in fact *word-clusters*. You should determine your own pattern for spacing words by varying your rate of presentation and judging in what way you communicate *all* your oral meanings best—by being deliberate, rapid, or varied in rate.

Voice quality, as we can readily observe from noting the "qualities" of musical instruments, is a complex trait. Two musical instruments may play a tone at the same pitch level and intensity level. Yet they "sound" different. This special sound of any tone producer is its quality. It results from a combination of the other basic elements. Because of differences in resonators, overtones appear in resonated sound with different intensity levels, and this interaction of pitches and intensities is what is perceived as *quality*. A pleasant vocal quality is helpful for speech communication. Some less pleasant vocal qualities may be described as breathiness, shrillness, hoarseness, and nasality. Each occurs as the result of some inefficient functioning of one of the sound producer-resonator controls, and each interferes to a greater or less extent with oral interaction.

Articulation has to do with the production of distinguishable speech sounds. English has about forty-five distinctive groups of speech sounds, or *pho-nemes*. These sounds are produced when the articulators of speech—tongue, teeth, lips, and palate—function together in close coordination to modify the breath stream as it is blocked by them or passes over them. Some cases of faulty articulation are severe enough to warrant a visit with a speech therapist. Your speech teacher will know when this is needed. But even among so-called "nor-mal" speakers, certain problems of articulation often occur. Because of bad speech habits, a speaker may mumble words. The articulation is not sharp and precise, and because of a "mushy" quality the sounds are not easy to distinguish. A tape recording of your speech will provide an objective sample of your articu-lation. If minor changes are needed, your speech teacher should be able to ad-vise you.

Pronunciation has to do with the choice of sounds. Sometimes a speaker will leave a sound out of a word, will substitute an incorrect sound, or will add a sound. When a speaker drops the "g" in "ing" endings, as in "goin'" and "doin'," he or she is really substituting sounds; as written with phonetic symbols, the speaker is substituting [n] for [ŋ]. Some eastern speakers frequently drop [r] sounds except as a link between vowels, where they may add it. Some New York-ers, for example, will say something like "fa" and "fam" for "far" and "farm," but will add [r] in "the idear of it."

Standards of pronunciation differ from area to area. If adaptation is easy, perhaps you should adapt. There is no virtue in refusing to go along with the way a person pronounces the name of an old home town. When in Cairo, Illinois, you might as well give it the local pronunciation (something like "kay'-row"). If you move from one region of the country to another, however, you may always be an outsider because of the dialect you learned elsewhere. This is like moving from one particular language community to another. If it is important to you, or neces-sary for your career, you may decide to learn the new language. Usually, how-ever, if you speak clearly and carefully, your dialect will not cause you great hard-ship. But slovenly articulation and pronunciation in any language or dialect will diminish your credibility for most listeners and, therefore, impair your effective-ness as a public speaker.

Pausing and *phrasing* are also very important elements in vocal delivery. We write in sentences, using commas, semicolons, periods, and the like for punc-tuation. As we have mentioned before, however, much of the time we speak in *phrases* or *word-clusters*, using pauses of varying lengths as punctuation. The phrase or word-cluster is a word or group of words spoken as one single breath unit and/or thought unit. Speakers all too frequently fight this characteristic of oral communication, and instead try to pause only at those places where they probably would find a comma or period in written discourse. This practice usually results in too much material being grouped within a single thought unit. This makes a communicative message difficult for the audience to follow because listeners are used to hearing the phrased patterns of *speech*. Other speakers may pause too frequently, uttering only two or three words per phrase. Often this can be traced to nervousness, which causes rapid, shallow breathing that cannot give enough support for the longer phrases in which speech patterns normally fall.

Try speaking the first sentence of the Gettysburg Address as indicated below. In each version, pause and breathe at each point where there is a dash (—), and *only* where there is a dash:

—*Fourscore and seven years ago our fathers brought forth on this continent a new nation conceived in liberty and dedicated to the proposition that all men are created equal*—

Did you make it? How meaningful was the statement? Try again:

—*Fourscore—and seven years—ago—our fathers—brought forth—on this—continent—a new—nation—conceived—in liberty—and—dedicated—to the—proposition—that—all men—are created—equal*—

This could be the phrasing of an extremely nervous speaker. It is not very communicative. What about the following?

—*Fourscore and seven years ago—our fathers—brought forth on this continent—a new nation—conceived in liberty—and dedicated to the proposition—that all men are created equal*—

It is not necessary—or even possible—of course, to breathe every time you pause. Go back over these three samples, making sure you pause at each (—), but breathing only when necessary. The pauses can be of different durations also. Finally, determine how you would phrase the sentence for the best possible effect. Where would you pause, and for how long? Where would you take a breath? After comparing the above versions, you should be better able to understand why pausing and phrasing are so important to effective speech communication.

"Twinkle, twinkle, little star, how I wonder . . . ." Say this well-known rhyme to yourself a few times and also have someone else try it. It will very probably be phrased the same each time. The delivery may be varied, but it will also be *patterned*. *Too* patterned. The variation is always the same; that is, the variation *itself* becomes a pattern—a pattern almost indistinguishable regardless of who utters it. We all tend to use the same melody—the same pattern. When we say delivery should be varied, we mean varied *and* variable, with variation determined by meaning. In our old rhyme, the melody is as important as the meaning. We know the rhyme linked with the melody, almost as we know a song.

Whenever a speech is presented with a patterned phrasing so obvious or evident that any listener could produce the phrasing for the next sentence, we say the speaker has a "sing-song" delivery. This means that the *pattern* has attracted audience attention, and listeners are distracted from the meaning. Many beginning speakers use a "sing-song" delivery for quotations. Unless you take time to consider the meaning of the quoted material, you will tend to adopt a patterned presentation. The way to avoid sing-song delivery is simple: Always keep the *thought* to be expressed central in your speaking, and don't heedlessly utter the words of a potential thought until you have a sense of its meaning.

In concluding this discussion of the auditory factors in oral presentation, let's consider another pitfall of speech delivery: the *vocalized pause,* or the habit of injecting a random and meaningless syllable between words and sentences. James Winans, a pioneer teacher of speech, strongly emphasized the old proverb that "Speech is silver; silence is golden" and pointed out that silence is never more golden than in the midst of speech. Unfortunately, however, pauses always seem much longer to a speaker than they do to a listener, and for this reason the speaker feels impelled to fill them in with some sort of pointless vocalization. But pauses in and of themselves *can* be most helpful. Let's look more closely at some of the reasons this is so:

1. Pauses provide *punctuation* to a speaker's thoughts; they can help give to utterance the "commas," "semicolons," "exclamation marks," "question marks," "quotation marks," "periods," and "ellipses" needed by listeners for *easy* and accurate interpretation of messages.

2. Pauses can serve well to establish *transitional intervals* between thoughts and units of thought material within the speech.

3. Pauses allow the listeners to relax and reflect on what they have heard, to associate statements just made with other aspects of the topic and with statements made by the speaker earlier in his or her presentation.

4. Pauses provide moments for the speaker to reflect on his or her next thought and get it clearly in mind before beginning to utter it.

5. Pauses, especially longer ones which precede or follow a point, give the strongest possible *emphasis* to the point.

Most beginning speakers, unless they work against it, will fill many of the needed "silent" periods in their speeches with noisy, distracting, vocalized "um's," "er's," "ah's," and "uh's." Sometimes these vocalized pauses are uttered more loudly than the rest of the speech. They may, in fact, be the most emphasized parts of the speech event. Again, read the following passage aloud:

> *Fourscore and—uh—seven years ago—er—our fathers brought forth—ah—on this—um—continent a new nation conceived in—ah—liberty and dedicated to—ah—the proposition that all—er—er—men are created—um—equal.*

With conscientious effort, any speaker can eliminate vocalized pauses. Do you believe it is worth the effort?

In essence, then, in working to improve your speech-presentation skills, pay careful attention to the *auditory* factors. Improve your vocal rate, vocal intensity, voice quality, pronunciation, and phrasing and timing by *practicing your speeches aloud*—so you can *hear yourself.* Listen for weaknesses in delivery and attempt to eliminate them *in practice.* Work for a generally fluent delivery with adequately precise (but never overprecise) articulation and pronunciation, vocal variety determined by the meaning of what you say, appropriate pausing and phrasing, and elimination of vocalized pauses. The usefulness of a tape recorder for such self-assessment should be *self-evident.* 3

Visual Factors

The second aspect of delivery is what the audience *sees* as you stand before it. Much of the meaning in speech communication is transmitted through the *visual* channel. You have only to consider the performance of a mime like Marcel Marceau to know the large amounts of meaning that can be transmitted by visual cues alone. Demosthenes reportedly used a large mirror to gain a sense of the visual impression he made upon his audiences. By using whatever means seems best to you, you should assess your visual presentation and work for improvement through practice. To this end, you should give attention to *posture, physical movement, gesture,* and *visual directness.*

Your *posture* as a speaker should be erect, poised, and relaxed. You "look better" that way; but, more importantly, this is the posture from which it is always easiest to *move* in order to express ideas and thought-variations. You should feel comfortable and free to move or gesture as you like. What is to be avoided is conflict between the information received by the listener from the visual and the auditory channels. This conflict occurs, for example, when a speaker

---

 Study Probe 3
Listening to Yourself

   a. Make a tape (if possible, *videotape*) recording of (1) a short passage of expository prose, (2) a lyric poem, and (3) a brief cutting of a scene from a play in which two or more characters interact. Listen critically to your articulation, voice quality, pitch variation, and use of pauses. Have your instructor and classmates comment on these same aspects of your speech. Which of the three passages indicated above did you find most difficult to read? What factors gave rise to this difficulty? Practice all three passages frequently over a period of several days, and then make a second recording. Have you improved in your reading? If so, in what specific characteristics?

says the topic being discussed is of the greatest importance, but slouches over the speaker's stand while saying it.

General *physical movement* is also important in your behavior and effectiveness as a public speaker. Some degree of movement will help reduce bodily tensions. Movement can also provide visual transitions in your speech as you move from one part of it to another. If, in concluding a main point, you pause and take a step or two away from the position you have been holding, the action harmonizes and is consistent with the shift of thought, and it emphasizes that shift in the perceptions of the listeners. But, for the reasons mentioned in the preceding paragraph, if you try to make a serious point and at the same time pace back and forth, or shuffle your feet noisily, or stand with your shoulders swaying back and forth like a little child caught stealing cookies, the incongruity between *what* you say and *how* you present it will work against your general effectiveness.

Gestures are an especially significant part of the visual information received by listeners. Doubtless, you have observed many different types of hand gestures. A "locative" gesture may be used to point to a particular section of a visual aid in order to direct attention to it. An "illustrative" gesture may be used to describe the curves of a model or the dimensions of an object. The most common gestures are the "emphatic" ones used to give added emphasis to a point. These gestures are often made with a pointed finger, a clenched fist, or the edge of a flat hand; but, of course, physical emphasis can also be achieved in a wide variety of other ways. Like all other aspects of delivery, gestures should be in harmony and in time with the thoughts being spoken. Some speakers never gesture and, as a consequence, appear reserved and stiff. Some speakers gesture too much. They flail away incessantly at the air about them. The impulse to gesture is for most people a natural one, especially if the speaker is at ease. You will be well advised, then, to view your attempts at developing gestural communication in terms of *growth,* avoiding frequent, aimless gestures or gesturing in a mechanical or patterned manner. You need also to be relaxed and free to gesture so that if

Lay out a practical program for future self-improvement. Provide your instructor with a copy and retain a copy for your use and reference.
b. Select a list of names from the telephone directory. Using variations in pitch and rate along with appropriate pauses, read this list of names in such a way that you appear to be (1) asking questions, (2) making assertions, (3) expressing doubt, or (4) displaying confidence. See if the other members of the class can detect the mood you are attempting to convey. If they can't, repeat the list until someone is able to identify the intended moods correctly.

the impetus or need to do so occurs or an idea requires it, you can respond freely—something you cannot do if you are leaning on your elbows or have your hands in your pockets.

Hand gestures are only a part of the communicative, gestural resources at your command. Equally important are head gestures and facial expressions. The expressionless "deadpan" may be fine for a game of poker, but speakers are supposed to be giving us *clues* to how they feel about their "cards." Their interest in a topic is usually revealed by lively facial expressions and head movements. As a speaker genuinely interested in communicating with your listeners, you will find that it is absolutely essential that you sustain a *visual directness*. If, while speaking, you turn your face away and refuse to look at your audience, you have no gauge by which to judge their reactions—no feedback to your message. And as we have repeatedly emphasized, especially in Chapter 7, if you are oblivious or indifferent to feedback, you cannot possibly make any adjustments to it. When members of an audience see a speaker looking intently at the floor, at the ceiling, or out the window, they sense immediately that this person is either ill-at-ease and/or unconcerned. And at this point real, productive interaction is seriously impeded.

In sum, work assiduously to improve your *visual* presentation of your public messages. Learn to talk warmly and directly with the people in your audience. Like you, they are living, breathing personalities; and they will appreciate your treating them as such, rather than as empty chairs or as faceless objects on the periphery of your consciousness. Remember, too, that visual directness is not just a perfunctory turning of your head from side to side, a mere mechanical sweeping back and forth of your glance as if you were watching a tennis match in slow motion. Obviously, you will probably look most closely and frequently at the people directly before you, but make sure also that from time to time you look

Study Probe 4
Studying Visual Factors

a.   Attend a speech, lecture, or sermon given on campus or in the community. Prepare for this listening experience by making a brief checklist of the aspects of visual delivery that we've been talking about—posture, gestures, and the like. Carefully observe the speaker with these points in mind. Do visual factors seem to add appreciably to the effectiveness of the address, or do they detract from it? Why? Report your findings in a brief paper.

If all members of the class attended the same speech event as a group, hold a general discussion of the speaker's use of visual factors. Is there common agreement about the effectiveness or ineffectiveness of the speaker in this respect? If not, on what particular points do differences occur?

into the faces of those seated toward the back and at the sides of the room. Try always to look at your audience—see them, see their reactions, and respond! 4

Using Visual Aids

An important but often neglected aspect of the speaker's physical or visual delivery concerns the handling of visual aids. Such aids, in the form of *charts, diagrams, pictures, slides, films,* or *working models,* may be of great help in clarifying complex processes or relationships, or in reinforcing a point the speaker wishes to make. To begin with, care should be exercised in the selection of the aid itself. Is the chosen picture or diagram *large enough* to be seen easily from all parts of the room in which the speech is presented? Is the chart *simple enough* so that its meaning or significance may be grasped quickly? Is the working model something that can be transported with ease and set up without undue difficulty? An aid too small for everyone to see or so complex that its meaning cannot be grasped without prolonged consideration will obviously be of little value. And if you can't transport it to the "scene of the action" or handle it once you get it there, it will be of no use at all.

It also is essential, however, that consideration be given to *when* and *how* the aid is to be introduced and shown. In this connection, the following directions should be observed:

Do not display the aid until you are ready to make direct reference to it. A brightly colored chart or intriguing picture visible to the audience while you are introducing your speech or discussing matters not directly related to it will split the listeners' attention away from what you are saying. In altogether too many instances people will be studying the chart or picture rather than listening to what you say.

b. Tune your television set to an evening newscast or to some other program in which the principal speaker remains seated. Turn off the "audio" elements of the telecast and study the speaker's facial expression, head and shoulder movements, and eye contact with viewers. Are you able to tell from changes in facial expression something of the content of the message being transmitted and of the speaker's attitude toward that content? When viewed silently, do the visual factors in the speaker's delivery seem graceful or awkward? Does the speaker appear alert or phlegmatic? Does the speaker appear to be looking at the viewers rather than at notes or a manuscript? Are notes and papers skillfully and unobtrusively handled? Can you estimate the extent to which the control of these visual factors accounts for the speaker's success as a television personality?

Make sure that you can handle the aid smoothly and without embarrassing mishaps or accidents. The cardboard-mounted diagram that will not stand up properly or the model that refuses to work when you wish to demonstrate it—rather than aiding you in communicating your ideas—will be a serious hindrance.

When presenting the aid, look at your listeners rather than at the aid itself. When referring or pointing to a visual aid, many speakers have a tendency to turn their backs on their listeners and talk to the aid they are explaining. Naturally, you will have to glance at the aid from time to time or will need to point to certain of its features. Your general orientation must, however, be toward the persons with whom you are communicating.

Do not block the audience's view of the aid by standing in front of it. Stand to one side of the aid or behind it. A visual presentation that cannot be fully and easily seen loses much, if not all, of its value.

Introduce only those aids that contribute in a direct and essential way to the message you wish to communicate. Sometimes speakers introduce visual aids not because they add materially to the ideas being communicated, but simply because they "dress up" a speech and make it more attractive. Or after a subject has been discussed at length, a speaker may hold up an aid as a sort of afterthought. Because the aid has nothing to do with the specific purpose of the speech, it actually is a distraction and might better be omitted.

A question which commonly arises concerning the use of visual aids is whether to prepare drawings or diagrams beforehand or to put them on a blackboard, chalkboard, or flip chart as the speech progresses. The answer to this question, as to so many other questions concerning the oral communication process, is "It all depends." If the drawing is to be a simple one, you may decide to produce it on the board while you are speaking. The board also may be preferable if you wish to change or add to your drawing as the speech progresses—to have the aid grow and develop along with your ideas. On the other hand, stopping to "sketch out" the aid while in the midst of the speech takes time and interrupts the natural flow of ideas. In addition, you may be forced to turn your back on your listeners for rather extended periods of time.

Similarly, if the aid takes the form of a small object or of a graph or table summarizing a mass of detailed data, you may need to decide on the advisability of passing it among the members of the audience or even providing each listener with a copy. Obviously, such a practice has the advantage of making the aid readily available to all for detailed inspection. The disadvantage is that all persons in the audience can't see or handle it at the same time or that they will become so engrossed in examining the aid that they won't pay attention to what you are saying. Here, then, as in the case of whether to prepare the aid beforehand, you must use good judgment, weighing the comparative advantages and disadvantages of the two methods. When presenting a detailed treasurer's report, you may wish to have a copy of the document in each listener's hands. When demonstrating a relatively small model or object, however, you may conclude that it would be better to retain control of the aid yourself, if necessary walking among the members of your audience so that each person may inspect it more closely. ⑤

Factors of Credibility

Having considered the auditory and visual factors in speech presentation, let us as a last step turn to the most important factors of all—those which establish the *credibility* of the speaker and, therefore, in the final analysis, determine how the speech message will be received. What do we mean by a speaker's "credibility"? Why is credibility so important a factor in winning acceptance of the speech message? How is credibility established?

Some 2,500 years ago in his classic treatise on rhetoric, the Greek philosopher Aristotle distinguished between two basic kinds of proofs or "persuasives"—inartistic and artistic. *Inartistic proofs,* he said, consist of such things as testimony, contracts, and laws. These come to the speaker complete and ready-made, and merely need to be "entered into" the text of the speech in their original form. *Artistic proofs,* on the other hand, are proofs which the speaker must create or manufacture out of the materials which are available.

According to Aristotle's analysis, artistic proofs fall into three classes: logical, emotional, and ethical. *Logical proofs* grow out of the subject matter treated in the speech, and are closely related to what we today think of as arguments based on evidence and reasoning. *Emotional proofs* are to be found in the feelings and passions of the listeners, and have as their purpose the winning of responses made under the influence of these emotional states. *Ethical proofs* lie in the *character* or—to use the Greek term—*ethos,* of the speaker. They are the persuasive powers that lie in the account the speaker gives of himself or herself as an honest, sincere, sympathetic, competent, and intelligent human being. Of these three kinds of artistic proofs, Aristotle declared without reservation, those of the ethical variety are most influential in winning belief or inspiring action.[3]

Not only has Aristotle's classification of the forms of artistic proof gener-

---

Study Probe 5
Evaluating Visual Aids

a. Collect several advertising brochures from automobile dealers, travel agencies, or appliance stores. Report to the class how the pictures and other visual aids used in these brochures help to attract attention, motivate the reader, and communicate the seller's message.

b. Select three different subjects on which you might speak to the class or to some imaginary audience: how the tax dollar is spent, basic plays in football, a rotary gasoline engine, etc. Tell what type of visual aid(s) you might develop for each speech. Explain why the kind of aid(s) you would plan to use would be particularly well adapted to the subject matter in question.

ally been adopted by later writers on the subject, but his estimate of the crucial position occupied by the speaker's credibility or *ethos* has generally been endorsed. Why this should be so is not difficult to understand if we reflect on the importance we place on sincerity, honesty, and competence in our dealings with other persons. The individual whose character is dubious, who is poorly informed on the subject under discussion, and who lacks poise and self-control makes an unfavorable impression and seldom inspires confidence.

To this general rule, the public speaking situation is no exception. Here, as elsewhere, speakers whose integrity is evident, who know what they are talking about, and who display assurance and skill tend to be accepted more readily. Obviously, the credibility a public speaker will have with any given audience is determined in part by the *established reputation* he or she brings to the speaking situation. If the speaker is known to be honorable, well informed on the subject, and earnestly concerned about communicating important ideas to others, the initial advantage will be great. But there are also many things a speaker can do while preparing and presenting a speech that will *enhance* credibility.

First, as we've already suggested, it is of prime importance that the speaker *know thoroughly the subject that he or she is talking about*—that the information presented in the speech be broad, up-to-date, and authoritative. Without this sort of evident knowledge as a base, other attributes will be of little avail. Second—and only slightly less in importance—the speaker must *evidence com-*

Study Probe 6
Establishing Credibility or Ethos

a. Certain professions tend to suffer from negative stereotypes. Encyclopedia salespersons, automobile dealers, real-estate promoters—to name a few— often meet sales resistance because people tend to distrust them. In teams of two in front of the class, role play an encounter between one of these salespersons and a potentially distrusting client. Then, discuss what the person playing the role of salesperson did to counteract suspicion and establish credibility. Can you suggest additional techniques that might have been used effectively? Refer again to Chapter 10, "Dyadic Communication."

b. Assume that one of your classmates intends to speak on the subject of motorcycles (or some other topic such as drugs, abortion, etc.). Assume also that you generally tend to distrust that classmate's knowledge of this subject—to think perhaps that you know more about it than he or she does. On the basis of these assumptions, write out a carefully thought-out set of specific suggestions as to what this speaker could do to establish credibility in your eyes. Hand the set of suggestions to your instructor; and then—with a classmate serving as the "motorcycle specialist"—role play a situation in which you discuss the problem with this person and orally communicate your suggested improvements to her or him in a way that should ensure acceptance and maintain good relationships.

mand of the speaking situation. As a rule, we tend to discount the ideas and distrust the judgment of individuals who have so little confidence in themselves that they can't stand before an audience with confidence and poise. Third, it is essential that the speaker appear *sincere and committed* in what he or she says. Signs of cynicism and indifference inevitably arouse suspicion. Fourth—and finally—credibility rests to a significant extent on what has been called "dynamism": a quality of *energy, animation, and enthusiasm* apparent in the speaker's attitude and manner. The speaker who is lethargic, colorless, and seemingly uninterested in what he or she is saying—who appears unconcerned about the outcome of the speech—can't expect to arouse enthusiasm or induce belief in the audience.

Needless to say, the qualities upon which credibility depends are not easy to acquire. You can, however, begin by always knowing your subject thoroughly and by sincerely believing in whatever subject you select. Moreover, you can earnestly try to communicate your ideas to your listeners, and to do so in a way that will serve their best interests. Poise and dynamism, the other major qualities on which credibility depends, will come with repeated practice in the one-to-many speaking situation. 6

Sometimes students ask, "Which is the more important factor in determining the success of a speech—good content or effective presentation?" The truth of the matter is that they are *equally* important. Without solid content, the speaker does not have anything worth talking about; without effective delivery, the speaker's ideas will not be attended to and understood, and, therefore, will be of no use to others. In the best kind of public communication, substance and presentation work hand in hand, each supplementing and reinforcing the other. As we emphasized in Chapter 6, they are inseparable. 7 Do not think, therefore, that the matters discussed in this chapter are less crucial than those covered earlier in the book. *It is only through extended and systematic practice that skill in*

Study Probe 7
Comparing Matter and Manner

Select two public figures—preferably candidates or office-holders on the national level—one of whom you dislike and one whom you like very much. Analyze your feelings about these persons as objectively as you can. How much of your like or dislike is rooted in the policies for which the individual stands? To what extent is your attitude the result of appearance and personality? Does the person's effectiveness or ineffectiveness as a speaker influence your judgment? It sometimes is said that most voters are swayed by personality or "image," rather than by issues. If this is true, how would you account for it?

Using your analysis as a foundation, prepare, practice, and present a six-minute *persuasive* public speech in which you influence your audience—the other members of the class—to accept your judgment of the two public figures.

speech presentation can be developed; and it is only through skill in presentation that the objectives of a speech can finally be realized.

EVALUATING PUBLIC SPEECH COMMUNICATION

From time to time in the foregoing pages—usually in the Study Probes—we have suggested that you prepare, practice, present, and analyze various kinds of public speeches in classroom settings and elsewhere. Invariably, a twofold task has been stated or implied: speaking *and* listening. In these communicative activities you will at times be functioning as a speaking agent and at other times as a listening agent. Fundamental to these functions—if growth, discernment, and improvement are to be made—is careful *evaluation*. To assist you in making your evaluations we have prepared and class-tested a Speech Evaluation Checklist. (See the sample on the two following pages.)

We suggest that you use the marked Sample Checklist as a model both of factors to consider in evaluating speeches and of comments that may prove productive for your analytical purposes.

In particular, as you listen and respond to the public speeches of your classmates and others, you will find that the eight component factors of the Checklist—*Specific Purpose, Introduction, Body, Conclusion, Facilitative Materials, Language Usage, Delivery,* and *Ethos Development* (and their several sub-elements) can serve usefully as guides to deriving your estimate of the *Overall Effectiveness* of the speech and the interaction which it is intended to create.

The "Evaluations" column should be filled in with a number from 1 to 7—along a continuum from "needs improvement" (1) to "well done" (7)—to indicate your evaluation of the successive component factors. In the "Comments" column should be written brief explanatory notes that reflect and amplify the reasons for your ratings.

SPEECH EVALUATION CHECKLIST

Factors	Evaluations	Comments
1. Specific Purpose		*Specific purpose was too broad for a short speech.*
Clear and to the point	2	
Appropriately narrowed in scope	2	
Appropriate for listener-agents	6	
Appropriate for context	6	
2. Introduction		*Introduction was very effective. It got my interest.*
Attention of listener-agents secured	6	
Interest of listener-agents developed	7	
Specific purpose related to listener-agents	7	
3. Body		*Too many main points. Except for third point, they were not adequately developed. More examples and illustrations needed.*
Main points fulfilled specific purpose	4	
Main points appropriately patterned	6	
Main points emphasized	2	
Main points unified and coherent	3	
Developmental materials varied and helpful	1	
Transitions effective	5	
Internal summaries helpful	5	
4. Conclusion		*Conclusion was fairly effective.*
Final summary effective	5	
Final appeal appropriate	5	

Factors	Evaluations	Comments
5. Facilitative Materials		*Use of visual aids would have helped speech.*
Visual aids helpful to purpose	1	
Visual aids used effectively	1	
Humor used effectively	5	
6. Language Usage		*Language was generally effective. Easy to understand, and appropriate.*
Language clear	6	
Language appropriate to listener-agents	6	
Language appropriate to context	6	
Language vivid	4	
7. Delivery		*Delivery was somewhat monotonous. Try to eliminate vocalized pauses. You slumped over lectern and therefore were unable to move freely or use gestures effectively.*
Vocal variety utilized	2	
Pronunciation and articulation appropriate	5	
Phrasing and pausing effective	5	
Vocalized pauses avoided	2	
Good posture practiced	2	
Ease of movement demonstrated	2	
Gestures natural	2	
Facial expressiveness varied	6	
8. Ethos Development		*You needed to demonstrate greater expertness and concern for your topic.*
Knowledge demonstrated	2	
Trustworthiness shown	5	
Dynamism / Magnetism shown	2	
OVERALL EFFECTIVENESS	4	*Next speech: Limit main ideas. Prepare developmental materials more carefully. Improve posture by practice.*

Suggested Readings

We can recommend the following sources for additional information on the topics discussed in this chapter:

Alan H. Monroe and Douglas Ehninger, *Principles and Types of Speech Communication,* 7th ed. (Glenview, Ill.: Scott, Foresman and Company, 1974), especially Chapters 5, 6, and the section entitled "Ethical Judgment," in Chapter 17, pages 457–463.

John F. Wilson and Carroll C. Arnold, *Public Speaking as a Liberal Art,* 3rd ed. (Boston: Allyn and Bacon, Inc., 1974), especially Chapters 10 and 11.

Reference Notes

[1]Robert G. Ingersoll's "Oration at His Brother's Grave" is available in *The World's Great Speeches,* ed. Lewis Copeland (Garden City, N.Y.: Garden City Publishing Co., Inc., 1942), pp. 324–325.

[2]Cicero, *De Oratore,* trans. H. Rackham, 2 vols. (Cambridge, Mass.: Harvard University Press, 1960 printing of Loeb Classical Library), v. II, p. 169.

[3]Aristotle, *Rhetoric,* trans. W. Rhys Roberts, in *The Basic Works of Aristotle,* ed. Richard McKeon (New York: Random House, Inc., 1941), p. 1329.

MASS
AND INTERCULTURAL
CONTEXTS
OF
SPEECH COMMUNICATION

floyd kalber
NEWSFIVE
5

Mr. Barboza
Counsel

Mr. Conyers
Chairman

Mr. McClory

Chapter 15

MASS ELECTRONIC COMMUNICATION

By Joseph M. Foley
Department of Communication, The Ohio State University

As users of mass electronic communication,
we may aim a message at an intended audience,
but we do not know who actually will receive
the message. This means we must plan messages
very carefully and have a working knowledge
of broadcast programming and policies.

As students of communication, we should understand the workings of the mass electronic media, mainly because we will need to use them as tools of communication but also because they are among our primary sources of information about the world. Moreover, we may become directly involved in their operation as announcers, program producers, or other broadcast station employees. In this chapter we'll survey the ways in which the mass electronic media function, and look also at some of the key factors affecting communication via radio and television.

PUTTING THE MEDIA IN PERSPECTIVE

As the term implies, there are two characteristics of all mass-media communication systems:

357

1. They reach out to a *mass* audience, which means that the communicating agent, even though aiming the message at *intended* receivers, does not know who *actually* will receive the message. Typically, a mass communicator has little control over which people receive the message and which do not. As we shall see, getting the message to the intended audience is a major problem in mass communication.

2. They use *media*—mechanical or electronic, as the case may be—to convey their messages. This means, of course, that there is an additional element in the communication context that affects the *flow* of the message between communicator and audience. This element is the *technological means* by which it is transmitted. Just as the print media—books, newspapers, magazines, and pamphlets—use *mechanical* technologies to present messages, the non-print mass media draw upon *electronic* technologies to convey their messages.

Radio, television, cable television, and satellite communication are the most widely used types of electronic mass communication. Motion pictures use a combination of mechanical, electronic, and optical technologies to communicate.

Some mass-media programming seeks to reach a very large audience; other types of mass-media programming are directed to a specialized audience. *Whether the audience is large or small, it is widely dispersed and not known directly and immediately by the communicator.* Some broadcast programs are designed to reach large numbers of people; for example, an Academy Awards program. Others aim for a much narrower or more limited group of people; for example, the public television series on aviation weather forecasts. In the first example, the program seeks to attract as many viewers as possible. In the second, the program is designed to reach the individuals throughout the country who have a specialized interest in the topic. This trend toward specialization has long been evident and significant in radio, as stations have developed music and news-program formats to appeal to particular segments of their communities. The specialized media retain the essential characteristics—and problems—of the mass media.

In both types—the generalized and the specialized—their messages are transmitted on the media and go to audiences who are unknown by the communicators.

Special Factors in the Mass Communication Process

Throughout our study of interpersonal communication processes (and especially in Chapter 6), we have learned that many factors determine the way in which listeners receive or accept a message. Many of these same factors are also present in mass communication. But there are two additional factors which—largely because of the unique character of print/electronic technologies—are important in determining the flow of mass communication messages. The first is the "gate keeper"; the second is the "opinion leader."

Gate keepers and control of message flow.   Gate keepers are individuals who control the flow of information in the media.[1] In the electronic media, they are the people who decide whether a program will be broadcast on a particular station. Since there are thousands of stations, there are wide differences in the kinds of information and programs which their gate keepers decide to carry.

There are national gate keepers as well as local gate keepers. The national gate keepers for the electronic media control which national stories, reportage, documentaries, etc., will be sent on to the local media gate keepers. The local gate keepers for the respective media then select from the material they receive items which are to be broadcast in their media.

Television network program executives—those at the top—are among the most important national gate keepers, for they determine which programs the networks will offer to the local stations. If a message is to receive national exposure, it must be selected by both national and local gate keepers. Therefore, if you want to get a message carried on the mass media, you must first convince the appropriate gate keepers that the message is valuable and *should* be carried. You may need to contact a number of people at several media outlets to insure that the message *will* be carried. It is with *these* people that you must interact directly and interpersonally—the ones you must influence first—if you want your messages to be communicated via the mass media.

Opinion leaders and information diffusion.   One of the ways to analyze the role which mass media play in society is to look at the ways they "communicate" information to people. Much of our knowledge of new products, new ideas, and new social problems comes to us by way of the media. Some research studies, in trying to analyze how this is accomplished, have suggested that all information does not flow *directly* from the media to their audiences. Rather it comes in stages, going first to some members of the mass audience—the so-called "opinion leaders"—then being repeated by them to other people. Thus, although only a small part of the public might initially hear or see a particular message, those who do receive it may very well talk with others and thereby spread the message to many. This process is called *information diffusion,*[2] and it operates like the second-level communication we discussed in Chapter 9. Simply put, *the information-diffusion process links the information flow through the mass media to individuals at successive levels of interpersonal communication.* A few people get information directly from the mass media, but most people get their information from other people. This process—an extension, really, of the disciple effect—has been characterized as an n-step flow,[3] in which people who get the information directly from the media tell other people, who in turn tell other people, who in turn tell other people, and so on until the message is widely spread.

People who get information directly from the media can, as we've suggested, serve as *opinion leaders.* An opinion leader, you'll remember from Chapter 9, is someone whose advice is respected by others. These individuals are most influential in persuading others. Usually, opinion leaders have influence only in a particular area of subject matter. For example, an auto mechanic might be influential in determining whether we decide to have some new gas-saving attachment installed on our car. But the mechanic probably would not be as influential in other areas, such as our decision about whether to undergo some new type of surgery to correct a medical problem. Because the information from the mass media can diffuse through the opinion leaders to many *beyond* the immediate audience for the message, when you are using the mass media as part of a communication effort, you should develop messages which will (*a*) influence opinion leaders to (*b*) influence other people. Thus, even though we may often think of audiences of the mass media as being an enormous "impersonal mass," we have to keep clearly in our minds the fact that the interpersonal communication processes of information-diffusion are extremely important in spreading the message.

Reasons People Use the Media

When we are producing a message for a mass audience, we like to think that people will want to listen to it because they want to be informed. Perhaps a few will, but most people in the audience probably will be there for other reasons—for *social-contacting* or for *escape,* to cite only a couple of possibilities. The media often serve as an important base of our continuing interactions with other speaking/listening agents. One example of this is when we watch television with other people. At such times the television becomes one part of the process of being in a group. At other times we may watch programs so we can discuss them with our friends the next day. This is often one of the uses made of sports programs and of late-night talk shows. For example, how many times have you heard conversations which begin, "Did you see X on television last night?" We know that the media will provide us with topics to discuss later. Since this aspect of the information-diffusing process is so significant in media communication, as media communicators we will want to build messages which people will want to talk about and enjoy discussing.

At other times we may use the mass media for *escape*—to help us forget the problems of our daily lives by enjoying a fantasy world for a time. We may turn to the media when we are seeking to avoid doing something: writing a term paper, studying for an exam, taking out the garbage, etc. When we use the media for escape, we select primarily programs which do not treat important problems. We prefer programs which are simply entertaining with no apparent message. When we are using the media for escape, we will ignore messages which directly relate to important social issues, although we might watch a dramatic program which touches on the problem. As communicators, we can reach the people viewing for escape only if we place our messages in an entertaining context.

Effects of the Mass Media

Many social critics have expressed concern about the influences of the mass electronic media. Broadly speaking, their concerns center upon two categories of effects: (1) the short-term effects—the impact of a particular message or set of messages, and (2) the long-term effects—the cumulative impact of continued exposure to a series of media messages.

Short-term effects of the mass media are those which result from a single program or message, or which result from a series of messages. Advertisers spend vast amounts of money to present their messages on the media, hoping to produce the short-term effect of having people try their products. We are bombarded with requests to use the "all new" something-or-other which is now "so much better" than any other product. Departments of business and advertising have conducted extensive research studies of the impact of particular commercials. This research has found many ways of shaping appeals for products. Most advertising is carefully designed to have maximum short-term impact on the potential users of the product.

The mass media have also been used extensively to produce short-term effects in political campaigns. They have unquestionably had a major impact on the political process in the United States. Candidates devote much effort to trying to get their messages on the mass media in the most persuasive form possible. Communication consultants play a major role in influencing the ways campaigns are conducted.[4] Political campaigns use the mass media in two ways. They depend on the mass media to present advertisements for their candidate; in this use they are much like other advertisers. They also use the mass media to try to present a favorable *image* of the candidate on news programs and other special programs. They try to get maximum media coverage of the candidate; and they try to insure that the candidate will always be seen in the most favorable situations.

Long-term effects of the mass media are those produced by the cumulative impact of viewing the media—especially television—for many hours each day and night. For some time, cities have studied and debated these long-term effects, and they have been particularly concerned about the influence of televised violence on young people. Children see a tremendous number of killings and fights on television. The impact of such programming on children is not clearly understood. Thus far, the findings of research on televised violence can be classified into two broad areas: (a) studies which have found that violent scenes on television tend to influence children to *imitate* these actions by being more aggressive in later play; and (b) studies which have found that violence on television has a "cathartic effect"—that after watching televised violence children are less likely to commit violent acts.[5]

Televised violence appears to have different impacts on different children. Apparently, too, it can influence an individual child in different ways at different times. Although the research is not yet conclusive, there is substantial evidence that televised violence can have the undesired effect of making some of its viewers more violent. However, this particular effect, like other long-term effects of the media, is difficult to assess in a rigorous, scientific way. Nevertheless, media communicators must be sensitive to possible negative side effects their messages may have.

Another area of concern with regard to the long-term effects of mass media has been the controversy over the kinds of *behavior models* they present. Critics have argued that the media provide us with examples of certain life styles and that this influences our ways of dealing with other people. These critics are particularly concerned because they believe television presents a relatively narrow range of socially acceptable roles. An example of this type of concern has been the criticism of the sex roles which are presented in the media. The media have been accused of giving the impression that men are interested only in gathering money and power, whereas women merely stay in the house, have babies, and work as servants for men. Many groups are now working to influence the media to change these images by presenting both women and men in a broader range of roles. Likewise, many racial and ethnic minority groups—feeling that the media present disproportionate numbers of white Anglo-Saxons—have sought to persuade the media to give their members more—and favorable—exposure.

The long-term effects of mass-media communication, clearly, present an important question with which we—as both citizens and communicators—must be continuously concerned and in which we should become actively involved. We are all certain to be affected by the influence they may be having upon our society. To work for constructive change, we need to understand how the media operate, how we may use the media, and how to influence media organizations to carry our messages for us.

CHALLENGES TO THE COMMUNICATOR

Suppose that you are involved in and committed to a social cause. You want to be heard, so you are attempting to develop some media messages dealing with the particular issue on which you have taken a definite position. You will be faced at the outset with two basic challenges: (1) selecting your audience and (2) developing a message that will reach and hold that audience.

Selecting the Target Audience

To reach an audience, of course, you must first select the audience you want to reach. In the mass media this truism becomes an extremely important part of planning the message. The audience you want to reach is often called the "target audience." In selecting this target audience, you need to deal with three general categories of people: (a) those who *agree* with your position, (b) those who have *not formed an opinion,* and (c) those who *disagree* with your position. For each of these target groups you will need to prepare different types of appeals. You want your messages to reinforce the beliefs of the people who already agree (certainly it would be unfortunate if you prepared messages which caused them to change their minds). Then you need to build messages which will persuade those who have not yet made a decision to accept your point of view. Finally, you will seek to convert those who disagree with you. Probably you will not want to *direct* many messages specifically to those who disagree, since most research studies have indicated that—through the mass media—it is very difficult to get such people to change viewpoints. But you should, nevertheless, be aware that they are "out there" and that some cognizance must be taken of their constituency. *Primarily, though, you will want to develop messages which will encourage the people who agree with you to become active in discussing their views with other people.* This will take maximum advantage of the information-diffusion process in spreading your message. The way you personally carry out your media campaign may cause a few of the people who have not formed an opinion to come to agree with you. But in most instances the direct, interpersonal contacts of information-diffusion will be much more influential.

Having identified the people in the target audience, you now need to analyze the ways the people in each of the three groups *use* the mass media. You need that information to help you identify the best ways for you to reach these people—the best media to use to get the results you desire. Obviously, there's no point in trying to place your messages in media in which they never will be seen or heard by the people you want to reach. Selecting the best media for your messages is more difficult than identifying your target audience. There are two problems: First, the members of your target audience probably use media in very different ways; it is unlikely that there will be a *single* medium that will reach all of them. Second, very often the media they are most likely to use are not the media on which you can get your messages placed. For this reason, you must carefully study the media uses of your target audience in order to find the *combination* of available media which will best reach them. Once you've determined what this combination is, usually you will find you must develop at least two types of messages: (a) messages for a *variety* of media and (b) mass-media messages *supplemented by interpersonal messages* to reach your target audience.

Developing a Message to Reach and Hold the Audience

Many of the techniques for developing messages for a mass audience are the same as the techniques for adapting a message to a listener or group of listeners in interpersonal communication, such as those discussed in Chapter 7 and in Chapter 13. The message should seek to reach the audience's interests; it should relate to things with which the audience is familiar; it should be easy for the audience to understand; and it should use a variety of psychological, motivational appeals to hold the audience's attention. But holding an audience through the mass media is for obvious reasons more difficult than holding an audience in a face-to-face situation. The many social conventions which hold listeners in a face-to-face encounter do not apply in the mass-media situation. The mass-media audience, for example, can easily tune out a radio announcement or stop watching a TV program with the turn or snap of a dial. In face-to-face communication, however, strong social pressure keeps the listeners present for the entire message. According to the social code of most cultures, to walk away while someone is speaking is considered very rude. Yet children are encouraged to change the television channels quickly if they don't like the program they are watching.

In view of these differences, communicators using the mass media must *constantly* strive to hold the attention of their audience. This means that the message must be developed in a way that draws the audience into it and *keeps the audience's attention steadily on the message.* In Chapter 7, where we were concerned with techniques for planning messages that would get and hold an audience, as well as with ways of adjusting messages to listeners during the communicative encounter, we discussed how to deal with situations in which listeners appear to lose interest and begin to fidget. The variety of techniques that may work to regain audience attention in a face-to-face situation—change of pace, added emphasis, humor, etc.—don't necessarily work in the mass-media context. In mass communication, the communicator never knows when the audience is tuning out. Having no feedback to guide an adjustment to the supposed audience, we can't know if and when we're losing attention. Then, having lost it, we have no chance of regaining it—we're simply tuned out. In mass-communication messages it therefore becomes all-important to strive constantly to *sustain* audience attention from the outset and never lose it.

When circumstances permit, it is well to try to determine how your listeners or viewers reacted to your message by conducting audience research. This point will be taken up later in the chapter.

GETTING YOUR MESSAGE ON THE MEDIA

After you have identified your communication goals, studied your target audience, and started to prepare your message, you should begin work on the next problem—getting your message on the media. To do this you must have some familiarity with the ways the media operate. You will find, first of all, that you need to convince the gate keepers that the media they control should carry your message. This means you must "sell" your idea to the media. To succeed in this you must be skilled in the kinds of interpersonal persuasive communication we've talked about in Chapter 7, and you must also understand how the media business works.

In getting your message on the mass media you are faced with a basic dilemma: The larger the audience for a program or station, the more difficulty you will have in getting your message on that program or station. Stations with large audiences are very cautious about changing their programming for fear of losing some of their established audience. Stations with smaller audiences are much more willing to try something different which may help *build* an audience. Generally, it is easier to get a message on radio than it is to get it on television. There are many more radio stations than there are television stations. Furthermore, radio stations do much of their own programming locally, whereas television stations get most of their programs from national sources. This gives radio stations more flexibility in introducing new local material. Finally, radio production costs are much lower than television costs, so radio stations are more accustomed to producing their results with limited resources.

Types of Exposure for Broadcast Messages

There are three major options for getting exposure for your messages in broadcasting: *incorporating your message into an existing program; producing "spot announcements"* (that is, commercials) for presenting your message; and *producing your own programs*. Each option has advantages and disadvantages.

Using existing programs. Most stations have some kind of *community discussion program* which is broadcast weekly or monthly. It may be possible to convince the producers of one of these programs to use your topic for a show. Probably this is the easiest way to get your message on the broadcast media. However, the people working on these programs always have more requests for time than they possibly can fill. They may be unable or unwilling, therefore, to treat your topic at a time when you want the issue covered. Moreover, since stations often broadcast these programs at times when very few people are in the audience (for example, early Sunday mornings), you may feel that this is not an effective way to reach your target audience.

News programs also provide an opportunity for getting your message presented. Before you contact station news departments, however, watch their newscasts so you know the kinds of stories they cover and are familiar with the individuals who report the stories. This knowledge and familiarity will allow you to adapt your request for coverage to the various ways stations present the news. The more thorough your advance preparations of this kind, the greater your chances of getting your message on the air. News coverage can be difficult to arrange. You must convince the station that you have something which is *newsworthy*. This is *basic*. Every day the station news departments are bombarded with many news releases and phone calls requesting coverage. To get on the news, you must have something which will be particularly appealing to the news department. Generally, stories are chosen either because of their importance as news events, or because they have some novelty interest. If you find a news event related to your message, you may be able to convince the stations to include your message when they cover that event.

But even if the news department assignment editor agrees to send a reporter to cover your story, you will probably have little influence over the way it is presented on the news. The editorial judgment about how to present the story will be exercised by the station personnel. They may decide to emphasize aspects of the event very different from the ones you would have chosen. You should, of course, feel free to tell the reporter what you think is important, but do not be too surprised if the story is reported in another way. Also bear in mind that most broadcast news stories are very short (less than a minute), and they will present only a few parts of the message. The amount of time given your story will depend on the station's evaluation of its importance relative to the importance of the other stories which need to be covered. On a "slow news day" (a day when there are few major stories) you may possibly get more time. Finally, when you use newscasts to carry your message, you need to analyze which parts of your target audience will probably be reached. Just getting your message on the news does not insure that it will get to the people you need to reach.

Using spot announcements. You can have complete control over the content of your messages if you produce them as spot announcements—the short (10-, 20-, 30-, or 60-second) commercials which support commercial broadcasting. If you decide to use spots, you will probably need to pay for the production costs. If your message originates with a non-profit organization, you may be able to get your announcements broadcast for no charge as "public service announcements" (PSA's). However, since stations usually have more requests for public service time than they have time available, you will need to convince them that running your messages is particularly important. If the station uses your messages as PSA's, you will have little control over when the messages are run. This, admittedly, is a drawback. Since the station audience changes at different times of the day, naturally you should make every effort to have your messages broadcast at times when your target audience is most likely to be watching. But this may not happen if your message is a PSA.

If you have considerable money available, you may want to buy time on the station to run your announcements. Under this arrangement, your spots will be treated like the commercials of other advertisers. You can select any available time you can afford to buy. If you are going to spend money in this way, you should carefully study all the available data on the audience for each program slot and determine how well it matches your target audience. Buying radio or television time is very expensive. It can be an effective way of reaching an audience, but its effectiveness must be weighed against its high costs.[6]

Producing your own programs. Usually people who are considering use of the mass media start by investigating the possibilities of doing a special program on their issue or area of interest. This is a good way to reach some target audiences, but it needs to be carefully evaluated in terms of the effort required. First among these considerations is the fact that most stations are unwilling to undertake the expense of producing a program. Since studio time and air time are very costly, station owners and managers are reluctant to use them for programs outside their regular schedule. Second, attracting and holding an audience for a special program is extremely difficult. And *risky*. People tend to tune out the station when specials (other than entertainment specials) are presented. Finally, because producing an entire program obviously requires a lot of very hard work, you must evaluate whether producing a program is the best way to use your energies and tie up your time. There may be better ways to communicate your message and reach your target audience without getting involved in the problems of producing a special program.

Even more complicated and costly than producing a single special program is the task of producing a program *series* dealing with the message material you wish to present to your target audience. About the only place this can be done is on public broadcasting, where there are some opportunities to broadcast such series. If you plan a series of programs, you will need substantial financial backing. Don't think of starting without it. One example of this type of effort is the Sesame Street series which has been produced for a target audience of preschool children. The producers of the series combined their message (preparing children for school) with a variety of entertaining devices to attract and hold their young audience. The series was financed by a variety of government and foundation sources, and wouldn't have been possible without that kind of support. If the programs are interesting enough, a series of programs is an excellent way to build and hold an audience for socially important messages. However, finding financing, producing a succession of programs, and getting stations to broadcast them on a regularly scheduled basis make producing such a series a massive undertaking.

In the final analysis, the primary advantage of producing your own program is that you will have greater control over the content of the program than you would have by using existing programs to present your message. The primary problems are the difficulty of getting your target audience to watch the program and the complexities and costs of getting the program produced and broadcast.

Selling Yourself and Your Idea to the Station

When you seek assistance from a radio or television station, it is important that you realize you are asking to use a scarce resource. Although broadcast stations are licensed to operate in the "public interest, convenience, and necessity," they are not required to respond to all the requests they receive. You must, therefore, find ways to make your request more important than the other requests being made of the station. You can do this more effectively, we believe, if you understand the station's position with regard to your request. The station's primary concern is attracting as large an audience as possible for its programs. It has to be extremely sensitive to the possibility that any changes in programming may cause listeners to turn to its competitors. Since the station depends on its listeners to get advertisers to buy time for their commercials, it can't afford to broadcast many programs which have small audiences. Thus, the best way to interest the station in beaming your message—its format and material—to listeners and/or watchers is to show that your proposal will draw an audience. Most people know this, yet every radio and television station gets many requests to do programs which have little hope of attracting an audience of satisfactory proportions. So if you want your request and proposal to be considered ahead of these other requests, you must show the station management that presenting your material is a sound programming decision.

The station's concern with audience size, of course, extends beyond the audience for your particular program. Stations have found that "audience flow" is an important factor in attracting large numbers of listeners/watchers to tune in and *stay* tuned in. Listeners tend to stay with one particular station rather than change to another. This is particularly true on radio. Radio listeners select a favorite station and stay with it for hours (or even weeks or years) before they change the radio dial to another station. On television, evening schedules are carefully planned to try to attract an audience early in the evening and then hold that audience *throughout* the evening. Programs before and after shows with high ratings tend to have large audiences. An extremely popular show like "All in the Family" can ensure an audience for that channel for an entire evening. A program with a smaller audience can seriously hurt the ratings of the programs that precede and follow it. Special "public issues" programs tend to have very small audiences, so radio and television stations are understandably reluctant to run these programs at times when they could have large audiences.

People to Contact at the Station

Fortified with a clear understanding of the station's needs and problems and having carefully worked out the content and format of the mass-media message you hope to communicate to your target audience, you are now ready to talk with somebody—the "right" person—at the station. But *whom?* Stations, as you will discover rather quickly, have a variety of organizational patterns. Usually the person in charge has a title something like "General Manager." Under the general manager are a variety of department heads: "Sales Director," "News Director," "Program Director," "Community Affairs Director." For each such "director," each station has its own set of titles and responsibilities; but the following general pattern of organization may be considered typical:

The *sales director* is in charge of the sales staff which sells the air time on the station to commercial sponsors. If you are planning to use paid spot advertisements, the sales director is the person to contact.

The *news director* is in charge of the news department. If you are trying to get your story or message on a newscast, contact the news director, the assignment editor (who assigns the reporters to stories), or one of the reporters.

The *program director* is in charge of the non-news programming of the station. If you want to try to develop a special program, the program director is the person to talk with.

The *community affairs director* usually is in charge of several programs having a community-problems orientation or base. If you want to get your message incorporated into one of these programs, or if you want to run a series of public-service announcements, the community affairs director is the person to contact.

When you deal with individual stations, you will find that this general organizational pattern is extensively modified in actual practice. Do some research to find out how the particular station you wish to contact is organized and who the individuals in the various positions are. There are several broadcast directories which can help you in this effort.[7] After checking the directories, place a call to the station's switchboard to be sure you have the current names and titles before you begin your contacts. Ask other people who have contacted the station recently who is most likely to be helpful for your project. Doing a little research of this kind will help you to contact the right people quickly. This, in turn, can make the station more responsive in dealing with you and your requests.

FCC Policies on Access to Station Channels

The Communications Act of 1934 requires that broadcast stations operate in the "public interest, convenience, and necessity." Compliance with this broad and vague requirement is governed by the Federal Communications Commission which oversees the licensing of broadcast stations. Station licenses expire periodically and must be renewed. If the FCC has reason to believe there are serious problems with the station's operation, the station may have to promise to improve in the future. In unusual situations the station may be fined or even lose its license. The FCC encourages public participation in the renewal process. If you believe the station is not treating your requests in a reasonable way, you could complain to the FCC.[8]

Stations are required to keep their renewal applications on file for public inspection. You can request to see this file to learn what commitments the station made in its last renewal. Stations are required to list the ten problems they believe are most important in their community and to indicate the type of programming they plan to use in combating these problems. Since the station is required to keep all letters of complaint in its public-inspection file, you can learn if other people in the community have also experienced difficulty getting their messages carried by the station.

Several sections of the FCC's regulations relate to access to the broadcast media. These can be grouped in four general categories: (1) the equal time provision, (2) the fairness doctrine, (3) the editorializing rules, and (4) the personal attack rule. As a potential mass-media communicator, you should of course have some understanding of these rules. Since they are revised from time to time, you should check their current status if you think one of them applies to your situation.

The equal time provision. Often called "Section 315" since that's how it's designated in the Communications Act of 1934, the equal time provision deals with broadcast appearances of candidates for public office. It applies only to appearances of the candidates themselves; it does not apply to people appearing on behalf of candidates, nor to non-candidates speaking on campaign issues. Basically the rule requires stations to provide the same amount of time, under the same conditions, to all candidates for a public office. If five minutes of free time is provided for one candidate for mayor, all candidates for mayor must be offered five free minutes. If one candidate for a council seat is sold time, all other candidates for that seat must be sold time at the same rate. The station is not required to provide time to any of the candidates for a given office; it can refuse to give or sell time if it refuses time to all candidates for that office. The equal time provision has an important exception—it does not apply to the coverage of candidates in news programs.

There has been heated debate over whether the equal time provision has provided increased access to air time for candidates, or whether it has restricted access for major candidates because stations do not want to have to give or sell time to minor candidates and write-in candidates. Congress has been studying proposals for revising Section 315 for many years. If you are working on a political campaign, you certainly should be familiar with the way the equal time provision applies to your candidate.[9]

The fairness doctrine.   The FCC requires, in what is known as *the fairness doctrine,* that stations which treat controversial issues of public importance must also present the opposing views on those issues. The station does not have to present the opposing views in a particular program, nor does it have to devote the same amount of time to each view. The station merely must show that the opposing views have been covered adequately somewhere in its programming. If you believe that a station is placing undue emphasis on one side of an issue, the fairness doctrine may help you persuade the station that it should provide more balanced coverage. Unlike the equal time situation, the fairness doctrine places the station under no obligation to provide time to any particular individual. The station can use its own staff to present the other side of the issue. The FCC's rules and the ensuing court decisions have made fairness a complex legal area. You will need a basic knowledge of the current interpretations of fairness to determine whether it can be helpful in encouraging a station to provide coverage for your point of view.

The editorializing rules.   When a station broadcasts an editorial, it is required to seek out people to speak for the point of view opposite that expressed in the editorial. If you wish to reply to an editorial, you must write the station promptly, and clearly show why you are the person who should give the reply. If the station happens to present an editorial on an issue with which you are concerned, you may be entitled to some time in which to respond to it.

The personal attack rule.   This rule requires that anyone who is verbally attacked on any of a station's programs must be notified of the attack and given time to reply. In other words, stations must try to be sure that no one using their facilities attacks someone else. If you are communicating your message on the air, for example, the station will want to be sure that any comments you make about other people do not constitute a personal attack requiring free-response time.

These, then, are the four major and specific policy guidelines to public access of station channels as administered by the Federal Communications Commission: the *personal attack* rule, the *editorializing* rule, the *fairness doctrine,* and the *equal time* provision. Aside from these regulations, the station management has broad discretion in selecting the material which is to be aired. The FCC is extremely reluctant to interfere with station decisions if the station proceeds in a reasonable manner. Getting access to the station (even access for paid announcements) can be controlled by the station. For the most part, you can request time, but you have no right to demand time.

The Use of Cable Television

In addition to broadcast television stations, cable-television systems also can provide a wide range of opportunities for the electronic communication of messages. Cable-television systems began by distributing broadcast signals to homes which could not receive them without prohibitively expensive antennas. Technology, developed in the 1960s, vastly increased the number of channels which can be brought into the home. Twenty-channel systems are now the minimum which the Federal Communications Commission will allow to be built. Some experimental systems have been developed with sixty or more channels. Since the FCC has limited the number of broadcast television stations which can be carried on cable television, the cable operators are seeking other uses for the additional channels. Some channels have been used for programs originating in local areas. If your target audience is served by a cable system which originates its own programming, you may be able to get your message on this channel. At least it's worth a try.

In 1972 the FCC required cable-television systems to provide a "public access channel" that would be available to anyone in the community on a first-come, first-served basis. Up to five minutes of studio time was to be provided at no charge, and additional time was to be made available at cost. The systems were also required to run videotapes provided by members of the community. These rules have been interpreted differently by various cable operators and may be revised by the FCC. If the access channel is available in your community, it may be a good way to reach your target audience. The cable system is required to keep a list of people who have requested access time; contact some of them and use their experiences for assistance in developing your ideas.

Where they are available, the cable-television access channels offer much more time than is currently being used. So getting a program on the channel presents little difficulty. However, the access channels usually have a very small audience. If you are going to use the access channel to carry your message, be sure to develop a promotional campaign to ensure that the members of your target audience will be aware of the program.

GOING ON THE AIR

Suppose you are going to be on television, either because you've convinced a station manager that your message should be televised or because you've been invited to appear on a program. With what kinds of procedures and problems do you need to be concerned? First, you will need to recognize some of the special demands of electronic communication. Then, you will need to adapt what you know about communicating effectively to the particular situation.

Special Demands of Electronic Communication

There are two primary differences between face-to-face communication and broadcast communication. The first is the *absence of direct and immediate audience feedback* which we discussed on pages 363–364. And the second difference is that the broadcast studio is *a very unnatural communication setting* for most people. In broadcasting, the equipment often dominates—even "overpowers"—the communication situation. The television studio is filled with lights, cameras, microphones, and a variety of sets and pieces of equipment. Off in one small area will be the "set" for the program on which you are to appear. The only part of the studio the *audience* will see in the camera shots will be related to your program, but the parts of the studio *you* will see as a performer will be filled with sets for other shows.

Your only audience will be the studio crew. For the most part, they will have to work at their own jobs and will have little opportunity to pay attention to the content of your communication. This situation might cause you to feel you have no audience for the things you are saying. Furthermore, since most of the people around you will be preoccupied with their own work, their movements and the movements of the equipment can become very distracting—especially when you are trying to think about what you want to say. You will have to concentrate on "communicating" with the camera and its little glass eye. In all, because the studio environment will probably be so very different from anything you're accustomed to, the first few times you work in it, you may find it not only uncomfortable but also downright nerve-wracking.

In radio there is much less equipment than in television, but the communication environment is equally strange. A typical radio studio is a small room with a table, a chair, and a microphone. If you are not comfortable sitting alone in a room talking to yourself (and few people are comfortable in that situation) you will feel uneasy the first few times you communicate over radio.

It takes time to become accustomed to working in broadcast communications because you have to *relearn* so many things you have come to expect from face-to-face communication. If you could know your audience quite well and specifically, you could plan carefully for feedforward. But because you can never be sure just who will be listening and watching, you have to rely on your own best judgment about what people want to hear, what they can understand, and what communication skills will help you get your message across. If you could address your listeners face-to-face, you could watch them closely and make necessary adjustments as you go along. But, as you now know, the electronic media make it imperative that you communicate *without* any immediate feedback. Imagine making a telephone call in which the person at the other end of the line says nothing but just lets you talk about whatever you want! This is similar to the situation a communicator faces in broadcasting. You never know if there is an audience "out there." To the extent that anything can aid you in situations of this kind, a thorough understanding of the processes of interpersonal communication—which have been stressed throughout this book—should enable you to understand better how to communicate over the media without the feedback cues which normally help us adjust to our audience. Only if we really understand communication can we be convincing and interesting when deprived of feedback.

Achieving Naturalness of Presentation

The best advice for broadcast communication is the same as for any other form of communication—*be natural in what you do*. This is extremely difficult advice to follow. Often, the more you think about being natural, the more difficult it becomes. Yet because broadcast studios are such unusual and unnatural communication settings, you must make a *special* effort to communicate naturally. One way to be more natural is to try to imagine that you are talking to a friend. Think of a person you would like to talk to about the subject of the program. Then try to communicate as though you were talking directly to that person. Don't let yourself think about the equipment and the other people in the studio who are working with the equipment. Imagine the friend to be standing where the television camera is, or think of the friend as standing behind the radio microphone; then talk to that person.

Communicating by radio or television is somewhat similar to communicating to a small group. The communicative styles used in speaking for the mass media are more like those used in carrying on a conversation than those used in giving a speech. Some of the techniques of the platform speaker appear decidedly out of place on the television screen. For example, public speakers sometimes use a wide range of speaking *volumes*—shouting one minute, whispering the next minute. In the electronic media, the sound volume is adjusted to keep a relatively constant level. If you speak softly, the audio operator will amplify your voice more; if you speak loudly, he or she will reduce the amplification. In either case, the volume reaching the audience will remain almost constant. This means that, in general, shouting to project a strong emotion is not a useful and effective technique for radio or television purposes. Similarly, trying to gain—or regain—the audience's attention by whispering probably won't be successful either.

There are, however, many delivery techniques which *are* very effective in broadcasting: changing the vocal pace by speaking rapidly or speaking slowly, varying the tone to indicate emphasis, and changing inflection patterns to highlight a point. Listen to some media performers who you think are particularly skillful and try to identify the ways they use their voices to make their communication more effective. Notice especially how they use their voices to give the impression that they are communicating directly and informally with a friend or a very small group of acquaintances.

Skillful and controlled use of *gestures* is another very important factor in communicating effectively on television. In the public speaking setting, as you know—especially when you're addressing a large audience—the use of broad, expansive gestures can be very useful and helpful. Large gestures are usually more effective there than small ones. On television, however, the large gestures of the platform speaker are inappropriate. The broad sweep of the hands, the arm thrust into the air, and other large gestures are likely to be lost because they extend beyond the edges of the camera shot. If the camera moves to a shot wide enough to include the broad gestures, the performer's head may become the size of a small dot on the screen. In presenting televised messages, small gestures close to the body are much more effective than wide, sweeping gestures. They allow the camera to stay on a shot which is "tight" enough to capture facial expressions as well as hand-and-arm gestures. Watch experienced television performers, and notice how they use their hands effectively but keep them close enough to the body to allow the camera to have a close shot. Notice how they use facial expressions to heighten the impact of their gestures.

Your *physical appearance* is still another important consideration when you're working on television. When you have a chance to stand before the critical eye of the studio camera, you will find yourself wondering "What should I wear?" Almost any clothes that are becoming to you will also enhance your appearance on television; ask the people at the studio if they have any special guidelines. There are two, in particular, which should merit concern: (1) Do not wear jewelry that sparkles unless you want the viewers to be distracted by bright flashes of light reflected from it. (2) Do not wear clothing with horizontal stripes. Stripes can make you look heavier—and television will make you look heavier anyway.

Wear whatever *makeup* you would normally wear. Applying professional makeup for television is an art which requires years of practice. So if you have a particular problem, seek the advice of someone who has experience in television makeup. For most of us, everyday makeup is satisfactory. But there are a few facial areas that may cause difficulties. The television lights tend to darken the areas around the *eyes.* If you normally wear dark eye shadow, you may want to use a lighter shade for television. Television also tends to emphasize *beard shadow.* If you have light skin and a dark beard, you may look as though you haven't had a shave for several days, even though you may have shaved shortly before the program. The best solution for this problem is to use some face powder that is the same shade as your skin. Oily skin or skin with perspiration can look very glossy on camera. This can sometimes be corrected by face powder. Check with people at the studio first, however. Applying the wrong shade of powder can have a detrimental effect.

Making the Program Interesting

The electronic media provide a variety of techniques which can be used to make a program more interesting. Proper choices of *music* and *sound effects* may help attract the audience to your message. Using *visual aids, slides,* and sections from *motion picture films* can add considerable interest to a television program. In utilizing these materials, however, remember that you must obtain permission to use copyrighted material. Since copyright is a very complex legal area, you should seek advice from a knowledgeable person at the studio to determine whether there is any problem with the material you wish to use.

Production techniques—if the studio staff are skilled in creating and handling them—can add much to your message-presentation. But they also can cause you to lose sight of your communicative purpose and your target audience. There is a real danger that you can become so interested in the clever ways to use the technology that you will lose sight of the primary purposes of your program. There are many programs which have numerous interesting technical gimmicks but have nothing to communicate. The key to attracting an audience, as we've emphasized, is to *have something important to say*. If you have an interesting message, production techniques can help it. But without an interesting message, even the most sophisticated use of production techniques won't save the show.

Following Up with Research on Audience Feedback

When your message finally is broadcast on the electronic media, you will want to gather as much information as possible about who received the message and if they perceived the message as you intended. This information will assist you in evaluating your efforts and designing follow-up messages to reach others in your target audience. One of the frustrating aspects, as we've said, of using the mass media to communicate your message is that you might never know who really received the message. Except for a few comments from friends, you may rarely hear directly from other people. There may be some limited feedback through the mail, but usually only from people who feel most strongly about the issues.

It is possible—and sometimes necessary—to conduct audience surveys to determine who was in the audience for the program and to learn whether your message has "come through." But such surveys are very costly. They become especially expensive if relatively few people were in the audience because so much effort will be needed to find a sufficiently large number of them for the results to be meaningful. But, despite these difficulties, audience research of some kind is needed to determine how well the messages are being received. We can't assume that simply getting our message constructed and on the air means that the target audience will automatically receive it. And just because we've worked carefully and conscientiously on the message in terms of listeners' needs, motives, beliefs, and values is no guarantee that our audience will respond as we expect they will. In conducting this type of research, do as much as you *can* do—and can *afford* to do. But, at the same time keep always in mind this important practical consideration: the money and time spent on audience research might be better spent on developing additional messages and placing them in the media. The effort spent in developing messages needs to be carefully balanced against the efforts made on audience research.

To sum it all up, if you wish to communicate via the mass media, preparing the media messages is just one part of the process. You need to identify an appropriate target audience, develop messages appropriate for that audience, find ways to get those messages on the media, ensure that the messages are well promoted so the target audience knows where to look for them, and construct messages that will utilize the information-diffusion process to get your message to a broad audience. After the presentation, be sure to follow through and learn who your audience was and how they reacted to the message. To do all of this, you must understand the media, but—even more important—you must have a meaningful message to present, and you must thoroughly understand the audience you are trying to reach.

Suggested Readings

Among the many good sources available on mass electronic communications are the books listed below. The Barnouw and Head works present general and historical perspectives on these media, and the Emery and Krasnow-Longley sources are especially helpful on the important topic of government regulation of the mass media.

Erik Barnouw, *A History of Broadcasting in the United States* (New York: Oxford University Press, 1966–1970).

Walter B. Emery, *Broadcasting and Government,* 2nd ed. (East Lansing: Michigan State University Press, 1971).

Sydney W. Head, *Broadcasting in America,* 3rd ed. (Boston: Houghton Mifflin Company, 1975).

Erwin G. Krasnow and Lawrence D. Longley, *The Politics of Broadcast Regulation* (New York: St. Martin's Press, 1973).

Reference Notes

[1] The gate keeper concept has been widely discussed in communication literature. It was introduced by David Manning White, "The 'Gate Keeper': A Case Study in the Selection of News," *Journalism Quarterly* 27 (1950):383–390.

[2] The information diffusion research is thoroughly reviewed in Everett M. Rogers and F. Floyd Shoemaker, *Communication of Innovations: A Cross-Cultural Approach* (New York: The Free Press, 1971).

[3] An early, clear description of the flow of information is given in Elihu Katz, "The Two-Step Flow of Communication: An Up-to-Date Report on an Hypothesis," *Public Opinion Quarterly* 21 (1957):61–78.

[4] Theodore H. White has written a series of books which trace the strategies of recent presidential campaigns. Also, Joe McGinniss, in *The Selling of the President 1968* (New York: Trident Press, 1969), presents an opinionated review of the media strategies used in the 1968 campaign of Richard Nixon.

[5] The research on media effects is reviewed in Wilbur Schramm and Donald F. Roberts, *The Process and Effects of Mass Communication* (Urbana: University of Illinois Press, 1971).

[6] Standard Rate and Data Service, Inc. (Skokie, Illinois) publishes a series of directories of advertising rates and audience figures for broadcast stations, magazines, and newspapers. If you are considering buying time, consult these directories to get an idea of costs and audience sizes. Then talk with a sales representative to get more detailed information.

[7] Two extensive annual directories are: *Broadcasting Yearbook* (Broadcasting Publications, Inc., Washington, D.C.) which covers radio and television, and *Television Factbook* (Television Digest, Inc., Washington, D.C.) which covers television and cable television.

[8] See "The Public and Broadcasting," *Federal Register* 39 (1974):32287–32296, in which the FCC summarizes its procedures. A less technical discussion of FCC procedures is found in Nicholas Johnson, *How to Talk Back to Your Television Set* (New York: Bantam Books, 1970).

[9] The FCC has published several question-and-answer guides to the equal time provision which are very helpful in explaining the many complex situations which develop.

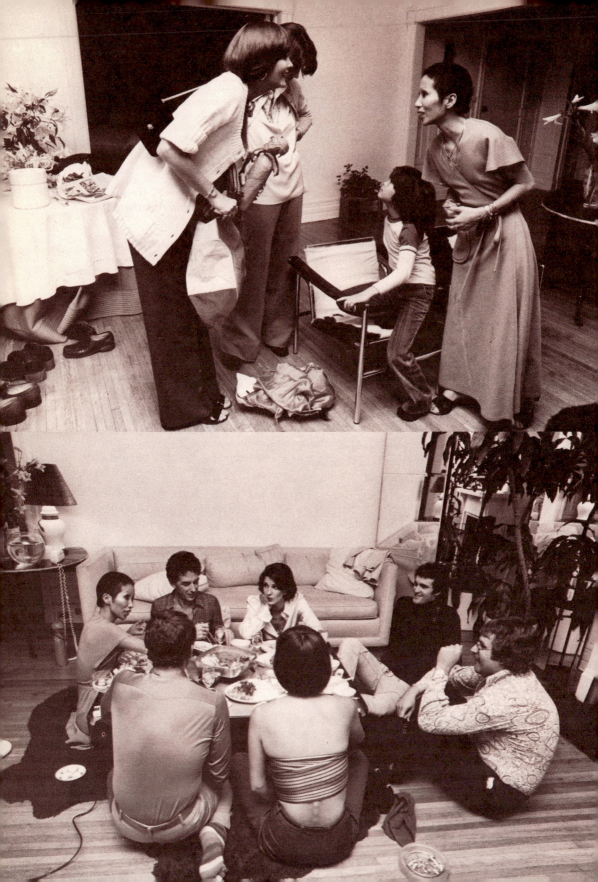

Chapter 16

INTERCULTURAL COMMUNICATION

By Gordon C. Whiting

Department of Communications, Brigham Young University

An *awareness* of the self as a culture
bearer, a *sensitivity* to verbal and nonverbal
patterns in other cultures, an *empathy*
in interpersonal interaction—these are
the special strengths you must have
for successful intercultural communication.

Everything we have said thus far about speech communication and human interaction takes on especial importance in the area to which we now turn our attention: communication across cultures. As the boundaries of our communicative world shrink, it is increasingly likely that we will be speaking and interacting in cultures other than our own. But what is different about intercultural communication? Why should we devote any extra time and effort to this subject?

INTERCULTURAL VS. INTRACULTURAL COMMUNICATION

Many people report no difference at all between communicating in their own culture and communicating in other cultures; they report having had no trouble with foreigners when they visit other lands. People, they say, are "pretty much the same all over." Interpersonal communication to them is completely unproblematical, something not worth becoming concerned about. The old saying—attributed to the Chinese—that "Talking to you is like playing a violin to a cow" [1] aptly describes such individuals. Their imperceptiveness to cultural nuances parallels their imperceptiveness to their own failures. In all but the least demanding intercultural situations and for all but the least delicatè purposes, these people are relatively unsuccessful, disliked, and ineffective.[2]

Some General Approaches to Other Cultures

People fall into several orientations when working in another culture.[3] Some, as we've indicated, attempt to ride roughshod over the culture and get things done regardless of obstacles or niceties. They may succeed if their purposes are simple and their power great, but they will not often achieve their goals and will fail to enrich their understanding. Another group tries to learn only what is necessary to manipulate members of the other culture to their advantage. They simulate in themselves the adaptations that they feel will help to get their job done. For example, they may insincerely convert to Islam to gain the confidence of an Islamic people. Besides running the risk of being found out or of misperceiving what it is they will need, they, too, shortchange themselves in their failure to glean values and insight from the culture.

Another approach is to "go native." Persons who adopt this approach reject their own culture and substitute in its place the values and procedures of the host culture. Sometimes people succeed in this. There is a story of an anthropologist studying an American Indian tribe who decided to join the tribe and eventually gave up and renounced anthropology. Often, however, these people can only be marginally accepted in the host culture. And they lose much of their ability to effect change there when they "go native."

Perhaps the best and most successful orientation, over the long haul, is to be a culture bearer but remain susceptible to change by contact with the alien culture. Maintain identity and uniqueness as well as allegiance to your own history and origins—not rigidly but with acceptance of what is good in the new culture. Some research suggests that this willingness to be changed as well as to change is the most important characteristic of those who succeed interculturally. It is superior to language skill, knowledge of culture, and even empathy[4]—all of which we shall consider in this chapter.

The characteristics of the self-actualizer mentioned in Chapter 3 tend also to be those of the successful intercultural communicator—with one proviso. Each of those characteristics must be modified by cultural awareness. Thus, what is regarded as "spontaneity of behavior" in your own culture may be misinterpreted as disrespect in another. "Problem-centeredness" is appropriate, provided you center on the same kinds of problems and in the same way. In some cultures, for instance, the paramount problem is survival of the in-group rather than solution of social problems. Even a sense of humor needs watching to be sure it is not misinterpreted as insult. America is one of the few countries in the world where nicknames, for instance, are not ordinarily a means of belittling others.

In intercultural communication the participants must expect error and misunderstanding, breakdown and difficulty, and they must take steps to pinpoint the areas of difficulty and remedy them. This chapter can't ensure error-free intercultural communication for every individual. But we do hope to make you more aware of the resources available for improving communication and of the points at which an intercultural communicator may wish to consciously choose whether to sacrifice being understood for some other more important goal.

The greatest enemy of intercultural communication, as of all communication, is *the illusion of its occurrence*. When you originate a message, you understand perfectly what you said and you know exactly what you meant. Consequently, you might suppose that the same levels of knowledge and understanding are true for the listening agent. While this position may have merit in some settings, it is one to guard against when messages cross cultures.

As pointed out in Chapter 1, James Winans argued that the difference between ordinary conversation and public speaking is one of degree, not of kind. A similar relationship could be claimed between intercultural communication and *intra*cultural communication. At a sufficiently abstract level, communication is the same, whether or not it crosses cultures. But there are important differences in the degree to which certain factors become relevant.

Edward Hall's treatment of cultural differences in the comfortable space associated with conversation, which was mentioned in Chapter 1 and also in Chapter 6, provides an example. You can depend fairly well on all reasonably socialized members of your culture to know intuitively how far to stand from you when they talk. They will also know whether and how to touch you during the conversation, how often to look you in the eye, and how to orient their bodies to yours during the conversation. If Hall is correct, none of these things can be taken for granted when the other party comes from and was socialized in a different culture.

Perhaps only a minority of the readers of this chapter will be like the cow listening to the violin. But even if you read with care and sensitivity you will not, from that alone, have the experience of moving and communicating successfully in a strange culture. Only that experience can give understanding, although if you are ill-prepared, it, too, will be wasted. What appears here can help you take advantage of and learn from mistakes you will make there. Some mistakes need not be made even once, and perhaps this material can help alert you to those.

Awareness of the Self as a Culture Bearer

The world is overrun with foreigners; in fact, 94 percent of it is non-American.* In other words, from the point of view of 94 percent of the people in the world it is *we* who behave strangely, boorishly, irrationally, and—yes—even inhumanly. The comments of a Chinese scholar on first seeing white people in his country a century and a half ago are apropos:

---

*The use of the terms *non-American* and *American* in this chapter gives evidence of how trapped we are in our own culture, since by "Americans" United States citizens mean themselves. They thereby give offense to the other inhabitants of North and South America. The terms are used here for efficiency in expression and because most of the readers would find "United States citizen" puzzling.

These "Ocean Men," as they are called, are tall beasts with deep sunken eyes and beaklike noses. The lower part of their faces, the backs of their hands, and, I understand, their entire bodies are covered with a mat of curly hair, much as are the monkeys of the southern forests. But the strangest part about them is that, although undoubtedly men, they seem to possess none of the mental faculties of men. The most bestial of peasants is far more human, although these Ocean Men go from place to place with the self-reliance of a man of scholarship and are in some respects exceedingly clever. It is quite possible that they are susceptible to training and could, with patience, be taught the modes of conduct proper to a human being.[5]

Definitions of culture are legion, but perhaps the one which is most helpful in intercultural communication is to regard every culture as a *way of being human.* The Chinese scholar just quoted recognized that those hairy "Ocean Men" were indeed *men,* although their modes of behavior were so alien as to make him dubious of their *humanity.* The discovery of culture is the discovery that there is more than one way to be human and that other people's ways seem as natural and rational to them as ours seem to us.

This approach to culture highlights its existence as well as its plural character. Most of the time, our culture operates outside of our awareness. We are as immersed in it as is a fish in water and so we are about as little prone to notice its existence and influence as a fish is to notice the medium in which it lives. One of the potential values of intercultural experience is the self-discovery involved. Such experience may force awareness that *every person, ourself included, is a culture bearer.* And this awareness is the first step toward becoming capable of controlling the intuitions and predispositions that culture instills in each of us.

Jean Piaget, the child psychologist, speaks of the child's "egocentrism." By this Piaget means the tendency of young children to be unaware that there is any perspective on reality other than their own. Egocentric children are not necessarily selfish; rather they are blissfully unaware that the world does not revolve about them or that others do not see precisely what they *see* or experience precisely what they experience.

These comments on egocentrism apply also to the concept of *ethnocentrism.* This is the tendency to suppose that there is but one way of being human— the way you have been taught and the way you will in turn teach the next generation. Ordinarily, feelings of superiority will accompany the contrasts which you draw with other cultures. Still, in most instances you will view the other culture as containing some good points as well as some bad ones. A study by Harry Triandis and Vasso Vassiliou found, for instance, that although both Greeks and Americans had a more positive evaluation of their own culture than of the alien culture, each found something in the other to applaud. The Americans saw the Greeks as *inefficient, competitive,* and *suspicious,* but also as *charming* and *witty.* The Greeks saw the Americans as *efficient,* but also as *dull* and *lacking in charm.* Later a detailed study by the same scholars and others showed that for the Americans the greater the contact, the stronger and clearer the stereotypes became and the more they tended to correspond to the Greeks' own view of themselves. Still, although accuracy improved, attractiveness did not.[6]

On the other hand, Greeks saw Americans rather differently than Americans saw themselves. To the Greeks, Americans were *arrogant, suspicious, sly,* and *competitive,* as well as *systematic, emotionally controlled,* and *flexible.*

Ethnocentrism reflects preference, even in the individual who has been blasted out of blasé complacency by the experience of another culture. Given a trade-off between being *forward-looking* and *efficient* versus being *witty* and *charming,* most Greeks, it seems, would prefer wit, and most Americans efficiency. Ethnocentrism is not a disease to be eradicated by trying to rid yourself of cultural preferences. Lack of awareness of the possibility of other ways of being human may make you less sensitive and prevent the improvement of your own humanity, but it cannot be combated by getting rid of your own way of being human. Rather, in the interest of communicative effectiveness, you need to learn to control the culture that you bear. This means: (a) recognizing that you are a culture bearer, (b) recognizing to what this may predispose you, and (c) undertaking to check out the impact of those predispositions. Knowing yourself as a culture bearer is part of knowing yourself generally. As we have stressed throughout this book, awareness and knowledge of your characteristics as a communicator can be used to improve your communication. So, awareness and knowledge of yourself as a culture bearer can improve intercultural communication.

Imagine that you have been asked to draw a picture of North America in this rectangle:

If you are like the faculty members of a certain well-known department of communication, you would attempt to draw a picture of the United States. Most of the faculty members wanted their drawings back when it was pointed out to them that the instructions had called for a picture of *North America* (which would, of course, include Canada, Mexico, and Central America). I know, for I was one of the majority who drew a picture of the United States.

Every known culture prepares the children born into it for assimilation into *its* culture. No culture prepares them to understand, enjoy, and positively evaluate large segments of an alien culture. Of course, some cultures do prepare their members more adequately for interaction with foreigners. The modern Dutch strike me as an instance. Children in Amsterdam seem to have mastered three or four languages by the time they reach the age of twelve. But this does not mean they would prefer being English, German, Flemish, or French to being Dutch.

Members of a culture may value some aspects of an alien culture without wishing to adopt the whole. Ragged Afghans who admire and mildly covet U.S. and Soviet technology do not want the arid secularism, vacuum of values, and infidel religious views that they see as also characterizing their technological benefactors.

Finally, it is probably best that each culture's bearers value and prefer their own ways in most things over the ways of the stranger. At least, it is easier to communicate with them if they feel positive about their own culture and consequently about themselves. The demise of allegiance to a culture spells the demise of that culture itself, thereby reducing a pluralism and diversity which is in most respects probably healthy for society at large.

To repeat, recognize yourself as a culture bearer and recognize that this means you have to be wary of your *reason, intuition,* and *feelings.* You cannot do away with them, but you can attempt to control them on the initial contact and to improve communication when that initial contact leads to misunderstandings, as it nearly always will. Since communication occurs only to the degree that the expectations concerning the meaning of messages and other matters mesh, and since this is less likely when messages cross cultures, you cannot depend on "what comes naturally."

CULTURAL NORMS AND EXPECTATIONS

One enduring problem in intercultural communication is the conflict between one's self-concept, which is bound up with values and derived from culture, and one's eventual knowledge about how things are done, what actions count for, and what members of the alien culture expect. For example, to the woman reader: You may *know* intellectually that for you to walk down the street with your head unbowed will be regarded as improper conduct for a woman in India. But you may also have your own convictions about how women should act and be treated. This particular cultural prescription may be too irritating to endure. So you may elect to retain your own values and identity rather than to fit yourself more perfectly into the alien culture's expectations.

You may further console yourself with the thought that cultures differ even in the extent to which they expect foreigners to be similar to them in preferences and behavior. Japanese, for example, are surprised that any non-Japanese should attempt to look, talk, dress, and behave like them in all respects, although they certainly expect aliens to conform to Japanese cultural procedures and rules in some areas. Americans may be at the other end of the continuum in expecting people to learn their language and adopt their customs. But even Americans allow the foreigner to retain identity as a foreigner in some aspects. Often, for example, we are charmed by foreign accents.

Some observers argue for complete flexibility and adaptation on the part of a person stepping into another culture. Clearly, this may be necessary for the achievement of certain purposes. If a spy is to pass for a native, he or she had better look, act, sound, and behave like a native in every way. But for a larger range of purposes it is wiser to be faithful to your own identity while retaining the flexibility and humility to learn from and adapt to the host culture in noncritical areas.

Margaret Mead's writings suggest to me that to act effectively in other cultures you must have a firm sense of identity and a stable core of cultural preferences plus flexibility. Without the core of cultural preferences, the experience of another culture can be psychologically overwhelming. Without the flexibility, the experience can be frustrating and unprofitable.[7] To borrow a Taoist analogy, the branch which bends and therefore sheds snow survives, whereas a more rigid branch will crack and break. But on the other hand, the flexible branch still requires inner cohesion and strength as well as resilience.

The Problem of Stereotypes and Values

There have been many attempts to list or categorize American values, including the one by Jurgen Ruesch (see Chapter 8, page 172). An equally interesting list is the one prepared by Robin Williams.* As you glance through the list, try to imagine the possibility of some other group which might, with complete internal consistency, reject each of the values listed and substitute in their stead a contrasting set. Also, ask yourself how well these describe the values of your culture. According to Williams, Americans value:

> Achievement and success
> A moral orientation (to life, to work, to interpersonal behavior)
> Purposefulness and self-discipline
> Humanitarianism and equality
> Efficiency and practicality
> Science and secular rationality
> Consumption and material comfort
> Freedom (but in the context of conformity to peer group norms)
> Democracy, patriotism, nationalism
> The individuality and personal identity of each

You probably have at least some disagreements with this list as a characterization of Americans. You might also realize that although the average (or perhaps the most frequent) view may correspond to each of these individually, you

---

*List of American Values from AMERICAN SOCIETY: A SOCIOLOGICAL INTERPRETATION, Second Edition, Revised, by Robin M. Williams, Jr. Reprinted by permission of Alfred A. Knopf, Inc.

would rarely find a person who represented all of them. Within America there are groups which champion values quite opposite to at least some of those on Williams' list.

This points to a problem with the use of stereotypes. They can be accurate for the group as a whole, although it is often assumed that they are not. But even given overall accuracy, general stereotypes fail to represent the diversity present in the culture. While we may feel that our culture is more diversified than many (and this is supported if we contrast it with "primitive" cultures), it would be a mistake to suppose that the value systems of alien cultures are uniformly shared among their members.

When an impressionistic analysis is employed, experts will be found to disagree about what the values of another culture are. Further, those values are also undergoing change. Values change more slowly than other aspects of the culture, but they do change nonetheless. Likewise, the average value of a group may fail to represent the particular value of any member of that group. But most important, the culture itself will not be homogeneous in values or behavior. Not all people who bear it will completely exemplify all its values.[8]

As Anthony Wallace has argued, cultures are not *replications of uniformity*. Rather they are particular ways of *organizing human diversity* and coordinating human activities. Even in studies of small and relatively primitive (technologically speaking) groups, Wallace found that careful analysis of cultural characteristics showed only a fraction of the culture's members conforming to *one* particular pattern. If the most frequent pattern contains only ten percent of the culture's members, we haven't much ground for describing the culture's nature in stereotypic terms.[9]

In trying to be culturally sensitive and learn from experience it is easy to make the mistake of basing your inferences on faulty data or on too small a set of observations. Some behaviors you observe in a culture will be *contrary* to cultural norms, just as some behaviors in our culture are. Some of what is observed will be permitted only to members of a particular class or only to full cultural members. Foreigners may not be permitted to participate. Some behaviors will be accepted in children but not in adults—for instance, eating on the street. Finally, some of your inferences will be simply incorrect, similar to the mistake latent in the statement "All Indians walk in single file . . . at least the one I saw did."[10]

Those who know a culture will find it difficult to give a brief and simple account of its values and ways. Every statement they make requires qualification, just as *every* simple statement about Americans would need qualification and explanation.

Despite these somewhat gloomy cautions about values and stereotypes we will see that the former are basic and central to understanding a culture and the latter can be very useful in improving communication accuracy. The trick is to go beyond mere impressions when it comes to characterizing values and to gain considerable detail before applying the multiple stereotypes appropriate to the situation.

The Role of Language

Language, which is crucial to intercultural communication of any complexity or detail, is an area which deserves a much more detailed and lengthy treatment than space permits. Each language tends to reflect the way in which the culture divides the pie of experience. At the same time, the structure of each language tends to make certain decisions obligatory. For instance, in English there is no singular possessive pronoun which is not marked for gender *(his, hers, its)*, and at the same time there is no plural possessive pronoun which is not *without* gender markings *(ours, yours, theirs)*. With our current sensitivity to woman's liberation, we either must encumber prose with phrases like "his and hers," and "he and she" or hope that the females in the audience will still be willing to read "his" and "he" generically.

The experience and research of two skilled translators, Eugene Nida and Charles Taber, have turned up the following kinds of principles when it comes to language's role in intercultural communication.[11] First, "to communicate effectively one must respect the genius of each language." Each language has its own unique character and capabilities. All are rich "in vocabulary for the areas of cultural focus, the specialities of the people, e.g. cattle (Anuaks in the Sudan), yams (Ponapeans in Micronesia), hunting and fishing (Piros in Peru), or technology (the western world)."

Secondly, "anything that can be said in one language can be said in another, unless the form is an essential element of the message." This is because, "to preserve the content of the message the form must be changed."[12] Linguistic equivalence rather than identity is what must be sought. If you are translating "white as snow" into a tropical language where there is no word for snow, you can try "white as egret feathers" or in other ways obtain an equivalent image.

Bible translators face interesting problems, however, when the cultural equivalents conflict with the linguistic equivalents. In one area of New Guinea, for instance, the cultural equivalent of a lamb is a young pig. Yet translating "the lamb of God" as "the piglet of God" is somehow disconcerting. Furthermore, these issues of equivalence shade over into questions of imparting unwarranted interpretations to a text. Thus, translation of Luke 13:11 as "a woman . . . who had an evil spirit in her that had kept her sick for eighteen years" is preferred to a translation of the same material along these lines: "a woman who for eighteen years had been ill from some psychological cause."[13] Our culture believes in psychological causes just as Luke's culture believed in evil spirits. If you wish to make an expression culturally as well as linguistically equivalent, you can do so, but you may need to import cultural ideas which are at least absent from, if not opposed to, the ideas in the original.

To summarize, in this section we have emphasized the importance of values and stereotypes in attempting to understand a culture, and have briefly suggested the role played by language in intercultural communication. In the following section, which has to do with verbal and nonverbal behavior as distinctive factors in the communicative process, we'll be concerned with some specifics of language use.

WHAT OUR MESSAGES IMPLY

The first order of business in inter- or intracultural communication, and one that receives continued reinforcement as interaction progresses, is that of developing a relationship between the participants. Psychiatrists have shown that every message implies a relationship between the communicators in addition to its substantive content.[14] (See pages 124–125.) This is the case even for messages which have as their content statements about relationship. For instance, the statement "I love you" also implies a relationship of being comfortable in or at least being allowed to express the relationship. In intercultural communication, important differences may exist in both the verbal and nonverbal behavior appropriate for a given situation. Language codes and rituals, gestures and movements, and the nearness of communicators to each other, for example, are keys to how each of them feels about the message being conveyed. Knowledge of the verbal and nonverbal behaviors appropriate to a given culture are needed if we are to get our message through.

Patterns of Verbal Behavior

In our culture we utilize our knowledge of what is appropriate in particular roles to help predetermine the appropriate relationships. Students know approximately how to treat professors and apply this knowledge when they initially interact with a strange person filling the professorial role. But we probably do this much less than many other cultures where the maintenance of harmonious relationships with other people is seen as crucial. We tend to rely considerably on the improvisation and the preferences of the individuals involved. This gives our encounters an excitement which may be lacking in other cultures, but it also results in conflict and inefficiency when the roles and expectations proferred by the parties fail to mesh.

Robert Oliver gives a delightful account of the manner in which the Chinese used to handle encounters among officials of equal rank.[15] The interaction formula stretches over a full printed page and contains five reciprocal cycles of deference. For example, "After you," "No, after you" would constitute one cycle. This contrasts dramatically with the formulas we are accustomed to, which may consist merely of a "Hi, how are you?" "Fine." "Whadaya think of the weather we've been having?" "I can't believe it for this time of year." "Yeah, me too." And then the participants get down to business.

Brief though we are, we contrast on another dimension with the Greeks when it comes to initial contacts. A Greek must seek to determine whether a stranger is the kind of person who should be admitted to the "in-group" or one to be regarded as a member of the "out-group." This is an extremely important decision so far as the treatment accorded a stranger is concerned. Treatment of the person admitted to the in-group will in many cases be exactly opposite to what it would be if he or she were relegated to the out-group. Out-groupers are fair game and must expect to take their lumps. Consequently, Greeks tend to be seen by Americans as initially hostile and suspicious. Their defenses are up, and they are probing for cues to know how to categorize the guest. If, as a guest, you show genuine concern for them and regard for their feelings and future, you are likely to be admitted to the in-group, with all its advantages and burdens. If you act in what for Americans is a more appropriate way—as an acquaintance who is not going to interfere in others' lives uninvited or upon the first meeting—you will probably appear cold and indifferent and so will be shuttled into the out-group.[16]

Interpretation of the messages exchanged during ceremonies needs to take the ceremonial setting into account. Words will not necessarily mean what they appear to mean or what they would mean if uttered in our culture. On parting, we may say to our acquaintances, "Come and see me any time," expecting that this will be "reasonably" interpreted. But what we mean by "reasonable" may be different from what people will understand if they come from another culture. Invitations, compliments, greeting ceremonies, and departure ceremonies all require special investigation of the literalness with which they are to be taken.

The Japanese are frequently cited as having a culture in which preliminary ceremony is very important. According to several accounts, numerous courtesy visits in which the reason for the visit is *not* mentioned by the visitor may be required before one can "get down to business." The Japanese participants must determine whether or not you are the *kind of person they want to do business with*.[17] And even when it is time to get down to business, the initial step may have to be made by an intermediary, perhaps the one who brought the two individuals together, who will return after one of the meetings has terminated to explain what it is that the visitor wanted.

It is interesting to realize that the Japanese are about as prone to interpret our behavior in their culture's terms as we are to project our culture onto them. Consider this account of a Japanese businessman explaining the subtle ceremonies of greeting that characterize American businessmen.

> . . . there is a lot of noise, they beat each other on the back; then as though by signal they both reach for cigars, which they offer each other. Both men will refuse each other's cigar, but ultimately the man of inferior status will accept the cigar of the man in the superior status.[18]

If we lack a well-defined ceremony for most encounters, the Japanese—reasoning from their own cultural preferences—will nonetheless discover one in our behavior.

Nonverbal Behavior

Nonverbal cues frequently have importance in establishing and maintaining relationships, as we discussed in Chapter 6. We often judge the sincerity of a profession of relationship by the "fit" of a person's words and actions. And if the "fit" is poor, we may be led to doubt that person's intentions. Even if we recognize that he or she is a foreigner—ignorant, perhaps, of our ways—we cannot be sure. It is easy to attribute immoral or insane intent to others whose nonverbal behavior puzzles us, especially if the symbols in which that behavior is expressed have for us some other cultural meaning. Thus, when we see two soldiers sauntering down the street hand in hand it may be hard to stifle the inference that they are homosexuals; we find it difficult to entertain the possibility that this is just the way friends behave in public. Even if, as a male, you withhold judgment on the issue, it is hard to bring yourself to hold hands with an American buddy in order to fit into the culture; and it may be a little difficult to remember not to hold hands with your fiancee or spouse in public places to avoid scandalizing the natives.

Robert Saitz and Edward Cervenka, two Fulbright professors in Colombia, had mastered Spanish even to the point of knowing its differences paralinguistically from English—differences in the meanings attributed to intonations, stress, and juncture. They could understand most of what was said to them and could make themselves understood. But they were not as effective as they wished to be. As they explained:

> In conversations with Colombians, our side of the talk seemed limp. We were making good points argumentatively, but they were winning, it seemed, aesthetically. Often at crucial points in discussions when we were sure that we sounded convincing, the audience laughed.[19]

Saitz and Cervenka provide several anecdotes of misunderstanding and difficulty due to misinterpretation of nonverbal signaling. For instance, one of them arrived half an hour later than the other guests at a party because, when the host's car came for him, his wife waved at the chauffeur to indicate a five-minute wait. "The chauffeur understood this as a dismissal gesture, and he merrily took off."[20]

They also give a balanced assessment of the relative importance of verbal and gestural languages in intercultural communication when they state:

> Although the absence or misuse of gestures may not result in serious cross-cultural misunderstandings, . . . the appropriate use of gesture, often an emphatic and colorful complement to speech, contributes to smoother communication and unstrained interchange.[21]

Some gestures, they found, have essentially the same meaning in two cultures. Other gestures are unique to a particular culture, and their absence in the other helps call the foreigner's attention to them. An example is the loose finger-flapping gesture which is used in Colombia to indicate chagrin, albeit a little humorously. Neither of these kinds of gestures are as troublesome as the third type—gestures which are identical in form but different in meaning. For example, North Americans may indicate the size of a person by holding their hand out, palm down. Colombians use this gesture only for animals. When the professor said his daughter was "about so tall" and indicated the height, his hosts laughed.

A further set of examples comes from gestures which are neutral in one culture but have sexual meaning in the other. The North American OK sign is an example. Imagine a visiting North American politician flashing that sign to a Latin audience. The response could be as icy as that accorded a Russian who applauds himself or uses his shoe to pound on the table.

Saitz and Cervenka provide many examples of interaction where outcomes depend on nonverbal codes. For instance, they present the communication problem between Alvaro, a Colombian, and Jim, a North American, depicted in dialogue form on pages 392–393.

Jim and Alvaro's problems in intercultural communication would have been reduced if both of them understood the meanings their gestures had in the other's culture. Still, they would probably have the greatest difficulty adjusting to gestures with different meaning. Such gestures, like Alvaro's *come-here* motion, are analogous to words which seem—but are not—similar in foreign and native languages. Skilled bilinguals find they can shift between languages with ease except when both languages use the same verbal symbol with slightly different meanings.[22] It is much harder, for example, for an American to learn that the meaning of the German word *bekommen* is "to receive" than it is to learn the meaning of the word *empfangen* (also "to receive") precisely because *bekommen* looks and even sounds a good deal like *become*.

Situations That Require Unlearning

Triandis notes the problem of familiar words with unfamiliar meanings and draws from it a principle of intercultural communication which, though it contradicts what we might intuitively expect, has received good research support. When what you do at home in a particular situation is exactly what is done in the alien culture, no new learning is required. When the social situation calls for different behavior from what you have learned, you can learn it if you are sufficiently perceptive and teachable. But when the behavior appropriate to a situation in an alien culture happens to be almost identical to what you have learned for a different situation, you've got a problem. Here you must not only learn but also first unlearn.

Triandis comments:

> . . . the greater the similarity between two cultures, the easier the contact when the same response is required and the more difficult the contact when a different response is required. When the cultures are very different, contact is always difficult but probably at an intermediate level between the extreme levels of difficulty found in contact among similar groups. . . . American businessmen with wide intercultural experience, . . . claim, for instance, that dealing with southern Europeans or Latin Americans is more difficult than dealing with the Chinese or Japanese.
>
> A further implication of this argument leads to the hypothesis that intercultural training is specific. One has to learn anew the subjective culture of each cultural group with which he comes into contact. Though

A COMMUNICATION PROBLEM

A problem described by Saitz and Cervenka* concerns Alvaro, a Colombian, and Jim, a North American. This situation takes place on the streets of Colombia.

Hello, Jim, how are you?
(*Alvaro extends his hand.*)

HI, Alvaro, how are you?
(*Jim's hands are in his pockets; he withdraws and extends one hand, too late.*)

Is it true you have a new girl friend?

Is it that tall girl I saw you with yesterday?
(*He extends his hand, palm vertical.*)

Yes, I do, as a matter of fact.

No, she's just a little girl.

(*He extends his hand, palm down. Alvaro laughs.*)

1

2

Because she was a doll.
(*He puts his finger to the skin just below his eye.*)

Uh?
(*Jim stares at Alvaro's eye, wondering what's wrong.*)

Well, I'll be seeing you.
(*He waves and walks away.*)

4

5

Well, I thought that tall girl I saw you with yesterday was lovely. I wonder if you could introduce me some time. *(Alvaro moves closer to Jim.)*

Sure, of course, sure, sure.
(Jim backs away.)

3

In this situation, there were no problems in oral communication; both speakers had excellent command of the pronunciation, the intonation and syntax of English, but it was an unsatisfactory exchange. Both speakers felt awkward, and at the end Alvaro felt offended.

The basis for Alvaro's offense was that Jim interpreted Alvaro's *come-here* gesture as the North American *goodbye* gesture. Part of the feeling of awkwardness came from Alvaro's expectation of a handshake, even among friends, and his feeling that they should stand a bit closer—at a distance, in fact, that Jim reserves for close friends of the opposite sex.

If either Alvaro or Jim were completely informed about the meaning of their gestures in the other's culture, their problems in communicating would have been reduced.

See ya, Alvaro.
(Jim keeps walking.)

Hey Jim. *(He motions with his hand for Jim to come closer, the fingers curving away from his body.)*

But . . . .

6

*Robert L. Saitz and Edward J. Cervenka. COLOMBIAN AND NORTH AMERICAN GESTURES: A CONTRASTIVE INVENTORY. Reprinted by permission.

some general sensitivity to interpersonal relations may facilitate cross-cultural interaction, it is not sufficient to overcome the communication barriers and intercultural misunderstanding. [*]

To summarize, communication problems may be greater in cultures which are in some respects similar to one's own because that very similarity leads us to overlook subtle differences and requires unlearning as well as learning. This is true not only for verbal but also for nonverbal behavior. Jim is more likely to discover the meaning of the finger-to-eye gesture than he is to discover the meaning of Alvaro's moving closer to him.

It is also true that experience and skill in one foreign culture do not automatically qualify a person for another. In fact, the expert's knowledge may be dangerous. It may lead a person to be overconfident in the inferences he or she draws when placed in the new culture.[23] To learn to make one's way will require learning anew the meaning of symbols, both in verbal and nonverbal codes, and to appreciate the situational meanings as they occur in culture. The more you know already, the more you may first have to unlearn.

LEARNING TO LEARN A NEW CULTURE: EMPATHY

With so much to know and so little time to learn it, the person who enters another culture needs to learn from the errors he or she will inevitably make. An indispensable skill for this learning is *empathy*. This skill is useful generally in communication, but it is especially important in intercultural communication.

There are many specifications of empathy as a concept, but the one which is most helpful defines it as a sort of "vicarious introspection."[24] It is not like projecting yourself with all your values, preferences, beliefs, and abilities into someone else's shoes. Such projection is in fact the enemy of empathy.[25] Rather, empathy is a capacity to put the *other* person, with all his or her inner characteristics, into *your* shoes and to understand what that person is feeling by feeling those same things inside yourself.

If Sherlock Holmes simply put himself in the criminal's shoes, he might attribute too much intelligence and calculation to his game. With the exception of Professor Moriarty, Holmes always had to take into account the other's inferior talents and then determine what he would do *if* he were just like that person. Although the difference is subtle, it is important. Putting yourself in another's shoes may lead to the discovery that the "shoes pinch" without leading to an understanding of the views, values, and opportunities of the person who "wears the shoes."

There are several stages, aspects, or steps to empathy. The empathic per-

[*]From THE ANALYSIS OF SUBJECTIVE CULTURE by Harry C. Triandis et al. Reprinted by permission of John Wiley & Sons, Inc.

son is first and foremost *perceptive:* alert to what may be subtle cues, recognizing that in the culture they may not be subtle at all.

Second, the empathic person is able to withhold judgment or the drawing of inferences—an ability you were urged to develop in Chapter 6. This capacity stands in tension with perceptiveness, for we are very prone to attempt to organize our perceptions and make immediate sense out of them rather than to allow uncertainty to grow. But to be empathic you must avoid jumping to unwarranted conclusions.[26]

Interculturally, the empathic person is less likely to fix quickly on an explanation and then gather confirming evidence. He or she is less prone to say "They are dishonest . . . " and so probe for confirmation, or to conclude "They are persecuting and making fun of me" and so act in ways that will come to make this misperception eventually accurate.

Third, and perhaps most mysteriously, the empathic person comes up with good hunches, good explanations, and good inferences about what things mean and count for. How is this accomplished? Perhaps by perceptiveness and avoidance of premature judgment. Perhaps also by careful use of the next step.

The empathic person has the good sense and the skills to put possible interpretations to the test. He or she finds out, by generating feedback from others, whether or not an interpretation is accurate. Let's take a look at some examples.

The empathic person is alert for and to some extent *expects* miscommunication when crossing cultures. He or she recognizes the symptoms of miscommunication.[27] Such a person notes wherein his or her emotional reactions seem to diverge from those of the hosts and wherein other people are not "living up to" expectations. Moreover, the empathic person will note wherein he or she is tempted to assign negative judgments. For example, "Brazilians are too political," "Indians talk too much and don't respect privacy," "Nigerians are too happy-go-lucky."

An empathic person seeks guidance from those who know the culture as natives rather than those of his or her own cultural group who may impart inaccurate stereotypes. Such a person tries to discover the interpersonal cues used in the culture so as to interpret the flow and content of communication. For example, the empathic person asks questions such as "How could you tell that they wanted to talk with us but were afraid to?" or "How do you know that they probably won't be at home even though they said they would be?" These questions are asked because the asker is seeking a designation of the cues the native is attending to rather than challenging how the cues are interpreted. Of course, the fact that there is this resource—a cooperative informant—implies that the individual has already managed to establish a trusting relationship with at least one person in the other culture.

An empathic person may know the language well but will recognize the need for an interpreter to assist in learning the interaction cues. Besides obtaining a good interpreter in these areas, the empathic person asks questions in the right way and makes good use of the answers. For instance, he or she avoids asking such leading questions as "It's OK if I wear my T-shirt on the street, isn't it?"

And an empathic person is sensitive to answers by indirection. For instance, "Yes, I suppose you can do so if you really want to." Or "It may be all right for an American; people will not be too surprised." Or "Most people would wear a shirt." To keep the flow of advice coming, an empathic person tends to follow it. People who trouble themselves to try to help an alien fit into the culture will cease to do so if they find their efforts are spurned.

The empathic person tries to control his or her presuppositions. To see how difficult this is, try answering the following questions:

1. Do they have a Fourth of July in England?
2. How many birthdays does the average person have?
3. Some months have 30 days, some have 31. How many have 28?
4. I have in my hand two United States coins which total 55 cents in value. One is not a nickel. What are the coins?
5. Divide thirty by half and then add ten. What is the answer?*

This brief exercise shows that it is hard to control presuppositions. But it also shows that communication depends on a meshing of what the sender *intends* to say with what the receiver *understands*. Everyone would get the five test questions right if they knew what the asker meant. Success in communication comes to those who already sense, in some measure, what the other is trying to indicate by the words and gestures he or she is using. When expectations do not mesh, communication fails.

Avoiding Communication Pitfalls

The empathic person is aware of possible areas of misunderstanding, possible causes of communication breakdown. John Parry has sketched seven such causes of communication breakdown,** and they take on new and additional dimensions when cultures are crossed.

The first cause of communication breakdown is *channel overload*. Generally, when we try to communicate too much, the eventual result is confusion. Information-processing habits and expectations differ culturally. We may overload and thus confuse and lose our audience. On the other hand, we may underload in some instances and thereby bewilder them.

The second cause is *distraction*. Foreignness itself is a distractor. People in a strange culture must listen with real effort to understand what is being said

---

*The answers:

1. Yes, and a third of July and a fifth, too.
2. One.
3. All.
4. A fifty-cent piece and a nickel; the fifty-cent piece is the one which is not a nickel.
5. Seventy. 30 / ½ = 60.

**From THE PSYCHOLOGY OF HUMAN COMMUNICATION by John Parry. Published 1967 by The University of London Press Limited.

with "that awful foreign accent." (It is interesting that we tend to find that our fellow nationals speak a foreign language with greater clarity of pronunciation than the natives. What this really means, of course, is that our fellow countrymen's accent falls on the ear more naturally than the proper sounds do.)

Receivers in the culture will differ greatly in their ability to discount the distractions you emit. Those with more experience and who are themselves multilingual will tolerate departures from language norms more readily than inexperienced monolinguals. But even if there are no distractions coming from you or if the receivers are already skilled at penetrating them and attending to what you are trying to say, they may be experiencing a range of distractions quite different from those which persons in a similar position in your culture would experience. For instance, they may have substantial family obligations and concerns distracting them which might not exist for persons like them in your culture.

Finally, take care that the materials you use to clarify and make your message memorable do not result in obscuring it or in leaving false trails as to meaning. Only by pretesting those materials on someone who will tell you if they mislead or confuse can you hope to avoid this error. In one instance, for example, natives who were shown a slide/sound presentation on the importance of controlling the flies in their area missed the whole point. They went away relieved that the flies in their country were tiny, rather than the giants they had seen on the screen.

The third cause of communication breakdown is the inability of receivers of a message to fill in *unstated assumptions*. If all assumptions had to be made explicit, communication would be impossible. But as an empathic communicator, you must recognize that there is a good chance that the receivers will not be able to fill in some of the assumptions you have supposed they would. This means you must gather evidence that they understand what you are saying, rather than falling prey to the "but I told them . . ." trap. You may not have told them in terms they understood, or worse, they may have interpreted what you said differently than you assumed they would.

When you have not been understood, it may help to try to say the same thing another way. But be sure the receivers understand that this is what you are trying to do, lest they have already understood you and now suppose that this is something new which they cannot distinguish from what has already been said.

The fourth cause of communication breakdown is probably the most important in all communication. It is like the unstated assumptions problem, but more complex. The way you experience and make sense out of the world may be incompatible or just plain different from the way your listeners do. The "schema" you use to map experience may not fit with theirs. Research shows that we are even subject to different perceptual illusions because of differing cultural backgrounds. This problem is difficult because we are necessarily selective in our perception and interpretations and ordinarily not at all aware of this selectiveness. Much of what we noted earlier about differences in culture fits into this general problem area of *incompatible schemas*.

Cultures may differ in the barriers which operate outside of communicator awareness. *Unconscious barriers,* the fifth kind of "contributors" to communication breakdown, can be extremely subtle, but the most obvious have to do with the elements of experience which are taboo and have been repressed. These are, of course, similar to the assumptions we do not make explicit, except that they may *not be available* to the native or to us to make explicit. This is certainly the case if they are truly unconscious.

Parry's sixth cause of breakdown is that of *confused or confusing presentations of messages.* The "extra wrinkle" is that we may not be able to anticipate that our planned presentation will be confusing to those in an alien culture. Often we lack the necessary knowledge of the ordinary rhetorical forms, the expected patterns of organization and presentation, and the favored forms of argument.

Robert Oliver provides a fascinating catalog of what he takes to be differences in the rhetorical orientation and expectations of Indians and Chinese in contrast to those cultures which draw upon an Aristotelian background.[28] The result is very instructive. As only one example from many, the Indians and Chinese tend to believe that a person's true nature is revealed by words rather than deeds. The opposite assumption characterizes us. Perhaps your initial response to their view is incredulity. Don't they realize a person can lie and dissemble? Of course they do, but since people control what they say more completely than they control all of what they do, their words give a better picture of what is in their hearts. Besides, for many aspects of others' natures, our only access is through careful scrutiny of what they say.

We can observe, further, that cultures differ in their *communication rules.* This extends not only to rules governing and constituting what counts as what, but also to rules which regulate the flow and structure of discourse and interaction. We should be aware of this as a possible area of difference that needs probing and exploration.

The seventh and final cause of communication breakdown, according to Parry, is simple—the message does not arrive. Absence of familiar channels or ignorance of alternative channels plagues the intercultural communicator. You may utilize less effective means of getting messages through when more effective ones are available because you are not aware of them. Perhaps rather than writing a formal letter which gets lost in the shuffle of a foreign bureaucracy, you should have used an intermediary. This topic is complex, and pitfalls for the unwary are many. The point is to be suspicious of the notion that the channels of communication which worked in one culture will also work in another. How can you tell? By trial and feedback, certainly; or perhaps more efficiently, by asking a knowledgeable native.

Using Sources to Facilitate Communication

As Harry Triandis has indicated, there are limits to how well you can prepare for contact with other cultures in general. Specific knowledge is needed. If you do not know that it is improper to open a gift in the presence of the giver when in Greece, you will probably open the gift. Not knowing that you should enter the home of a Greek friend with the right foot first rather than just walking in with the left or right may give rise to another discourtesy. Yet how can you know these things? It is no solution to avoid doing anything in a culture until advised about how to do it, for there are cultural sins of omission as well as sins of commission.

Given enough lead time, you can visit the library and find materials that will help you communicate in other cultures. For some cultures these have been structured into efficient training manuals. For instance, Uriel Foa and his associates have prepared the *Thai Culture Assimilator,* a set of volumes containing small cultural vignettes that lead to a decision point.* The reader is asked to select among four possible acts or interpretations. A correct selection is rewarded with praise. An incorrect selection results in further explanation and clarification; then the reader goes back to try again.

How it works can be seen quickly by examining materials in the same source designed to help Thais understand Americans:

> An American professor was 20 minutes late for an appointment that he had made with two of his graduate students. The students were looking at their watches when the professor finally came into the room. The professor said, "I am terribly sorry I am late." The two graduate students jokingly replied, "Better late than never." The professor laughed, and after a few more informal exchanges of conversation the group enthusiastically got down to the business that the appointment had been scheduled for.
>
> Judging from the behavior exhibited in this incident, which one of the following do you see as the accurate description of what that behavior mainly signifies?
>
> 1. The students do not have the proper respect for their professor.
> 2. No Americans like to be kept waiting 20 minutes for an appointment, regardless of what the status of the person who is late may be.
> 3. The professor is asserting his status and authority over the students by making them wait until it is convenient for him to meet with them.
> 4. The professor felt that the students were rude in their manner and remarks.**

By moving through several hundred of these incidents and the accompanying explanations, the learner can begin to fathom the culture's nature and the meaning of various behaviors in it. Of course, the value of such a series is dependent on the accuracy of the author's understanding of the culture and the care that has gone into selecting the critical incidents to be taught.

In a sense, what is sought by these means is the development of an accu-

---

*A similar set of documents has been prepared by Triandis and others to assist whites and blacks in understanding one another in our nation. Intersubcultural communication can be as difficult and multifaceted as intercultural communication.

**From THAI CULTURE ASSIMILATOR, Book 1, by Uriel Foa et al. Reprinted by permission of the University of Illinois.

rate, detailed, and situationally located set of stereotypes to aid anyone who aspires to effective communication in the culture. H. C. Smith has amassed a great deal of evidence to the effect that accurate and sufficiently detailed stereotypes are extremely valuable tools for increasing a communicator's sensitivity to others.[29] The approach utilized by those who construct training materials similar to the *Thai Culture Assimilator* is essentially one of training the student in such stereotypes.

If a recognition of the problems in intercultural communication seems to be emphasized in this chapter, that may perhaps be a healthy antidote for too much naive enthusiasm about the "quaint culture" you are heading for. Being culturally sensitive does not require that you like and approve of all the ways or all the people you meet in another culture, since there are disagreeable people and disagreeable habits abroad as well as at home. The anthropologist who failed to complete his field work because he couldn't stand the way they kicked the dogs is an example of one person who found some.

Still, the intercultural experience is a potential gold mine for the prepared individual. Success interculturally tells us something quite complimentary about ourselves, and in that respect is its own reward. Communication that crosses cultures successfully can be every bit as gratifying as successful communication with those of our own culture.

Suggested Readings

John C. Condon and Yousef Fathi, *Introduction to Intercultural Communication* (Indianapolis: The Bobbs-Merrill Company, Inc., 1975). Rich in examples and broad in scope, this introduction should prove useful to student and traveler alike. The authors are particularly interested in values but include chapters on nonverbal problems, differences in rhetoric and reasoning, and most of the issues in interpersonal, intercultural communication.

Robert T. Oliver, *Communication and Culture in Ancient India and China* (Syracuse, N.Y.: Syracuse University Press, 1971). The opening and closing chapters of this book provide excellent summaries of the impact of culture on the social uses of communication in public settings. The principles are clear and well stated.

Anthony F. C. Wallace, *Culture and Personality,* 2nd ed. (New York: Random House, Inc., 1970). Well written, challenging, and innovative, this anthropologically oriented book discusses the psychic unity of human beings and provides brief but very perceptive summaries of research in a variety of areas.

Eugene A. Nida and Charles R. Taber, *The Theory and Practice of Translation* (Leiden, The Netherlands: E. J. Brill, 1974). First published in 1969, this is the eighth volume in a series intended especially for Bible translators. Very well written, it pulls together translation principles and illustrates problems and difficulties with exercises in Bible translation. Although occasionally too technical for the general reader, it is a very articulate and thorough book made for anyone who wants to be well informed about the possible and the impossible in translation.

Harry C. Triandis, *The Analysis of Subjective Culture* (New York: John Wiley & Sons, Inc., 1972). This is a brilliant scientific scrutiny of a range of psychological factors impinging on intercultural communication. Chapter 7, where values of Japanese, American, Indian, and Greek students are compared and analyzed, and Chapter 9, with an integrated picture of Greek culture, are particularly interesting.

Michael H. Prosser, *Intercommunication Among Nations and Peoples* (New York: Harper & Row, Publishers, 1973); and Larry A. Samovar and Richard E. Porter, *Intercultural Communication: A Reader* (Belmont, Calif.: Wadsworth Publishing Co., 1972). The selections in both of these volumes were compiled with undergraduates in mind. Prosser has collected more selections on mass communication, whereas Samovar and Porter have focused on interpersonal communication. Readers who prefer to "pick and choose" will find a variety of materials in these two books.

Reference Notes

[1]Elizabeth Schattner, *Making It Abroad (And at Home)*, USAF (TAC) Special Operations School, 1971, Introduction.

[2]Ibid., p. 2.

[3]This material is in part suggested by a portion of David Berlo's analysis of "Empathy and Managerial Communication" in Charles Press and Alan Arian (eds.), *Empathy and Ideology: Aspects of Administrative Innovation* (Skokie, Ill.: Rand McNally & Company, 1966), pp. 130–145. See especially pp. 142–145.

[4]Lawrence H. Fuchs, "The Role and Communication Task of the Change Agent—Experiences of the Peace Corps Volunteers in the Philippines," in Daniel Lerner and Wilbur Schramm (eds.), *Communication and Change in the Developing Countries* (Honolulu: East West Center Press, 1967), pp. 235–278.

[5]Robert T. Oliver, *Communication and Culture in Ancient India and China* (Syracuse, N.Y.: Syracuse University Press, 1971), pp. 4–5.

[6]Harry C. Triandis, et al., *The Analysis of Subjective Culture* (New York: Wiley-Interscience, 1972), p. 301.

[7]Margaret Mead, "Professional Problems of Education . . . ," *Journal of Negro Education* 15, No. 3 (1946):347.

[8]Howard P. Holladay, "The Value System—A False Prophet for Intercultural Communication," Western Speech Communication Association, 1972.

[9]Anthony F. C. Wallace, *Culture and Personality*, 2nd ed. (New York: Random House, Inc., 1970).

[10]Fernando Diaz-Plaja, *Los Sete Pecados Capitales U.S.A.*, Ediciones Marte 1969, Concilio de Trento D. Galerias Comerciales, 18, Barcelona.

[11]Eugene A. Nida and Charles R. Taber, *The Theory and Practice of Translation* (Leiden, The Netherlands: E. J. Brill, 1974, published for the United Bible Societies), pp. 3–4.

[12]Ibid., pp. 4–5.

[13]Ibid., p. 134.

[14]Paul Watzlawick, Janet Beavin, and Don Jackson, *The Pragmatics of Human Communication* (New York: W. W. Norton & Co., Inc., 1967), pp. 51–54.

[15]Oliver, op. cit., p. 151.

[16]Triandis, op. cit., pp. 334–335.

[17]Schattner, op. cit., p. 8.

[18]Ibid., p. 16.

[19]Robert L. Saitz and Edward J. Cervenka, *Colombian and North American Gestures: A Contrastive Inventory* (Bogota: Centro Colombo Americano, 1962), p. 4.

[20]Ibid., p. 10.

[21]Ibid., p. 77.

[22]Triandis, op. cit., p. 347.

[23]Henry Clay Smith, *Sensitivity to People* (New York: McGraw-Hill Book Company, 1966), Ch. 5.

[24]Robert L. Katz, *Empathy: Its Nature and Uses* (New York: The Free Press, 1963), p. 93.

25Ibid., p. 170.

26Smith, op. cit., Ch. 4.

27The following paragraphs draw upon examples provided by Raymond L. Gordon, "Tools for Learning to Operate in a Foreign Culture." Paper given at ACTFL preconvention culture workshop, Chicago, Ill., 1971.

28Oliver, op. cit., Ch. 1, 14.

29Smith, op. cit., Ch. 8.

APPENDIX

**Sample Speeches
for Analysis**

The New Furies:
Skepticism, Criticism, and Coercion
by John A. Howard   **407**

Women in Leadership and
Decision Making:
A Shift in Balance
by Virginia Y. Trotter   **413**

THE NEW FURIES:
SKEPTICISM, CRITICISM,
AND COERCION

A speech by John A. Howard,

President, Rockford College,

delivered at The Prairie School,

Racine, Wisconsin,

June 6, 1974.*

Y ou may recall in Greek mythology there were three Avenging Furies, super-natural beings who tracked down the wayward folk, pursuing them until they ei-ther redeemed themselves or were consigned to the underworld for proper eter-nal torment. The name for these inexorable bloodhounds was the Erinnyes. According to some sources, people called them the Eumenides, which means "The kindly ones," which of course they weren't, but nobody wanted to call them by their real names for fear of offending them. I doubt if any of the simple souls who used the substitute name fooled the Furies, but they evidently deceived themselves rather successfully.　/ 1

As I considered what might be helpful to say to a graduating class in anno Domini 1974, it seemed to me that we have a trio of self-deceptions operating in our time which, while they may not pursue their victims on into an afterlife, are certainly making things miserable for everybody in the life that is going on now. The sad thing, and the pertinent thing about them, is that they are rather widely regarded as beneficial influences, particularly in the intellectual community.　/ 2

Since a number of you are going on to college, and since forewarned is believed to be forearmed, I thought I would like to offer some perspective on these New Furies, so that you may at least recognize them when you encounter

*Speech by John A. Howard, "The New Furies" from VITAL SPEECHES OF THE DAY, Vol. 40, No. 19 (July 15, 1974), pp. 599–601. Reprinted by permission.

them and, hopefully, give a second thought before you embrace them as your friends. / **3**

The first is skepticism, a fundamental attitude of doubting everything. Several years ago the *Harvard Bulletin* published excerpts from a student discussion. All the participants were quite critical of their university experience. Toward the end of the discussion, one of the participants said to another, "But you've acquired a healthy skepticism. Isn't that a great reward?" The student to whom the question was directed, responded, "Sure! But I'm not sure Harvard gave me that." Both agreed, however, that healthy skepticism was a great reward. / **4**

Here we see an example of one of the principal articles of faith of the academic community. The assumption seems to be that if the college does nothing else, it will have earned its tuition by making all of its students into doubting Thomases. This presumed virtue must, I think, be reexamined. The success of higher education in recent years in producing large numbers of committed skeptics is probably not in question. But are they healthy? Is it a triumph or a disaster to have skepticism as the identifying mark of the educated man? / **5**

The circumstances of our times, and the popular inclination to challenge whatever is and has been, need no help from the school or the college to stimulate the student's capacity to doubt and to question. That talent needs no organized help in its development. In my judgment, this is one academic priority which needs to be turned upside-down. The great need, instead, is for the college to help the student find solid bases for hope and courage, and to help the student identify fundamental principles and worthy objectives to which he can commit himself with confidence and joy. Skepticism is no friend to anybody. / **6**

The second New Fury I wish to identify is a proper cousin of the first. It is criticism. Skepticism and criticism are reenforcing partners. If one does not have some broad base of belief and commitment, if there is perceived to be no grounds for faith and affirmation, then the person's moral energy is all bottled up. It is my conviction that *every* person is possessed of a transcendent spark of desire to be helpful to others. This is one of the identifying marks of mankind, helpfulness. In a society where there are no general standards of what is good, no accepted norms of what is right, where skepticism prevails, the moral spark is prevented from burning brightly *in behalf of* something. The person who says, "Look, everybody, this is a good thing. Let us nourish it and foster it and make it grow," that person is likely to be resented for trying to impose his beliefs on others. And so fewer and fewer people proclaim themselves in behalf of institutions and values. / **7**

That is the situation today. It is very pronounced on the college campuses. The Daniel Yankelovitch survey, just released, indicates that only 28 percent of today's college students consider religion to be a very important value, only 34 percent place a high priority on leading a clean moral life, and a scant 19 percent consider patriotism a matter of great significance. Standing for something is not in vogue today. / **8**

Given this circumstance, the moral tendencies, discouraged from affirmative activity, spew forth in majestic proportions into critical activity. There are still certain things that are generally considered to be bad, so we find ourselves in the midst of an era when everybody is pointing the finger at someone else. It really doesn't take any brains or special talent to complain. Indeed, some fairly dull people make whole careers out of complaining. There is a sense of superiority in identifying what someone else is doing wrong, and it is a lot more fun to complain about somebody else than it is to mend one's own ways.   / **9**

I suggest it is not the fault-finders of history who make us proud to belong to the human race. Indeed, none of us, if we could help it, would choose a chronic complainer for a husband or a wife, a neighbor, an employer, an employee, or much of anything else.   / **10**

One is reminded of King Gama in the operetta, *Princess Ida*. He sings a song that starts out:

> *If you'll give me your attention, I will tell you what I am*
> *I'm a genuine philanthropist, all other kinds are sham.*
> *Each little fault of temper and each social defect*
> *In my erring fellow creatures, I endeavor to correct.*
>
> *To all their little weaknesses, I open people's eyes*
> *And little plans to snub the self-sufficient, I devise.*
> *I love my fellow creatures, I do all the good I can,*
> *Yet everybody says I'm such a disagreeable man*
> *And I can't think why.*   / **11**

The complainer may at times serve a useful function, but such a function is for petty people. The giants of this world are those who stand for, not against. Criticism is the second New Fury.   / **12**

The third is coercion. It is closely related to the first two. Having identified the serious faults of someone else, the next step of the self-righteous soul is to try to force the offender to change his ways. This, too, is a pronounced characteristic of our times. The first response of many people to any problem is to try to get a new law passed to fix whatever it is that concerns them. The legislative machinery at every level is glutted with proposals to prevent or change this, that or the other thing. In a way, it almost seems too bad that the legislative machinery hasn't broken down completely. So many laws have already been enacted that a very large and still growing portion of our population is employed full-time doing nothing but administering and enforcing the laws. Millions and millions of people now earn their livelihood trying to get the citizens to live their lives differently, by carrying out the carrot laws which provide grants to encourage people to do certain things, and the stick laws which discourage people from doing certain things, and there seem to be some points at which the one set of laws is in conflict with the other.   / **13**

A second and equally dismaying aspect of the propensity to change society by legislation is that there are now so many laws governing the operation of any enterprise, that more and more time, energy, personnel and financial resources must be diverted away from productive activity into meeting the requirements of public statutes. This problem is just as true of an educational institution or a hospital as it is of a small or a large commercial enterprise. There is, I believe, a very real question of how much further we can go in governmental interference and regulation before the whole system simply collapses from the burden of having to meet all the statutory requirements.   / **14**

The current enthusiasm for coercion, however, is not restricted to the thrust for more and more laws. The most grievous acts of coercion that appeared on the campuses in the sixties—arson, vandalism, terrorism and the occupation of buildings—have largely abated, but the coercive efforts to discredit or silence the opposition still continue in the form of picketing, character assassination and an occasional mob scene that prevents a speaker from being heard.   / **15**

I would like to suggest to you that if one genuinely wishes to bring about a change in society or a change in the performance of an individual, legal coercion and mob coercion should be regarded at best as instruments of last resort, and more often, as grievously counterproductive. Human nature, having a recalcitrant streak, tends to react to a law by producing the minimum change that the enforcement of the law will require. If someone says, "Do this" or "Do that," the first reaction is usually, "That's the last thing I'm going to do." Ideally, one would hope to persuade the citizens why it is a good idea to do something differently and influence them to behave accordingly as a matter of conscience. Where this is possible, the objectives are far better served than they are by legal constraint.   / **16**

This, of course, is what democracy is all about. It is a form of government which can only work if the population is disciplined by an informed conscience. To the extent that the conscience of the citizenry falters, freedom must yield to the dictatorship of controlled behavior.   / **17**

With regard to the efforts to win converts to a point of view by silencing or denouncing the spokesmen for a contrary view, these are the tactics of the barbarian. What is needed is a massive effort to train our people in the necessity for both sides to listen, truly listen, to each other so that some accommodation may be found that attends as far as possible to the legitimate concerns of both. It seems to me that one of the monumental causes for rejoicing in this era when there isn't much to rejoice about is the example our Secretary of State, Henry Kissinger, has recently provided of calm and patient and rational negotiation of one of the most intractably unresolvable issues of human history. If objective negotiation can bring peace between Arab and Jew, it can move mountains. True harmony among individuals and true peace among nations is seldom achieved by jamming the point of view of the stronger down the throat of the weaker. Coercion is the enemy of good relationships, a Fury much in evidence today.   / **18**

Some time ago a cartoon was published, I think in *The New Yorker*, which showed a mother and child standing in an art gallery. The child was pointing to a painting entitled "Black on Black" or some such thing, and was saying, "Oh, look, Mommy, it lost its picture."   / **19**

To a very great extent, I think our society, and particularly the intellectual community, has lost its picture. The picture is still there to be put back in focus and enjoyed. Today we speak of gremlins rather than Furies which hound us in our perplexities, but by whatever name you choose to call them, I hope you will be alert to the true nature and the consequences of these destructive forces of our day, Skepticism, Criticism and Coercion.   / **20**

Let me conclude by suggesting that if you will invert these three hostile forces and if you will guide your own life by their opposites—an unwavering faith in the principles you believe to be sound, instead of a corrosive skepticism; a persistent encouragement for that which is right, instead of criticism for that which is wrong; and a friendly persuasion, rather than angry coercion to advance the causes you believe in—if you can order your life by an affirmative rather than a negative posture, you will be surprised by how much you can accomplish and perhaps equally surprised by how much fun you have in accomplishing it and how many friends you make along the way.   / **21**

Good luck to you. May God be with you. And may you be with God.   / **22**

WOMEN IN LEADERSHIP
AND DECISION
MAKING: A SHIFT
IN BALANCE

A speech delivered by Virginia Y. Trotter,

Assistant Secretary for Education,

Department of Health, Education, and Welfare,

to the Academic Woman Conference,

Kansas State University,

February 15, 1975.*

I'm delighted to be here with you today. As you know, all of my working life has been in the field of education, and this occasion gives me the unique opportunity to share some of my concerns on the future of women in leadership and decision-making positions in education.   / **1**

It was almost 200 years ago that Abigail Adams wrote to her husband John at the Constitutional Convention:

> *Dear John:*
> *By the way, in the new code of law I desire you would remember the ladies and be more generous and favorable to them, than were your ancestors. Remember, all men would be tyrants if they could.*
>
> *Your loving wife, Abigail*

*Speech by Virginia Y. Trotter, "Women in Leadership and Decision Making" from VITAL SPEECHES OF THE DAY, Vol. 41, No. 12 (April 1, 1975), pp. 373–376. Reprinted by permission.

413

He answered: *Depend on it my dear wife. We men know better than to re-peal our masculine system.* / **2**

When you think of it, America was already 144 years old before women received the right to vote. Fifty years ago our institutions were totally male domi-nated. And what is the situation today—50 years later? Out of a female popu-lation of about 107 million, there are not today 100 women in posts of command or in high supervisory or policymaking positions. Only three women have been elected to the Senate and 78 women have been chosen as representatives to the House. There have been only three women governors, two women cabinet mem-bers, and 14 women ministers and ambassadors. / **3**

Today, there are no women in the cabinet, no women in the Senate, one woman governor, and only 18 women representatives. The picture is the same in finance, business, and the media. / **4**

Almost all of the mass circulation women's magazines were once edited by women. Today most are edited by men. / **5**

Yesterday, most of the presidents of women's universities were women. Today, many have been replaced by men. One statistic alone suffices to reveal the situation in the world of education. In 1972, women comprised 57.6 percent of the professional educators in New York City public schools but only 1.7 per-cent of the high school principals were women. The University Council for Edu-cational Administration determined in 1972 that only 2 percent of all professors of educational administration were women—and although women make up about 40 percent of the work force, only about 10 percent of them are managers at most. Perhaps nothing epitomizes the need for sensitivity and consciousness-rais-ing among educators more—than at a recent convention of school administrators in which there were two panel discussions relating to women:

> One—From Adam's Rib to Women's Lib—You've Come A Long Way Baby
> Two—The Superintendent's Wife—Some Do's and Don'ts and Maybe's / **6**

It's true that a resolution was passed to identify women who are potential leaders, but nevertheless these titles say a lot about attitudes. / **7**

The truth of it is we have continued to maintain relatively undisturbed all the ancient edicts about the superiority of males and the inferiority of females. In short—what we call today the Women's Liberation Movement is only the most re-cent aspect of the struggle that began with Mary Wollstonecraft's *Vindication of the Rights of Women* in 1795. / **8**

I received just before I left for Kansas a report from the National Center for Education Statistics which will be sent to the President showing that the sala-ries of women relative to men have not significantly improved either in private or public institutions of higher education. Women's salaries were 82.9 percent of men's salaries in 1972, and they were 83.2 percent in 1974. Women were also disadvantaged in the tenure situation where 26.7 percent of the women and 57 percent of the men had tenure. In academic rank, for example, in 1972, the total number of full women Professors was 9.8 percent and in 1974, 10.3 percent; women Associate Professors in 1972 numbered 16.3 percent and in 1974, 27.1 percent. The complete survey will be published at a later date, and I'd be very happy to send it to you.   / **9**

Considering this gloomy picture, you may well ask what there is to look forward to in the future. But there is much to look forward to. Since 1970 there has been a *legislative explosion*—as Congress has recognized the necessity to end sex discrimination on the campus. Title IX now prohibits discrimination on the basis of sex in all Federally-assisted education programs, and after over 10,000 responses, the regulations are finally being prepared for release.   / **10**

I believe the second great breakthrough favoring the goal of sex equality is the opening of the doors of higher education to women. Today, a girl can be admitted to college and get the same education as a boy, and she is free to study for any career that she aspires to. At least society now has access to women's brains and talents instead of only men's—but it is still woefully underutilized. As I have traveled from state to state, I see the development of new research centers and resource centers on women's studies. I see women faculty and students coming together to examine their status on the campus. I see an interchange and communication between diverse people, older and younger women, government and volunteer organizations, industry taking the initiative in new management training courses for women, Carnegie and Ford Foundation are funding research projects on career aspirations. There are new innovative programs in recruitment and training procedures. Our own Fund for the Improvement of Post-Secondary Education has initiated a most creative approach for career counseling for women, establishment of a woman's center for career and life planning, and a unique grant for research on reducing the attrition of women students in the sciences—to mention just a few.   / **11**

However, the effort to change education and employment patterns for women are part of a larger social concern. What we need to know is information about women who have aspired but failed, the conditions under which more women are likely to aspire, the specific job descriptions which detract from its desirability for women and what are the professional aspirations of women entering the universities. In fact, career aspiration has been identified as the crucial issue in women's education.   / **12**

One of the greatest challenges is to convince women themselves that they can go beyond the role stereotype that was formed in them virtually since birth. Little boys are given toys that challenge the mind and teach manual dexterity. Their sisters are given dolls and teacups and dreams of motherhood.   / **13**

It has been said that girls become less intelligent as they grow older, that thousands of females who are positively brilliant in grade school become merely bright in high school, simply very good in college, and finally, almost mediocre in graduate school. But I doubt that any of us here accept that.   / **14**

I believe as a result of the women's movement, more and more young women are rethinking their goals and aspirations and are planning lives that include active careers.   / **15**

I believe women not only have the capacity to accept leadership but need to question themselves on what do women need to learn from men and what do men need to learn from women. Women in the working world must accept the responsibility of being assertive and to accept the reality of the demands of the job.   / **16**

As women we must realize three fundamentals:

1. A woman must be competent in whatever she decides to do because opportunity means nothing if we're not prepared to take advantage of it.
2. Women as well as men must be aware of their prejudices against women in responsible positions. We absolutely cannot afford to maintain artificial barriers of race—sex—or creed—artificial barriers that prevent full use of all human resources.
3. Women must become convinced within themselves that they can do what they most want to do—and they must expect to be looked upon as persons and be willing to accept the same responsibilities within a job that men are expected to accept.   / **17**

This means living with the same professional strains and stresses that men live with—there is a difference—we have to be better, because most of us don't have "a wife" at home.   / **18**

If we play our role as liberated women to the fullest—the future is going to hold a more honest and happier relationship between women and men—and between men and women and their country.   / **19**

The seesaw—or the escalator—is an excellent image in that as the new gains and setbacks take effect, the sexes will only hamper progress if they see themselves at opposite ends of a seesaw, one falling as the other rises. It is recognizing our mutual stakes in abandoning stereotypes that we can turn the seesaw into an escalator for lifting everybody as it goes along. It was stated eloquently by Dr. Matina Horner, President of Radcliffe College, who went to the heart of what is necessary, no matter what the ups and downs of governmental decree—when she said:

> There is an increasing awareness that the genuine experiences of equality between men and women depend not only on the opportunities and barriers society has to offer—but also and perhaps more importantly—on the reaction and beliefs that those men and women involved have about themselves and each other. Since people differ from each other as individuals—more than men and women do as groups—those who choose to

pursue traditional careers or family patterns should be encouraged to do
so with pride—without guilt, discomfort, or apology—as those who seek
nontraditional fulfillment and life patterns must also enjoy and exercise
their options freely—without fear of retribution and loss of self-esteem. / **20**

But even if all job discrimination were to end tomorrow—nothing very drastic would change. For job discrimination is only part of the problem. It does impede women who choose to go higher up in industry, academia or government—but it does not by itself help us to understand why so many women *choose* to be aides instead of physicians—assistants instead of executives—instructors instead of deans. / **21**

Discrimination frustrates choices already made—and something more *pernicious perverts* the motivation to choose. *That something* is an unconscious ideology about the nature of the female, an ideology which constricts the emerging self-image of a female child and the nature of her aspirations from the very first. / **22**

So long as those responsible for the education of children believe sexual stereotypes to be innate rather than culturally induced, so long will the conditioning continue. / **23**

We now know that children's aspirations are developed at a very early age—through the visual stimuli of mass communication. Through their interaction with role models, and through direct and indirect verbal messages children learn who is smart, who is powerful, who can be creative, who can be independent, who will be successful, and who will fail. / **24**

In school the expectation of "feminine" behavior is steadily reinforced by adult attitudes, curriculum materials, and various kinds of separate activities for boys and girls. But, lest you think that stereotyping is limited to men, let me assure you this is not the case. A study was made recently showing that women are equally guilty of self-defeating prejudice. / **25**

An equal number of professional monographs by male and female authors were selected. The articles covered a variety of subjects, and all were adjudged in advance to be of equal merit. But in order to test the reaction of college women who took part in the study, changes were made in the authors' names. Half of the articles written by a man were labeled with the name of a woman. Half of those written were labeled with a man's name. All of the articles purportedly written by men received a higher rating than those labeled as having a woman author. The results confirmed that these college women attribute a higher level of competence to the professional work of men than to that of their female counterparts. / **26**

Last Friday at a meeting with publishers of college books, a similar story was told of a young woman who chose to publish her book under her initials rather than her first name. She felt it would be more saleable. Maybe so—but this is a great area of weakness. If we can't comprehend the fact that we're all in this together—then it can never work. We are all part of a movement interested in obtaining equality and equity for all *human beings*—and that is what is important. And that is why I believe that it is up to *you*—because it is the colleges and universities which are the key to any effort on the part of women to awaken more people to the whole matter of discrimination and understand why society perpetuates it.   / **27**

I agree with John Stuart Mill when he said "The knowledge men can acquire of women even as they have been and are without reference to what they might be is wretchedly imperfect and superficial and will always be so until women themselves have told us all they have to tell." But to consult only women when writing about women would be, I believe, to invite some of the same disabilities that would afflict a dominantly male approach to the subject. / **28**

It was of great interest to read about the Michael Korda book, *Male Chauvinism and How It Works.* He is a successful business executive who replays the games one by one that men play to keep women at the bottom of the organizational ladder. Some of you here today, I'm sure, are familiar how the table of organization can be changed to undercut a successful woman and what attitudes, language, and demands some men employ to hold women down. But what is *encouraging* is the *realization* that when men realize that they are seeing other people as stereotypes—whether from fear or habit—they make stereotypes of themselves.   / **29**

Certainly the employment of increased numbers of women faculty members and administrators at high levels would have a considerable impact upon lessening discriminatory practices. Such a policy would give men and women students role models of successful and respected academic women.   / **30**

No one woman speaks for women, but I must say it is a great time to be a woman and to be part of one of the great challenges of our time. As teachers and administrators we have an unparalleled opportunity to affect change. Your roles on the transmission of values and on the preparation of men and women for careers make this opportunity a responsibility. Legislation can support equality but without the involvement of men and women together to give the law life and momentum, meaning and action, then nothing we can do in Washington can make a real difference.   / **31**

The task of teaching, reorientation, and facilitation are the primary tasks for women and will remain so until the goals we seek have become interwoven into the fabric of social consciousness.   / **32**

How do we begin? First, by listening to ourselves, listening to our experiences, by listening deeply and humbly—but with a sense of trust and confidence that we can understand what our experience shows we require, for that is what the new image must incorporate. The old model of a "good woman" has become insufficient for life today. The old image has grown so small and narrow, and if women are not prepared to believe and to understand their own lives better than do men, they will not have the courage and stamina to change them.   / **33**

What we have at this moment is the statement of history that it is necessary, that social change demands it. I believe it is important to realize how vital a new image of women is for humanity as a whole. A new image of women as active participants and leaders in society does not mean women will desert the emotional validity of personal relations as we move into the world of action. We will bring it along with us to a place where it is badly needed. What we need is the gift of a new image—one that shows men and women honestly and realistically, interrelating and active in all phases of life.   / **34**

I am reminded of what Elizabeth Cady Stanton, at age 72, said in speaking to the International Council of Women, in the year 1888:

> *The younger women are starting with great advantages over us. They have the results of our experience; they have superior opportunities for education; they will find a more enlightened public sentiment for discussion; they will have more courage to take the rights which belong to them. . . . Thus far women have been the mere echoes of men. Our laws and constitutions, our creeds and codes, and the customs of social life are all of masculine origin. The true woman is as yet a dream of the future.*   / **35**

I know and you know that the dream is possible because here we are today sharing these thoughts, caring about each other as men—as women—and caring how we effectively utilize together the greatest source of energy that our country possesses—ourselves!

I'm proud the Federal government has provided the leadership and the opportunity for America's women to reach their highest potential—and it's only the beginning.   / **36**

In two years our country will be celebrating its 200th birthday. Today, just as 200 years ago, we are at a crucial turning point in our history. It is a time in which we must reaffirm our faith and commitment to the ideas and values upon which the United States of America was founded—not as an end in itself but as a means to rekindle the American tradition of individual initiative, restore pride in what we do and how we do it. Never has there been a more propitious time for change than the present. All the rest of history has been different in the sense that man and woman together have never had the power to take total destiny in their laps.   / **37**

The grand leaps of the creative intelligence and resolute determination that pushed back the American frontier can now be put to work on the most magnificent project of all—men and women working together to create a world congenial not just to human physical presence but also to the human spirit.   / **38**

STUDY PROBES

Chapter 11 **Small Group Communication**

Chapter 12 **Managing Conflict in Interaction**

Chapter 13 **Speech Planning and Preparation**

Chapter 14 **Speech Practice and Presentation**

INDEX